KAEGI'S
GREEK GRAMMAR

WITH

TABLES FOR REPETITION

BY
ADOLF KAEGI, Ph.D.

ADAPTED & TRANSLATED BY
JAMES A. KLEIST, S.J.

TWENTY-FIRST EDITION

BOLCHAZY-CARDUCCI PUBLISHERS, INC.
Wauconda, Illinois, USA

Formerly published by B. Herder Book Co. as
A Short Grammar of Classical Greek

CONTENTS

Cover Illustration:
Chiron with the young Achilles
wall painting from Herculaneum

Cover Design:
Catherine R. Bogan

BOLCHAZY-CARDUCCI PUBLISHERS, INC.
1000 Brown Street, Unit 101
Wauconda, Illinois, USA
WWW.BOLCHAZY.COM

Printed in the United States of America
2002
by United Graphics, Inc.

ISBN 0-86516-281-6

Reprint of the 1926 B. Herder Book Co. edition

FOREWORD

The reprint of Adolf Kaegi's *Short Grammar* is an important event in modern classical Greek studies. A short, attractively laid-out grammar has been needed for many years. The grammars currently available, Abbott & Mansfield, Goodwin and Gulick, and Smyth, are somewhat disarranged in their layout or are, like Smyth, too long for quick reference. Kaegi's *Grammar* will appeal to the elementary and intermediate (even the more advanced) student of Greek because it provides the answers to questions about forms or syntax easily, quickly and clearly.

The presentations of morphology and syntax are well displayed with intelligible definitions, clearly listed examples and ample margins. Particularly attractive are the "Tables for Repetition" with a "Syntax" section for each verb. The syntactical uses of verbs are stated in plain terms and are much easier to locate than in the crowded pages of Liddell & Scott's *Lexicon*. Given the emphasis of modern linguistics on a syntactic view of vocabulary, Kaegi's *Grammar* is surprisingly modern in form. "Vocabulary may indeed be due for a revival in language teaching, not just through the traditional technique of frequency of usage, but through ideas of syntactic specification of lexical items," according to Vivian Cooke (in *Perspective on Pedagogical Grammar*, ed.Terence Odlin, 1994 p.44).

A classical Greek grammar with easy-to-understand sentences and a neatly arranged format is long overdue. Adolf Kaegi's *Short Grammar* with its logical and user friendly arrangment will be a welcome experience for students and scholars alike. As a result, classical Greek studies will benefit and, one hopes, expand.

EDWARD S. PHINNEY

University of Massachusetts at Amherst
February 12, 1995

iii

PREFACE.

This *Short Grammar of Classical Greek* is an adaptation of the *Kurzgefasste Griechische Schulgrammatik* of Dr. Adolf Kaegi, Professor in Zurich University, Switzerland. It will be accompanied by an English edition of the Exercise Books of the same author.

The reasons that seem to justify an attempt at making Prof. Kaegi's books accessible to English-speaking students of Greek are of a threefold nature: (1) The peculiar character of Kaegi's Grammar and Exercise Books, (2) the fact that both are based upon the **same** method of strict criticism, and (3) their favorable reception throughout Europe.

1. It was in the year 1884 that Prof. Kaegi published his *Griech. Schulgrammatik*. Some forty Greek grammars were then in use at the *Gymnasia* of German speaking countries, and the author could scarcely venture to add a new one, unless he was convinced that the characteristic features of his own book would justify its appearance and win for it a prominent place among the books that served a similar purpose.

What then are the merits of Kaegi's **School** Grammar?

Of late years, but especially since the issue of the *Lehrpläne für die höheren Schulen Preussens*, it was deemed necessary by men of authority on school **matters** **to reduce the amount of grammar** that had to be mastered during the college course by the students of Greek. Accordingly, there soon appeared in Germany a number of grammars which, especially in their etymological parts, discarded much of what was formerly required. The authors of these new text-books were guided by the correct principle that " it is useless and a loss of time to burden the mind of the young student with material he never or seldom meets with in the authors read at college."

Thus a considerable advance was made in the line of *short* school grammars. In many cases, however, the intended reduction was *not methodical*. It was not always based on an accurate knowledge of what frequently occurred in school authors and thus became necessary, or what but rarely occurred and was in consequence dispensable, in a **school** grammar. On the contrary, a thorough examination convinced Prof. Kaegi that much had been dropped in a merely *eclectic* manner, because it *seemed* superfluous to the authors of these books.

Against such eclecticism Prof. Kaegi made a resolute stand.

In order to find a *reliable basis* for his own School Grammar, in which he intended to omit all the useless ballast of **rare** forms, exceptions, finesses, etc., the author went over the whole range of classical literature as far as it came within the reading-scope of German *Gymnasia*, with the avowed purpose of preparing upon the above principle a **school** grammar and sifting the matter to be incorporated into it.

iv

This long protracted labor put a vast amount of grammatical matter at the disposal of the author, and as he correctly thought that *the teaching of grammar must be subservient to, and determined by, the reading-matter*, he either omitted all the peculiarities and irregularities which are **seldom** met with in classical authors, or marked them by small print, or put them in special notes or chapters for reference.

Thus it is that Kaegi's *Schulgrammatik* shared on the one hand from its very first appearance *the advantage of brevity* with other grammars, and on the other far surpassed them, because his system of reducing the grammar was not at all eclectic, but *strictly methodical*.

Such is a brief sketch of the history of the *Schulgrammatik*.

In the first edition of this book the author said: " I wish to lay particular stress on this point, that the **reduction of the matter** might be carried much further, if the circle of classical **school** authors were drawn still closer than I have purposely done. It would be most useful, especially for a concentration of the teaching of Greek in our schools, if a list of the **Standard School Authors** (*ein Canon der Schulautoren*) were fixed upon by competent men."

The wished-for list appeared in the *Lehrpläne* for the Secondary Schools of Prussia in January, 1892.

These new regulations **prescribe as obligatory** the reading of: —

Xenophon's Anabasis, Hellenica, Memorabilia.

Plato and *Thucydides.*

Demosthenes' Olynthiacs and *Philippics.*

Herodotus, Homer, and *Sophocles.*

To these is usually added *Lysias.*

The time had therefore come for Prof. Kaegi to take a step further, and as the result of his studies he offered in October, 1892, the first edition of the *Kurzgefasste Griech. Schulgrammatik.*

In this *Short Grammar of Classical Greek* the author remained faithful to his principle that *the study of grammar is but to aid the reading of Greek.* Accordingly, all the peculiarities and irregularities that are only occasionally met with in the prescribed authors were **either** dropped or placed for *reference* in special chapters (60 and 113).

2. Those who appreciate Prof. Kaegi's grammatical methods will readily admit that an English edition of his Exercise Books was equally advisable.

Authors of grammars sometimes fail to publish corresponding readers. Teachers must consequently use grammars and exercise books of different authors. The disadvantages of such an expedient stand to reason : grammars and readers, not written to aid each other, will in many particulars pursue different ends. For instance, the exercise book will contain words, forms, and rules which are not learned in the grammar, or the latter will insist upon rules for the practice of which the former fails to furnish suitable reading-matter.

We are spared all these inconveniences in the present case; for besides his Grammar, we are indebted to Prof. Kaegi for two Exercise Books, which have been carefully worked out *upon the same method of criticism* that characterizes his Grammar. Indeed, they are so perfectly based upon the latter, that they furnish abundant material, both in unconnected sentences and in narratives, for the practice of such words only as are *current* in the same *School* Authors from which the material was taken for his Grammar, as well as of such rules only as must be perfectly familiar to the student who wishes to read with ease the classical authors specified in the list of the Standard School Authors.

In view of these characteristic features of Kaegi's Grammar and Readers, it is hoped that they will prove a help for many a beginner in the study of Greek at the High Schools, Academies, and the High School (or Academical) Departments of Colleges in this country.

3. A word remains to be said on the extraordinary success of the books of Prof. Kaegi. The *Griechische Schulgrammatik* made its first appearance in 1884. It has since passed through the second, third, fourth, and fifth editions in the years 1889, 1892, 1896, and 1900 respectively. Soon after the publication there appeared a Bohemian, a Russian, a French, and a Polish edition.

The *Short Grammar* was received still more favorably. It first appeared in October, 1892, then in March, 1894, next in April of the same year, again in January and April, 1895, the sixth edition came out in January, 1896, the seventh in January, 1897, the eighth in January, 1898, the ninth in January, 1899, the tenth in January, 1900, the eleventh in January, 1901, the twelfth in January, 1902; in a word, within only ten years it has gone through twelve editions, the last of which comprised eight thousand copies. Nor should it be overlooked that Kaegi's Grammar appeared at a time when, to a superficial observer, there seemed little call for a new Greek grammar in Germany.

The Exercise Books have met with a similar success: within ten years Exercise Book I has been published six times, Exercise Book II has, within seven years, passed through five editions.

4. The present *Short Grammar* is not a mere translation, but to some extent an adaptation of Kaegi's Grammar, inasmuch as the translator has been forced in more than one chapter to depart from the German original, in order to answer the requirements of idiomatic English. Besides several minor changes, some paragraphs were dropped, as they seemed superfluous in an English edition, others were inserted where idiomatic considerations seemed to call for an addition to the German text. These changes are nearly all confined to the Syntactical Part of the work.

In order to conform to the present usage of this country, all Latin expressions, such as *genetivus qualitatis, accusativus cum infinitivo*, etc., have been superseded by their English equivalents.

In accordance with the latest researches, the translator has followed the author in adopting the spellings ἀνύτω, ἀποθνήσκω, μιμνήσκω, οἰκτίρω, μείγνυμι, μείξω, τείσω (of τίνω), etc., although they have not as yet found their way into all text-editions. The same applies to Ξεῖ, πεῖ, φεῖ, χεῖ, ψεῖ.

In the present work, the name of *first perfect* is extended only to those active perfects that end in the formative syllable -κα; all others, including aspirated forms, are designated as *second* perfects.

The *Tables for Repetition*, containing a list of verbs and a summary of the chief rules of Syntax, have been added as an appendix to the Grammar. In the *List of Verbs* those which are of comparatively rare occurrence are marked by smaller print. They may be omitted when the verbs are learned for the first time, but should not be passed over in the repetition. On the other hand, the *regular* forms of certain verbs that do *not* occur in the Standard School Authors have been added from purely practical considerations.

The Tables contain, moreover, a column of *Syntactical Remarks*. They are arranged alphabetically alongside of, and for the most part in connection with, the list of verbs. They may be used exclusively for reference, or for repetition after the study of Syntax, or they may be studied with the respective verbs. In the latter case, the study of Syntax would be prepared and facilitated.

The *Chief Rules of Syntax* are intended to furnish a *brief* and *concise* sketch of the main features of Greek Syntax. They contain those syntactical peculiarities with which a student should be familiar after a few years' study of Greek. Teachers who have little time at their disposal, and indeed all who want to gain time for reading after the study of etymology, will do well to proceed at once to the Chief Rules and leave the Syntax of the Grammar (114–207) to those who wish to pursue it at greater length.

The translator has availed himself of such works as he found of assistance in his task, notably the Greek-English Lexicon of *Liddell* and *Scott*, the Dictionary to Xenophon's Anabasis by Professors *John W. White* and *Morris H. Morgan*, as well as the grammars of Professors *Basil L. Gildersleeve* and *William W. Goodwin*. The treatise on the Ethical Dative was enlarged according to *K. W. Krueger's* Sprachlehre.

All who have kindly assisted the translator in preparing the Grammar are asked to accept this public expression of his gratitude. A fair criticism and the suggestions of those who are engaged in teaching will enable him to make this *Short Grammar of Classical Greek* as perfect as a text-book for students should be, for whom only the best is good enough, and to make it worthy of its author, Dr. Adolf Kaegi, who has done so much for the advancement of the study of Greek.

JAMES A. KLEIST, S. J.

St. Louis University,
St. Louis, Mo., June 6, 1902.

TO THE SECOND EDITION.

In this second edition a thorough revision of the former has been carefully made. Those who are familiar with the first edition of the *Short Grammar* will be pleased to find that there is hardly a page in the Syntactical Part of the work which does not bear traces of improvement. I take pleasure in publicly expressing my grateful appreciation for the kindness of all those Professors of Greek at various Colleges of the country who have generously assisted me in the task of revision. My special thanks are due to Professor John J. Toohey, S.J., of Loyola College, Baltimore, Md., for several letters containing criticisms of the first edition, and many practical hints which I have followed to make the book more useful.

Some critics have suggested that **all the Greek quotations** I have **used to exemplify the rules of Syntax** be **done into English.** As a translation of these sentences, no doubt, greatly facilitates the study of the rules they are intended to illustrate, I have gladly availed myself of this suggestion. The plates of the first edition were to be left intact; hence the translation could not be inserted in the text, but will be found, in the form of an Appendix, on pages 241 sqq. of this volume. No pains have been spared to furnish a translation which would be of real help to the student. Due regard has been paid to the context, which ever lends to the expression of a thought a specific, individual coloring. In elaborating my translation I have freely drawn hints and helps from such excellent works as: *Goodwin's* Moods and Tenses, *Gildersleeve's* Syntax of Classical Greek, *Thompson's* Greek Grammar, *Goodwin's* and *White's* Anabasis. The translations of quotations from Plato are, in most cases, from *Jowett's* classical version of that author. For a careful perusal of the Appendix I am indebted to my friend and colleague James J. O'Brien, S.J., Spring Hill College, Mobile, Ala.

The purpose of the *Appendix*, containing a List of Verbs and a Summary of the Chief Rules of Syntax, has been misjudged by some critics. These I beg to refer to my Preface to the first edition, where they will find the scope of the Appendix explained. The Appendix is not, of course, an integral part of the Grammar. It has been designed for the convenience of those teachers who would be satisfied with a more cursory view of the most important rules of Syntax. Besides, such a summary may not come amiss to students for purposes of repetition.

JAMES A. KLEIST, S.J.

COLLEGE OF THE SACRED HEART,
PRAIRIE DU CHIEN, WIS., May 15, 1905.

PART I.: ON THE SOUNDS.

LETTERS: THEIR FORM AND PRONUNCIATION.

1. 1. The Greek alphabet consists of these twenty-four letters:

FORM		SOUND	NAME	
Capitals or Uncials	Small Cursives			
Α	α	ă (*father*)	Alpha	Ἄλφα
Β	β	b	Bēta	Βῆτα
Γ	γ	g (*g*old)	Gamma	Γάμμα
Δ	δ	d	Delta	Δέλτα
Ε	ε	ĕ (b*e*d)	Epsīlon	Ἔ ψῑλόν
Ζ	ζ	ds (be*ds*)	Zēta	Ζῆτα
Η	η	ē (*ai*r)	Ēta	Ἦτα
Θ	θ	t'h (ho*th*ouse)	Thēta	Θῆτα
Ι	ι	ĭ (r*i*m), ī (*e*ve)	Iōta	Ἰῶτα
Κ	κ	k	Kappa	Κάππα
Λ	λ	l	Lambda	Λάμβδα
Μ	μ	m	Mü	Μῦ
Ν	ν	n	Nü	Νῦ
Ξ	ξ	ks, x (a*x*e)	Xi	Ξεῖ
Ο	ο	ŏ (h*o*t)	Omīkron	Ὄ μῑκρόν
Π	π	p	Pi	Πεῖ
Ρ	ρ	r	Rho	Ῥῶ
Σ	σ, ς	s (*s*ing), z (*z*ero)	Sigma	Σίγμα
Τ	τ	t	Tau	Ταῦ
Υ	υ	ŭ (d*u*ne in French)	Upsīlon	Υ̓́ ψῑλόν
Φ	φ	p'h (u*ph*old)	P'hi	Φεῖ
Χ	χ	k'h (in*kh*orn)	K'hi	Χεῖ
Ψ	ψ	ps	Psi	Ψεῖ
Ω	ω	ō	Omĕga	Ὦ μέγα

2. The form σ is used at the beginning of, and within, a word; the form ς at the **end**; thus,

σάκος, σεισμός. Also εἰς-βάλλω besides εἰσ-βάλλω, etc.

Note 1.—The letter ϝ (*digamma, double gamma*) was in primitive Greek used for the sound *v* (as in ha*v*e); *e.g.* ϝοῖκος = *vīcus*, ὄϝις = *ŏvis*.

Note 2.—The only trace of another letter which originally belonged to the Greek alphabet, the semivowel *j*, *Iōd*, is to be found in certain grammatical facts, which could not otherwise be accounted for. See 77, 3.

3. Note the following points for **pronunciation** :

γ before γ, κ, χ, ξ is sounded as ṇ before *c, g, ch, x ;*

as ἄγγελος aṇgelus, *angel,*	Ἀγχίσης *Anchises,*
ἄγκῦρα aṇcora, *anchor,*	Σφίγξ *Sphinx.*

ζ is equivalent in sound to *ds* in be*ds*.

θ is neither like *t* in *t*ell, nor like *th* in *th*ing, but like *t'h*, i.e. *t* followed by *h* ; thus θείνω *strike* differs from τείνω *stretch*.

φ is like *p* followed by *h*, as in u*ph*old, χ like *k* followed by *h*, as in in*kh*orn.

ι is sounded as the vowel *i* in *i*nk, not as the consonant *y* in *y*onder; hence Ἰωνία *I-onia*.

τι is always like *ti* in *ti*n.

σ and ς have the hissing sound, as *s* in *s*ing, but are pronounced like *z* before the liquids λ, μ, ν, ρ, or the middle mutes (2, 4) γ, β, δ; *e.g.* Σμύρνα *Zmyrna*.

ου has the sound of *u* in r*u*le, αυ that of *ow* in br*ow*n.

Each vowel is distinctly heard in αι, ει, ευ, and οι.

CLASSIFICATION OF SOUNDS.

2. 1. As to quantity, the simple **vowels** are either short (ε, ο) or long (η, ω) or doubtful (ᾰ, ῐ, ῠ).

2. Proper **diphthongs** are

αι, ει, οι, υι, as in Μαῖα, Δαρεῖος, Κροῖσος, Ἅρπυιαι,

αυ, ευ, ου, ηυ, as in Γλαῦκος, Ζεύς, Μοῦσα, ηὔξανον.

3. **Improper diphthongs** arise from a combination of one of the long vowels, ᾱ, η, ω, with a following, (now) silent, ι; hence,

ᾳ, ῃ, ῳ with *iota subscript; e.g.* ᾄδω, ᾖδον, ᾠδή,

Αι, Ηι, Ωι, with *iota adscript; e.g.* Ἅιδης, Ὠιδεῖον.

4. The **simple consonants** are classified according to the part of the organ of speech which produces them and according to their characteristic sound, as follows:

Characteristic Sound	Orders of Sounds	Gutturals Throat Sounds (κ-Sounds)	Labials Lip Sounds (π-Sounds)	Dentals Tooth Sounds (τ-Sounds)
Mutes Momentary Sounds	Smooth Mutes	κ	π	τ
	Middle Mutes	γ	β	δ
	Rough Mutes	χ	ϕ	θ
Semivowels Continuous Sounds	Liquids	λ	ρ	
	Nasals	$\gamma = ng$	μ	ν
	Spirants	j	$ϝ$	σ

Note. — The term Liquids is often applied to both the liquids proper and the nasals μ and ν, hence to λ, μ, ν, ρ.

5. **Double consonants** are $\xi = \kappa\sigma$, $\psi = \pi\sigma$, $\zeta = ds$.

BREATHINGS AND ACCENTS.

3. 1. Every initial vowel or diphthong is marked by a breathing or *spiritus*, which is either

    a) **rough**, *spiritus asper* (‘), as the English *h*:
        ἥρως *hero*, Αἵμων *Haemon;* or

    b) **smooth**, *spiritus lenis* (’), which is not pronounced:
        Ἔρως *Eros*, Αἴγινα *Aegina.*

2. Every initial ρ is aspirated, *i.e.* marked by the *spiritus asper;*
    e.g. ῥήτωρ *rhetor*, Ῥόδος *Rhodos.*

Double ρ in the middle of a word takes either both or neither of the breathings;
    e.g. Πύρρος or Πύῤῥος *Pyrrhus.*

3. There are three **accents** to mark the tone or pitch of voice:

    a) the **circumflex** (ˆ) indicates a lengthened, drawn out tone:
        Ἆγις, Ἀθῆναι, ὀρθῶς.

    b) the **acute** (´) indicates a high pitch of voice:
        ἄγω, ἀγέλη, ὀρθός.

    c) the **grave** (`) indicates a low pitch of voice:
        ὀρθὸς ἦν ὁ λόγος. See 6, 3.

Note. — The Greek accents originally conveyed a *musical* meaning; we now treat them simply as *stress* accents.

4. Position of Breathings and Accents. — They are placed
in case of small letters over the vowel : ὁ ἀνήρ,
in case of capitals before the vowel at the top : ἡ Ἑλλάς,
in proper diphthongs over the second vowel : Αἰγαί, εἰ,
εὐποίητος.

When breathing and accent fall on the same vowel, the breathing
is placed before the acute or grave, but under the circumflex,

e.g.   Αἴας ὤμοσεν, ὃς ἄριστος ἦν.

When improper diphthongs (2, 3) are used as capitals, they take
breathing and accent before the first vowel : Ἅιδης, Ὠιδεῖον —
ᾄδω, ᾠδή.

OTHER READING AND PUNCTUATION SIGNS.

4. 1. The sign of diaeresis (¨) shows that two vowels do
not form a diphthong, but are to be pronounced separately,

e.g.   Ἀτρεΐδης, πραΰνω.

The double dot need not be written, whenever accent and breathing sufficiently mark the diaeresis, as in αὐτή, ὄις.

2. **Punctuation Signs.** — The Greek uses the period (.) and
the comma (,) as the English ; its colon and semicolon is a dot
above the line (·) ; its interrogation point is like our semicolon (;).

DIVISION AND QUANTITY OF SYLLABLES.

5. 1. Every single consonant and every combination of consonants, which can begin a Greek word, is joined to the following
vowel. *E.g.* ἔ-χο-μεν, ἐ-σθής, ὅ-πλον, δε-σμός, νυ-κτός, ἔ-στροφα, —
but δελ-φίς, ἅρ-μα, ἀν-δρός — Πύρ-ρος, ἀγ-γέλ-λω — Βάκ-χος.

2. Compound words are divided according to their component
parts : συν-έχω, προσ-άπτω, ἀπ-έρχομαι, ὥσ-περ.

3. A syllable is **short by nature**, when it has a short vowel followed by only one simple consonant : ἄ-γο-μεν, ἔ-χο-μεν, γέ-νε-σις.

4. A syllable is **long by nature**, when it has a long vowel or a
diphthong : ἥ-ρως, Εὐ-ρώ-πη, ᾠ-δή.

5. A syllable is **long by position**, when it has a short vowel followed by two or more consonants or a double consonant : ἄχθος,
ὀρθός, ἐχθρός, ἄξων, ἔζομαι, ὄψομαι.

6. The pronunciation of syllables which are long by nature **must**
be carefully distinguished from that of syllables which are **only long**
by position. Thus there is a difference between

πράσσω and τάσσω,   πρᾶξις and τάξις,
πρᾶγμα and τάγμα,   μᾶλλον and κάλλος,
βέβηκε and ἕνεκα,   ἄνθρωπος and ῥήτορες.

ACCENTUATION.

6. Nearly every Greek word (see 8) has one or other of the accents mentioned in 3, 3.

General Principles :

1. The **acute** can stand on short and long syllables. The **circumflex** is confined to syllables which are long by nature.

2. The **acute** can stand on any one of the last three syllables, but on the antepenult only when the ultima is short; *e.g.* πόλεμος, πολέμιος, σώματα.

3. An acute on the final syllable of a word which is not separated from the following word by some sign of punctuation is changed to the **grave**; hence Οἱ μὲν αὐτῶν ἦσαν ἀγαθοί, οἱ δὲ κακοί.

Note.— Exceptions are τίς, τί (67, 1).

4. The **circumflex** can stand on either of the last two syllables, but on the penult only when the ultima is short; *e.g.* δῶρον, δῶρᾰ, φεῦγε.

5. Every accented penult must have the circumflex, provided it is long by nature and followed by a short ultima; hence,

θήρ,   but θῆρες,   πολίτης, but πολῖτᾰ,
σώφρων, but σῶφρον,   φεύγω,   but φεῦγε.

Note.— Exceptions are given in 9, note 3.

6. In compound words the accent generally recedes toward the beginning of the word as far as the above rules will allow (*recessive* accent);

e.g.   ὁ φίλος *the friend,* but ἄφιλος *friendless,*
              ἡ τιμή *the honor,*   "   ἄτιμος *dishonored,*
              ὁ νοῦς *the mind,*   "   εὔνους *well-minded,*
              ἑκών *willing,*   "   ἄκων (ἀέκων) *unwilling.*

CLASSIFICATION OF WORDS ACCORDING TO THEIR ACCENT.

7. A word

with the acute on the ultima is called Oxytone : τιμή, ὁδός.

with the acute on the penult is called Paroxytone : λόγος.

with the acute on the antepenult is called Proparoxytone: ἄνθρωπος.

with the circumflex on the ultima is called Perispōmenon: τιμῶν.

with the circumflex on the penult is called Properispōmenon : δῶρον.

without any accent on the ultima is called Barytone : λόγος, δῶρον.

PROCLITICS or WORDS THAT HAVE NO ACCENT.

8. 1. Ten monosyllables are called Atonics (*toneless*) or Proclitics (*leaning forward*) because they attach themselves so closely to the following word as to have no accent of their own. The proclitics are :

    a) the four forms of the article : ὁ, ἡ, οἱ, αἱ.

    b) the three prepositions : εἰς, ἐν, and ἐκ (ἐξ).

    c) the two conjunctions : εἰ (*if*) and ὡς (*how, that, as*).

    d) the negative : οὐ (οὐκ, οὐχ).

  2. Still these proclitics sometimes take an accent :

    a) All are accented, when followed by an enclitic (9 *seqq.*): ὅδε, εἴτε, οὔτε.

    b) Besides, the negative οὐ is accented before a punctuation mark, *i.e.* at the end of a sentence where it has no following word to lean upon : φὴς ἢ οὔ ; — Χειρίσοφος τὸν ἡγεμόνα ἔπαισε μέν, ἔδησε δ᾽ οὔ.

ENCLITICS.

9. 1. Some few words of one or two syllables are called Enclitics (*leaning upon*) because they attach themselves so closely to the preceding word as generally either to lose their own accent or to throw it as an acute upon the preceding word. The enclitics are :

    a) nine forms of the personal pronoun : μοῦ, μοί, μέ — σοῦ, σοί, σέ — οὗ, οἷ, ἕ, 61 ; 62.

    b) the indefinite pronoun τὶς, τὶ in all its cases, 67, 2.

    c) the indefinite adverbs πού, ποί, ποθέν, πώς, πή, ποτέ, 69.

    d) the present indicatives of φημί and εἰμί, except φής and εἶ, 104, 1. 3.

    e) the particles γέ, τέ, τοί, νύν, πέρ, πώ.

    f) the inseparable suffix -δε in ὅδε, τοσόσδε, οἰκόνδε, etc.

  2. The following rules illustrate the different **cases of enclisis** :

    a) The accent of the enclitic is lost

      1. after a perispomenon :   { σοφῶν τις, σοφῶν ἐστιν.

2. after an oxytone or an atonic word; { σοφός τις,
   these, however, receive the acute { σοφοί εἰσιν,
   (not the grave): { οὔτε — οὔποτε.

3. after a proparoxytone or a properi- } ἄνθρωπός τις,
   spomenon, which, in addition to } ἀνθρωποί εἰσιν,
   their own accent, receive an acute } δῶρά ἐστιν.
   on their ultima: }

b) After a paroxytone, enclitics of one { λόγος τις,
   syllable lose their accents, enclitics of { λόγοι τινές,
   two syllables keep them: { λόγων τινῶν.

Note 1.—In the use of enclitics it never happens that more than two syllables remain without an accent;

hence σοφοί τινες and σοφῶν τινων,
but λόγοι τινές and λόγων τινῶν.

Note 2.— When several enclitics follow in succession, each throws its accent as acute upon the preceding: εἴ πώς τίς τινά ποι πέμποι.

Note 3.— By joining certain of the enclitics to the preceding words, compounds arise whose accents deviate from the rule given in 6, 5; e.g. οὔτε, μήτε, ὥστε, οὔτις.

10. Enclitics are accented or orthotoned:

a) according to 9, 2 b: after paroxytones, when the enclitic is dissyllabic.

b) according to 9, note 2: before other enclitics.

c) when special stress is required: σὺν σοί, πρὸς σέ (61, 1).

d) when the syllable upon which the accent was to fall is elided (17); e.g. καλὸς δ᾽ ἐστίν.

e) at the beginning of a sentence; e.g. εἰσὶν ἑκάστοις λόγοι — φαμὲν τοίνυν.

For οἱ, σφίσιν see 62; for ἔστιν see 104, 3, 1. 2.

THE PRINCIPAL PHONETIC LAWS.

11. **Changes of Vowels.** — A certain regularity in the change of vowels often appears in words which belong to the same stem, both in regard to the quantity and the quality of the vowel.

1. Change of Quantity (" *Weakening* or *Shortening of Vowels* "). — The following examples show a substitution of weaker (short) for stronger (long) sounds, or the reverse:

ᾱ and ᾰ: ἐάσω, ἐάω.　　　　　ει and ῐ: λείπω, λιπεῖν.
η and ᾰ: τιμήσω, τιμάω.　　　　ῑ and ῐ: τρίβω, τρῐβή.
η and ε: ποιήσω, ποιέω.　　　　ευ and ῠ: φεύγω, φῠγή.
ω and ο: δουλώσω, δουλόω.　　　ῡ and ῠ: λύσω, λυτός.

2. **Change of Quality** (*Ablaut*). — In like manner there is a change of quality between ε and ο, αι and οι, ευ and ου, η and ω.

e.g. ε and ο: λέγω, λόγος,   νέμω, νομή,   τεκεῖν, τέτοκα.
εἰ and οι: λείπω, λοιπός,   κεῖμαι, κοίτη,   πείθω, πέποιθα.
ευ and ου: σπεύδω, σπουδή, κέλευθος, ἀκόλουθος.
η and ω: ἀρήγω, ἀρωγός, πτήσσω, πτωχός,   ῥήγνυμι, ἔρρωγα.

3. The following table results from a combination of either change:

QUANTITY.		QUALITY.	
Strong.	Weak.	Ablaut.	
η	ᾰ	ω:	φήμη, φᾰτός, φωνή — βῆναι, βᾰσις, βωμός.
η	ε	ω:	θημών, θετός, θωμός — ἥσω, ἑτός, ἀνέωμαι.
ει	ῐ	οι:	λείπειν, λῐπεῖν, λοιπός — πείθειν, πεπῐθεῖν, πέποιθα.
ευ	ῠ	ου:	σεύω, ἔσσῠμαι, ἔσσονα — ἐλεύσομαι, ἤλῠθον, εἰλήλουθα.

Moreover, the proximity and influence of the liquids cause the interchange of

ε   ᾰ   ο: τρέπω, τρᾰπεῖν, τρόπος— στέλλω, στᾰλῆναι, στόλος.
τέμνω, ταμίας, τομή   — μένος, μᾰνῆναι, μέμονα.

12. The Lengthening of Vowels in the Nominative. — The long vowels η and ω in the nominative singular are often due only to a lengthening of ε and ο, which reappear in the other cases;

e.g. ποιμήν, but ποιμέν-ος, etc.,   δαίμων, but δαίμον-ος, etc.,
χιών, but χιόν-ος, etc.,   ῥήτωρ, but ῥήτορ-ος, etc.

13. Compensative Lengthening is the lengthening of a vowel to make up for the loss of consonants. A short vowel with two or three consonants is replaced by a long vowel with one consonant, and consequently a vowel long by position is replaced by one long by nature. This compensative lengthening changes

ᾰ mostly to ᾱ:	thus	παντ-ς	λυσαντ-σι	ἐμιαν-σα	μελαν-ς
	becomes πᾶς,	λύσᾱσι,	ἐμίᾱνα,	μέλᾱς.
more rarely to η:	thus	ἐφαν-σα			
	becomes ἔφηνα.				
ε always to ει:	thus	χαριεντ-ς	λυθεντ-σι	ἐστελ-σα	ἐν-ς
	becomes χαρίεις,	λυθεῖσι,	ἔστειλα,	εἶς.
ο always to ου:	thus	διδοντ-ς	γεροντ-σι	παιδευοντ-σι	
	becomes διδούς,	γέρουσι,	παιδεύουσι.	
ῐ always to ῑ:	thus	ἐκριν-σα			
	becomes ἔκρῑνα.				
ῠ always to ῡ:	thus	φυντ-ς	δεικνυντ-σι	ἤμυν-σα.	
	becomes φύς,	δεικνῦσι,	ἤμῡνα.	

14. Syncope (*a cutting up* or *short*) consists in dropping within a word a short vowel between consonants; *e.g.* γίγνομαι, stem γεν, for γιγένομαι. Compare *gigno*, *genui*.

15. Metathesis (*transposition*) consists in placing a short vowel after a simple liquid (λ, μ, ν, ρ) instead of before the same. The vowel is generally lengthened;

e.g. θάρσος, κάλ-έω, τέμ-νω, θάν-ατος, πορ-εῖν,
　　　θρᾶσος, κλη-τός, τμῆ-σις, θνη-τός, πέ-πρω-ται.

16. 1. Contraction unites in one long vowel or diphthong two vowels that follow each other within a word. Thus τιμά-ων becomes τιμῶν, πλό-ου becomes πλοῦ, γένε-ος becomes γένους.

For the different modes of contraction, see the treatise on Inflection.

2. The contracted syllable receives an accent, if either of the two contracted vowels was accented: the circumflex, if the accent was on the first, the acute, if it was on the second vowel. Thus

τίμαε	becomes τίμᾱ,	ἐτίμαον	becomes ἐτίμων,
τιμάων	becomes τιμῶν,	βεβαώς	becomes βεβώς,
τιμάετε	becomes τιμᾶτε,	τιμαέτω	becomes τιμάτω.

17. 1. Elision consists in dropping a short final vowel before a word beginning with a vowel. The sign of elision is the apostrophe (’); *e.g.* ἐπ’ αὐτῷ for ἐπὶ αὐτῷ, ἀλλ’ ἐγώ for ἀλλὰ ἐγώ, ἀπέχω from ἀπό and ἔχω.

Note.— The vowel υ,— α and ο in monosyllables,— ῐ in περί, ἄχρι, μέχρι, τί τὶ and ὅτι are never elided.

2. Elision influences the accent as follows:

　　a) in oxytone prepositions and conjunctions it is lost:
　　　　thus ἐπ’ ἐμοί for ἐπὶ ἐμοί, ἀλλ’ ἐγώ for ἀλλὰ ἐγώ.

　　b) in all other oxytones it recedes as acute upon the preced
　　　　ing syllable: Εἰ δείν’ ἔδρασας, δεινὰ καὶ παθεῖν σε χρή, —
　　　　τὰ ἀγάθ’ ἦν for τὰ ἀγαθὰ ἦν, φήμ’ ἐγώ for φημὶ ἐγώ.

　　c) in all barytones it remains unchanged:
　　　　οὔτε σοὶ οὔτ’ ἐμοὶ ταῦτ’ ἔλεγον.

18. 1. Crasis (*mixture*) is the contraction of the final vowel or diphthong with the initial vowel of the following word.[1] Its sign is the coronis (’).

The contracted vowel receives an iota subscript, if the last of the vowels to be contracted was an ι; thus ἐγῷμαι for ἐγὼ οἶμαι, but κἄν for καὶ ἄν.

---

[1] Elision, therefore, serves to avoid an hiatus which occurs when the final and the initial vowel of two successive words collide. Crasis serves the same purpose, 18. See also 24.

2. Crasis is most frequent with the article, the relative and with καί and πρό.

ὁ ἀνήρ, τὰ ἄλλα, ἃ ἐγώ, καὶ ἐν, καὶ ἄν, προέλεγον,
becomes ἀνήρ, τἆλλα, ἀγώ, κἀν, κἄν, προὔλεγον.

3. The accent of the first word is generally lost, that of the second determines which syllable is to have the accent after the contraction.

19. Concurrence of Consonants. — Two or more adjoining consonants are hardly ever left unchanged. They are subject to certain modifications according to definite principles. The second consonant is generally left unaltered and a change is produced only in the first of the two sounds. This euphonic change is especially brought about by assimilation (*change to a like sound*), dissimilation (*change to a different sound*), and elision (*suppression of a sound*).

Special attention is due to the euphonic changes :

a) in the nom. sg. and dat. pl. of the 3d decl., 38 *seqq.*

b) in the third class of verbs (with -*jω* in the present), 77, 3.

c) in the formation of tenses of mute verbs, 82 ; 83.

d) in the final consonants of prepositions in compounds, as in 20.

20. Before the **rough breathing** a smooth mute is changed to the corresponding rough :

thus οὐκ οὗτος, ἀπ' οὗ, ἀντ' ὧν, ἐπ' and ὁδός,
becomes οὐχ οὗτος, ἀφ' οὗ, ἀνθ' ὧν, ἔφοδος.

21. Changes in the Rough Mutes. —

1. If two successive syllables begin each with a rough mute, generally one of the two is changed to the corresponding smooth ; in particular

the first is changed in the reduplication : πεφύτευκα — τίθημι, 74, 1.

and in the aor. pass. of θύω and τίθημι : ἐτύθην, ἐτέθην.

the second is changed in the aor. imper. pass. : παιδεύθη-τι for παιδεύθηθι, 78, 8.

In other cases, however, both rough mutes remain unchanged. Thus in ὠρθώθην, ηὐθύνθην, ἐθέλχθην, ἐφάνθην, πεφάνθαι, ἐκαθάρθην. κεκαθάρθαι, φάθι, ἐχύθην, etc.

2. Whenever in several monosyllabic stems the **final rough** mute is dropped, the initial consonant is changed to the corresponding rough ; thus in the stems ταφ-, ταχ-, τρεφ-, τρεχ-, τρυφ- and τριχ-.

Compare τάφος, ταχύς, τρέφω, τρέχω, τρυφή, τρίχες, with θάπτω, θάττων, θρέψω, ἔθρεξα, θρύπτω, θριξίν.

There are initial and final rough mutes in τεθράφθαι (from τρέφω, but τετράφθαι from τρέπω), τεθάφθαι and ἐθάφθην (from θάπτω).

22. Initial ρ **is doubled** when a **short vowel** precedes it whether as augment or as reduplication:

ἔρριπτον, ἔρριψα, — ἔρριφα, ἔρρωμαι.

Thus also in composition: ἐπιρρίπτω, διαρρήγνυμι, ἄρρωστος, ἀπόρρητος.

23. Rule for Consonantal Termination. — No Greek word can end in any other consonant than ν, ρ, or σ (ξ, ψ). Consequently, other consonants which by rights should stand at the end of a word must be dropped. Thus παῖ is for παιδ, σῶμα for σωματ.

Note. — The two particles ἐκ and οὐκ are only apparent exceptions; for these proclitics (8) attach themselves so closely to the following word as to coalesce into one; consequently, κ must be considered as being in the *middle* of the word thus formed. Compare οὐκέτι, and 24, 2. 3.

MOVABLE FINAL CONSONANTS.

24. 1. N movable (ν ἐφελκυστικόν *drawn after*) is added [1]
   a) to third persons in -ε(ν) and -σι(ν) : ἐπαίδευε(ν), ἐπαίδευ-σε(ν), παιδεύουσι(ν), δίδωσι(ν), διδόασι(ν), εἰσί(ν).
   b) to datives and locatives in -σι(ν) : πᾶσι(ν), ᾿Αθήνησι(ν).
   c) to some other words with similar endings : εἴκοσι(ν), — ἐστί(ν).

This ν may or may not stand before a following consonant,
      it must stand before a following vowel, as well as
            before punctuation marks.

2. Σ movable is taken by οὕτω *thus*, and ἐκ *out;* the spelling is οὕτως and ἐξ before vowels.

E.g. οὕτω γράφω, but οὕτως ἔγραφον — ἐκ τοῦ οἴκου, but ἐξ οἴκου.

3. A movable guttural is sometimes added to the negative οὐ.
Use οὐκ before vowels with the smooth breathing : οὐκ ἀγαθόν,
      οὐχ before vowels with the rough breathing : οὐχ ἁπλῶς,
      οὐ before all consonants : οὐ καλῶς, οὐ ῥᾳδίως.

Note. — Before a punctuation mark, οὐ is accented, οὔ (8, 2), even when followed by a vowel:

᾿Εξικνοῦντο γὰρ οὔ, οὐδ᾿ ἔβλαπτον οὐδέν.
Εἴτε μηνύουσιν εἴτε καὶ οὔ· ἀμφότερα γὰρ εἰκάζεται.

_____
[1] See foot-note on page 9.

PART II.: INFLECTION.

1. INFLECTION OF NOUNS AND ADJECTIVES.

PRELIMINARY NOTES.

25. 1. Unlike the Latin, the Greek language has a special form for the **dual** number (71 ; 96), but none for the ablative case.

2. Note the following rules of **gender** :

a) The names of males are masculine. So are those of rivers, winds and months.

b) The names of females are feminine. So are those of trees, countries, islands and towns.

c) Most diminutives are neuter, even when they denote persons: τὸ παιδίον *the little boy, little girl.*

3. **Neuters** have in each number but one form for the nominative, accusative and vocative. These cases always end in the plural in -ᾰ.

4. The **vocative** and **nominative** plural are always, the vocative and nominative singular are often, alike in form.

5. The **accent** remains, as long as the general rules of accentuation (6) allow, on that syllable which has it in the nom. sing. Final -αι and -οι are accounted short.

Note. — A few exceptions are mentioned in 36, 6. 7 and 67, 2.

6. In the genitive and dative cases, such final syllables as are long and accented generally have the circumflex. In other cases they take the acute.

The circumflex on the ultima in the nom., acc. and voc. is met with only in some monosyllables and in contracted words.

THE ARTICLE.

26. Like the English, the Greek has a definite article, but, unlike our idiom, it has a separate form for each gender : ὁ ἡ τό *the.*

12

Sing. Nom.	ὁ ἡ τό	*the*	Plur. Nom.	οἱ αἱ τά
Gen.	τοῦ τῆς τοῦ	*of the*	Gen.	τῶν τῶν τῶν
Dat.	τῷ τῇ τῷ	*to (for) the*	Dat.	τοῖς ταῖς τοῖς
Acc.	τόν τήν τό	*the*	Acc.	τούς τάς τά

Note.— The article has no form for the vocative; in its place the interjection
ὦ is used in all numbers.

A–DECLENSION.

27. It includes all words with stems in -a, which in certain cases
of the singular is changed to η. The A-declension corresponds in
general to the first declension in Latin; it contains masculines and
feminines.

28. FEMININES IN -ᾱ, -η, AND ᾰ.

Stems:	οἰκῐᾱ- *house*	χωρᾱ- *country*	στρατιᾱ- *army*	δοξᾰ- *opinion*	Μουσᾰ- *Muse*
Sing. N.V.	ἡ, ὦ, οἰκίᾱ	χώρᾱ	στρατιά	δόξᾰ	Μοῦσᾰ
G.	τῆς οἰκίας	χώρας	στρατιᾶς	δόξης	Μούσης
D.	τῇ οἰκίᾳ	χώρᾳ	στρατιᾷ	δόξῃ	Μούσῃ
A.	τὴν οἰκίαν	χώραν	στρατιάν	δόξᾰν	Μοῦσᾰν
Plur. N.V.	αἱ, ὦ, οἰκίαι	χῶραι	στρατιαί	δόξαι	Μοῦσαι
G.	τῶν οἰκιῶν	χωρῶν	στρατιῶν	δοξῶν	Μουσῶν
D.	ταῖς οἰκίαις	χώραις	στρατιαῖς	δόξαις	Μούσαις
A.	τὰς οἰκίας	χώρας	στρατιάς	δόξας	Μούσας

Stems:	μᾰχᾱ- *battle*	νῑκᾱ- *victory*	τῑμᾱ- *honor*	θαλαττᾰ- *sea*	γεφῡρᾱ- *bridge*
Sing. N.V.	ἡ, ὦ, μάχη	νίκη	τιμή	θάλαττᾰ	γέφυρᾰ
G.	τῆς μάχης	νίκης	τιμῆς	θαλάττης	γεφύρας
D.	τῇ μάχῃ	νίκῃ	τιμῇ	θαλάττῃ	γεφύρᾳ
A.	τὴν μάχην	νίκην	τιμήν	θάλαττᾰν	γέφυρᾰν
Plur. N.V.	αἱ, ὦ, μάχαι	νῖκαι	τιμαί	θάλατται	γέφυραι
G.	τῶν μαχῶν	νικῶν	τιμῶν	θαλαττῶν	γεφυρῶν
D.	ταῖς μάχαις	νίκαις	τιμαῖς	θαλάτταις	γεφύραις
A.	τὰς μάχας	νίκας	τιμάς	θαλάττας	γεφύρας

1. **Change of a to η in the singular.**

   a) An *a* in the nominative after ε, ι, ρ remains throughout
      the singular (*a, as, ᾳ, αν, a*).

b) An η in the nominative is likewise retained throughout the singular (η, ης, ῃ, ην, η).

c) An a in the nominative after other consonants than ρ is changed in the genitive and dative to η (a, ης, ῃ, αν, a).

2. Quantity. — The ending -ας is always long.

3. Rule of Accent. — In the genitive plural the a of the stem is contracted with the case ending -ων. Consequently, all nouns of the A-declension are in the genitive plural perispomena in -ῶν.

29. MASCULINES IN -ᾱς AND -ης.

Stems:	νεᾱνῐᾱ- youth	πολῑτᾱ- citizen	δικαστᾱ- judge	᾿Ατρειδᾱ- Atreus' son
Sing. Nom.	ὁ νεανίας	πολίτης	δικαστής	᾿Ατρείδης
Gen.	τοῦ νεανίου	πολίτου	δικαστοῦ	᾿Ατρείδου
Dat.	τῷ νεανίᾳ	πολίτῃ	δικαστῇ	᾿Ατρείδῃ
Acc.	τὸν νεανίαν	πολίτην	δικαστήν	᾿Ατρείδην
Voc.	ὦ νεανία	πολῖτᾰ	δικαστᾰ	᾿Ατρείδη
Plur. N. Voc.	οἱ, ὦ, νεανίαι	πολῖται	δικασταί	᾿Ατρεῖδαι
Gen.	τῶν νεανιῶν	πολιτῶν	δικαστῶν	᾿Ατρειδῶν
Dat.	τοῖς νεανίαις	πολίταις	δικασταῖς	᾿Ατρείδαις
Acc.	τοὺς νεανίας	πολίτας	δικαστάς	᾿Ατρείδας

1. Masculines differ from feminines only in the nom. and gen. sing. The final ᾱ of the stem remains after ε, ι, ρ; otherwise it is changed to η (28, 1).

2. The voc. sing. ends in the same vowel, -ᾱ or -η, which occurs in the last syllable of the nom. :

hence ὦ νεανίᾱ, ὦ ᾿Ατρείδη.

All words in -της, however, have a short -ᾰ :

ὦ πολῖτα, ὦ Σπαρτιᾶτα, ὦ ᾿Ορέστᾰ.

So have national names in -ης :

ὦ Πέρσᾰ, Σκύθα, Σπαρτιᾶτα.

3. Some Doric and very many foreign proper names in -ᾱς have -ᾱ in the gen. sing. (Doric Genitive) :

Φοιβίδᾱ, Εὐρώτᾱ — ᾿Αβροκόμᾱ, Μάσκᾱ, ᾿Ορόντᾱ.

30. CONTRACTS OF THE A-DECLENSION.

Stems:	Ἀθηναα, Ἀθηνᾱ- Athena	γεα, γη- earth	Ερμεα, Ἑρμη- Hermes, plur. Hermes Pillars.	
Sing. N.	ἡ Ἀθηνᾶ	ἡ γῆ	ὁ Ἑρμῆς	οἱ Ἑρμαῖ
G.	Ἀθηνᾶς	γῆς	Ἑρμοῦ	Ἑρμῶν
D.	Ἀθηνᾷ	γῇ	Ἑρμῇ	Ἑρμαῖς
A.	Ἀθηνᾶν	γῆν	Ἑρμῆν	Ἑρμᾶς
V.	Ἀθηνᾶ	γῆ	Ἑρμῆ	Ἑρμαῖ

-ᾰᾱ is contracted to -ᾶ, -έᾱ after ρ to -ᾶ, otherwise to -ῇ; before vowels or diphthongs a and ε are absorbed: Ἑρμαῖ, Ἑρμῶν.

Rule of Accent. — All the cases are perispomena.

O–DECLENSION.

31. 1. It comprises words with stems in -ο, besides some in -ω. Thus it corresponds in general to the second declension in Latin. It contains masculines and neuters, and a number of feminines.

Stems:	λογο- word, speech	δημο- people	ἀνθρωπο- human being, man	ὁδο- way, road	δωρο- gift
Sing. N.	ὁ λόγος	ὁ δῆμος	ὁ ἄνθρωπος	ἡ ὁδός	τὸ δῶρον
G	τοῦ λόγου	δήμου	ἀνθρώπου	τῆς ὁδοῦ	τοῦ δώρου
D.	τῷ λόγῳ	δήμῳ	ἀνθρώπῳ	τῇ ὁδῷ	τῷ δώρῳ
A.	τὸν λόγον	δῆμον	ἄνθρωπον	τὴν ὁδόν	τὸ δῶρον
V.	ὦ λόγε	δῆμε	ἄνθρωπε	ὦ ὁδέ	ὦ δῶρον
Plur. N.V.	οἱ λόγοι	δῆμοι	ἄνθρωποι	αἱ ὁδοί	τὰ δῶρα
G.	τῶν λόγων	δήμων	ἀνθρώπων	τῶν ὁδῶν	τῶν δώρων
D.	τοῖς λόγοις	δήμοις	ἀνθρώποις	ταῖς ὁδοῖς	τοῖς δώροις
A.	τοὺς λόγους	δήμους	ἀνθρώπους	τὰς ὁδούς	τὰ δῶρα

2. The following are feminine nouns in -ος. See 25, 2 b.

ἡ παρθένος maiden,   ἡ νῆσος island,   ἡ Αἴγυπτος Egypt,
ἡ ἄμπελος vine,   ἡ Δῆλος Delos,   ἡ Κόρινθος Corinth,
ἡ ἤπειρος mainland, ἡ Ἤπειρος Epirus,   ἡ Πελοπόννησος Peloponnesus.

ADJECTIVES OF THE A- AND O–DECLENSIONS.

32. 1. The feminine form has in the singular -ā after ε, ι, ρ, otherwise η. *E.g.* :

νέος, νέα, νέον *new, young,*
δίκαιος, δικαία, δίκαιον *just,*
πατρῷος, πατρῴα, πατρῷον *paternal,*
αἰσχρός, αἰσχρά, αἰσχρόν *shameful,*

φίλος, φίλη, φίλον *dear,*
ὀλίγος, ὀλίγη, ὀλίγον *little,*
λίθινος, λιθίνη, λίθινον *of stone,*
ἀγαθός, ἀγαθή, ἀγαθόν *good.*

Stems :	ἀγᾰθο-,	ἀγᾰθᾱ-, good	ἀγᾰθο-,	δῐκαιο-,	δῐκαιᾱ-, just	δῐκαιο-,
Sing. N.	ἀγαθός	ἀγαθή	ἀγαθόν	δίκαιος	δικαία	δίκαιον
G.	ἀγαθοῦ	ἀγαθῆς	ἀγαθοῦ	δικαίου	δικαίας	δικαίου
D.	ἀγαθῷ	ἀγαθῇ	ἀγαθῷ	δικαίῳ	δικαίᾳ	δικαίῳ
A.	ἀγαθόν	ἀγαθήν	ἀγαθόν	δίκαιον	δικαίαν	δίκαιον
V.	ἀγαθέ	ἀγαθή	ἀγαθόν	δίκαιε	δικαία	δίκαιον
Plur. N. V.	ἀγαθοί	ἀγαθαί	ἀγαθά	δίκαιοι	δίκαιαι	δίκαια
G.	ἀγαθῶν	ἀγαθῶν	ἀγαθῶν	δικαίων	δικαίων	δικαίων
D.	ἀγαθοῖς	ἀγαθαῖς	ἀγαθοῖς	δικαίοις	δικαίαις	δικαίοις
A.	ἀγαθούς	ἀγαθάς	ἀγαθά	δικαίους	δικαίας	δίκαια

2. The accent of the nom. and gen. plur. fem. of barytone adjectives and participles in -ος, -η(-α), -ον is the same as that of the masculine.

E.g. δίκαιος, nom. pl. masc. δίκαιοι, gen. pl. masc. δικαίων,
δικαία, nom. pl. fem. δίκαιαι, gen. pl. fem. δικαίων

(against 25, 5 not δικαῖαι; nor δικαῶν, see 28, 3).

3. Many, and especially almost all compound, adjectives in -ος have but two endings.

E.g. βάρβαρος, -ον *foreign,*
ἥμερος, -ον *tame,*
ἥσυχος, -ον *quiet,*
φρόνιμος, -ον *prudent,*

πρᾶος, -ον *mild, tame,*
ἄβᾰτος, -ον *impassable,*
ἔντῑμος, -ον *honored,*
παράνομος, -ον *unlawful.*

Note ἐν-αντίος, -α, -ον *opposite, opposed.*

4. Other adjectives have sometimes two, sometimes three endings.

E.g. βέβαιος, 2. and 3., *firm,*
ἔρημος, 2. and 3., *deserted,*

χρήσιμος, 2. and 3., *useful,*
ὠφέλιμος, 2. and 3., *profitable.*

Also some compounds, as ἀν-άξιος, *unworthy,* and ἀν-αίτιος, *guiltless.*

33. CONTRACTS OF THE O-DECLENSION.

Stems :	νοο- = νου- mind		ὀστεο- = ὀστου- bone		εὐνοο- = εὐνου- well-minded		
					masc. fem.		neut.
Sing. N.	ὁ΄ νόος	νοῦς	τὸ ὀστέον	ὀστοῦν	εὔνους		εὔνουν
G.	νόου	νοῦ	ὀστέου	ὀστοῦ	εὔνου		
D.	νόῳ	νῷ	ὀστέῳ	ὀστῷ	εὔνῳ		
A.	νόον	νοῦν	ὀστέον	ὀστοῦν	εὔνουν		εὔνουν
Plur. N.	οἱ νόοι	νοῖ	τὰ ὀστέα	ὀστᾶ	εὖνοι		εὔνοα
G.	νόων	νῶν	ὀστέων	ὀστῶν	εὔνων		
D.	νόοις	νοῖς	ὀστέοις	ὀστοῖς	εὔνοις		
A.	νόους	νοῦς	ὀστέα	ὀστᾶ	εὔνους		εὔνοα

1. -εο and -οο are contracted to -ου, -εᾰ to -ᾱ; ε and ο before long vowels or diphthongs are absorbed.

2. The nom. and acc. pl. neut. of the adjectives of this class are never contracted: εὔνοα, ἄνοα, κακόνοα.

3. **Rule of Accent.** — Simple words are in all the cases perispomena; compound words retain the accent on the same syllable upon which it falls in the nom. sg. : ἔκπλοι, περίπλων, εὖνοι (accent against 16, 1), εὔνων, εὔνοις, εὔνους, εὔνοα.

CONTRACTED ADJECTIVES OF THE A- AND O-DECLENSIONS.

34. 1. The only adjectives which admit contraction are :

   a) adjectives in -εος, denoting material or color.

   b) multiplicatives in -πλόος (= -fold, -plex, 70, 4).

2. The contraction is the same as in the nouns ; the feminine sg. has -α after ρ, otherwise -η (28, 1 ; 29, 1).

3. **Rule of Accent.** — All the cases are perispomena.

For the compounds of νοῦς and πλοῦς, see 33, 3.

'Αργυροῦς, silver, and χρυσοῦς, golden, are thus declined :

ἀργύρεος, ἀργύρεᾱ, ἀργύρεον silver					
S. N. V.	ἀργυροῦς ἀργυρᾶ ἀργυροῦν	P. N. V.	ἀργυροῖ	ἀργυραῖ	ἀργυρᾶ
G.	ἀργυροῦ ἀργυρᾶς ἀργυροῦ	G.	ἀργυρῶν	ἀργυρῶν	ἀργυρῶν
D.	ἀργυρῷ ἀργυρᾷ ἀργυρῷ	D.	ἀργυροῖς	ἀργυραῖς	ἀργυροῖς
A.	ἀργυροῦν ἀργυρᾶν ἀργυροῦν	A.	ἀργυροῦς	ἀργυρᾶς	ἀργυρᾶ

χρύσεος, χρῡσέα, χρύσεον *golden*						
S. N.V.	χρυσοῦς	χρυσῆ	χρυσοῦν	P. N.V.	χρυσοῖ χρυσαῖ χρυσᾶ
G.	χρυσοῦ	χρυσῆς	χρυσοῦ	G.	χρυσῶν χρυσῶν χρυσῶν
D.	χρυσῷ	χρυσῇ	χρυσῷ	D.	χρυσοῖς χρυσαῖς χρυσοῖς
A.	χρυσοῦν	χρυσῆν	χρυσοῦν	A.	χρυσοῦς χρυσᾶς χρυσᾶ

THE ATTIC DECLENSION.

35. 1. It includes substantive and adjective stems in -ω.

Stems:	νεω- temple	ἵλεω- propitious	
Sing. N. V.	ὁ νεώς	ἵλεως	ἵλεων
G.	νεώ	ἵλεω	
D.	νεῴ	ἵλεῳ	
A.	νεών	ἵλεων	ἵλεων
Plur. N. V.	οἱ νεῴ	ἵλεῳ	ἵλεα
G.	νεών	ἵλεων	
D.	νεῴς	ἵλεῳς	
A.	νεώς	ἵλεως	ἵλεα

2. The ω is retained through all the cases and absorbs the case-endings as far as possible. The ι is always subscript.

3. Ἡ ἕως *the dawn* is thus declined: ἕως, ἕω, ἕῳ, ἕω (without ν!).

4. Adjectives have -ᾰ in the nom., voc. and acc. plur. neut.

5. **Rule of Accent.** — The accent of the nom. sing. is retained through all the cases; the ω is counted as short in determining the accent of the barytones, hence Μενέλεως, ἔκπλεώς ἐστιν, ἵλεῴ εἰσιν.

THE CONSONANTAL DECLENSION.
INTRODUCTORY NOTES.

36. 1. This declension includes all the stems that end in a consonant, or in -ι, -υ, and diphthongs, with a few in -ω and -ο. It corresponds, therefore, in general to the third and fourth declensions in Latin.

2. For the regular case-endings see the declension of ἅλς, 37.

Note. — -α and -ας, -ι and -σι are short.

As not all successive consonants can remain unchanged (19), and no other consonant except ν, ρ and ς can end a Greek word (23), certain changes must take place in the nom. sing. and in the dat. plur. before the endings -ς and -σι, as well as in the final consonants of the pure stem.

3. The **nom. sing.** masc. and fem. is formed either with or without -ς. In the latter case the vowel of the stem is lengthened (12).

Neuters show their pure stems in the nom., acc. and voc. sing. as far as the rule for final consonants will allow (23).

4. In the **acc. sing. and plur.** masc. and fem., consonant stems have, as a rule, -ἄ and -ἄς added to them, vowel stems -ν and (-ν)ς.

The acc. plur. masc. and fem. of the -ς, -ι, and the adjective -υ stems is the same as the nom.: οἱ and τοὺς εὐγενεῖς, αἱ and τὰς πόλεις, οἱ and τοὺς ἡδεῖς.

5. The **voc. sing.** masc. and fem. is either the same as the nom.:

ὦ φύλαξ, ὦ Ἄραψ, ὦ ποιμήν,

or the same as the pure stem, as far as the rule for consonantal termination allows:

ὦ ῥῆτορ, ὦ παῖ (for παιδ), ὦ γέρον (for γέροντ).

6. **Rule of Accent.** — Monosyllables have the accent on the ending in the gen. and dat. of all three numbers:

θηρός, θηρί — θηρῶν, θηρσί(ν).

7. Contrary to this rule, the stem is accented:

    a) in all the cases of participles: ὄντος, ὄντι, θέντων, θεῖσι(ν).

    b) in the gen. and dat. plur. of the word πᾶς (*omnis*),
        hence παντός, παντί, but πάντων, πᾶσι(ν) (41, 3).

    c) in the gen. plur. of the words
        ὁ παῖς παιδός *boy*, τὸ οὖς ὠτός *ear*;
        hence παιδός, παιδί, παισί(ν), but παίδων,
        ὠτός, ὠτί, and ὠσί(ν), but ὤτων.

37. STEMS IN LIQUIDS (-λ, -ρ). (See ὕδωρ 39; ὄναρ, πῦρ 50; ἦρ 60.)

Stems:	ἀλ- *sal* salt	θηρ- *beast*	κρᾱτηρ- *mixing bowl*	ῥητορ- *orator*
Sing. N.	ὁ ἅλ-ς	ὁ θήρ	ὁ κρατήρ	ὁ ῥήτωρ
G.	ἀλ-ός	θηρ-ός	κρατῆρ-ος	ῥήτορ-ος
D.	ἀλ-ί	θηρ-ί	κρατῆρ-ι	ῥήτορ-ι
A.	ἅλ-α	θῆρ-α	κρατῆρ-α	ῥήτορ-α
V.	ἅλ-ς	θήρ	κρατήρ	ῥῆτορ
Plur. N. V.	οἱ ἅλ-ες	οἱ θῆρ-ες	οἱ κρατῆρ-ες	οἱ ῥήτορ-ες
G.	ἀλ-ῶν	θηρ ῶν	κρατῆρ-ων	ῥητόρ-ων
D.	ἀλ-σί(ν)	θηρ-σί(ν)	κρατῆρ-σι(ν)	ῥήτορ-σι(ν)
A.	ἅλ-ας	θῆρ-ας	κρατῆρ-ας	ῥήτορ-ας

38. STEMS IN GUTTURALS (-κ, -γ, -χ) AND LABIALS (-π, -β, -φ).

Stems:	φυλακ- *watchman*	αἰγ- *goat*	γῦπ- *vulture*
Sing. N. V.	ὁ, ὦ φύλαξ	ἡ, ὦ αἴξ	ὁ, ὦ γύψ
G.	φύλακ-ος	αἰγ-ός	γῦπ-ός
D.	φύλακ-ι	αἰγ-ί	γῦπ-ί
A.	φύλακ-α	αἰγ-α	γῦπ-α
Plur. N. V.	οἱ φύλακ-ες	αἱ αἰγ-ες	οἱ γῦπ-ες
G.	φυλάκ-ων	αἰγ-ῶν	γῦπ-ῶν
D.	φύλαξι(ν)	αἰξί(ν)	γῦψί(ν)
A.	φύλακ-ας	αἰγ-ας	γῦπ-ας

With -σ, any guttural becomes ξ, any labial becomes ψ:
st. φυλακ-, N. S. φύλαξ; comp. Lat. stem *duc-*, N. S. *dux;*
st. Ἀραβ-, D. P. Ἄραψι; comp. Lat. *scripsi* of *scribo*.

39. STEMS IN DENTALS (-τ, -δ, -θ).

Stems	γυμνητ- *light-armed soldier*	ἐλπῐδ- *hope*	σωμᾰτ- *body*
Sing. N.	ὁ γυμνής	ἡ ἐλπῐς	τὸ σῶμα
G.	γυμνῆτ-ος	ἐλπῐδ-ος	σώμᾰτ-ος
D.	γυμνῆτ-ι	ἐλπῐδ-ι	σώμᾰτ-ι
A.	γυμνῆτ-α	ἐλπῐδ-α	σῶμα
V.	γυμνής	ἐλπῐς	σῶμα
Plur. N. V.	γυμνῆτ-ες	ἐλπῐδ-ες	σώμᾰτ-α
G.	γυμνήτ-ων	ἐλπῐδ-ων	σωμάτ-ων
D.	γυμνῆ-σι(ν)	ἐλπῐ-σι(ν)	σώμᾰ-σι(ν)
A.	γυμνῆτ-ας	ἐλπῐδ-ας	σώμᾰτ-α

1. Before σ simple dentals are dropped:
ἐσθής, ἐσθῆσι(ν) (for ἐσθητς, ἐσθητσι(ν)); cf. Lat. *dos, dotis*.
Final dentals are also dropped: σῶμα (for σωματ) (23).

2. Barytones with dental stems in -ις and -υς form the acc.
sing. (like the -ι and -υ stems, 46 seqq.) in -ιν and -υν.

E.g. ἡ ἐλπῐς, *hope*, ἐλπῐδος, ἐλπῐδι, ἐλπῐδα,
but ἡ χᾰρῐς, *grace*, χᾰρῐτος, χᾰρῐτι, χᾰριν,
ἡ ἔρῐς, *strife*, ἔρῐδος, ἔρῐδι, ἔρῐν.

3. The following words show an irregularity only in the nom. sing.:

ὁ πούς, ποδός *foot, pēs,*　　　　　τὸ γόνυ, γόνᾰτος *knee,*
τὸ οὖς, ὠτός *ear* (36, 7. c),　　　τὸ δόρυ, δόρᾰτος *spear,*
τὸ φῶς, φωτός (only sing.) *light,*　τὸ ὕδωρ, ὕδᾰτος *water,*
τὸ κέρας, κέρᾱτος *horn, wing of an army.*

4. **Adjectives** have partly two endings, as ἄχαρις, -ι *unpleasant* (G. ἀχάριτος, D. ἀχάριτι, A. ἄχαριν, -ι); partly only one, as πένης, -ητος *poor;* φυγάς, -άδος *fugitive, exiled.*

40. STEMS IN -ν.

Stems:	Ἑλλην- *Greek*	ποιμεν- *shepherd*	δαιμον- *deity*	εὐδαιμον- *happy*		
				m. fem.		neut.
S. N.	ὁ Ἕλλην	ὁ ποιμήν	ὁ δαίμων	εὐδαίμων		εὔδαιμον
G.	Ἕλλην-ος	ποιμέν-ος	δαίμον-ος	εὐδαίμονος		
D.	Ἕλλην-ι	ποιμέν-ι	δαίμον-ι	εὐδαίμονι		
A.	Ἕλλην-α	ποιμέν-α	δαίμον-α	εὐδαίμονα		εὔδαιμον
V.	Ἕλλην	ποιμήν	δαῖμον	εὔδαιμον		εὔδαιμον
Pl. N.V.	Ἕλλην-ες	ποιμέν-ες	δαίμον-ες	εὐδαίμονες		εὐδαίμονα
G.	Ἑλλήν-ων	ποιμέν-ων	δαιμόν-ων	εὐδαιμόνων		
D.	Ἕλλη-σι(ν)	ποιμέ-σι(ν)	δαίμο-σι(ν)	εὐδαίμο-σι(ν)		
A.	Ἕλλην-ας	ποιμέν-ας	δαίμον-ας	εὐδαίμονας		εὐδαίμονα

1. Before σ, ν is simply dropped: ποιμέσι, δαίμοσι, μέλᾱσι.
2. **Adjectives** have recessive accent: εὔδαιμον, 6, 6.
3. Besides the forms in -ονα and -ονες, -ονας, the **comparatives** in -ων, -ον (57 and 58) have also the shorter ones in -ω and -ους.

Stem: κακῑον- *worse*					
	masc. fem.	neut.			
Sing. N.	κακίων	κάκῑον	Plur. N.	κακίονες	κακίονα
G.	κακίονος		V.	κακίους	κακίω
D.	κακίονι		G.	κακιόνων	
A.	κακίονα / κακίω	κάκῑον	D.	κακίοσι(ν)	
V.	κάκῑον		A.	κακίονας / κακίους	κακίονα / κακίω

41. STEMS IN -ντ.

Stems:	γιγαντ- *giant*	ὀδοντ- *tooth*	γεροντ- *old man*
Sing. Nom.	ὁ γίγᾱς	ὁ ὀδούς	ὁ γέρων
Gen.	γίγαντ-ος	ὀδόντ-ος	γέροντ-ος
Dat.	γίγαντ-ι	ὀδόντ-ι	γέροντ-ι
Acc.	γίγαντ-α	ὀδόντ-α	γέροντ-α
Voc.	γίγαν	ὀδούς	γέρον
Plur. N. V.	γίγαντ-ες	ὀδόντ-ες	γέροντ-ες
Gen.	γιγάντ-ων	ὀδόντ-ων	γερόντ-ων
Dat.	γίγᾱ-σι(ν)	ὀδοῦ-σι(ν)	γέρου-σι(ν)
Acc.	γίγαντ-ας	ὀδόντ-ας	γέροντ-ας

1. Before σ, ντ is dropped with compensative lengthening (13)

both in the nom. sing.: γίγᾱς for γιγἄντς, ὀδούς for ὀδοντς,
and in the dat. plur.: γίγᾱσι for γίγαντσι, γέρουσι for γέροντσι.

2. Nouns with stems in -ντ are all masculine.

3. PARADIGMS OF ADJECTIVES AND PARTICIPLES.

Stems:	ἀκοντ- *unwilling*			λυθεντ- *loosed*		
S. N.V.	ἄκων	ἄκουσα	ἆκον	λυθείς	λυθεῖσα	λυθέν
G.	ἄκοντ-ος	ἀκούσης	ἄκοντ-ος	λυθέντ-ος	λυθείσης	λυθέντ-ος
D.	ἄκοντ-ι	ἀκούσῃ	ἄκοντ-ι	λυθέντ-ι	λυθείσῃ	λυθέντ-ι
A.	ἄκοντ-α	ἄκουσαν	ἆκον	λυθέντ-α	λυθεῖσαν	λυθέν
Pl. N.V.	ἄκοντ-ες	ἄκουσαι	ἄκοντ-α	λυθέντ-ες	λυθεῖσαι	λυθέντ-α
G.	ἀκόντ-ων	ἀκουσῶν	ἀκόντ-ων	λυθέντ-ων	λυθεισῶν	λυθέντ-ων
D.	ἄκου-σι(ν)	ἀκούσαις	ἄκου-σι	λυθεῖ-σι(ν)	λυθείσαις	λυθεῖ-σι(ν)
A.	ἄκοντ-ας	ἀκούσας	ἄκοντ-α	λυθέντ-ας	λυθείσας	λυθέντ-α

Stem:	παντ- *all, whole*					
S. N.V.	πᾶς	πᾶσα	πᾶν	**Pl.** N.V.	πάντ-ες πᾶσαι πάντ-α
G.	παντ-ός	πάσης	παντ-ός	G.	πάντ-ων πασῶν πάντ-ων
D.	παντ-ί	πάσῃ	παντ-ί	D.	πᾶ-σι(ν) πάσαις πᾶ-σι(ν)
A.	πάντ-α	πᾶσαν	πᾶν	A.	πάντ-ας πάσας πάντ-α

4. Adjectives with stems in -εντ, as χαρίεις *graceful, agreeable*, have some
of their forms from a shorter stem in -ετ, to wit:

the dat. plur. masc. and neut.: χαρίεσι(ν) for χαρίεϝσι(ν),
and the whole of the feminine: χαρίεσσα for χαριετ-ϳα, 77, 3.

42. SYNCOPATED LIQUID STEMS.

Stems:	πατερ- *father*	μητερ- *mother*	θυγατερ- *daughter*	γαστερ- *belly*	ἀνερ- *man*
S. N.	ὁ πατήρ	ἡ μήτηρ	ἡ θυγάτηρ	ἡ γαστήρ	ὁ ἀνήρ
G.	πατρός	μητρός	θυγατρός	γαστρός	ἀνδρός
D.	πατρί	μητρί	θυγατρί	γαστρί	ἀνδρί
A.	πατέρα	μητέρα	θυγατέρα	γαστέρα	ἄνδρα
V.	πάτερ	μῆτερ	θύγατερ		ἄνερ
P. N. V.	πατέρες	μητέρες	θυγατέρες	γαστέρες	ἄνδρες
G.	πατέρων	μητέρων	θυγατέρων	γαστέρων	ἀνδρῶν
D.	πατράσι	μητράσι	θυγατράσι	γαστράσι	ἀνδράσι
A.	πατέρας	μητέρας	θυγατέρας	γαστέρας	ἄνδρας

1. Πατήρ, μήτηρ, θυγάτηρ and γαστήρ drop the ε by syncope (14) in the gen. and dat. sing. and in the dat. plur., which ends in -τράσι(ν).

2. Ἀνήρ drops the ε entirely, except in the voc. sing., and inserts δ between ν and ρ.

Σ– OR ELIDING STEMS.

43. The stem characteristic -σ remains only when final, but it is dropped by elision (17) between vowels, which are then always contracted.

NOUNS.

44. 1. Neuters in -ος, st. in -ος and -εσ-; *e.g.* τὸ γένος *genus.*

Stems: γενος and γενεσ- *race*					
Sing. N. V.	τὸ γένος		Plur. N. V.	τὰ γένεα	γένη
G.	γένεος	γένους	G.	γενέων	γενῶν
D.	γένεϊ	γένει	D.	γένεσι(ν)	
A.	γένος		A.	γένεα	γένη

γένεσ-ος [*gener-is*] becomes γένους, etc.; γένεσι stands for γένεσ-σι.

Note. — The gen. plur. sometimes remains uncontracted: ὀρέων, κερδέων.

2. Neuters in -ας, stem in -ασ-. The most important are:
τὸ κρέας *meat:* κρέως, κρέᾳ; plur. κρέᾶ, κρεῶν, κρέᾱσι(ν),
τὸ γῆρας *old age:* γήρως, γήρᾳ.

3. Ἡ αἰδώς *shame, reverence,* stem αἰδοσ-, is thus inflected:
ἡ αἰδώς, αἰδοῦς, αἰδοῖ, αἰδῶ (for αἰδοσος, etc.).

45. ADJECTIVES. — PROPER NAMES.

Stems	εὐγενεσ- of noble birth					Διογενεσ- Diogenes	Περικλεεσ- Pericles
	Sing.			Plur.			
	m.	fem.	neut.	m. fem.	neut.		
N.	εὐγενής	εὐγενές	εὐγενεῖς	εὐγενῆ	ὁ Διογένης	ὁ Περικλῆς
G.	εὐγενοῦς		εὐγενῶν		Διογένους	Περικλέους
D.	εὐγενεῖ		εὐγενέσι(ν)		Διογένει	Περικλεῖ
A.	εὐγενῆ	εὐγενές	εὐγενεῖς	εὐγενῆ	Διογένη	Περικλέᾱ
V.	εὐγενές	εὐγενές	εὐγενεῖς	εὐγενῆ	Διόγενες	Περίκλεις

1. Adjectives with a vowel before the final -εσ contract -έα to -ᾶ instead of to -ῆ. Thus ἐνδεής *needy* has ἐνδεᾶ, εὐκλεής *renowned* has εὐκλεᾶ, ὑγιής *healthy* has ὑγιᾶ.

2. **Barytones** have recessive accent:

εὔηθες, σύνηθες, αὔταρκες — συνήθων, τῶν τριήρων.

Exceptions to this are the neuters of adjectives in -ώδης and -ήρης:

εὐῶδες *fragrant*,	ζημιῶδες *ruinous*,
εὐῆρες *well-fitted*,	ποδῆρες *reaching to the feet*.

3. **Proper names** in -ης, gen. -ους, have, besides the regular acc. sing. in -η, a form in -ην (after the A-declension).

E.g. Διογένη and Διογένην, Σωκράτη and Σωκράτην,
Κλεομένη and Κλεομένην, Δημοσθένη and Δημοσθένην.

4. **Proper names** in -κλῆς (from τὸ κλέος *glory*, stem κλέεσ-) contract twice in the dat. sing., elsewhere but once:

(-κλέης) Περικλῆς, (-κλέεᾰ) Περικλέᾱ,
(κλέεος) Περικλέους, (-κλεες) Περίκλεις.
(-κλέεϊ to -κλέει) Περικλεῖ,

46. STEMS IN -ι.

Stems:	στᾰσι- and στᾰσε- rising, sedition		αἰσθησι- and αἰσθησε- perception	
N.	ἡ στᾰσι-ς	αἱ στάσεις	ἡ αἴσθησι-ς	αἱ αἰσθήσεις
G.	στάσε-ως	στάσε-ων	αἰσθήσε-ως	αἰσθήσε-ων
D.	στάσει	στάσε-σι(ν)	αἰσθήσει	αἰσθήσε-σι(ν)
A.	στάσι-ν	στάσεις	αἴσθησι-ν	αἰσθήσεις
V.	στάσι	στάσεις	αἴσθησι	αἰσθήσεις

1. In the endings -ως and -ων, ω is accounted short.

2. All words in -ις, -εως are barytone. Most of them are femi-

nines in -σις and denote action, as ἡ λύσις *the loosing, ransoming,
release;* ἡ πρᾶξις *the doing, deed.*

47. STEMS IN -υ.

Stems:	συ- *swine*	'Ερίνυ- *avenging goddess*	ἡδυ- } ἡδεια- { ἡδυ- ἡδε- } *sweet* { ἡδε-		
Sing. N.	ὁ ἡ σῦ-ς	ἡ 'Ερινύ-ς	ἡδύ-ς	ἡδεῖα	ἡδύ
G.	σῦ-ός	'Ερινύ-ος	ἡδέ-ος	ἡδείας	ἡδέ-ος
D.	σῦ-ί	'Ερινύ-ι	ἡδεῖ	ἡδείᾳ	ἡδεῖ
A.	σῦ-ν	'Ερινύ-ν	ἡδύ-ν	ἡδεῖαν	ἡδύ
Plur. N. V.	σύ-ες	'Ερινύ-ες	ἡδεῖς	ἡδεῖαι	ἡδέ-α
G.	σῦ ῶν	'Ερινύ-ων⁻	ἡδέ-ων	ἡδειῶν	ἡδέ-ων
D.	σῦ-σί(ν)	'Ερινύ-σι(ν)	ἡδέ-σι(ν)	ἡδείαις	ἡδέ-σι(ν)
A.	σῦ-ς	'Ερινῦ-ς	ἡδεῖς	ἡδείας	ἡδέ-α

1. In **nouns** in -υς, the stem characteristic -υ remains throughout (cf. 2); the acc. plur. ends in -ῡς (for -ŭνς).

2. Τὸ ἄστυ *the city* (esp. of Athens) is inflected like ι-stems:

τὸ ἄστυ,   ἄστεως,   ἄστει,   ἄστυ,
τὰ ἄστη,   ἄστεων,   ἄστεσι(ν),   ἄστη.

3. **Adjectives** have two stems in the masc. and neut.:
ἡδυ- in the nom., acc., voc. sing.; everywhere else ἡδε- (for ἡδεϝ-).

48. STEMS ENDING IN DIPHTHONGS.

Stems: βασιλευ- and βασιλε- *king*			
Sing. N.	ὁ βασιλεύ-ς	Plur. N.	οἱ βασιλεῖς
G.	βασιλέ-ως	G.	βασιλέ-ων
D.	βασιλεῖ	D.	βασιλεῦ-σι(ν)
A.	βασιλέ-ᾱ	A.	βασιλέ-ᾱς
V.	βασιλεῦ	V.	βασιλεῖς

1. All words in -ευς are **masculine oxytones**.
Note the quantity of the endings -ως, -ᾱ and -ᾱς.

2. In old Attic the nom. plur. ends in -ῆς: οἱ βασιλῆς. In poetry, and occasionally in prose, the acc. plur. ends in -εῖς: τοὺς γονεῖς.

3. Words in -εύς with a **preceding vowel** are often contracted in the gen. and acc. sing. and plur., and thus

-έω becomes -ῶ: τοῦ Πειραιῶς, τῶν Εὐβοῶν,
-έᾱ becomes -ᾶ: τὸν Πειραιᾶ, τοὺς 'Ερετριᾶς.

4. 'Ο ἡ βοῦς (*bōs, bŏvis*) *ox, cow* retains the stem βου- **only** when the ending is, or begins with, a consonant: βοῦ-ς, βοῦ-ν, βου-σί(ν);

but otherwise changes it to (βοϝ) βο-, without admitting contraction; hence ὁ ἡ βοῦς,   βοός,   βοΐ,   βοῦν,

βόες,   βοῶν,   βουσί(ν),   βοῦς.

49. STEMS IN -ω AND -ο.

Stems:	ἡρω- *hero*				πειθο- *persuasion*	
Sing. N.	ὁ ἥρω-ς	Plur. N.	οἱ ἥρω-ες	Sing. N.	ἡ πειθώ	
G.	ἥρω-ος	G.	ἡρώ-ων	G.	πειθοῦς	
D.	ἥρω-ι	D.	ἥρω-σι(ν)	D.	πειθοῖ	
A.	ἥρω-α	A.	ἥρω-ας	A.	πειθώ	
V.	ἥρω-ς	V.	ἥρω-ες	V.	πειθοῖ	

1. The few stems in -ω do not admit of contraction.

2. Words with stems in -ο are feminine oxytones, and mostly proper names; they are found in the singular only.

IRREGULAR NOUNS.

50. Irregularities in the declension of nouns arise chiefly from the fact that the cases of a word are formed from two different stems. The following are the most common irregular nouns:

1. ἡ γυνή *woman* derives all its other forms from the stem γυναικ-. The accentuation is that of monosyllabic consonant stems (36, 6): ἡ γυνή,   γυναικός,   γυναικί,   γυναῖκα,   γύναι,

γυναῖκες,   γυναικῶν,   γυναιξί(ν),   γυναῖκας,   γυναῖκες.

2. Ζεύς *the god Zeus* (stems Ζευ- and Δι-):

Ζεύς,   Διός,   Διΐ,   Δία,   Ζεῦ.

3. ὁ ἡ κύων *dog* (stems κυον- and κῠν-):

ὁ ἡ κύων,   κυνός,   κυνί,   κύνα,   κύον,

κύνες,   κυνῶν,   κυσί(ν),   κύνας,   κύνες.

4. ὁ μάρτυς *witness* (stems μαρτῠ- and μαρτῡρ-):

ὁ μάρτυς,   μάρτυρος,   μάρτυρι,   μάρτυρα,

μάρτυρες,   μαρτύρων,   μάρτυσι(ν),   μάρτυρας.

5. ἡ ναῦς *ship* (stem ναυ-, νᾱϝ-, νᾱυ-ἱς, νηϝ-):

ἡ ναῦς,   νεώς,   νηΐ,   ναῦν,

νῆες,   νεῶν,   ναυσί(ν),   ναῦς.

6. τὸ ὄναρ *dream* (stems ὀναρ- and ὀνειρατ-):

τὸ ὄναρ,   ὀνείρατος,   ὀνείρατι,   ὄναρ,

τὰ ὀνείρατα,   ὀνειράτων,   ὀνείρασι(ν),   ὀνείρατα.

Also ὁ ὄνειρος and τὸ ὄνειρον are found.

7. ὁ πρεσβευτής *ambassador* borrows the plural from πρέσβυς *old, venerable.* Hence

ὁ πρεσβευτής, -τοῦ, -τῇ, -τήν, -τά,
οἱ πρέσβεις, πρέσβεων, πρέσβεσι(ν), πρέσβεις.

8. τὸ πῦρ *fire* is inflected in the singular according to the consonantal, in the plural according to the O-, declension:

τὸ πῦρ,   πῦρ-ός,   πῦρ-ί,
τὰ πῦρ-ά,   πῦρ-ῶν,   πῦρ-οῖς, *watchfires.*

9. ὁ σῖτος *corn, food* is neuter in the plural:

τὰ σῖτα,   σίτων,   σίτοις.

10. τὸ στάδιον *stadium* (a measure of length) has in the plur. both οἱ στάδιοι and τὰ στάδια.

11. ὁ υἱός *son* (besides the regular forms according to the O-declension) forms some cases from the stem υἱε- (compare ἡδύ-ς):

in the sing.   υἱέ-ος,   υἱεῖ,
in the plur. υἱεῖς,   υἱέ-ων,   υἱέ-σι(ν),   υἱεῖς.

12. ἡ χείρ *hand* is regular, except in the dat. plur.: χερ-σί(ν)

LOCAL CASE ENDINGS.

51. These are mostly applied to the stem:

-θεν denoting : *whence,*
-ι and -θι in the sing., } denoting : *where,*
-σι(ν) in the plural,
-δε, -σε, -ζε denoting : *whither.*

E.g. οἴκοθεν *from home,*   οἴκοι *at home,*   οἴκαδε *home(ward),*
ἄλλοθεν *aliunde,*   ἄλλοθι *alibi,*   ἄλλοσε *alio,*
Ἀθήνηθεν *from Athens,*   Ἀθήνησι(ν) *at Athens,* Ἀθήναζε *to Athens,*
πάντοθεν *from all sides,*   Μαραθῶνι *at Marathon,* Μέγαράδε *to Megara* (9, 1. f.),
χαμᾶθεν *from the ground,* χαμαί *humi,*   χαμᾶζε *to or on the ground.*

Note.— The forms in -ι are *relics of an original locative* sing., those in -σι(ν), of a locative plur.

CLASSIFICATION OF ADJECTIVES.

a) ADJECTIVES OF THREE ENDINGS.

52. The masculine and the neuter of these adjectives are formed from the same stem. The feminine always follows the A-Declension.

1. Stems in -o. Decl. 32.

ἀγαθός,   ἀγαθή,   ἀγαθόν   *good,*
δίκαιος,   δικαία,   δίκαιον   *just.*

2. Contracted adjectives with stems in -o. Decl. 34.

ἀργυροῦς,	ἀργυρᾶ,	ἀργυροῦν	silver,
χρῡσοῦς,	χρῡσῆ,	χρῡσοῦν	golden,
ἁπλοῦς,	ἁπλῆ,	ἁπλοῦν	simple.

3. Stems in -ν. Decl. 40.

μέλᾰς,	μέλαινα,	μέλᾰν	black,
τάλᾱς,	τάλαινα,	τάλαν (poet.)	wretched.

4. Stems in -ντ. Decl. 41.

πᾶς,	πᾶσα,	πᾶν	whole, all,
ἄκων,	ἄκουσα,	ἆκον	unwilling,
ἑκών,	ἑκοῦσα,	ἑκόν	willing,
λυθείς,	λυθεῖσα,	λυθέν	loosed.

5. Stems in -υ (almost all oxytone). Decl. 47.

ἡδύς,	ἡδεῖα,	ἡδύ	sweet,
ἥμισυς,	ἡμίσεια,	ἥμισυ	half.

b) ADJECTIVES OF TWO ENDINGS.

53. The stem is the same for all genders; the masculine and feminine are alike in form.

1. Stems in -o (especially compound adjectives). 32, 3. *seqq.*

βάρβαρος, -ον	foreign,	ἄτῑμος, -ον	dishonored,
ἥσυχος, -ον	quiet,	ἔντῑμος, -ον	honored,
φρόνιμος, -ον	prudent,	παράνομος, -ον	unlawful,
πρᾶος, -ον	mild, tame,	πανοῦργος, -ον	cunning.

Note. — Adjectives of two and three endings are mentioned in 32, 4.
βέβαιος, 2. and 3., *firm, stable,*   ὠφέλιμος, 2. and 3., *profitable.*

2. Contract adjectives with stems in -o. Decl. 33.
εὔνους, εὔνουν *well-disposed,*   σύμπλους, σύμπλουν *sailing with.*

3. Stems in -ω (according to the Attic decl.). Decl. 35.
ἵλεως, ἵλεων *propitious.*   ἔκπλεως, ἔκπλεων *full.*

4. Stems in dental mutes (esp. compounds of nouns). 39.
ἄχαρις, -ι *unpleasant* (ἀχάριτος, ἀχάριτι, ἄχαριν, -ι).
εὔελπις, -ι *hopeful* (εὐέλπιδος, εὐέλπιδι, εὔελπιν, -ι).
ἄπολις, -ι *homeless* (ἀπόλιδος, ἀπόλιδι, ἄπολιν, -ι).

5. Stems in -ν. Decl. 40.

εὐδαίμων,	εὔδαιμον *happy,*	κακίων,	κάκιον *worse,*
σώφρων,	σῶφρον *prudent,*	ἄρρην,	ἄρρεν *male.*

6. Stems in -εσ. Decl. 45.

εὐγενής, -ές of noble race,   συνήθης, σύνηθες customary,
ἐνδεής, -ές   needy,   ὑγιής, -ές   healthy.

c) ADJECTIVES OF ONE ENDING.

54. A few adjectives have but one termination for all three genders. On account of their meaning, however, they are rarely used in the neuter. They have nearly all a dental stem.

φυγάς, φυγάδος fugitive, exiled,   πένης, πένητος needy, poor,
μάκαρ, μάκαρος blessed, happy.

Note. — Masculine only is the adjective ἐθελοντής, -οῦ voluntary, volunteer. Feminine only are the adjectives in -ίς, -ίδος, as συμμαχίς, -ίδος allied, Ἑλληνίς, -ίδος a Grecian woman, ἡ πατρίς (sc. γῆ) one's native country.

d) IRREGULAR ADJECTIVES.

55. The two adjectives μέγας, μεγάλη, μέγα great, tall,
        and πολύς, πολλή, πολύ much, pl. many,
derive all their forms, except the nom. and acc. sing. masc. and neut., from the stems μεγαλο- and πολλο- respectively.

Stems:	μεγα- and μεγαλο- great			πολυ- and πολλο- much		
Sing. N.	μέγας	μεγάλη	μέγα	πολύς	πολλή	πολύ
G.	μεγάλου	μεγάλης	μεγάλου	πολλοῦ	πολλῆς	πολλοῦ
D.	μεγάλῳ	μεγάλῃ	μεγάλῳ	πολλῷ	πολλῇ	πολλῷ
A.	μέγαν	μεγάλην	μέγα	πολύν	πολλήν	πολύ
Plur. N.	μεγάλοι	μεγάλαι	μεγάλα	πολλοί	πολλαί	πολλά
G.	μεγάλων	μεγάλων	μεγάλων	πολλῶν	πολλῶν	πολλῶν
D.	μεγάλοις	μεγάλαις	μεγάλοις	πολλοῖς	πολλαῖς	πολλοῖς
A.	μεγάλους	μεγάλας	μεγάλα	πολλούς	πολλάς	πολλά

II. COMPARISON OF ADJECTIVES.

56. 1. Comparison is **mostly** expressed
        by -τερος, -τέρα, -τερον in the comparative degree,
        by -τατος, -τάτη, -τατον in the superlative degree.

These endings are joined to the stem of the masculine.

E.g. δίκαιος just,   st. δικαιο-,   c. δικαιό-τερος, s. δικαιό-τατος,
     μέλᾱς   black,   μελαν-,   μελάν-τερος,   μελάν-τατος,
     σαφής   clear,   σαφεσ-,   σαφέσ-τερος,   σαφέσ-τατος,
     εὐκλεής renowned,   εὐκλεεσ-,   εὐκλεέσ-τερος,   εὐκλεέσ-τατος,

βραχύς short,   st. βραχυ-,   c. βραχύ-τερος, s. βραχύ-τατος,
πρέσβυς old,   πρεσβυ-,   πρεσβύ-τερος,   πρεσβύ-τατος.

2. The stems in -ο lengthen this vowel to · -ω, whenever the preceding syllable is short.

E.g. δεινός   terrible,   δεινό-τερος,   δεινό-τατος,
       ἔντῑμος   honored,   ἐντῑμό-τερος,   ἐντῑμό-τατος,
       πικρός   bitter,   πικρό-τερος,   πικρό-τατος,
       ἔνδοξος   renowned,   ἐνδοξό-τερος,   ἐνδοξό-τατος,
but   σοφός   wise,   σοφώ-τερος,   σοφώ-τατος,
       ἄξιος   worthy,   ἀξιώ-τερος,   ἀξιώ-τατος,
       πολεμῐκός warlike,   πολεμικώ-τερος,   πολεμικώ-τατος.

3. The following adjectives drop their stem characteristic -ο :

       γεραιός   old,   γεραί-τερος,   γεραί-τατος,
       φίλος   dear,   φίλ-τερος,   φίλ-τατος.

4. -έσ-τερος and -έσ-τατος are added to the stem
   a) of the adjectives in -ων, -ον.

E.g. εὐδαίμων   happy,   εὐδαιμον-έσ-τερος,   εὐδαιμον-έσ-τατος,
        σώφρων   wise,   σωφρον-έσ-τερος,   σωφρον-έσ-τατος.

   b) of the contracted adjectives in (-οος), -ους, after dropping
      the final stem vowel.

E.g. ἁπλοῦς simple,   st. ἁπλο-ο-,   ἁπλούστερος,   ἁπλούστατος,
        εὔνους well-disposed,   εὐνο-ο-,   εὐνούστερος,   εὐνούστατος,
from ἁπλο-έσ-τερος, εὐνο-έσ-τατος, etc.

   c) of ἐρρωμένος strong, which also drops final -ο : ἐρρωμεν-έσ-
      τερος, -έσ-τατος.

Note. — Adjectives often form their comparative by prefixing μᾶλλον, *magis*,
more, to the positive, and their superlative by μάλιστα, *maxime*, *most*.

E.g. μᾶλλον φίλος = φίλτερος, μάλιστα σοφός = σοφώτατος, etc.

57. 1. Comparison is **less frequently** expressed by
   -ίων, -ίων, -ιον,   stem -ιον-, in the comparative,
   -ιστος, -ίστη, -ιστον, stem -ιστο-, in the superlative.

2. Besides the irregular adjectives (58) there are especially six
other adjectives in Greek prose that follow this manner of comparison. Three of them drop the final vowel of their stems before the
endings, three form their degrees from a kindred stem :

       κακός   bad,   κακίων,   κάκιον,   κάκιστος, 3.
       ἡδύς   sweet,   ἡδίων,   ἥδῑον,   ἥδιστος, 3.
       ταχύς   quick,   θάττων,   θᾶττον,   τάχιστος, 3.
                      (θάττων from ταχ-jων.)

καλός   beautiful,   καλλίων, κάλλῑον,   κάλλιστος, 3.
                                                        (τὸ κάλλος beauty).

αἰσχρός   base,   αἰσχίων, αἴσχῑον,   αἴσχιστος, 3.
                                                        (τὸ αἶσχος disgrace).

ἐχθρός   hostile,   ἐχθίων, ἔχθῑον,   ἔχθιστος, 3.
                                                        (τὸ ἔχθος enmity).

3. For the declension of the comp., see 40, 3; of the sup., 32.

IRREGULAR COMPARISON.

58. The comparative and superlative of the following adjectives are derived from one or more stems, which differ from that of the positive degree.

1. ἀγαθός good,   ἀμείνων, ἄμεινον,   ἄριστος, 3.
                                                 (clever, brave, ἀρ-ετή),
                       βελτίων, βέλτῑον,   βέλτιστος, 3.
                                                 (morally good, virtuous),
                       κρείττων, κρεῖττον,   κράτιστος, 3.
                                                 (strong, superior, τὸ κράτος).

2. κακός bad,   κακίων, κάκῑον,   κάκιστος, 3.
                                                 (worse, peior),
                       χείρων, χεῖρον,   χείριστος, 3.
                                                 (less good, deterior),
                       ἥττων, ἧττον,   ἥκιστα (adv. least!)
                                                 (weaker, inferior).

3. μέγας great,   μείζων, μεῖζον,   μέγιστος, 3.

4. μικρός small,   μικρότερος, 3,   μικρότατος, 3.
                       ἐλάττων, ἔλαττον,   ἐλάχιστος, 3.

5. ὀλίγος little,   ἐλάττων, ἔλαττον,   ἐλάχιστος, 3.
                       μείων, μεῖον,   ————

6. πολύς much,   πλείων, πλέον,   πλεῖστος, 3.
                                                 (πλέ-ως, τὸ πλῆ-θος).
           genit. etc. πλείονος and πλέονος.

7. ῥᾴδιος easy,   ῥᾴων, ῥᾷον,   ῥᾷστος, 3.
                                                 (facilis).

Note. — Defective comparatives are:

(πρό before),	πρότερος	prior,	πρῶτος	primus,
(ὑπέρ above),	ὑπέρτερος	superior,	ὑπέρτατος	supremus,
————	ὕστερος	posterior,	ὕστατος	postremus,
(ἐξ out),	————		ἔσχατος	extremus.

III. ADVERBS.

59. 1. Formation. — Adverbs derived from adjectives have the ending -ως. With the exception of the final consonant, ς, they perfectly agree in form and accent with the genitive plur. masc. of the respective adjectives.

E.g. σοφός *wise,* gen. plur. σοφῶν, adv. σοφῶς,
     δίκαιος *just,*   δικαίων,   δικαίως,
     ἁπλοῦς *simple,*   ἁπλῶν,   ἁπλῶς,
     πᾶς *all,*   πάντων,   πάντως,
     εὐδαίμων *happy,*   εὐδαιμόνων,   εὐδαιμόνως,
     σαφής *clear,* gen. plur. σαφῶν, adv. σαφῶς,
     συνήθης *customary,*   συνήθων,   συνήθως,
     ἡδύς *sweet,*   ἡδέων,   ἡδέως.

2. Sometimes the neuter of an adjective serves as adverb, *e.g.* ταχύ *quickly,* πολύ *much,* μικρόν *a little;* ἀγαθός *good* has εὖ *well, bene.*

3. **Comparison.** — The degree of comparison in adverbs which are derived from adjectives is expressed

     in the comparative by the acc. sg. neut.,
     in the superlative by the acc. pl. neut. of the adjective.

E.g. σοφῶς *wisely,* σοφώτερον, σοφώτατα,
     ἁπλῶς *simply,* ἁπλούστερον, ἁπλούστατα,
     εὐδαιμόνως *happily,* εὐδαιμονέστερον, εὐδαιμονέστατα,
     σαφῶς *clearly,* σαφέστερον, σαφέστατα.

So also

εὖ *well,*   ἄμεινον,   ἄριστα,
μάλα *much, very,* μᾶλλον *more, rather,* μάλιστα (*the*) *most, especially.*

4. Rare are such forms of comparison as μειζόνως (besides μεῖζον) and πλουσιωτέρως (besides πλουσιώτερον), ἐχθροτέρως (besides the more common ἔχθιον).

5. Local adverbs too may be compared. Their degrees often end in -ω.

E.g. ἐγγύς *near,*   ἐγγύτερον,   ἐγγύτατα,
        and ἐγγυτέρω,   ἐγγυτάτω,
    πόρρω *far off,* πορρωτέρω,   πορρωτάτω.

60. Irregularities of the Inflection of Nouns and Adjectives occasionally met with in Attic Prose, alphabetically arranged for Reference.

ἀδελφός, ὁ *brother;* voc. ὦ ἄδελφε better than ὦ ἀδελφέ.
ἀθρόος, 3. *crowded,* has in the fem. ἀθρόα agt. 32, 1.
ἀλγεινός, 3. *painful:* comp. reg., besides ἀλγίων, ἄλγιστος.
ἄπλους, 2. *not navigable:* comp. ἁπλοώτερος *less fit for sea.*
Ἀπόλλων, -ωνος, ὁ *Apollo:* reg.; also τὸν Ἀπόλλω (40, 3) and ὦ Ἄπολλον.
Ἄρης, ὁ *Ares:* Ἄρεως and -εος, Ἄρει, Ἄρη and -ην.
ἄστυ, -εως, τό: 47, 2; the gen. ἄστεος is Ionic.
ἄφθονος, 2. *ungrudging, plentiful:* ἀφθονέστερος, and -νώτερος.
βλάξ, -ᾱκός *sluggish, effeminate:* -κότερος, -κότατος or -κίστατος.
βορέας, -έου, ὁ *north wind,* reg.; also βορρᾶς, -ᾶ (29, 3), -ᾷ, -ᾶν
γέρας, τό *gift of honor:* γέρως, γέρᾳ; γέρᾱ, γερῶν, γέρασι; 44, 2.

γραῦς, ἡ old woman: γρᾱός, γρᾱΐ, γραῦν etc.; see ναῦς 50, 5.

δάκρυον, τό tear, reg.; dat. pl. also δάκρυσιν of δάκρυ (poet.).

δεῖνα, ὁ ἡ τό such a one: τοῦ δεῖνος, τῷ δεῖνι, τὸν δεῖνα, τῶν δείνων.

δένδρον, τό tree, reg.; dat. pl. also δένδρεσιν of τό δένδρος (Ion.).

δεσμός, ὁ bond, fetter, plur. besides δεσμοί also δεσμά, 50, 9. 10.

δεσπότης, ὁ lord, master: has in the voc. ὦ δέσποτα.

Δημήτηρ, ἡ Demeter: Δήμητρος, Δήμητρι, Δήμητρα, Δήμητερ; 42, 1.

δόρυ, -ρατος, τό: 39, 3; collat. forms are δορός, δορί.

ἐπίπεδος, 2. on a level with, flat; comp. ἐπιπεδέστερος; 56, 4. c.

ἐσχατώτατος (as it were: the lastest), the very last; sup. of ἔσχατος the last; 58. note.

εὔδιος, 2. genial, cheerful: comp. εὐδιαίτερος; 56, 3.

Εὐθύφρων, -ονος, ὁ Euthyphron, voc. Εὐθύφρον, agt. 40, 2.

ἦρ, τό spring: ἦρος, ἦρι (besides ἔαρος, ἔαρι), apparently agt. 36, 6.

ἥρως, ὁ: 49; also τῷ ἥρῳ, τὸν ἥρω, ὦ ἥρως — τοὺς ἥρως.

ἥσυχος, 2. quiet; comp. reg. or ἡσυχαίτερος (of ἡσυχαῖος 56, 3).

θρίξ, τριχός, ἡ hair: τριχί etc.; dat. pl. θριξίν 21, 2.

κέρας, κέρᾱτος, τό: 39, 3; also τοῦ κέρως, τῷ κέρᾳ, τὰ κέρα, τῶν κερῶν; **44, 2.**

Κέως, ἡ Ceos, see 35; acc. also τὴν Κέω (like τὴν ἔω 35, 2).

κλέπτης, -ου thief, thievish: sup. κλεπτίστατος.

κνέφας, τό darkness: gen. κνέφους, dat. κνέφᾳ, accdg. to 42, 2.

Κῶς, ἡ Cos, see 35; acc. also τὴν Κῶ (like τὴν ἔω 35, 2).

λαγῶς (or λαγώς), ὁ hare: 35; acc. sg. also λαγῶ (λαγώ) accdg. to 35, 2.

λῴων, λῷον better, and λῷστος, 3. best; a rare comparison of ἀγαθός.

μακρός, 3. comp. reg.; also (chiefly in poetry) μάσσων and μήκιστος, cf. 57.

Μίνως, ὁ Minos: now accdg. to 35 (acc. also Μίνω, 35, 2), now accdg. to 49.

μόσσυν, -υνος, ὁ wooden tower; dat. pl. by metaplasm also μοσσύνοις.

ὄις, ὁ ἡ ovis: οἰός, οἰΐ, οἶν — οἶες, οἰῶν, οἰσίν, οἶς, 48, 4.

ὅτων and ὅτοις, collat. with ὧντινων and οἷστισιν, as ὅτου and ὅτῳ, 67, 4. note 1.

ὄψιος, 3. late; sup. ὀψιαίτατος accdg. to 56, 3.

ὀψοφάγος, 2. eating meat, lickerish, dainty; sup. -φαγίστατος.

παλαιός, 3. ancient; comp. reg. or παλαίτερος, -αίτατος, 56, 3.

πέλεκυς, ὁ axe; is inflected (like ἄστυ 47, 2) after the ι-stems: πελέκεως, πελέκει,
    πέλεκυν; plur. πελέκεις, πελέκεων, πελέκεσιν.

πένης, -ητος poor, 54: comp. πενέστερος, sup. πενέστατος, see 56, 4.

πέρᾱ or πέρᾳ on the other side; comp. περαιτέρω beyond, farther than.

πέρας, τό end: πέρατος etc. reg.; nom. sing. like κέρας, 39, 3.

πῆχυς, ὁ forearm, cubit: inflected (like ἄστυ 47, 2) accdg. to the ι-stems: πήχεως,
    πήχει, πῆχυν, plur. πήχεις, πήχεων, πήχεσι(ν).

-πηχυς: adj. in -πηχυς have in the neut. plur. also -πήχη (agt. 47) besides -πήχεα:
    διπήχη, τριπήχη.

πλεονέκτης greedy: sup. πλεονεκτίστατος.

πλέως full: accdg. to 35; fem. also πλέα, and neut. pl. also τὰ ἔκπλεω.

πλησίον near, adv., forms πλησιαίτερος, -αίτατος, cf. 56, 3.

Πνύξ, ἡ Pnyx: Πυκνός, Πυκνί, Πύκνα.

πονηρός, 3. bad, wicked; adv. πονηρῶς, but πονήρως laboriously.

Ποσειδῶν, -ῶνος, ὁ reg.; besides also τὸν Ποσειδῶ and ὦ Πόσειδον.

-πους: adj. in -πους have in the acc. sing. now -ποδα, now -πουν.

πραΰς, πραεῖα, πραΰ collat. with πρᾶος (32, 3); gen. pl. πραέων accdg. **to 47, 3.**

προὔργου serviceable, profitable, useful; comp -γιαίτερος.

πρωΐ and πρῴ, adv. *early in the day;* degrees: πρωϊαίτερος, -αίτατος and πρῳαίτερος etc. (formed from the Ionic and poetic positive πρώϊος or πρῷος, accdg. to 56,3) ; also πρῴτερον and πρῴτατα.

σκότος, -ους, τό *darkness,* reg. accdg. to 44 ; besides also ὁ σκότος, -ου.

στενός, 3. *narrow;* στενότερος, στενότατος (στεινός in the Ionic dialect!).

σχολαῖος, 3. *slow:* has σχολαίτερος, σχολαίτατος, 56, 3.

σῶς, σῶν *safe and sound, salvus;* collat. with (σῶος, σῶα, σῶον, or) σῶος, σώα, σῶον, forms τὸν τὴν τὸ σῶν, οἱ αἱ σῷ, τοὺς τὰς σῶς, τὰ σᾶ (35).

τάν or τᾶν, indecl.: ὦ τάν (τᾶν), *my good friend, my good sir.*

τέρας, τό *prodigy, sign, portent:* τέρατος etc. reg. (vide κέρας 39, 3) ; besides also τὰ τέρᾱ, 44, 2.

Τισσαφέρνης, -ους, ὁ *Tissaphernes;* voc. ὦ Τισσαφέρνη.

Τρώς, Τρωός, ὁ *Trojan,* accdg. to 49 ; gen. pl. Τρώων accdg. to 36, 7. c.

ὑβριστής *wanton, insolent* forms ὑβριστότερος, -ιστότατος.

υἱός : 50, 11 ; acc. pl. also υἱέας.

φρέαρ, τό *well, cistern:* gen. φρέατος etc.; cf. ὕδωρ 39, 3.

χαρίεις, -εσσα, -εν *pleasing, charming:* χαριέστερος, χαριέστατος from a shorter stem χαριετ-, 41, 4.

χρέος, τό and τὸ χρέως *debt:* τοῦ χρέους, τὰ χρέα, τῶν χρεῶν.

χρώς, χρωτός, ὁ *skin,* reg.; also χροός, χροΐ and χρῷ (ἐν χρῷ properly : *close to the skin,* i.e. *close by, hard by*).

IV. PRONOUNS.

61. PERSONAL PRONOUNS.

	I. Person		II. Person		III. Person supplied by αὐτός			
S. N.	ἐγώ	ego	σύ	tu	———	———	———	
G.	ἐμοῦ, μου	mei	σοῦ, σου	tui	αὐτοῦ	αὐτῆς	αὐτοῦ	eius
D.	ἐμοί, μοι	mihi	σοί, σοι	tibi	αὐτῷ	αὐτῇ	αὐτῷ	ei
A.	ἐμέ, με	me	σέ, σε	te	αὐτόν	αὐτήν	αὐτό	eum, eam, id
Pl. N.	ἡμεῖς	nos	ὑμεῖς	vos	———	———	———	
G.	ἡμῶν	nostri, -um	ὑμῶν	vestri, -um	αὐτῶν	αὐτῶν	αὐτῶν	eorum, earum
D.	ἡμῖν	nobis	ὑμῖν	vobis	αὐτοῖς	αὐταῖς	αὐτοῖς	iis
A.	ἡμᾶς	nos	ὑμᾶς	vos	αὐτούς	αὐτάς	αὐτά	eos, eas, ea

1. The accented forms (ἐμοῦ, ἐμοί, ἐμέ — σοῦ, σοί, σέ) are emphatic. Hence they are used

    a) in contrasts: οὐκ ἐμοί, ἀλλὰ σοὶ ἀρέσκει.

    b) with prepositions: ἐπ' ἐμοί *upon me,* πρὸς σέ *before you.*

Otherwise the enclitic forms are used. (See 9 ; 10.)

2. Very emphatic are ἔγωγε, ἐμοῦγε, ἔμοιγε, ἐμέγε, σύγε, etc.
3. For the meaning of the nom. of αὐτοῦ, see 63.

4. The true pers. pron. of the third person, οὗ, οἷ, etc., is in standard prose restricted to a reflexive sense. See 62 and 125.

62. REFLEXIVE PRONOUNS.

	I. Person	II. Person	III. Person				
	Subj.: *I*	Subj.: *thou, you*	Subj.: *he, she, it*				
S. N.	——	——	——		——		
G.	ἐμαυτοῦ, -ῆς	σεαυτοῦ, -ῆς	ἑαυτοῦ, -ῆς			[οὗ]	*sui*
D.	ἐμαυτῷ, -ῇ	σεαυτῷ -ῇ	ἑαυτῷ, -ῇ			οἷ	*sibi*
A.	ἐμαυτόν, -ήν	σεαυτόν, -ήν	ἑαυτόν, -ήν, -ό			[ἕ]	*se*
	Subj.: *we*	Subj.: *you*	Subj.: *they*				
Pl. N.	——	——	——	——	——	σφεῖς	*ipsi*
G.	ἡμῶν αὐτῶν	ὑμῶν αὐτῶν	σφῶν αὐτῶν or ἑαυτῶν			σφῶν	*sui*
D.	ἡμῖν αὐτοῖς, -αῖς	ὑμῖν αὐτοῖς, -αῖς	σφίσιν αὐτοῖς or ἑαυτοῖς, etc.			σφίσι(ν)	*sibi*
A.	ἡμᾶς αὐτούς, -άς	ὑμᾶς αὐτούς, -άς	σφᾶς αὐτούς or ἑαυτούς, etc.			σφᾶς	*se*

1. Instead of σεαυτοῦ, etc., ἑαυτοῦ, etc., ἑαυτῶν, etc. you may also use σαυτοῦ, etc., αὑτοῦ, etc., αὑτῶν, etc.

2. For the use and meaning of the refl. pron. see 125.

3. οὗ, οἷ, ἕ are enclitic. 9, 1. a. See 61, 1.

Ἄλλος. THE INTENSIVE AND RECIPROCAL PRONOUNS.

63. 1. Αὐτός, αὐτή, αὐτό has the regular inflection of the adjective, except in the nom. and acc. sing. neut., which drop the -ν. See 61. Its meanings (see 127) are:

  a) self, ipse; *e.g.* ὁ υἱὸς αὐτός *filius ipse.*
  b) in the oblique cases: of him, eius (never heading a sentence); *e.g.* ὁ υἱὸς αὐτοῦ *filius eius,* στέργω αὐτόν *amo eum.*
  c) with the article: the same, idem; *e.g.* ὁ αὐτὸς υἱός *idem filius.*

Note.— By crasis with the article (18) arise the forms αὑτός, αὑτή, ταὐτό and ταὐτόν (68, 2), ταὐτοῦ, ταὐτῇ, ταὐτά, etc.

2. Like αὐτός is declined: ἄλλος, ἄλλη, ἄλλο, *alius, alia, aliud.*

3. The reciprocal pronoun wants the singular and the nominative case; it is thus declined:

Pl. Gen. ἀλλήλων   ἀλλήλων   ἀλλήλων   *of one another, each other,*
  Dat. ἀλλήλοις   ἀλλήλαις   ἀλλήλοις   *to each [one an]other,*
  Acc. ἀλλήλους   ἀλλήλας   ἄλληλα   *each [one an]other.*

POSSESSIVE PRONOUNS. (See 126.)

64. 1. Ἐμός, ἐμή, ἐμόν *my, mine, meus,* ἡμέτερος, -ᾱ, -ον *our, ours, noster.*

σός, σή, σόν *your, yours, tuus,* ὑμέτερος, ᾱ, -ον *your, yours, vester.*

2. The possessive pronoun of the third person is supplied by

the gen. ἑαυτοῦ, etc., in attributive position (refl.). See 120.

the gen. αὐτοῦ, etc., in predicate position (not refl.). See 121.

3. The relation of property is most frequently expressed by means of the possessive pronouns and the possessive genitive of the personal pronouns as follows:

a) In a sense not reflexive.

1. Less emphatic.	2. More emphatic.
ὁ φίλος μου,	ὁ ἐμὸς φίλος,
ὁ φίλος σου,	ὁ σὸς φίλος,
ὁ φίλος αὐτοῦ (αὐτῆς),	ὁ τούτου (ἐκείνου) φίλος,
ὁ φίλος ἡμῶν,	ὁ ἡμέτερος φίλος,
ὁ φίλος ὑμῶν,	ὁ ὑμέτερος φίλος,
ὁ φίλος αὐτῶν.	ὁ τούτων (ἐκείνων) φίλος.

b) In a reflexive sense.

1. Less emphatic.	2. More emphatic.
στέργω τὸν ἐμὸν φίλον,	στέργω τὸν ἐμαυτοῦ (-ῆς) φίλον,
στέργεις τὸν σὸν φίλον,	στέργεις τὸν σεαυτοῦ (-ῆς) φίλον,
στέργει τὸν ἑαυτοῦ (-τῆς) φίλον,	στέργει τὸν ἑαυτοῦ (-ῆς) φίλον,
στέργομεν τὸν ἡμέτερον φίλον,	στέργομεν τὸν ἡμέτερον αὐτῶν φ.,
στέργετε τὸν ὑμέτερον φίλον,	στέργετε τὸν ὑμέτερον αὐτῶν φ.,
στέργουσι τὸν ἑαυτῶν φίλον.	στέργουσι τὸν ἑαυτῶν φίλον.

DEMONSTRATIVE PRONOUNS.

65. 1. ὅδε, ἥδε, τόδε *this, this one here* — points ahead (see 128),

οὗτος, αὕτη, τοῦτο *this, that, he (who)* — points back,

ἐκεῖνος, ἐκείνη, ἐκεῖνο *that, yonder, that* — over there — points to things absent or remote.

2. ὅδε is composed of the article and the enclitic -δε (9, 1. f) which has a demonstrative force (*here, there*); it is therefore declined like the article.

3. οὗτος too grows out of the article, with which it shares both the initial sound (spir. asper or τ: οὗτος, αὕτη, τοῦτο, ταῦτα) and the middle sound (ου corresp. to the ο-, αυ to the α-sound in the article).

Sing. N.	οὗτος	αὕτη	τοῦτο	Plur. N.	οὗτοι	αὗται	ταῦτα
G.	τούτου	ταύτης	τούτου	G.	τούτων	τούτων	τούτων
D.	τούτῳ	ταύτῃ	τούτῳ	D.	τούτοις	ταύταις	τούτοις
A.	τοῦτον	ταύτην	τοῦτο	A.	τούτους	ταύτας	ταῦτα

4. Ἐκεῖνος is declined regularly like αὐτός, αὐτή, αὐτό, 61.

5. Note the predicate position in:

ὅδε ὁ ἀνήρ　　or ὁ ἀνὴρ ὅδε *this man here,*
οὗτος ὁ ἀνήρ or ὁ ἀνὴρ οὗτος *this (that, the said) man,*
ἐκείνη ἡ γυνή or ἡ γυνὴ ἐκείνη *yonder woman.* (See 128.)

RELATIVE PRONOUNS.

66. 1. Ὅς, ἥ, ὅ *who, which, that* is thus declined :

Sing. N.	ὅς	ἥ	ὅ	Plur. N.	οἵ	αἵ	ἅ
G.	οὗ	ἧς	οὗ	G.	ὧν	ὧν	ὧν
D.	ᾧ	ᾗ	ᾧ	D.	οἷς	αἷς	οἷς
A.	ὅν	ἥν	ὅ	A.	οὕς	ἅς	ἅ

2. More emphatic is ὅσπερ, ἥπερ, ὅπερ, οὗπερ, etc. *even (precisely, just) he who, the very person who.*

3. Ὅστις, ἥτις, ὅτι *quisquis, quicumque, any one who, whoever, whatever, whoso.* (See 67, 3.)

4. Notice the article in : ὁ φίλος, οὗ τὸν υἱὸν παιδεύω *the friend whose son I educate.*

INTERROGATIVE AND INDEFINITE PRONOUNS.

67. 1. Τίς, τί is an interrogative pronoun = *quis? quid? Who? what? which?*

It always accents the stem-syllable and takes no accent but the acute.

2. Τὶς, τὶ is an indefinite pronoun = *aliquis, quidam :*

　　Any (one), some (one), (a person), a certain (a kind of).

It is enclitic throughout and never takes an accent but upon the ultima (9, 2. b).

3. Ὅστις is: a) an indirect interrog. pronoun = *quis;*
　　　　　　b) an indefinite relative = *quicunque;* 66, 3.

4. They are declined as follows :

Sing. N.	τίς ;	τί ;	τὶς	τὶ	ὅστις	ἥτις	ὅ,τι
G.	τίνος ;		τινός		οὗτινος	ἧστινος	οὗτινος
D.	τίνι ;		τινί		ᾧτινι	ᾗτινι	ᾧτινι
A.	τίνα ;	τί ;	τινά	τὶ	ὅντινα	ἥντινα	ὅ,τι
Plur. N.	τίνες ;	τίνα ;	τινές	τινά	οἵτινες	αἵτινες	ἅτινα
G.	τίνων ;		τινῶν		ὧντινων	ὧντινων	ὧντινων
D.	τίσι(ν) ;		τισί(ν)		οἷστισι(ν)	αἷστισι(ν)	οἷστισι(ν)
A.	τίνας ;	τίνα ;	τινάς	τινά	οὕστινας	ἅστινας	ἅτινα

Note 1.— The following collateral forms are of frequent occurrence :
for τίνος : τοῦ ; for τινός : του encl., for οὗτινος mostly : ὅτου,
for τίνι : τῷ ; for τινί : τῳ encl., for ᾦτινι mostly : ὅτῳ,
for the neuter τινά : ἄττα (not encl.). for ἅτινα : ἄττα.

Note 2.— To distinguish the conjunction ὅτι that, becau-e from the neut. of
the relat. and interrog. pronoun ὅτι, the latter is sometimes written ὅ,τι.

CORRELATIVE PRONOUNS.

68. 1. ποῖος, ποία, ποῖον; *qualis? of what description? what
sort of?*

πόσος, πόση, πόσον ; *quantus? how large? how much?* pl. *quot?
how many?*

πότερος, ποτέρα, πότερον ; *uter? which of the two?*

INTERROGATIVE		INDEF.		RELATIVE	
direct and indirect	only indirect	encl.	DEMONSTRATIVE	limited (129, 1.)	unlimited (129, 1.)
πο-	ὁπο-	πο-	(το-)	ὁ-	ὁπο-
τίς ;	ὅστις	τὶς	ὅδε, οὗτος, ἐκεῖνος	ὅς	ὅστις
ποῖος ;	ὁποῖος	(ποιός)	(τοῖος) τοιόσδε τοιοῦτος	οἷος	ὁποῖος
πόσος ;	ὁπόσος	(ποσός)	(τόσος) τοσόσδε τοσοῦτος	ὅσος	ὁπόσος
πότερος ;	ὁπότερος		ἕτερος		ὁπότερος

2. τοιόσδε, τοιάδε, τοιόνδε and τοσόσδε, τοσήδε, τοσόνδε are declined
regularly, τοιοῦτος and τοσοῦτος like οὗτος, hence :

τοιοῦτος, τοιαύτη, τοιοῦτο	τοιοῦτοι, τοιαῦται, τοιαῦτα,
τοιούτου, τοιαύτης, τοιούτου, etc.	τοιούτων, τοιούτων, τοιούτων, etc.

Besides τοιοῦτο, τοσοῦτο and ταὐτό (63, 1, note), also τοιοῦτον, τοσοῦτον and
ταὐτόν are used as neuter forms.

Note.— By crasis, ὁ ἕτερος is changed to ἅτερος, τὸ ἕτερον to θάτερον. See 18.

69. CORRELATIVE ADVERBS.

INTERROGATIVE		INDEFIN. (all enclit.)	DEMONSTRA-TIVE	RELATIVE	
direct and indirect	indirect only			limited (129, 1.)	unlimited (129, 1.)
ποῦ; *ubi? where?*	ὅπου	πού *alicubi somewhere*	ἐνθάδε *hic* αὐτοῦ *ibidem* ἐνταῦθα *ibi* ἐκεῖ *illic*	οὗ *ubi* ἔνθα	ὅπου *ubi*

CORRELATIVE ADVERBS. — *Concluded.*

INTERROGATIVE		INDEFIN.	DEMONSTRA-	RELATIVE	
direct and indirect	indirect only	(all enclit.)	TIVE	limited (129, 1.)	unlimited (129, 1.)
ποῖ; *quo?* whither?	ὅποι	ποί *aliquo*	ἐνθάδε *huc* αὐτόσε *eo* ἐνταῦθα *eo* ἐκεῖσε *illuc*	οἷ *quo* ἔνθα	ὅποι *quo*
πόθεν; *unde?* whence?	ὁπόθεν	ποθέν *ali-cunde*	ἐνθένδε *hinc* αὐτόθεν *inde* ἐντεῦθεν *inde* ἐκεῖθεν *illinc*	ὅθεν *unde* ἔνθεν	ὁπόθεν *unde*
πότε; *quando?* when?	ὁπότε	ποτέ *ali-quando*	τότε *tum*	ὅτε *cum*	ὁπότε *cum*
πῶς; *quo modo?* how?	ὅπως	πώς	(ὥς) ὧδε οὕτω(ς)	ὡς, ὥσπερ	ὅπως
πῇ; *quā? how?* which way?	ὅπῃ	πῄ	τῇδε ταύτῃ	ᾗ, ᾗπερ	ὅπῃ

Note 1. — ἔνθα and ἔνθεν are mostly relative (*where, whither* and *whence*), but have demonstrative force in such expressions as ἔνθα δή *on that (very) occasion, just then, then indeed,* and others.

Note 2. — καὶ ὥς (ὥς) *even so;* οὐδ᾽ ὥς *not even so, ne sic quidem.*

70. V. NUMERALS.

		Cardinal	Ordinal	Adverbs
α′	1	εἷς, μία, ἕν	πρῶτος, -η, -ον	ἅπαξ *once*
β′	2	δύο	δεύτερος, -α, -ον	δίς *twice*
γ′	3	τρεῖς, τρία	τρίτος, -η, -ον	τρίς *three times*
δ′	4	τέτταρες, -ρα	τέταρτος	τετράκις
ε′	5	πέντε	πέμπτος	πεντάκις
ϛ′	6	ἕξ	ἕκτος	ἑξάκις
ζ′	7	ἑπτά	ἕβδομος	ἑπτάκις
η′	8	ὀκτώ	ὄγδοος	ὀκτάκις
θ′	9	ἐννέα	ἔνατος	ἐνάκις
ι′	10	δέκα	δέκατος	δεκάκις

NUMERALS. — *Concluded.*

		Cardinal	Ordinal	Adverbs
ια΄	11	ἕνδεκα	ἑνδέκατος	ἑνδεκάκις
ιβ΄	12	δώδεκα	δωδέκατος	δωδεκάκις
ιγ΄	13	τρεῖς (τρία) καὶ δέκα	τρίτος καὶ δέκατος	τρισκαιδεκάκις
ιδ΄	14	τέτταρες (-ρα) καὶ δέκα	τέταρτος καὶ δέκατος	τετρακαιδεκάκις
ιε΄	15	πεντεκαίδεκα	πεντεκαιδέκατος	etc.
ιϛ΄	16	ἑκκαίδεκα	ἑκκαιδέκατος	
ιζ΄	17	ἑπτακαίδεκα	ἑπτακαιδέκατος	
ιη΄	18	ὀκτωκαίδεκα	ὀκτωκαιδέκατος	
ιθ΄	19	ἐννεακαίδεκα	ἐννεακαιδέκατος	
κ΄	20	εἴκοσι(ν)	εἰκοστός	εἰκοσάκις
λ΄	30	τριάκοντα	τριακοστός	τριακοντάκις
μ΄	40	τετταράκοντα	τετταρακοστός	etc.
ν΄	50	πεντήκοντα	πεντηκοστός	
ξ΄	60	ἑξήκοντα	ἑξηκοστός	
ο΄	70	ἑβδομήκοντα	ἑβδομηκοστός	
π΄	80	ὀγδοήκοντα	ὀγδοηκοστός	
ϟ΄	90	ἐνενήκοντα	ἐνενηκοστός	
ρ΄	100	ἑκατόν	ἑκατοστός	ἑκατοντάκις
σ΄	200	διᾱκόσιοι, -αι, -α	διακοσιοστός	διακοσιάκις
τ΄	300	τριᾱκόσιοι, -αι, -α	τριακοσιοστός	etc.
υ΄	400	τετρᾱκόσιοι	τετρακοσιοστός	
φ΄	500	πεντᾱκόσιοι	πεντακοσιοστός	
χ΄	600	ἑξᾱκόσιοι	ἑξακοσιοστός	
ψ΄	700	ἑπτᾱκόσιοι	ἑπτακοσιοστός	
ω΄	800	ὀκτᾱκόσιοι	ὀκτακοσιοστός	
ϡ΄	900	ἐνᾱκόσιοι	ἐνακοσιοστός	
͵α	1,000	χίλιοι, -αι, -α	χιλιοστός	χῑλιάκις etc.
͵β	2,000	δισχίλιοι, -αι, -α	δισχιλιοστός	
͵ι	10,000	μύριοι, -αι, -α	μυριοστός	μυριάκις
͵ια	11,000	μύριοι καὶ χίλιοι		

1. All **ordinals** and the **cardinals** from 200 upwards are adjectives of three terminations; of the others, only the first four are declined:

N. 1. εἷς   μία   ἕν   2. δύο   3. τρεῖς τρία   4. τέτταρες τέτταρα
G.   ἑνός μιᾶς ἑνός   δυοῖν   τριῶν   τεττάρων
D.   ἑνί   μιᾷ ἑνί   δυοῖν   τρισί(ν)   τέτταρσι(ν)
A.   ἕνα μίαν ἕν.   δύο.   τρεῖς τρία.   τέτταρας τέτταρα.

Οὐδείς (μηδείς) *no one* is inflected like εἷς, ἄμφω like δύο.

S. οὐδείς   οὐδεμία οὐδέν *none*, Pl. Masc. οὐδένες   ἄμφω *both*.
   οὐδενός οὐδεμιᾶς οὐδενός   οὐδένων   ἀμφοῖν
   οὐδενί   οὐδεμιᾷ οὐδενί   οὐδέσι(ν)   ἀμφοῖν
   οὐδένα οὐδεμίαν οὐδέν.   οὐδένας.   ἄμφω.

2. **Rule for the combination of units, tens, etc.:**

If the smaller number precedes, καί must be inserted between;
if the larger number precedes, καί may be used or omitted.

Thus 235 may be expressed

by πέντε καὶ τριάκοντα καὶ διακόσιοι,
or διακόσιοι καὶ τριάκοντα καὶ πέντε,
or διακόσιοι τριάκοντα πέντε.

The same holds for ordinals: τριακοστὸς πέμπτος or τριακοστὸς καὶ πέμπτος, but only πέμπτος καὶ τριακοστός.

3. Instead of τρεῖς (τρία) καὶ δέκα, τέτταρες (τέτταρα) καὶ δέκα, τρίτος καὶ δέκατος, τέταρτος καὶ δέκατος, the other forms: τρισκαίδεκα, τετταρακαίδεκα, τρισκαιδέκατος, τετταρακαιδέκατος are also met with; so also ἕβδομος καὶ δέκατος besides ἑπτακαιδέκατος, etc.

Note.— Δύο is sometimes used indeclinably. Μύριοι, μυρίαι, μυρία *very many, countless, numberless* (compare *mille* and *sescenti*) is different both in meaning and accent from μύριοι, μύριαι, μύρια.

4. Besides the cardinal and ordinal numbers and the numeral adverbs, the Greek has

numeral adj. in -πλοῦς = -fold, -plex (34, 1. b);

e.g. ἁπλοῦς *simple*, διπλοῦς *twofold, double*, etc.

and in -πλάσιος; e.g. διπλάσιος *twice the size of;* and
numeral subst. in -άς, -άδος: ἡ μονάς *unit*, ἡ δεκάς, *decad;*
   ἡ μυριάς *the number 10,000, a myriad.*

THE DUAL IN DECLENSION.

71.. It has but two forms,
   one for the nom., acc., and voc. cases,
   the other for the genit. and dative cases.

Its terminations are in N. A. V.　　G. D.

in the I. decl.　　-ā̆,　　　-αιν,

" II. "　　　-ω,　　　-οιν,

" III. "　　　-ε,　　　-οιν.

E.g. τὼ χώρα, τοῖν χώραιν — τὼ τιμά, τοῖν τιμαῖν,

τὼ θεώ, τοῖν θεοῖν — τὼ ἀνθρώπω, τοῖν ἀνθρώποιν,

τὼ θῆρε, τοῖν θηροῖν — τὼ φύλακε, τοῖν φυλάκοιν,

τὼ ἄνδρε, τοῖν ἀνδροῖν — τὼ γυναῖκε, τοῖν γυναικοῖν,

τὼ χεῖρε, τοῖν χεροῖν — τὼ ὦτε, τοῖν ὤτοιν (50, 12 ; 36, 7. c).

τὼ πόλει, τοῖν πολέοιν — τὼ σκέλει, τοῖν τειχοῖν.

of ἐγώ : νώ, νῷν — of σύ : σφώ, σφῷν.

Note.— The masculine dual forms τώ and τοῖν are generally used for τά and ταῖν.

VI. INFLECTION OF THE VERB (CONJUGATION).

INTRODUCTORY REMARKS.

72. 1. The Greek verb appears to some advantage when contrasted with the Latin verb, because it has

an additional number :　　the **dual**, see 96 ;

an additional voice :　　the **middle**,

an additional tense :　　the **aorist**,

an additional mood :　　the **optative**,

and two **verbal adjectives**.

2. The **middle voice** has indeed an active meaning, but involves a reference of the action to the agent; παιδεύω, for instance, means *I educate*, παιδεύομαι *I educate for my own sake or benefit* (*mihi*, dative), or, *I educate myself* (*me ipsum*, accusative). See 165.

3. The middle and the passive voices are the same in form, except in the future and aorist.

Note.— Deponents with the aorist in the middle form are called **middle deponents** (D.M.) ; deponents with the aorist in the passive form are called **passive deponents** (D.P.).

4. The indicative of the **aorist** has its proper place in narrative. It corresponds to the historical perfect in Latin.

5. The **optative** is used in wishes : παιδεύοιμι *may I educate*, *I wish I were educating*. However, this is not the only purpose it serves; see 174, 2 ; 176, 4.

6. There are six **tenses** in Greek, which are divided

into principal } tenses { present, future, perfect,

and historical } { imperfect, aorist (ind.), pluperfect.

The historical tenses are also called preterit or augmented tenses.

7. The **Verb Stem** and the **Present Stem.** All forms of the verb grow out of the verb stem, which almost always appears enlarged or strengthened in the present tense.

For the manner of enlarging the verb stem, see 77 and 107–111.

8. There are two forms of **conjugation** in Greek, that of verbs
in -ω, **with** a thematic vowel; *e.g.* τιμά-ο μεν, τιμά-ε-τε.
in -μι, **without** a thematic vowel; *e.g.* ἵστα-μεν, ἵστα-τε.

9. The **mood suffixes** are not the same for all the moods:

a) the subjunctive lengthens the thematic vowels -ο- and -ε- ;

for example: indic. παιδεύ-ο-μεν, παιδεύ-ε-τε,
subj. παιδεύ-ω-μεν, παιδεύ-η-τε.

b) the optative adds a suffix of its own: -ι- or -ιη- (·ιε-);
for example: indic. παιδεύ-ο-μεν, ἵστα-τε,
opt. παιδεύ-οι-μεν, ἱστα-ίη-τε.

10. The **personal endings** are of two kinds: principal and historical;

principal for the indicative of the princ. tenses, and the subjunctive,

historical for the indicative of the historical tenses, and the optative; in other words:

for all augmented forms and optatives.

11. **Rule of Accent** for the inflection of verbs:

In all forms of the verb, the accent is thrown back as far as possible (the verb has *recessive* accent). Still it can never recede beyond the augment. Hence εἴσαγε, but εἰσῆγε. -αι and -οι are counted as short, except in the optative.

12. Special points to be noticed:

a) Contracted forms retain the accent on the contracted syllable, if either of the contracted vowels was accented: ἐποιούμεθα (from ἐποιε-όμεθα), βαλοῦ (from βαλέ-ο), παιδευθῶ (from παιδευθέ-ω), διδῶ (from διδό-ω).

b) Optatives of passive aorists and of verbs in -μι have the accent, if possible, on that syllable which contains the mood suffix -ι- : παιδευθεῖμεν, παιδευθεῖεν—τιθεῖμεν, ἱεῖτε, διδοῖεν, ἱσταῖντο.

c) Infinitives, participles and verbal adjectives, which are in reality verbal nouns or adjectives, do not fall under the above rule; participles retain the accent, if possible, upon the syllable which is accented in the nom. sing. masc. (25, 5).

d) Exceptions to the above rule for the verbal accent are consequently only such forms of second aorists act. and mid. as have the thematic vowel accented (see 86, 1 with note); hence

the 2 ps. sg. of the aor. imp. mid.: βαλοῦ (from βαλέ-ο, see a),
and a few active imperatives, as: εἰπέ (but ἄπειπε, ἔξειπε).

AUGMENT.

73. 1. The augment (*augmentum, increase*) is the sign of the past (historical, 72, 6) tenses. It is only used in the **indicative** of these tenses (imperfect, aorist, pluperfect), and never in any other moods or forms of the verb.

There is a syllabic and a temporal augment.

2. Verbs beginning with a consonant take the syllabic augment. It consists of the prefix ἐ; thus

παιδεύω: ἐ-παίδευον, ἐπαιδευσάμην.

Initial ρ is doubled after ε: ἔρριπτον *I threw* (22).

3. Verbs beginning with a vowel or diphthong take the temporal augment. It consists in the lengthening of the initial vowel. The breathing, however, is not changed. Thus

a	is lengthened to η	: ἄγω	lead,	impf. ἦγον,
ε	" "	" η : ἐλπίζω	hope,	" ἤλπιζον,
ο	" "	" ω : ὁπλίζω	arm,	" ὥπλιζον,
ῐ	" "	" ῑ : ἱδρύω	erect,	" ἵδρυον,
ῠ	" "	" ῡ : ὑβρίζω	am insolent,	" ὕβριζον,
αι	" "	" ῃ : αἰσχύνω	put to shame,	" ᾔσχυνον,
ᾳ	" "	" ῃ : ᾄδω	sing,	" ᾖδον,
αυ	" "	" ηυ : αὐξάνω	increase,	" ηὔξανον,
οι	" "	" ῳ : οἰκτίρω	pity,	" ᾤκτιρον.

4. Verbs beginning with a long ῑ, ῡ, ω or ου, and sometimes those beginning with ει or ευ, are **not** augmented;

e.g. οὐτάζω *wound,* impf. οὔταζον,
εἰκάζω *conjecture,* " ᾔκαζον (εἴκαζον),
εὔχομαι *pray, vow* " ηὐχόμην (εὐχόμην).

REDUPLICATION.

74. The **reduplication** enters into the **perfect** stem, and consequently appears in the **perfect, pluperfect** and **future perfect.** Reduplication takes place as follows:

1. Verbs beginning with one simple consonant (except ρ) repeat the same with ε, a rough mute being replaced by its corresponding smooth;

e.g.　παιδεύω　　educate,　　perf. πε-παίδευκα,
　　　χορεύω　　dance,　　　"　κε-χόρευκα,
　　　φυτεύω　　plant,　　　"　πε-φύτευκα,
　　　θηρεύω　　hunt,　　　"　τε-θήρευκα.

2. Verbs beginning with a mute followed by a liquid
(λ, μ, ν, ρ) repeat only the mute with ε;

e.g.　κλείω　　shut,　　　perf. κέ-κλεικα,
　　　δράω　　do,　　　　"　δέ-δρακα.

3. In all other cases the reduplication is the same as the augment;

e.g.　ἄγω　　　lead,　　　impf. ἦγον,　　perf. ἦχα,
　　　ὁπλίζω　　arm,　　　"　ὥπλιζον,　　"　ὥπλικα,
　　　κτίζω　　found,　　　"　ἔκτιζον,　　"　ἔκτικα,
　　　στρατεύω　take the field,　"　ἐστράτευον,　"　ἐστράτευκα,
　　　ζητέω　　look for,　　aor. ἐζήτησα,　　"　ἐζήτηκα,
　　　ψαύω　　touch,　　　"　ἔψαυσα,　　"　ἔψαυκα,
　　　ῥίπτω　　throw,　　　"　ἔρρῑψα,　　"　ἔρρῑφα,
only κτάομαι　acquire,　　has usually　"　κέ-κτημαι.

AUGMENT AND REDUPLICATION IN COMPOUNDS.

75. 1. In prepositional compounds, the simple form is augmented and reduplicated;

e.g. εἰς-άγω,　　　εἰς-ῆγον,　　　εἰς-ῆχα.
　　　ἐκ-στρατεύω,　ἐξ-εστράτευον,　ἐξ-εστράτευκα.

2. Before the augment (or augment-like reduplication):
prepositions ending in a consonant resume their original form, if
　it has been changed in the present tense;
prepositions ending in a vowel (except περί and πρό) drop it;

e.g.　ἐμβάλλω　　throw into,　　impf. ἐν-έβαλλον,
　　　συλλέγω　　gather,　　　　"　συν-έλεγον,
　　　συστέλλω　　draw together,　"　συν-έστελλον,
　　　ἀποβάλλω　　throw away,　　"　ἀπ-έβαλλον,
　　　ἐπιβάλλω　　throw upon,　　"　ἐπ-έβαλλον,
　　　παραβάλλω　throw beside,　　"　παρ-έβαλλον,
but περι-βάλλω　throw around,　　"　περι-έβαλλον,
　　　περιρρέω　　flow around,　　"　περι-έρρεον,
　　　προβάλλω　　throw before,　　"　προΰβαλλον,
　　　　　　　　　　　　　　　　　(or προ-έβαλλον, 18, 2).

3. Such denominative verbs as are derived from nounal compounds have the augment and the reduplication at the beginning;

e.g. ἀδικέω *do wrong,* ἠδίκησα, ἠδίκηκα (from ἄδικος),
ἀθυμέω *lack courage,* ἠθύμησα, ἠθύμηκα (from ἄθυμος),
δυστυχέω *am unhappy,* ἐδυστύχησα, δεδυστύχηκα (fr. δυστυχής),
εὐτυχέω *am happy.* ηὐτύχησα, ηὐτύχηκα (fr. εὐτυχής).

A. FIRST CONJUGATION: VERBS IN -ω.

CLASSIFICATION OF VERBS.

76. ACCORDING TO THE FINAL CONSONANT OF THE VERB STEM.

1. **Pure Verbs.** — The stem ends in a vowel (or diphthong);

e.g. παιδεύ-ω *educate,* λύ-ω *loose,* τί-ω *value,*
τιμά-ω *honor,* ποιέ-ω *make,* δουλό-ω *enslave.*

2. **Mute Verbs.** — The stem ends in a mute :

e.g. διώκ-ω *pursue,* λέγ-ω *say,* τρέχ-ω *run,*
τρέπ-ω *turn,* τρίβ-ω *rub,* τρέφ-ω *feed,*
ψεύδ-ω *cheat,* σπένδ-ω *pour out,* πείθ-ω *persuade.*

3. **Liquid Verbs.** — The stem ends in a liquid;

e.g. στέλ-λ-ω *send,* δέρ-ω *flay,* σπείρ-ω *sow,*
νέμ-ω *allot,* μέν-ω *stay,* κρίν-ω *judge.*

77. ACCORDING TO THE MANNER IN WHICH THE PRESENT STEM IS FORMED FROM THE VERB STEM. See 72, 7.

1. **First or ω-Class :** Present in -ω.

The verb stem is enlarged by the thematic vowel -ο, -ε. Almost all pure verbs (see 76, 1), very many mute verbs, and a few liquid verbs belong to this class :

παιδεύ-ω *educate,* διώκ-ω *pursue,* τρέφ-ω *feed,*
παύ-ω *stop,* λέγ-ω *say,* ψεύδ-ω *deceive,*
μηνί-ω *am angry,* ἄρχ-ω *rule,* πέρθ-ω *sack,*
μηνύ-ω *inform,* τρέπ-ω *turn,* δέρ-ω *flay.*

2. **Second or τ-Class :** Present in -τω.

The verb stem is enlarged by the suffix -το, -τε. This class consists almost exclusively of labial verbs :

τύπτω *strike,* stem τυπ- (ὁ τύπ-ος *blow*),
βλάπτω *damage,* " βλαβ- (ἡ βλάβη *damage*),
κρύπτω *hide,* " κρυφ- (κρύφ-α *secretly*),
θάπτω *bury,* " ταφ- (ὁ τάφ-ος *grave,* cf. 21, 2).

Note. — Exceptional formations are

τίκτω *beget,* stem τεκ- (τὸ τέκ-νον *child*),
ἀνύτω *accomplish,* " ἀνυ- (collat. ἀνύω, ἀνύω).

3. **Third or Iod-Class** : Present in -jω (1, 2, note 2).
The verb stem is enlarged by the formative syllable
-jo, -jε.   The concurrence of *j* with the final consonant of the stem
makes a variety of euphonic changes necessary.

a) A guttural (κ, γ, χ) with *j* becomes ττ (σσ):

e.g. φυλάττω   watch,   stem φυλᾰκ- (ἡ φυλακ-ή *watch*),
       τάττω   arrange,   "   τᾰγ-   (ὁ τᾰγ-ός *commander*),
       ταράττω disturb,   "   ταρᾰχ- (ἡ ταραχ-ή *tumult*).

Note.— A dental with *j* becomes ττ (σσ) in

    ἁρμόττω regulate,   stem ἁρμοτ- (ὁ ἁρμοστής *he who regulates*),
    πλάττω   form, mold,   "   πλᾰτ-   (τὸ πλάσμα *anything molded*).

b) δ with *j* becomes ζ:

e.g. ἐλπίζω   hope,   stem ἐλπῐδ- (ἡ ἐλπίς *hope*),
       καθ-έζομαι take a seat,   "   ἑδ-   (τὸ ἕδ-ος *seat*),
       ὄζω   smell of,   "   ὀδ-   (ἡ ὀδ-μή *od-or*).

Note.— In some verbs, such especially as denote a sound, a guttural underlies the ζ.

e.g. στενάζω   moan,   st. στενᾰγ- (ὁ στεναγ-μός *moaning*),
       οἰμώζω   lament,   "   οἰμωγ-   (ἡ οἰμωγ-ή *wailing*).

c) λ with *j* becomes λλ (compare μάλα, μᾶλλον) ;

e.g. ἅλλομαι   leap,   st. ἁλ-   (τὸ ἅλ-μα *leap, sal-io*),
       ἀγγέλλω   announce,   "   ἀγγελ- (ὁ ἄγγελ-ος *messenger*).

Note.— Only the stem ὀφελ- forms ὀφείλω (see d).

d) -ανjω, -ενjω, -ινjω, -ῠνjω and -αρjω, -ερjω, -ἰρjω, -ῠρjω
become -αίνω, -είνω, -ίνω, -ύνω and -αίρω, -είρω, -ίρω, -ύρω ;

e.g. φαίνω   show,   stem φᾰν- (φαν-ε-ρός *visible*),
       καθαίρω cleanse,   "   καθᾰρ- (καθαρ-ός *pure*),
       τείνω   stretch,   "   τεν-   (ἀ-τεν-ής *stretched*),
       σπείρω sow,   "   σπερ- (τὸ σπέρ-μα *seed*),
       κρίνω   judge,   "   κρῐν- (fut. κρῐν-ῶ),
       ἀμύνω   ward off,   "   ἀμῠν- (fut. ἀμῠν-ῶ),
likewise ὀφείλω am indebted, "   ὀφελ- (aor. II. ὤφελ-ον, 86).

Note.— In καίω (besides κάω) *burn*, st. καυ- (τὸ καῦ-μα *heat*),
      and κλαίω (besides κλάω) *weep*, st. κλαυ- (ὁ κλαυ-θμός *weeping*),
the stem remains unchanged before consonants; their presents are formed from
ϝᾰϝ-jω and κλᾰϝ-jω. 92, 2; 97, 44. 45.

For the remaining five classes, see the irregular conjugation,
107–112.

1. PURE

Active Voice

		Indicative		Subjunctive
		Principal Tenses	Historical Tenses	
Pres. and Impf.		*I educate* *	*I educated*	(that) [7] *I may educate*
	S. 1.	παιδεύ-ω	ἐ-παίδευ-ο-ν	παιδεύ-ω
	2.	παιδεύ-εις	ἐ-παίδευ-ε-ς	παιδεύ-ῃς
	3.	παιδεύ-ει	ἐ-παίδευ-ε(ν)	παιδεύ-ῃ
	P. 1.	παιδεύ-ο-μεν	ἐ-παιδεύ-ο-μεν	παιδεύ-ω-μεν
	2.	παιδεύ-ε-τε	ἐ-παιδεύ-ε-τε	παιδεύ-η-τε
	3.	παιδεύ-ουσι(ν) [1]	ἐ-παίδευ-ον	παιδεύ-ωσι(ν) [2]
Future		*I shall educate*		
	S. 1.	παιδεύ-σω		
	2.	παιδεύ-σεις		
	3.	παιδεύ-σει etc.		
		same as in present		
I Aorist			*I educated* (168, 2. a)	(that) [6] *I may educate*
	S. 1.		ἐ-παίδευ-σα	παιδεύ-σω
	2.		ἐ-παίδευ-σα-ς	παιδεύ-σῃς
	3.		ἐ-παίδευ-σε(ν)	παιδεύ-σῃ
	P. 1.		ἐ-παιδεύ-σα-μεν	παιδεύ-σω-μεν
	2.		ἐ-παιδεύ-σα-τε	παιδεύ-ση-τε
	3.		ἐ-παίδευ-σα-ν	παιδεύ-σωσι(ν)
Perfect, Pluperfect		*I have educated*	*I had educated*	(that) [6] *I may have educated*
	S. 1.	πε-παίδευ-κα	ἐ-πε-παιδεύ-κει-ν [4]	πε-παιδεύ-κω
	2.	πε-παίδευ-κα-ς	ἐ-πε-παιδεύ-κει-ς [4]	πε-παιδεύ-κῃς etc.
	3.	πε-παίδευ-κε(ν)	ἐ-πε-παιδεύ-κει [4]	same as in present, or :
	P. 1.	πε-παιδεύ-κα-μεν	ἐ-πε-παιδεύ-κε-μεν [5]	
	2.	πε-παιδεύ-κα-τε	ἐ-πε-παιδεύ-κε-τε [5]	πεπαιδευκὼς ὦ, ῇς, ῇ etc.
	3.	πε-παιδεύ-κᾶσι(ν) [3]	ἐ-πε-παιδεύ-κε-σαν [5]	

Note. — For the forms of the II Aorist

* In the paradigms only one meaning out of a variety

Remarks. — Note in the subj. the iota

[1] from παιδεύ-ο-ντι, παιδεύ-ο-νσι.
[2] from παιδεύ-ω-ντι, παιδεύ-ω-νσι.
[3] from πεπαιδεύ-κα-ντι, πεπαιδεύ-κα-νσι.
[4] early collat. form ἐπεπαιδεύκη, -κης, -κει(ν) [from -εα, -εας, -εε(ν)].

VERBS.

παιδεύω *I educate*

Active Voice

Optative	Imperative	Infinitive and Participle
may I educate παιδεύ-οι-μι παιδεύ-οι-ς παιδεύ-οι παιδεύ-οι-μεν παιδεύ-οι-τε παιδεύ-οιε-ν	 παίδευ-ε *educate* παιδευ-έ-τω *let him* [=*he* *should*] *educate* παιδεύ-ε-τε παιδευ-ό-ντων[7]	 παιδεύ-ειν *to educate* παιδεύ-ων, -οντος παιδεύ-ουσα, -ούσης παιδεῦ-ον, -οντος *one that educates*
(saying that) *I should educate* 169, 4. note παιδεύ-σοι-μι παιδεύ-σοι-ς παιδεύ-σοι etc. same as in present		παιδεύ-σειν (*to educate in future*) παιδεύ-σων, -οντος etc. *one that will* [*is about to*] *educate*
may I educate παιδεύ-σαι-μι παιδεύ-σαι-ς, -σειας παιδεύ-σαι, -σειε(ν) παιδεύ-σαι-μεν παιδεύ-σαι-τε παιδεύ-σαιε-ν, -σειαν	 παίδευ-σον *educate* παιδευ-σά-τω *let him edu- cate* παιδεύ-σα-τε παιδευ-σά-ντων[8]	παιδεῦ-σαι *to educate* or: *to have educated*, 169, 4. παιδεύ-σᾱς, -σαντος παιδεύ-σᾱσα, -σάσης παιδεῦ-σαν, -σαντος *one that educated*
may I have educated πε-παιδεύ-κοι-μι πε-παιδεύ-κοι-ς etc. same as in present, or: πεπαιδευκὼς εἴην, εἴης, εἴη etc.		πε-παιδευ-κέ-ναι *to have educated* πε-παιδευ-κως, -κότος πε-παιδευ-κυῖα, -κυίας πε-παιδευ-κός, -κότος *one that has educated*

and the II Perfect Active see 86 ; 88.

is given.   For a full explanation see Syntax, 167 *seqq.*

subscript: παιδεύῃς, παιδεύῃ.

[5] late collat. form ἐπεπαιδεύ-κειμεν, -κειτε, -κεισαν.
[6] *that* = *in order that* (implying intention, as in final clauses).
[7] late collat. form παιδευ-έ-τωσαν.
[8] "   "   "   παιδευ-σά-τωσαν.

Middle Voice   **PURE VERBS**

		Indicative		Subjunctive
		Principal Tenses	**Historical Tenses**	
Pres. and Impf.		*I educate (for my own sake)*, 165, 1. b.	*I educated (for my own sake)*	(that) *I may educate (for my own sake)*
	S. 1.	παιδεύ-ο-μαι	ἐ-παιδευ-ό-μην	παιδεύ-ω-μαι
	2.	παιδεύ-ῃ [1] (-ει) [3]	ἐ-παιδεύ-ου [4]	παιδεύ-ῃ [2]
	3.	παιδεύ-ε-ται	ἐ-παιδεύ-ε-το	παιδεύ-η-ται
	P. 1.	παιδευ-ό-μεθα	ἐ-παιδευ-ό-μεθα	παιδευ-ώ-μεθα
	2.	παιδεύ-ε-σθε	ἐ-παιδεύ-ε-σθε	παιδεύ-η-σθε
	3.	παιδεύ-ο-νται	ἐ-παιδεύ-ο-ντο	παιδεύ-ω-νται
Future		*I shall educate (for my own sake)*		
	S. 1.	παιδεύ-σο-μαι		
	2.	παιδεύ-σῃ		
	3.	παιδεύ-σε-ται		
	P. 1.	παιδευ-σό-μεθα		
	2.	παιδεύ-σε-σθε		
	3.	παιδεύ-σο-νται		
I Aorist			*I educated (for my own sake)*	(that) *I may educate (for my own sake)*
	S. 1.		ἐ-παιδευ-σά-μην	παιδεύ-σω-μαι
	2.		ἐ-παιδεύ-σω [5]	παιδεύ-σῃ
	3.		ἐ-παιδεύ-σα-το	παιδεύ-ση-ται
	P. 1.		ἐ-παιδευ-σά-μεθα	παιδευ-σώ-μεθα
	2.		ἐ-παιδεύ-σα-σθε	παιδεύ-ση-σθε
	3.		ἐ-παιδεύ-σα-ντο	παιδεύ-σω-νται
Perf. and Pluperf.		*I have educated (for my own sake)*	*I had educated (for my own sake)*	(that) *I may have educated (for my own sake)*
	S. 1.	πε-παίδευ-μαι	ἐ-πε-παιδεύ-μην	πε-παιδευ-μένος ὦ
	2.	πε-παίδευ-σαι	ἐ-πε-παίδευ-σο	——— ᾖς
	3.	πε-παίδευ-ται	ἐ-πε-παίδευ-το	——— ᾖ
	P. 1.	πε-παιδεύ-μεθα	ἐ-πε-παιδεύ-μεθα	πε-παιδευ-μένοι ὦμεν
	2.	πε-παίδευ-σθε	ἐ-πε-παίδευ-σθε	——— ἦτε
	3.	πε-παίδευν-ται	ἐ-πε-παίδευ-ντο	——— ὦσι(ν)

Note. — For the forms of

[1] from παιδεύ-ε-σαι, παιδεύ-ε-αι } hence iota subscript.
[2] from παιδεύ-η-σαι, παιδεύ-η-αι }
[3] the later form παιδεύει is often used in the indic. for the earlier form παιδεύῃ.
[4] from ἐπαιδεύ-ε-σο, ἐπαιδεύ-ε-ο.
[5] from ἐπαιδεύ-σα-σο, ἐπαιδεύ-σα-ο.

— *Continued.*

Middle Voice

Optative	Imperative	Infinitive and Participle
may I educate (*for my own sake*) παιδευ-οί-μην παιδεύ-οι-ο [1] παιδεύ-οι-το παιδευ-οί-μεθα παιδεύ-οι-σθε παιδεύ-οι-ντο	*educate* (*for your own sake*) παιδεύ-ου [2] παιδευ-έ-σθω παιδεύ-ε-σθε παιδευ-έ-σθων [3]	παιδεύ-ε-σθαι *to educate* (*for one's own sake*) παιδευ-ό-μενος παιδευ-ο-μένη παιδευ-ό-μενον *one that educates* (*for his own sake*)
(*saying that*) *I should educate* (*for my own sake*) 169, 4. note παιδευ-σοί-μην παιδεύ-σοι-ο [1] παιδεύ-σοι-το παιδευ-σοί-μεθα παιδεύ-σοι-σθε παιδεύ-σοι-ντο		παιδεύ-σε-σθαι *to educate* (*for one's own sake*) *in future* παιδευ-σό-μενος παιδευ-σο-μένη παιδευ-σό-μενον *one that will educate* (*for his own sake*)
may I educate (*for my own sake*) παιδευ-σαί-μην παιδεύ-σαι-ο [1] παιδεύ-σαι-το παιδευ-σαί-μεθα παιδεύ-σαι-σθε παιδεύ-σαι-ντο	*educate* (*for your own sake*) παιδεύ-σαι παιδευ-σά-σθω παιδεύ-σα-σθε παιδευ-σά-σθων [4]	παιδεύ-σα-σθαι *to educate* (*have educated*, 169, 4) (*for one's own sake*) παιδευ-σά-μενος παιδευ-σα-μένη παιδευ-σά-μενον *one that educated* (*for his own sake*)
may I have educated (*for my own sake*) πεπαιδευμένος εἴην ———— εἴης ———— εἴη πεπαιδευμένοι εἴημεν ———— εἴητε ———— εἴησαν	*have educated* (*for your own sake*) πε-παίδευ-σο πε-παιδεύ-σθω πε-παίδευ-σθε πε-παιδεύ-σθων [5]	πε-παιδεῦ-σθαι *to have educated* (*for one's own sake*) πε-παιδευ-μένος πε-παιδευ-μένη πε-παι·δευ-μένον *one that has educated* (*for his own sake*)

the II Aor. Middle, see 86.

[1] from παιδεύ-οι-σο (fut. παιδεύ-σοι-σο, aor. παιδεύ-σαι-σο).
[2] from παιδεύ-ε-σο, παιδεύ-ε-ο.
[3] later collat. form παιδευ-έ-σθωσαν.
[4] "   "   "   παιδευ-σά-σθωσαν.
[5] "   "   "   πεπαιδεύ-σθωσαν.

PURE VERBS

Passive Voice

		Indicative		Subjunctive
		Principal Tenses	Historical Tenses	
Pres. and Impf.		*I am educated*	*I was educated*	(that) *I may be educated*
	S. 1.	παιδεύ-ο-μαι	ἐ-παιδεν-ό-μην	παιδεύ-ω-μαι
	2.	παιδεύ-ῃ (-ει)	ἐ-παιδεύ-ου	παιδεύ-ῃ
	3.	παιδεύ-ε-ται	ἐ-παιδεύ-ε-το	παιδεύ-η-ται
	P. 1.	etc.	etc.	etc.
	2.			
	3.		same as in the middle	
Future		*I shall be educated*		
	S. 1.	παιδευ-θή-σο-μαι		
	2.	παιδευ-θή-σῃ (-σει)		
	3.	παιδευ-θή-σε-ται		
	P. 1.	παιδευ-θη-σό-μεθα		
	2.	παιδευ-θή-σε-σθε		
	3.	παιδευ-θή-σο-νται		
I Aorist			*I was educated*	(that) *I may be educated*
	S. 1.		ἐ-παιδεύ-θη-ν	παιδευ-θῶ
	2.		ἐ-παιδεύ-θη-ς	παιδευ-θῇς
	3.		ἐ-παιδεύ-θη	παιδευ-θῇ
	P. 1.		ἐ-παιδεύ-θη-μεν	παιδευ-θῶ-μεν
	2.		ἐ-παιδεύ-θη-τε	παιδευ-θῆ-τε
	3.		ἐ-παιδεύ-θη-σαν	παιδευ-θῶσι(ν)
Perf. and Plupert.		*I have been educated*	*I had been educated*	(that) *I may have been educated*
	S. 1.	πε-παίδευ-μαι	ἐ-πε-παιδεύ-μην	πεπαιδευμένος ὦ
	2.	πε-παίδευ-σαι	ἐ-πε-παίδευ-σο	——— ᾖς
	3.	πε-παίδευ-ται	ἐ-πε-παίδευ-το	——— ᾖ
	P. 1.	etc.	etc.	etc.
	2.			
	3.		same as in the middle	

Note. — For παιδεύῃ, παιδεύει, ἐπαιδεύου, παιδεύοιο and παιδεύου, see the notes, pp. 50 and 51.

— *Concluded.*

Passive Voice

Optative	Imperative	Infinitive and Participle
may I be educated παιδεύ‐οί‐μην παιδεύ‐οι‐ο παιδεύ‐οι‐το etc.	*let yourself be educated* παιδεύ‐ου παιδεύ‐έ‐σθω etc.	παιδεύ‐ε‐σθαι *to be educated* παιδευ‐ό‐μενος *one that is educated*

same as in the middle

(saying that) *I should be educated* (some time in the future),169,4.n. παιδευ‐θη‐σοί‐μην παιδευ‐θή‐σοι‐ο παιδευ‐θή‐σοι‐το παιδευ‐θη‐σοί‐μεθα παιδευ‐θή‐σοι‐σθε παιδευ‐θή‐σοι‐ντο		παιδευ‐θή‐σε‐σθαι *to be educated (at some future time)* παιδευ‐θη‐σό‐μενος παιδευ‐θη‐σο‐μένη παιδευ‐θη‐σό‐μενον *one that will be educated*
may I be educated παιδευ‐θείη‐ν παιδευ‐θείη‐ς παιδευ‐θείη παιδευ‐θείη‐μεν, ‐θεῖμεν παιδευ‐θείη‐τε, ‐θεῖτε παιδευ‐θείη‐σαν, ‐θεῖεν	*let yourself be educated* παιδεύ‐θη‐τι παιδευ‐θή‐τω παιδεύ‐θη‐τε παιδευ‐θέ‐ντων [1]	παιδευ‐θῆ‐ναι *to be educated (to have been educated)*, 169, 4. παιδευ‐θείς,　‐θέντος παιδευ‐θεῖσα, ‐θείσης παιδευ‐θέν,　‐θέντος *educated, one that was (is) educated*
may I have been educated πεπαιδευμένος εἴην ——　εἴης ——　εἴη etc.	*be educated* πε‐παίδευ‐σο πε‐παιδεύ‐σθω	πε‐παιδεῦ‐σθαι *to have been educated* πε‐παιδευ‐μένος *(one who has been) educated*

same as in the middle

[1] Later collateral form παιδευ‐θή‐τωσαν; compare the notes on pp. 49 and 51.

79. FORMATION OF THE TENSE

1. **Pres. and Impf. Act., Mid., and Pass.** Formative syllables are the thematic vowels -ο, -ε,
   -ο before μ, ν and in the optative,
   -ε before σ, τ and before vowels ;
   -ειν in the infinitive arises from -ε-εν.

2. **Fut. Act. and Mid.** Formative syllables: -σο, -σε.
   Same inflection as in the present.
   Subjunctive and imperative are wanting.

3. **I Aor. Act. and Mid.** Formative syllable: -σα.
   The subjunctive has the same endings as the present.
   To be distinguished: παίδευσον and παιδεῦσον;
   παίδευσαι, παιδεύσαι, παιδεῦσαι.
   [or λῦσαι, 2. and λύσαι — γράψαι, 3.]

4. **I Perf. Active** Formative syllable is -κα, added to the redupl. stem.
   Subj. and opt. have the same endings as in the present.

5. **I Pluperf. Active** Formative syllable: -κει, -κε, added to the redupl. stem.
   Perfects with ε- as reduplication take no extra augment.

SYNOPSIS OF THE FORMATION

80. The stems of pure verbs, from the future the verbs in -άω have after ε, ι, ρ : ᾱ (28, 1 ; 29, 1 ; 34, 2). otherwise : η.

1.	Present	Active Mid., Pass.	θηρά-ω hunt θηρά-ο-μαι	τιμά-ω honor τιμά-ο-μαι
2.	Future	Active Middle	θηρά-σω θηρά-σο-μαι	τιμή-σω τιμή-σο-μαι
3.	Aorist	Active Middle	ἐ-θήρᾱ-σα ἐ-θηρᾱ-σά-μην	ἐ-τίμη-σα ἐ-τιμη-σά-μην
4.	Perfect	Active Mid., Pass.	τε-θήρᾱ-κα τε-θήρᾱ-μαι	τε-τίμη-κα τε-τίμη-μαι
5.	Aorist } Future } Pass.		ἐ-θηρά-θη-ν θηρᾱ-θή-σομαι	ἐ-τιμή-θη-ν τιμη-θή-σομαι
6.	Verb. Adjectives		θηρᾱ-τός, 3. θηρᾱ-τέος, 3.	τιμη-τός, 3. τιμη-τέος, 3.

For peculiarities of

STEMS FROM THE VERB STEMS.

6. **Perf. and Plup. Mid. and Pass.**	**Without formative syllable.** The endings are applied **directly** to the **reduplicated** stem. The infin. and part. have the accent throughout on the penult.
7. **Future Perfect**	The act. is expressed by the pf. part. and ἔσομαι.(104, 3) ; thus πεπαιδευκὼς ἔσομαι *I shall have educated.* The **pass.** adds to the **redupl.** stem the middle endings -σομαι, etc. ; thus πεπαιδεύσομαι *I shall have been educated.*
8. **I Aor. and I Fut. Pass.**	Formative syllable: -θη, before vowels or -ντ: -θε, to be contracted with the thematic vowel of the subjunctive. The aorist passive has active, the future pass. has middle endings. Mark as imper. παιδεύθητι for παιδεύθηθι (21, 1).
9. **Verbal Adjectives**	Formative syllables are -τός, -τή, -τόν and -τέος, -τέα, -τέον. παιδευτός, 3. *(capable of being) educated,* παιδευτέος, 3. *that must be educated, educandus.*

OF TENSES OF PURE VERBS.

onward, end in a long vowel as follows:
the verbs in -έω: η,   the verbs in -όω: ω,
the verbs in -ῠω: ῑ,   the verbs in -ῠω: ῡ.

ποιέ-ω *make* ποιέ-ο-μαι	δουλό-ω *enslave* δουλό-ο-μαι	μηνῠ́-ω *make known* μηνῠ́-ο-μαι
ποιή-σω ποιή-σο-μαι	δουλώ-σω δουλώ-σο-μαι	μηνῠ́-σω μηνῠ́-σο-μαι
ἐ-ποίη-σα ἐ-ποιη-σά-μην	ἐ-δούλω-σα ἐ-δουλω-σά-μην	ἐ-μήνῡ-σα ἐ-μηνῡ-σά-μην
πε-ποίη-κα πε-ποίη-μαι	δε-δούλω-κα δε-δούλω-μαι	με-μήνῡ-κα με-μήνῡ-μαι
ἐ-ποιή-θη-ν ποιη-θή-σομαι	ἐ-δουλώ-θη-ν δουλω-θή-σομαι	ἐ-μηνῠ́-θη-ν μηνῡ-θή-σομαι
ποιη-τός, 3. ποιη-τέος, 3.	δουλω-τός, 3. δουλω-τέος, 3.	μηνῡ-τος, 3. μηνῡ-τέος, 3.

pure verbs see 91.

81. PRESENT AND IMPERFECT

1. Paradigm τιμάω : I honor.

a + E-sound(ε, η, ει, ῃ) gives ᾱ (ᾳ),
a + O-sound (ο, ω, οι, ου) gives ω (ῳ),
original ι becomes iota subscript.

		Active			Middle and Passive	
Indicative	S. 1.	τιμάω	τιμῶ		τιμάομαι	τιμῶμαι
	2.	τιμάεις	τιμᾷς		τιμάῃ (-ει)	τιμᾷ
	3.	τιμάει	τιμᾷ		τιμάεται	τιμᾶται
	P. 1.	τιμάομεν	τιμῶμεν		τιμαόμεθα	τιμώμεθα
	2.	τιμάετε	τιμᾶτε		τιμάεσθε	τιμᾶσθε
	3.	τιμάουσι(ν)	τιμῶσι(ν)		τιμάονται	τιμῶνται
Imperfect	S. 1.	ἐτίμαον	ἐτίμων		ἐτιμαόμην	ἐτιμώμην
	2.	ἐτίμαες	ἐτίμᾱς		ἐτιμάου	ἐτιμῶ
	3.	ἐτίμαε(ν)	ἐτίμᾱ		ἐτιμάετο	ἐτιμᾶτο
	P. 1.	ἐτιμάομεν	ἐτιμῶμεν		ἐτιμαόμεθα	ἐτιμώμεθα
	2.	ἐτιμάετε	ἐτιμᾶτε		ἐτιμάεσθε	ἐτιμᾶσθε
	3.	ἐτίμαον	ἐτίμων		ἐτιμάοντο	ἐτιμῶντο
Subjunctive	S. 1.	τιμάω	τιμῶ		τιμάωμαι	τιμῶμαι
	2.	τιμάῃς	τιμᾷς		τιμάῃ	τιμᾷ
	3.	τιμάῃ	τιμᾷ		τιμάηται	τιμᾶται
	P. 1.	τιμάωμεν	τιμῶμεν		τιμαώμεθα	τιμώμεθα
	2.	τιμάητε	τιμᾶτε		τιμάησθε	τιμᾶσθε
	3.	τιμάωσι(ν)	τιμῶσι(ν)		τιμάωνται ·	τιμῶνται
Optative	S. 1.	τιμάοιμι	τιμῷμι -ῴην		τιμαοίμην	τιμῴμην
	2.	τιμάοις	τιμῷς -ῴης		τιμάοιο	τιμῷο
	3.	τιμάοι	τιμῷ -ῴη		τιμάοιτο	τιμῷτο
	P. 1.	τιμάοιμεν	τιμῷμεν -ῴημεν		τιμαοίμεθα	τιμῴμεθα
	2.	τιμάοιτε	τιμῷτε -ῴητε		τιμάοισθε	τιμῷσθε
	3.	τιμάοιεν	τιμῷεν		τιμάοιντο	τιμῷντο
Imper.	S. 2.	τίμαε	τίμᾱ		τιμάου	τιμῶ
	3.	τιμαέτω	τιμάτω		τιμαέσθω	τιμάσθω
	P. 2.	τιμάετε	τιμᾶτε		τιμάεσθε	τιμᾶσθε
	3.	τιμαόντων	τιμώντων		τιμαέσθων	τιμάσθων
Infinitive		τιμάειν	τιμᾶν		τιμάεσθαι	τιμᾶσθαι
Participle		τιμάων	τιμῶν, -ῶντος		τιμαόμενος	τιμώμενος
		τιμάουσα	τιμῶσα, -ώσης		τιμαομένη	τιμωμένη
		τιμάον	τιμῶν, -ῶντος		τιμαόμενον	τιμώμενον

Note 1.— As the ending of the inf. act. ειν arises from a contraction of ε-εν, and consequently does not contain an original ι, the contracted inf. is τιμᾶν (not τιμᾷν) and δουλοῦν (not δουλοῖν).

OF CONTRACT VERBS.

2. Paradigm ποιέω: *I make.*

ε + ε gives ει,

ε + ο gives ου,

ε before a long vowel or diphthong is absorbed.

			Active		Middle and Passive	
Indicative	S.	1.	ποιέω	ποιῶ	ποιέομαι	ποιοῦμαι
		2.	ποιέεις	ποιεῖς	ποιέῃ(-ει)	ποιῇ(-εῖ)
		3.	ποιέει	ποιεῖ	ποιέεται	ποιεῖται
	P.	1.	ποιέομεν	ποιοῦμεν	ποιεόμεθα	ποιούμεθα
		2.	ποιέετε	ποιεῖτε	ποιέεσθε	ποιεῖσθε
		3.	ποιέουσι(ν)	ποιοῦσι(ν)	ποιέονται	ποιοῦνται
Imperfect	S.	1.	ἐποίεον	ἐποίουν	ἐποιεόμην	ἐποιούμην
		2.	ἐποίεες	ἐποίεις	ἐποιέου	ἐποιοῦ
		3.	ἐποίεε(ν)	ἐποίει	ἐποιέετο	ἐποιεῖτο
	P.	1.	ἐποιέομεν	ἐποιοῦμεν	ἐποιεόμεθα	ἐποιούμεθα
		2.	ἐποιέετε	ἐποιεῖτε	ἐποιέεσθε	ἐποιεῖσθε
		3.	ἐποίεον	ἐποίουν	ἐποιέοντο	ἐποιοῦντο
Subjunctive	S.	1.	ποιέω	ποιῶ	ποιέωμαι	ποιῶμαι
		2.	ποιέῃς	ποιῇς	ποιέῃ	ποιῇ
		3.	ποιέῃ	ποιῇ	ποιέηται	ποιῆται
	P.	1.	ποιέωμεν	ποιῶμεν	ποιεώμεθα	ποιώμεθα
		2.	ποιέητε	ποιῆτε	ποιέησθε	ποιῆσθε
		3.	ποιέωσι(ν)	ποιῶσι(ν)	ποιέωνται	ποιῶνται
Optative	S.	1.	ποιέοιμι	ποιοῖμι -οίην	ποιεοίμην	ποιοίμην
		2.	ποιέοις	ποιοῖς -οίης	ποιέοιο	ποιοῖο
		3.	ποιέοι	ποιοῖ -οίη	ποιέοιτο	ποιοῖτο
	P.	1.	ποιέοιμεν	ποιοῖμεν -οίημεν	ποιεοίμεθα	ποιοίμεθα
		2.	ποιέοιτε	ποιοῖτε -οίητε	ποιέοισθε	ποιοῖσθε
		3.	ποιέοιεν	ποιοῖεν	ποιέοιντο	ποιοῖντο
Imper.	S.	2.	ποίεε	ποίει	ποιέου	ποιοῦ
		3.	ποιεέτω	ποιείτω	ποιεέσθω	ποιείσθω
	P.	2.	ποιέετε	ποιεῖτε	ποιέεσθε	ποιεῖσθε
		3.	ποιεόντων	ποιούντων	ποιεέσθων	ποιείσθων
Infinitive			ποιέειν	ποιεῖν	ποιέεσθαι	ποιεῖσθαι
Participle			ποιέων	ποιῶν, -οῦντος	ποιεόμενος	ποιούμενος
			ποιέουσα	ποιοῦσα, -ούσης	ποιεομένη	ποιουμένη
			ποιέον	ποιοῦν, -οῦντος	ποιεόμενον	ποιούμενον

Note 2. — In the optative sing. the forms with η, in the plural those without η prevail.

PRESENT AND IMPERFECT OF CONTRACT VERBS. — *Concluded.*

3. Paradigm δουλόω : *I enslave.*

ο + ε or ο or ου gives ου,

ο + η or 'ω gives ω,

ο + ι-diphthong (ει, οι, ῃ) gives οι.

			Active		Middle and Passive	
Indicative	S.	1.	δουλόω	δουλῶ	δουλόομαι	δουλοῦμαι
		2.	δόυλόεις	δουλοῖς	δουλόῃ(-ει)	δουλοῖ
		3.	δουλόει	δουλοῖ	δουλόεται	δουλοῦται
	P.	1.	δουλόομεν	δουλοῦμεν	δουλοόμεθα	δουλούμεθα
		2.	δουλόετε	δουλοῦτε	δουλόεσθε	δουλοῦσθε
		3.	δουλόουσι(ν)	δουλοῦσι(ν)	δουλόονται	δουλοῦνται
Imperfect	S.	1.	ἐδούλοον	ἐδούλουν	ἐδουλοόμην	ἐδουλούμην
		2.	ἐδούλοες	ἐδούλους	ἐδουλόου	ἐδουλοῦ
		3.	ἐδούλοε(ν)	ἐδούλου	ἐδουλόετο	ἐδουλοῦτο
	P.	1.	ἐδουλόομεν	ἐδουλοῦμεν	ἐδουλοόμεθα	ἐδουλούμεθα
		2.	ἐδουλόετε	ἐδουλοῦτε	ἐδουλόεσθε	ἐδουλοῦσθε
		3.	ἐδούλοον	ἐδούλουν	ἐδουλόοντο	ἐδουλοῦντο
Subjunctive	S.	1.	δουλόω	δουλῶ	δουλόωμαι	δουλῶμαι
		2.	δουλόῃς	δουλοῖς	δουλόῃ	δουλοῖ
		3.	δουλόῃ	δουλοῖ	δουλόηται	δουλῶται
	P.	1.	δουλόωμεν	δουλῶμεν	δουλοώμεθα	δουλώμεθα
		2.	δουλόητε	δουλῶτε	δουλόησθε	δουλῶσθε
		3.	δουλόωσι(ν)	δουλῶσι(ν)	δουλόωνται	δουλῶνται
Optative	S.	1.	δουλόοιμι	δουλοῖμι -οίην	δουλοοίμην	δουλοίμην
		2.	δουλόοις	δουλοῖς -οίης	δουλόοιο	δουλοῖο
		3.	δουλόοι	δουλοῖ -οίη	δουλόοιτο	δουλοῖτο
	P.	1.	δουλόοιμεν	δουλοῖμεν -οίημεν	δουλοοίμεθα	δουλοίμεθα
		2.	δουλόοιτε	δουλοῖτε -οίητε	δουλόοισθε	δουλοῖσθε
		3.	δουλόοιεν	δουλοῖεν	δουλόοιντο	δουλοῖντο
Imper.	S.	2.	δούλοε	δούλου	δουλόου	δουλοῦ
		3.	δουλοέτω	δουλούτω	δουλοέσθω	δουλούσθω
	P.	2.	δουλόετε	δουλοῦτε	δουλόεσθε	δουλοῦσθε
		3.	δουλοόντων	δουλούντων	δουλοέσθων	δουλούσθων
Infinitive			δουλόειν	δουλοῦν	δουλόεσθαι	δουλοῦσθαι
Participle			δουλόων	δουλῶν, -οῦντος	δουλοόμενος	δουλούμενος
			δουλόουσα	δουλοῦσα, -ούσης	δουλοομένη	δουλουμένη
			δουλόον	δουλοῦν, -οῦντος	δουλοόμενον	δουλούμενον

Note 3. — For the inf. act. δουλοῦν see note 1, page 56.

Note 4. — Contracted forms of the 3. p. sg. have no ν ἐφελκυστικόν: ἐτίμα, ἐποίει, ἐδούλου.

2. MUTE VERBS.

82. Their tenses are formed by means of the same formative syllables and endings as those of pure verbs. Special attention is due only to the euphonic changes to which those suffixes are subject when brought into contact with the final consonants of the stem.

1. **Dental stems**

drop their final consonants (δ, τ, θ) before σ and κ (see ἐλπίσιν 39, 1), but change them to σ before μ or other dentals.

Note. — σπένδω takes compensative lengthening (13) throughout:
σπένδω, σπείσω, ἔσπεισα, (ἔσπεικα), ἔσπεισμαι, ἐσπείσθην.

2. **Guttural** and **labial stems.** Here

with σ: any guttural becomes ξ, any labial ψ (38),
before μ: "   "   "   γ,   "   "   μ,
before τ: "   "   "   κ,   "   "   π,
before θ: "   "   "   χ,   "   "   φ.

These stems have no first perf. act. (in -κα); if they have any perf. act. at all, it is the second (88).

3. Synopsis of the Formation of Tenses.

	γυμναδ- *train*	ἁρμοτ- *join*	πραγ- *do*	κρυφ- *hide*
Pres. Act.	γυμνάζω	ἁρμόττω	πράττω	κρύπτω
Fut.	γυμνά-σω	ἁρμό-σω	πράξω	κρύψω
Aor.	ἐγύμνα-σα	ἥρμο-σα	ἔπραξα	ἔκρυψα
Perf.	γεγύμνα-κα	ἥρμο-κα	(88, 3. b.)	(88, 3. a.)
Perf. Mid. Pass.	γεγύμνασ-μαι	ἥρμοσ-μαι	πέπραγ-μαι	κέκρυμ-μαι
Aor. Pass.	ἐγυμνάσ-θην	ἡρμόσ-θην	ἐπράχ-θην	ἐκρύφ-θην
III. Fut.	——	——	πεπράξομαι	κεκρύψομαι
Verbal Adj.	γυμνασ-τός	ἁρμοσ-τός	πρᾱκ-τός	κρυπ-τός
	γυμνασ-τέος	ἁρμοσ-τέος	πρᾱκ-τέος	κρυπ-τέος

INFLECTION OF THE PERF. AND PLUP. MID. AND PASS.

83. 1. As the final consonant of the stem must be assimilated to the initial sound of the endings and σ be dropped between two consonants, the following are the only combinations possible:

in dent. stems   in gutt. stems   in lab. stems

σμ   γμ   μμ

σ   ξ   ψ

στ   κτ   πτ

σθ   χθ   φθ.

2. The endings -νται and -ντο cannot be added to consonant stems; the third person plural, therefore, is always formed by the perfect participle passive, with

εἰσί(ν), neuter ἐστί(ν), in the perfect,
ἦσαν, neuter ἦν, in the pluperfect.

3. Paradigms.

		PERF. INDIC.	PLUPERFECT	PERF. IMPER.	INF. AND PART.
ψεύδω *deceive*	st. ψευδ-	ἔψευσ-μαι ἔψευ-σαι ἔψευσ-ται ἐψεύσ-μεθα ἔψευ-σθε ἐψευσ-μένοι εἰσί(ν)	ἐψεύσ-μην ἔψευ-σο ἔψευσ-το ἐψεύσ-μεθα ἔψευ-σθε ἐψευσ-μένοι ἦσαν	ἔψευ-σο ἐψεύ-σθω ἔψευ-σθε ἐψεύ-σθων	ἐψεῦ-σθαι ἐψευσ-μένος ἐψευσ-μένη ἐψευσ-μένον
πράττω *do*	st. πρᾱγ-	πέπρᾱγ-μαι πέπρᾱξαι πέπρᾱκ-ται πεπράγ-μεθα πέπρᾱχ-θε πεπρᾱγ-μένοι εἰσί(ν)	ἐπεπράγ-μην ἐπέπρᾱξο ἐπέπρακ-το ἐπεπράγ-μεθα ἐπέπραχ-θε πεπραγ-μένοι ἦσαν	πέπρᾱξο πεπράχ-θω πέπραχ-θε πεπράχ-θων	πεπρᾶχ-θαι πεπρᾱγ-μένος πεπρᾱγ-μένη πεπρᾱγ-μένον
γράφω *write*	st. γράφ-	γέγρᾰμ-μαι γέγραψαι γέγραπ-ται γεγράμ-μεθα γέγραφ-θε γεγραμ-μένοι εἰσί(ν)	ἐγεγράμ-μην ἐγέγραψο ἐγέγραπ-το ἐγεγράμ-μεθα ἐγέγραφ-θε γεγραμ-μένοι ἦσαν	γέγραψο γεγράφ-θω γέγραφ-θε γεγράφ-θων	γεγράφ-θαι γεγρᾰμ-μένος γεγρᾰμ-μένη γεγρᾰμ-μένον

4. The three verbs στρέφω *turn*, τρέπω *turn*, τρέφω *nourish*, change their stem vowel ε to ᾰ:

ἔστραμμαι, τέτραμμαι, τέθραμμαι (21, 2).

5. An accumulation of consonants is avoided; *e.g.* in πέπεμμαι, πεπεμμένος (instead of πέπεμμ-μαι, πεπεμμ-μένος) from πέμπω. Nor is this the only instance.

3. LIQUID VERBS.

Future and First Aorist Act. and Mid.

84. 1. The future adds to the verb stem the endings

(-έσω, -έω): -ῶ, -εῖς, etc.

It is inflected like contract verbs in -έω (*Futurum contractum*); see 3.

2. In the **first aorist** the σ drops out with compensative lengthening (13) of the last syllable of the stem. Thus
ᾰ after ι, ρ becomes ᾱ: μιαίνω stain, st. μιᾰν- f. μιᾰνῶ, a. ἐμίᾱνα,
περαίνω finish, περᾰν- περᾱνῶ, ἐπέρᾱνα,
elsewhere η:· φαίνω show, φᾰν- φᾰνῶ, ἔφηνα,
ε becomes ει: δέρω flay, δερ- δερῶ, ἔδειρα,
ῐ becomes ῑ: κρίνω judge, κρῑν- κρῑνῶ, ἔκρῑνα,
ῠ becomes ῡ: ἀμύνω ward off, ἀμῡν- ἀμῡνῶ, ἤμῡνα.

3. Paradigm: στέλλω *I send.*

		Indicative	Subjunctive	Optative	Imperative	Infin., Participle
Future	Active	στελῶ στελεῖς στελεῖ στελοῦμεν στελεῖτε στελοῦσι(ν)		στελοῖμι -οίην στελοῖς -οίης στελοῖ -οίη στελοῖμεν στελοῖτε στελοῖεν		στελεῖν στελῶν -οῦντος στελοῦσα -ούσης στελοῦν -οῦντος
Future	Middle	στελοῦμαι στελῇ (-εῖ) στελεῖται στελούμεθα στελεῖσθε στελοῦνται		στελοίμην στελοῖο στελοῖτο στελοίμεθα στελοῖσθε στελοῖντο		στελεῖσθαι στελούμενος στελουμένη στελούμενον
I Aorist	Active	ἔστειλα ἔστειλας ἔστειλε(ν) ἐστείλαμεν ἐστείλατε ἔστειλαν	στείλω στείλῃς στείλῃ στείλωμεν στείλητε στείλωσι(ν)	στείλαιμι στείλαις -ειας στείλαι -ειε(ν) στείλαιμεν στείλαιτε στείλαιεν -ειαν	στεῖλον στειλάτω στείλατε στειλάντων	στεῖλαι στείλας -αντος στείλασα -άσης στείλαν -αντος
I Aorist	Middle	ἐστειλάμην ἐστείλω ἐστείλατο ἐστειλάμεθα ἐστείλασθε ἐστείλαντο	στείλωμαι στείλῃ στείληται στειλώμεθα στείλησθε στείλωνται	στειλαίμην στείλαιο στείλαιτο στειλαίμεθα στείλαισθε στείλαιντο	στεῖλαι στειλάσθω στείλασθε στειλάσθων	στείλασθαι στειλάμενος στειλαμένη στειλάμενον

The Remaining Tenses.

85. 1. They are formed in the usual manner with the necessary changes:

a) final ν before κ becomes γ;
b) final ν before μ becomes σ;
c) σ between two consonants is dropped;
d) the ε of **mono**syllabic stems becomes α (cf. **11, 3.** extr.).

2. Synopsis of the Formation of Tenses.

Stems:	φᾰν- *show*	ἀγγελ- *announce*	στελ- *send*	σπερ- *sow*
Pres. Act.	φαίνω	ἀγγέλλω	στέλλω	σπείρω
Fut.	φᾰν-ῶ, -εῖς	ἀγγελ-ῶ, -εῖς	στελ-ῶ, -εῖς	σπερ-ῶ, -εῖς
Aor.	ἔ-φηνα	ἤγγειλα	ἔ-στειλα	ἔ-σπειρα
Perf.	πέ-φαγ-κα	ἤγγελ-κα	ἔ-σταλ-κα	ἔ-σπαρ-κα
Perf. M. & P.	πέ-φασ-μαι	ἤγγελ-μαι	ἔ-σταλ-μαι	ἔ-σπαρ-μαι
Aor. Pass.	ἐ-φάν-θην	ἠγγέλ-θην	ἐ-στάλ-ην	ἐ-σπάρ-ην (87, 3)
Verb. Adj.	φαν-τός	ἀγγελ-τός	σταλ-τός	σπαρ-τός
	φαν-τέος	ἀγγελ-τέος	σταλ-τέος	σπαρ-τέος

3. Inflection of the Perfect and Pluperfect Mid. and Pass.

	PERF. INDIC.	PLUPERFECT	PERF. IMPER.	INF. AND PART.
φαίνω *show* st. φᾰν-	πέφασ-μαι	ἐπεφάσ-μην		πεφάν-θαι
	πέφαν-σαι	ἐπέφαν-σο	πέφαν-σο	
	πέφαν-ται	ἐπέφαν-το	πεφάν-θω	πεφασ-μένος
	πεφάσ-μεθα	ἐπεφάσ-μεθα		πεφασ-μένη
	πέφαν-θε	ἐπέφαν-θε	πέφαν-θε	πεφασ-μένον
	πεφασ-μένοι εἰσί(ν)	πεφασ-μένοι ἦσαν	πεφάν-θων	
ἀγγέλλω *announce* st. ἀγγελ-	ἤγγελ-μαι	ἠγγέλ-μην		ἠγγέλ-θαι
	ἤγγελ-σαι	ἤγγελ-σο	ἤγγελ-σο	
	ἤγγελ-ται	ἤγγελ-το	ἠγγέλ-θω	ἠγγελ-μένος
	ἠγγέλ-μεθα	ἠγγέλ-μεθα		ἠγγελ-μένη
	ἤγγελ-θε	ἤγγελ-θε	ἤγγελ-θε	ἠγγελ-μένον
	ἠγγελμένοι εἰσί(ν)	ἠγγελ-μένοι ἦσαν	ἠγγέλ-θων	

4. Liquid verbs lack the future perfect.

5. For βάλλω, κλίνω, κρίνω, τείνω see 92, 4. 6. 7 with note.

4. SECOND TENSES.

I. SECOND AORIST ACTIVE AND MIDDLE.

86. 1. Formative syllables are -ο, and -ε, to be added to the verb stem. Thus the endings of the indicative are the same as those of the imperfect, those of the other moods the same as those of the respective forms of the present. However, four forms have a different accent:

in the active: the inf. and the part.: **βαλεῖν, βαλών.**
in the middle: the 2. p. imper. and the inf.: **βαλοῦ, βαλέσθαι.**

Note. — The compounds too have the accent on the thematic vᴏwel in these forms:

ἀποβαλεῖν, ἀποβαλών, ἀποβαλοῦ, ἀποβαλέσθαι.

2. Paradigm.

	INDICATIVE	SUBJUNCTIVE	OPTATIVE	IMPERATIVE	INF. AND PART.
Active	ἔ-βαλ-ο-ν	βάλ-ω	βάλ-οι-μι		βαλ-εῖν
	ἔ-βαλ-ε-ς	βάλ-ῃς	βάλ-οι-ς	βάλ-ε	
	ἔ-βαλ-ε(ν)	βάλ-ῃ	βάλ-οι	βαλ-έ-τω	βαλ-ών,　-όντος
	ἐ-βάλ-ο-μεν	βάλ-ω-μεν	βάλ-οι-μεν		βαλ-οῦσα, -ούσης
	ἐ-βάλ-ε-τε	βάλ-η-τε	βάλ-οι-τε	βάλ-ε-τε	βαλ-ό-ν,　-όντος
	ἔ-βαλ-ο-ν	βάλ-ωσι(ν)	βάλ-οιε-ν	βαλ-ό-ντων	
Middle	ἐ-βαλ-ό-μην	βάλ-ω-μαι	βαλ-οί-μην		βαλ-έ-σθαι
	ἐ-βάλ-ου	βάλ-ῃ	βάλ-οι-ο	βαλ-οῦ	
	ἐ-βάλ-ε-το	βάλ-η-ται	βάλ-οι-το	βαλ-έ-σθω	βαλ-ό-μενος
	ἐ-βαλ-ό-μεθα	βαλ-ώ-μεθα	βαλ-οί-μεθα		βαλ-ο-μένη
	ἐ-βάλ-ε-σθε	βάλ-η-σθε	βάλ-οι-σθε	βάλ-ε-σθε	βαλ-ό-μενον
	ἐ-βάλ-ο-ντο	βάλ-ω-νται	βάλ-οι-ντο	βαλ-έ-σθων	

3. The following second aorists of regular verbs are the most important in Attic prose:

τίκτω	bring forth,	st. τεκ-	ἔτεκον,
ἀνα-κράζω	cry out,	" κράγ-	ἀν-έκρᾱγον,
βάλλω	throw,	" βᾰλ-	ἔβᾰλον,
κατα-καίνω	kill,	" κᾰν-	κατ-έκᾱνον,
ὀφείλω	owe,	" ὀφελ-	ὤφελον utinam ego, *would that I,* with inf., 172, 2. note.

Some have a peculiar formation; as

ἄγω	lead,	st. ἀγ-	ἤγᾰγον (redupl.),
τρέπομαι	turn, intr.,	" τρεπ-	ἐτρᾰπόμην (ablaut, 11, 2).

Among the irregular verbs II aorists are very numerous.

II. SECOND AORIST AND SECOND FUTURE PASSIVE.

87. 1. The formative syllable is -η, before vowels or ντ -ε, to be added to the verb stem. These tenses arᵉ inflected like the I aor. and fut. pass. (79, 8), except that in the 2d person sing. of the imper. the ending -θι remains unchanged: στάλη-θι.

2. Several II aor. have an intransitive meaning.

3. In Attic prose, the following II aorists are almost exclusively used:

γράφω	write,	st. γρᾰφ-	II aor. ἐγράφην,
βλάπτω	damage,	βλᾰβ-	ἐβλάβην,
θάπτω	bury,	τᾰφ-	ἐτάφην,
κόπτω	cut,	κοπ-	ἐκόπην,
σκάπτω	dig,	σκᾰφ-	ἐσκάφην,
ἀλλάττω	change,	ἀλλᾰγ-	ἠλλάγην,
σφάττω	slay,	σφᾰγ-	ἐσφάγην,
σφάλλω	deceive,	σφᾰλ-	ἐσφάλην, pass. & intr.
μαίνομαι	rage,	μᾰν-	ἐμάνην,
φαίνομαι	appear,	φᾰν-	ἐφάνην.

The stem-vowel ε is changed to ᾰ:

τρέπω	turn,	st. τρεπ-	II aor. ἐτράπην, pass. & intr.
στρέφω	twist,	στρεφ-	ἐστράφην, pass. & intr.
τρέφω	nourish,	τρεφ-	ἐτράφην,
δέρω	skin, flay,	δερ-	ἐδάρην,
στέλλω	send,	στελ-	ἐστάλην,
σπείρω	sow,	σπερ-	ἐσπάρην,
δια-φθείρω	spoil,	φθερ-	δι-εφθάρην, pass. & intr.
only συλ-λέγω	collect,	λεγ-	has συν-ελέγην.

Note 1. — To be distinguished:

> ἐφάνην *appeared*, of φαίνομαι *appear*,
> ἐφάνθην *was shown*, of φαίνω *show*.

Note 2. — A II aor. pass. occurs in such verbs only as lack a II aor. act.; the verb τρέπω, however, has all the aorists possible:

> in the act. ἔτρεψα and ἔτραπον *turned*,
> in the mid. ἐτρεψάμην *put to flight*,
>   and ἐτραπόμην *took to flight*,
> in the pass. ἐτρέφθην *was turned*,
>   and ἐτράπην *was turned* and *turned myself*.

III. SECOND PERFECT AND SECOND PLUPERFECT ACTIVE.

88. 1. Formative syllables are **-α** and **-ει**, to be added directly to the reduplicated verb stem.

E.g. γράφω *write*, st. γρᾰφ-,   II pf. γέγρᾰφ-α,
                                   II plupf. ἐ-γεγράφ-ειν.

Such II perfects and II plupf. active (without κ[1]) are found only in mute verbs and in some few liquid verbs.

---

[1] In the present work, only such perfects as end in **-κα** are called I perfects, all others, including aspirated forms, are designated as II perfects.

These tenses are inflected throughout like the I tenses:

pf. ind. γέγραφ-α, -ας, -ε(ν), etc.   plupf. ἐγεγράφ-ειν, -εις, -ει, etc.
subj. γεγράφ-ω, -ῃς, -ῃ, etc.   opt. γεγράφ-οιμι, -οις, -οι, etc.
inf. γεγραφ-έ-ναι.   part. γεγραφ-ώς, -υῖα, -ός,
                                      -ότος, -υίας, -ότος.

2. It may happen that the verb stem remains unchanged in the second perfect (3, a). But more frequently it is changed as follows:

final gutturals and labials are altered to the corresponding rough mutes (3, b.);

short vowels of the stem undergo certain changes (3, c.);

or both aspiration and change of vowel take place (3, d.).

Several II perfects have an intransitive meaning.

3. Of regular verbs the following II pf. are the most common:

a) No change in the verb stem is made in:

κύπτω   stoop,   st. κῡφ-   perf. κέ-κῡφ-α,
γράφω   write,   st. γρᾰφ-   perf. γέ-γρᾰφ-α.

b) The final consonant becomes rough in:

ἄγω   lead,   ἀγ-   ἦχ-α,
τάττω   arrange,   τᾰγ-   τέ-τᾰχ-α,
πράττω do,   πρᾱγ-   πέ-πρᾱχ-α,
κόπτω   cut,   κοπ-   κέ-κοφ-α.

c) In the following the stem vowel is changed (see 11):

a becomes η in: μαίνομα-ι rage,   μᾰν-   μέ-μην-α *am mad*,
                   φαίνομαι appear, φᾰν-   πέ-φην-α *have app.*,
ε becomes ο in: στρέφω   turn,   στρεφ- ἔ-στροφ-α,
                 τρέφω   nourish, τρεφ-   τέ-τροφ-α,
                 ἀπο-κτείνω kill,   κτεν-   ἀπ-έ-κτον-α.

d) both aspiration and ablaut (11, 2) take place in:

πέμπω   send,   πεμπ-   πέ-πομφ-α,
τρέπω   turn,   τρεπ-   τέ-τροφ-α.

Note the difference between (see 87, 3. note 1):

πέφηνα *have appeared*, of φαίνομαι *appear*,
and πέφαγκα *have shown*, of φαίνω   *show*.

5. PECULIARITIES IN THE INFLECTION OF REGULAR VERBS IN -ω.

A. Augment and Reduplication.

89. 1. Six verbs originally beginning with a consonant have not η but ει (from ε-ε) for their augment and reduplication:

F

ἔχω have, ἕλκω pull, draw, ἕπομαι sequor,
ἐάω allow, ἐθίζω accustom, ἐργάζομαι work.
E.g. εἶχον, εἷλκον, εἱπόμην — εἴων, εἴθισα, εἴθικα, etc.

Note. — For the same reason, ὠθέω (originally ϝωθέω) and ὠνέομαι (orig. ϝωνέομαι) take the syllabic augment 111, 3; 112, 18; 209, 7.

2. Both the syllabic and the temporal augment are found in

impf. ἑώρων, aor. ——   perf. ἑώρακα (112, 6), of ὁράω see,
  ἀν-έ-ῳγον,   ἀν-έ-ῳξα,   ἀνέῳχα (88, 3. b), of ἀν-οίγω open,
       (subj. ἀν-οίξω)
pass. ἀν-ε-ῳγόμην,   ἀν-ε-ῴχθην,   ἀν-έ-ῳγμαι.
       (inf. ἀν-οιχθῆναι).

3. Ἔοικα resemble, am (look) like, seem, which is a defective II perfect of εἴκω, has in a similar manner in the plup. ἐῴκειν.

The participle ἐοικώς similar, must not be confounded with εἰκός meet, fitting, right, adv. εἰκότως.

4. The following verbs have εἰ- instead of the reduplication :

δια-λέγομαι speak with, perf.   δι-είλεγ-μαι (aor. δι-ελέχ-θην),
συλ-λέγω   gather,   pf. act. συν-είλοχα, pf. pass. συν-είλεγ-μαι,

similarly the defective II pf. εἴωθα, plup. εἰώθειν am, was wont.

5. There is the so-called Attic reduplication in :

ἀκήκοα and ἠκηκόειν   of ἀκούω hear,
ὀρώρυχα and ὠρωρύγμην of ὀρύττω dig.

In this reduplication, the first two letters of the stem are repeated before the temporal augment.

6. Some verbs that are compounded with prepositions came to be treated like simple verbs and, in consequence, take their augment before the preposition :

ἐν-αντιόομαι withstand, oppose,   impf. ἠναντιούμην,
καθ-έζομαι take a seat,   "   ἐκαθεζόμην,
καθ-ίζω   seat and take a seat,   "   ἐκάθιζον, aor. ἐκάθισα,
καθ-εύδω sleep,   "   ἐκάθευδον.

7. Both the verb and the preposition are augmented in
ἀν-έχομαι bear up against : ἠνειχόμην, ἠνεσχόμην. See 112, 5.

B. Peculiarities in the Formation of Tenses.

FUTURE AND AORIST.

90. 1. Some verbs drop σ in the future act. and mid. and are then treated like contract verbs (the Attic **Future**). Thus βιβάζω *cause to go,* fut. (βιβάσω) : βιβῶ, -ᾷς, etc. ;

καλέω *call, name,* " (καλέσω) : καλῶ, -εῖς, etc. ;

τελέω *finish,* " (τελέσω) : τελῶ, -εῖς, etc.

2. Verbs in -ίζω of more than two syllables regularly take the Attic future, which in the active ends in -ιῶ, 　　　-ιεῖς, etc.,

in the middle 　　　in -ιοῦμαι, -ιῇ (-ιεῖ), etc.

E.g. νομιῶ, -εῖς, νομιοίην, νομιεῖν, νομιῶν, -οῦσα, -οῦν, νομιοῦμαι, -ῇ, νομιοίμην, νομιεῖσθαι, νομιούμενος, 3.

3. The aorist of αἴρω *lift up,* [st. ἀρ- (from ἀερ-)] has ᾱ instead of η : fut. ἀρῶ, -εῖς ; aor. ἦρα (augment!), ἄρω, ἄραιμι, ἆρον, ἆραι, ἄρας, 84.

PURE VERBS.

91. 1. χράομαι *use,* changes ᾰ to η in spite of the ρ (agt. 80):

χρήσομαι, ἐχρησάμην, κέχρημαι.

2. ζάω *live,* and χράομαι *use,* have η wherever ᾱ would result from contraction :

ζῶ, ζῇς, ζῇ, 　　　ζῆτε, 　　　ἔζης, ἔζη, ἐζῆτε, ζῆν,

χρῶμαι, χρῇ, χρῆται, χρῆσθε, ἐχρῆτο, ἐχρῆσθε, χρῆσθαι.

3. **Mono**syllabic stems in -ε contract only to -ει :

πλέω, πλεῖς, πλεῖ, πλέομεν, πλεῖτε, πλέουσιν, πλέῃς, ἔπλεον, ἔπλεις, ἔπλει, ἐπλέομεν, ἐπλεῖτε, πλέοιμι, πλεῖν.

4. The following verbs retain the **short** final vowel of the stem through all the tenses. Moreover, in the perf., plupf. and aor. pass. and in the verb. adj., they insert σ before the endings beginning with -μ, -τ and -θ.

γελάω	laugh pass.	γελάσομαι γελασθήσομαι	ἐγέλᾰσα ἐγελάσθην	γεγέλᾰκα γεγέλασμαι	γελαστός laughable
σπάω	draw	σπάσω σπασθήσομαι	ἔσπᾰσα ἐσπάσθην	ἔσπᾰκα ἔσπασμαι	σπαστός drawn
τελέω	finish	τελῶ, -εῖς τελεσθήσομαι	ἐτέλεσα ἐτελέσθην	τετέλεκα τετέλεσμαι	ἀτέλεστος unfinished
αἰδέομαι D.P.	stand in awe of	αἰδέσομαι	ᾐδέσθην	ᾔδεσμαι	
ἀρκέω	suffice	ἀρκέσω	ἤρκεσα	———	

5. The compounds of αἰνέω, *speak in favorable terms of,* approve, retain the short vowel through all the tenses that are most in use, but have no σ inserted. Thus especially

ἐπ-αινέω   praise,   ἐπ-αινέσομαι, ἐπ-ήνεσα, ἐπ-ήνεκα, ἐπ-ηνέθην,
παρ-αινέω encourage, παρ-αινέσω,   παρ-ήνεσα, παρ-ήνεκα, παρ-ηνέθην.

6. There is a short vowel in some tenses, but without σ, in:

δέω	bind	δήσω	ἔδησα	δέδεκα	δετός
	pass.	δεθήσομαι	ἐδέθην	δέδεμαι	
θύω	sacrifice	θύσω	ἔθῦσα	τέθῠκα	
		τῠθήσομαι	ἐτύθην 21,1	τέθῠμαι	
λύω	loose	λύσω	ἔλῡσα	λέλῠκα	λῠτός
		λῠθήσομαι	ἐλύθην	λέλῠμαι	
δύω trans.	cause to sink	δύσω	ἔδῡσα	——	
		δῠθήσομαι	ἐδῠθην	δέδῠμαι	
δύομαι intr.	sink	δύσομαι	ἔδῡν 102	δέδῡκα	

7. Some verbs have σ after the lengthened vowel or diphthong (either in all, or at least in some forms of the passive):

κελεύω   bid,   κεκέλευσμαι, ἐκελεύσθην,   κελευστός,
κλείω (κλήω) shut,   κέκλειμαι,   ἐκλείσθην,   κλειστός,
χρίω   anoint,   κέχρῑμαι,   ἐχρίσθην,   χρῑστός,
χράομαι   use,   κέχρημαι, mid., ἐχρήσθην, pass., χρηστός.

92. Verbs with several of the above Peculiarities.

They are formed from stems that are not altogether different.

1. ἕλκω	pull, drag	ἑλκ	ἕλξω	εἵλκῠσα	εἵλκῠκα
		ἑλκυ(σ)	ἑλκυσθήσομαι	εἱλκύσθην	εἵλκυσμαι
2. καίω	burn, trans.,	και	καύσω	ἔκαυσα	κέκαυκα
κάω	(often κατα-)	κᾱ	κανθήσομαι	ἐκαύθην	κέκαυμαι
never contracted		καυ			ἄκαυ(σ)τος
3. σῴζω	save	σῳδ	σώσω	ἔσωσα	σέσωκα
mid.	save for my-self	σω	σώσομαι	ἐσωσάμην	
pass.	am saved, save myself		σωθήσομαι	ἐσώθην	σέσωσμαι (σέσω[σ]μαι)
4. βάλλω	throw	βᾰλ	βαλῶ, -εῖς	ἔβαλον	βέβληκα
mid.		βλη	βαλοῦμαι, -ῇ	ἐβαλόμην	βέβλημαι
pass.			βληθήσομαι	ἐβλήθην	
5. καλέω	call, name	κᾰλ	καλῶ, -εῖς	ἐκάλεσα	κέκληκα
mid.		κλη	καλοῦμαι, -ῇ	ἐκαλεσάμην	κέκλημαι
pass.			κληθήσομαι	ἐκλήθην	κέκλημαι my name is

6. κρίνω	judge	κρῖν	κρῐνῶ, -εῖς	ἔκρῑνα	κέκρῐκα
	pass.	κρῐ	κρῐθήσομαι	ἐκρῐθην	κέκρῐμαι
7. τείνω	stretch	τεν	τενῶ, -εῖς	ἔτεινα	τέτᾰκα
	pass.	τᾰ	τᾰθήσομαι	ἐτάθην	τέτᾰμαι

Note. — κλαίω is inflected like καίω, κλίνω like κρίνω: 97, 45. 49.

C. Peculiarities in the Use of the Voices.

TRANSITIVE AND INTRANSITIVE MEANING.

93. Whenever there is a fluctuation between transitive and intransitive meaning in the forms of a verb,

the I. aor. and the I. perf. have the trans. meaning of the act.,
the II. aor. and the II. perf. have the intr. meaning of the mid.-pass. (95, 3.);

whenever only one perfect occurs, it is intransitive. Examples:

φαίνω	show,	fut. φανῶ, -εῖς	aor. ἔφηνα	pf. πέφαγκα
φαίνομαι	appear,	φανοῦμαι, -ῇ	ἐφάνην	πέφηνα
δύω	cause to sink,	δύσω	ἔδῡσα	——
δύομαι	sink, intr.	δύσομαι	ἔδῡν (102)	δέδῡκα
ἐνδύω	put on (another),	ἐνδύσω	ἐνέδυσα	——
ἐνδύομαι	put on (myself),	ἐνδύσομαι	ἐνέδυν	ἐνδέδυκα
καταδύω	cause to sink,	καταδύσω	κατέδυσα	——
καταδύομαι	sink, intr.	καταδύσομαι	κατέδυν	καταδέδυκα
φύω	produce,	φύσω	ἔφυσα	——
φύομαι	am born,	φύσομαι	ἔφυν (102)	πέφῡκα
				am by nature.

Compare ἵστημι 100, 2 and 106, 9–11; 108, 1.

MIDDLE FUTURES IN ACTIVE AND PASSIVE SENSE.

94. 1. Many active verbs have a middle future with **active** meaning:

e.g.   ἀκούω   hear,   ἀκούσομαι,   γελάω   laugh,   γελάσομαι,
       βοάω   shout,   βοήσομαι,   διώκω   pursue,   διώξομαι, etc.

2. Some active verbs employ the middle future in a **passive** sense; thus

ἀξιώσομαι shall be deemed worthy,   βλάψομαι shall be injured,
πολιορκήσομαι shall be blockaded,   ὠφελήσομαι shall be aided, etc.

3. A few verbs employ both the middle and the passive forms in a **passive** sense:

e.g. ἀπο-στερήσομαι and ἀποστερηθήσομαι shall be deprived,
      τιμήσομαι   and τιμηθήσομαι   shall be honored, etc.

DEPONENTS AND MIDDLE–PASSIVES.

95. 1. **Middle deponents** (72, 3 note) have in the p a s s i v e form of the aorist a p a s s i v e meaning, in the perfect both an a c t i v e and a p a s s i v e meaning;

e.g. αἰτιάομαι *accuse :* ᾐτιασάμην *accused,* ᾐτιάθην *was accused,*
ᾐτίαμαι *have and have been accused.*

Thus βιάζομαι *force,*   ἰάομαι *heal,*   μιμέομαι *imitate,*
δέχομαι *receive,*   λογίζομαι *reason,*   χειρόομαι *overpower,*
ἐργάζομαι *work,*   μέμφομαι *blame,*   ἐν-τέλλομαι *enjoin,*
ἀπο-κρίνομαι *reply,*   μετα-πέμπομαι *send for,*   κατα-στρέφομαι *subdue.*

2. **Passive deponents** (72, 3 note) are especially verbs denoting m o t i o n, f e e l i n g or m e n t a l a c t i o n. They have generally a m i d d l e future.

E.g.   ἐναντιόομαι   *oppose,*   ἐναντιώσομαι,   ἠναντιώθην.
ἐράω, ἔραμαι *love,*   ἐρασθήσομαι,   ἠράσθην.
ἥδομαι   *rejoice,*   ἡσθήσομαι,   ἥσθην.
ἡττάομαι   *am defeated,*   ἡττήσομαι,   ἡττήθην.
ἐν-θυμέομαι   *consider,*   ἐν-θυμήσομαι,   ἐν-εθυμήθην.
προ-θυμέομαι *am anxious,*   προ-θυμήσομαι,   προ-εθυμήθην.
δια-νοέομαι *intend,*   δια-νοήσομαι,   δι-ενοήθην.

For passive deponents of irregular verbs, see 111.

3. **Middle-Passives.** — Some (chiefly direct) m i d d l e s (165, 1) have passed from a reflexive into the intransitive and passive meaning, and consequently some of their tenses are p a s s i v e. They are called m i d d l e-p a s s i v e s. *E.g.*

αἰσχύνω *make ashamed,*   m.-p. *am ashamed,*   αἰσχυνοῦμαι, -ῇ   ᾐσχύνθη .
κοιμάω *lay to rest,*   m.-p. *go to sleep,*   κοιμήσομαι   ἐκοιμήθη .
ὀργίζω *make angry,*   m.-p. *grow angry,*   ὀργιοῦμαι, -ῇ   ὠργίσθηι
ὁρμάω *urge on,*   m.-p. *set out,*   ὁρμήσομαι   ὡρμήθην.
πείθω *persuade,*   m.-p. *obey,*   πείσομαι   ἐπείσθην.
πειράω *try* (trans.),   m.-p. *try (my own skill),*   πειράσομαι   ἐπειράθην.
πλανάω *lead astray,*   m.-p. *go astray,*   πλανήσομαι   ἐπλανήθην.
πορεύω *convey,*   m.-p. *march, travel,*   πορεύσομαι   ἐπορεύθην.
φοβέω *scare,*   m.-p. *am scared, fear,*   φοβήσομαι   ἐφοβήθην.
φαίνω *show,*   m.-p. *appear,*   φανοῦμαι, -ῇ ⎫ ἐφάνην.
and φανήσομαι ⎭

THE DUAL IN CONJUGATION.

96. It has but two forms, one for the 2., the other for the 3. person; the 1. person dual is always the same as the 1. person plural.

The endings are

		Act. and Aor. Pass.	Mid. and Pass.
1. in the principal tenses and the subj.:	2. p. -τον	-σθον
	3. p. -τον	-σθον
2. in the historical tenses and optatives,	2. p. -τον	-σθον
or in the augmented forms:	3. p. -την	-σθην
3. in the imperatives	2. p. -τον	-σθον
	3. p. -των	σθων ;

hence:

			Act. and Aor. Pass.	Mid. and Pass.
Active:	pres.	ind.	παιδεύω	παιδεύε-τον	παιδεύε-τον
		impf.	ἐπαίδευον	ἐπαιδεύε-τον	ἐπαιδευέ-την
		subj.	παιδεύω	παιδεύη-τον	παιδεύη-τον
		opt.	παιδεύοιμι	παιδεύοι-τον	παιδευοί-την
		imp.	παίδευε	παιδεύε-τον	παιδευέ-των
	aor.	ind.	ἐπαίδευσα	ἐπαιδεύσα-τον	ἐπαιδευσά-την
		subj.	παιδεύσω	παιδεύση-τον	παιδεύση-τον
		opt.	παιδεύσαιμι	παιδεύσαι-τον	παιδευσαί-την
		imp.	παίδευσον	παιδεύσα-τον	παιδευσά-των
Aor. Pass.		ind.	ἐπαιδεύθην	ἐπαιδεύθη-τον	ἐπαιδευθή-την
		subj.	παιδευθῶ	παιδευθῆ-τον	παιδευθῆ-τον
		opt.	παιδευθείην	παιδευθεῖ-τον	παιδευθεί-την
		imp.	παιδεύθητι	παιδεύθη-τον	παιδευθή-των
Mid. and Pass.	pres.	ind.	παιδεύομαι	παιδεύε-σθον	παιδεύε-σθον
		impf.	ἐπαιδευόμην	ἐπαιδεύε-σθον	ἐπαιδευέ-σθην
		subj.	παιδεύωμαι	παιδεύη-σθον	παιδεύη-σθον
		opt.	παιδευοίμην	παιδεύοι-σθον	παιδευοί-σθην
		imp.	παιδεύου	παιδεύε-σθον	παιδευέ-σθων
	perf.	ind.	πεπαίδευμαι	πεπαίδευ-σθον	πεπαίδευ-σθον
		plupf.	ἐπεπαιδεύμην	ἐπεπαίδευ-σθον	ἐπεπαιδεύ-σθην
		imp.	πεπαίδευσο	πεπαίδευ-σθον	πεπαιδεύ-σθων
Aor. Mid.		ind.	ἐπαιδευσάμην	ἐπαιδεύσα-σθον	ἐπαιδευσά-σθην
		subj.	παιδεύσωμαι	παιδεύση-σθον	παιδεύση-σθον
		opt.	παιδευσαίμην	παιδεύσαι-σθον	παιδευσαί-σθην
		imp.	παίδευσαι	παιδεύσα-σθον	παιδευσά-σθων.

The same holds for the verbs in -μι.

97. TABLE SHOWING THE FORMATION

Present		Verb Stem	Future	Aorist Act.
a. Pure Verbs				
1. παιδεύω	educate	παιδευ-	παιδεύσω	ἐπαίδευσα
2. θηράω	hunt	θηρᾱ-	θηράσω	ἐθήρᾱσα
3. τιμάω	honor	τιμη-	τιμήσω	ἐτίμησα
4. ποιέω	make	ποιη- ⎫ 80.	ποιήσω	ἐποίησα
5. δουλόω	enslave	δουλω- ⎭	δουλώσω	ἐδούλωσα
b. Mute Verbs				
6. γυμνάζω	train	γυμνᾰδ-	γυμνᾰσω	ἐγύμνᾰσα
7. ἁρμόττω	set in order	ἁρμοτ-	ἁρμόσω	ἥρμοσα
8. πείθω	persuade	πειθ-	πείσω	ἔπεισα
9. πείθομαι	obey	πειθ-	πείσομαι	
10. ψεύδω	deceive	ψευδ-	ψεύσω	ἔψευσα
11. ψεύδομαι	lie	ψευδ-	ψεύσομαι	ἐψευσάμην lied
12. σπένδω	pour (a libation)	σπενδ-	σπείσω [13. 82, 1. note;	ἔσπεισα
13. πράττω	do	πρᾱγ-	πράξω	ἔπρᾱξα
14. τάττω	arrange	τᾰγ-	τάξω	ἔτᾰξα
15. ἄρχω	rule, begin	ἀρχ-	ἄρξω	ἦρξα
16. ἄγω	lead	ἀγ-	ἄξω	ἤγαγον 86, 3.
17. πέμπω	send	πεμπ-	πέμψω	ἔπεμψα
18. γράφω	write	γρᾰφ-	γράψω	ἔγραψα
19. κόπτω	cut	κοπ-	κόψω	ἔκοψα
20. βλάπτω	damage	βλᾰβ-	βλάψω	ἔβλαψα
21. θάπτω	bury	τᾰφ-	θάψω 21, 2.	ἔθαψα
22. ῥίπτω	throw	ῥῑπ-	ῥίψω	ἔρρῑψα
23. τρέπω	turn	τρεπ-	τρέψω	ἔτρεψα ⎱ 87, 3. ἔτραπον ⎰ note 2
24. τρέφω	feed	τρεφ-	θρέψω 21, 2.	ἔθρεψα
25. στρέφω	turn, twist	στρεφ-	στρέψω	ἔστρεψα

OF TENSES OF THE REGULAR VERB.

Perfect Active	Perfect Mid. and Pass.	Aorist Passive	Verbal Adjective
πεπαίδευκα	πεπαίδευμαι	ἐπαιδεύθην	παιδευτός, -τέος
τεθήρᾱκα	τεθήρᾱμαι	ἐθηράθην	θηρᾱτός
τετίμηκα	τετίμημαι	ἐτιμήθην	τιμητός
πεποίηκα	πεποίημαι	ἐποιήθην	ποιητός
δεδούλωκα	δεδούλωμαι	ἐδουλώθην	δουλωτός
γεγύμνᾰκα	γεγύμνᾰσμαι	ἐγυμνάσθην	γυμναστός
ἥρμοκα	ἥρμοσμαι	ἡρμόσθην	ἁρμοστός
πέπεικα	πέπεισμαι	ἐπείσθην was persuaded	πειστός
	πέπεισμαι	ἐπείσθην obeyed	πειστέον
ἔψευκα	ἔψευσμαι	ἐψεύσθην was deceived	ψευστός
	ἔψευσμαι	ἐψεύσθην was mistaken	
ἔσπεικα	ἔσπεισμαι	ἐσπείσθην	σπειστέον
πέπρᾱχα 88, 3.	πέπρᾱγμαι	ἐπράχθην	πρᾱκτός
τέτᾰχα	τέτᾰγμαι	ἐτάχθην	τᾰκτός
ἦρχα	ἦργμαι	ἤρχθην	ἀρκτός
ἦχα	ἦγμαι	ἤχθην	ἀκτός
πέπομφα	πέπεμμαι	ἐπέμφθην	πεμπτός
γέγραφα	γέγραμμαι	ἐγράφην 87, 3.	γραπτός
κέκοφα	κέκομμαι	ἐκόπην	κοπτός
βέβλαφα	βέβλαμμαι	ἐβλάβην	βλαπτός
τέταφα	τέθαμμαι	ἐτάφην	ἄ-θαπτος
ἔρρῑφα	ἔρρῑμμαι	ἐρρίφθην	ῥιπτός
τέτροφα	τέτραμμαι 83, 4.	ἐτράπην ἐτρέφθην	τρεπτός
τέτροφα	τέθραμμαι	ἐτράφην	θρεπτός
ἔστροφα	ἔστραμμαι	ἐστράφην	στρεπτός

TABLE SHOWING THE FORMATION OF

Present		Verb Stem	Future	Aorist Act.
c. Liquid Verbs				
26. μιαίνω	*stain*	μιᾰν-	μιᾰνῶ, -εῖς	ἐμίᾱνα
27. καθαίρω	*purify*	καθᾰρ-	καθαρῶ, -εῖς	ἐκάθηρα
28. φαίνω	*show*	φᾰν-	φανῶ, εῖς	ἔφηνα
29. φαίνομαι	*appear*	φᾰν-	φανοῦμαι, -ῇ ⎫ φανήσομαι ⎭	
30. ἀγγέλλω	*announce*	ἀγγελ-	ἀγγελῶ, -εῖς	ἤγγειλα
31. δέρω	*flay, skin*	δερ-	δερῶ, -εῖς	ἔδειρα
32. στέλλω	*send*	στελ-	στελῶ, -εῖς	ἔστειλα
33. σπείρω	*sow*	σπερ-	σπερῶ, -εῖς	ἔσπειρα
34. ἀπο-κτείνω	*kill*	κτεν-	ἀποκτενῶ, -εῖς	ἀπέκτεινα
d. Verbs with certain peculiarities :				
35. νομίζω	*believe*	νομιδ-	νομιῶ, -εῖς	ἐνόμισα
36. σπάω	*draw*	σπα(σ)-	σπᾱσω	ἔσπᾰσα
37. τελέω	*finish*	τελεσ-	τελῶ, -εῖς	ἐτέλεσα
38. δέω	*bind*	δη-, δε-	δήσω	ἔδησα
39. χράομαι	*use*	χρη(σ)-	χρήσομαι	ἐχρησάμην
40. κελεύω	*command*	κελευ(σ)-	κελεύσω	ἐκέλευσα
41. ἀκούω	*hear*	ἀκου(σ)-	ἀκούσομαι	ἤκουσα
42. κλείω	*shut*	κλει(σ)-	κλείσω	ἔκλεισα
43. χρίω	*anoint*	χρῑ(σ)-	χρῑσω	ἔχρῑσα
44. καίω, κάω	*burn*, trans.	καυ(σ)-, κᾱ-	καύσω	ἔκαυσα
45. κλαίω, κλάω	*weep*	κλαυ(σ)-, κλᾱ-	κλαυσομαι	ἔκλαυσα
46. σῴζω	*save*	σῳδ-, σω-	σώσω	ἔσωσα
47. αἴρω	*lift up*	ἀρ-, (ἀερ-)	ἀρῶ, -εῖς	ἦρα (ἆραι)
48. κρίνω	*judge*	κρῐν-, κρῐ-	κρῑνῶ, -εῖς	ἔκρῑνα
49. κλίνω	*lean, incline*	κλῐν-, κλῐ-	κλῐνῶ, -εῖς	ἔκλῑνα
50. τείνω	*stretch*	τεν-, τᾰ-	τενῶ, -εῖς	ἔτεινα
51. βάλλω	*throw*	βαλ-, βλη-	βαλῶ, -εῖς	ἔβαλον
52. καλέω	*call, name*	καλ-ε-, κλη	καλῶ, -εῖς	ἐκάλεσα

TENSES OF THE REGULAR VERB. — *Concluded.*

Perfect Active	Perfect Mid. and Pass.	Aorist Passive	Verbal Adjective
μεμίαγκα	μεμίασμαι	ἐμιάνθην	ἀ-μίαντος
κεκάθαρκα [shown	κεκάθαρμαι	ἐκαθάρθην	καθαρτός
πέφαγκα have	πέφασμαι	ἐφάνθην was shown	ἄ-φαντος
πέφηνα have ap-		ἐφάνην appeared	
[peared			
ἤγγελκα	ἤγγελμαι	ἠγγέλθην	ἀγγελτός
δέδαρκα	δέδαρμαι	ἐδάρην	δαρτός
ἔσταλκα	ἔσταλμαι	ἐστάλην	σταλτέον
ἔσπαρκα	ἔσπαρμαι	ἐσπάρην	σπαρτός
ἀπέκτονα	—	—	—
νενόμικα	νενόμισμαι	ἐνομίσθην	νομιστέος
ἔσπᾰκα	ἔσπασμαι	ἐσπάσθην	σπαστός
τετέλεκα	τετέλεσμαι	ἐτελέσθην	τελεστός
δέδεκα	δέδεμαι	ἐδέθην	δετός
	κέχρημαι	ἐχρήσθην	χρηστός
κεκέλευκα	κεκέλευσμαι	ἐκελεύσθην	κελευστός
ἀκήκοα	ἤκουσμαι	ἠκούσθην	ἀκουστός
κέκλεικα	κέκλειμαι	ἐκλείσθην	κλειστός
κέχρῑκα	κέχρῑμαι	ἐχρίσθην	χριστός
κέκαυκα	κέκαυμαι	ἐκαύθην	ἄ-καυ(σ)τος
κέκλαυκα	κέκλαυμαι	ἐκλαύ(σ)θην	ἄ-κλαυ(σ)τος
σέσωκα	σέσωσμαι	ἐσώθην	ἄ-σωτος
ἦρκα	ἦρμαι	ἤρθην	ἀρτέον
κέκρῐκα	κέκρῐμαι	ἐκρίθην	κρῐτός
κέκλῐκα	κέκλῐμαι	ἐκλίθην	κλῐτός
τέτᾰκα	τέτᾰμαι	ἐτάθην	τᾰτός
βέβληκα	βέβλημαι	ἐβλήθην	βλητός
κέκληκα	κέκλημαι	ἐκλήθην	κλητός

B.　SECOND CONJUGATION:

1.　Verbs in -μι with

98.　THE PARADIGMS

τίθημι *put*,　　　pres. stem τιθη-, τιθε-,　　verb stem θη-, θε-,
ἵημι　*send*,　　　　"　　ἱη-, ἱε-,　　　　"　ἡ-, ἑ-,

1.　PRESENT AND IMPERFECT ACTIVE.

St.	τιθη- and τιθε-	ἱη- and ἱε-	διδω- and διδο-	ἱστη- and ἱστᾰ-
Indicative	τί-θη-μι	ἵ-η-μι	δί-δω-μι	ἵ-στη-μι
	τί-θη-ς	ἵ-η-ς	δί-δω-ς	ἵ-στη-ς
	τί-θη-σι(ν)	ἵ-η-σι(ν)	δί-δω-σι(ν)	ἵ-στη-σι(ν)
	τί-θε-μεν	ἵ-ε-μεν	δί-δο-μεν	ἵ-στᾰ-μεν
	τί-θε-τε	ἵ-ε-τε	δί-δο-τε	ἵ-στᾰ-τε
	τι-θέ-ᾱσι(ν)	ἱ-ᾶσι(ν)	δι-δό-ᾱσι(ν)	ἱ-στᾶ-σι(ν)
Imperfect	ἐ-τί-θη-ν	ἵ-ει-ν (ἵ !)	ἐ-δί-δου-ν	ἵ-στη-ν (ἵ !)
	ἐ-τί-θει-ς	ἵ-ει-ς	ἐ-δί-δου-ς	ἵ-στη-ς
	ἐ-τί-θει	ἵ-ει	ἐ-δί-δου	ἵ-στη
	ἐ-τί-θε-μεν	ἵ-ε-μεν	ἐ-δί-δο-μεν	ἵ-στᾰ-μεν
	ἐ-τί-θε-τε	ἵ-ε-τε	ἐ-δί-δο-τε	ἵ-στᾰ-τε
	ἐ-τί-θε-σαν	ἵ-ε-σαν	ἐ-δί-δο-σαν	ἵ-στᾰ-σαν
Subjunctive	τι-θῶ (τι-θέ-ω)	ἱ-ῶ (ἱ-έ-ω)	δι-δῶ (δι-δό-ω)	ἱ-στῶ (ἱ-στά-ω)
	τι-θῇς	ἱ-ῇς	δι-δῷς	ἱ-στῇς
	τι-θῇ	ἱ-ῇ	δι-δῷ	ἱ-στῇ
	τι-θῶ-μεν	ἱ-ῶ-μεν	δι-δῶ-μεν	ἱ-στῶ-μεν
	τι-θῇ-τε	ἱ-ῇ-τε	δι-δῶ-τε	ἱ-στῆ-τε
	τι-θῶσι(ν)	ἱ-ῶσι(ν)	δι-δῶσι(ν)	ἱ-στῶσι(ν)
Optative	τι-θείη-ν	ἱ-είη-ν	δι-δοίη-ν	ἱ-σταίη-ν
	τι-θείη-ς	ἱ-είη-ς	δι-δοίη-ς	ἱ-σταίη-ς
	τι-θείη	ἱ-είη	δι-δοίη	ἱ-σταίη
	τι-θείημεν, -θεῖμεν	ἱείημεν, -εῖμεν	διδοίημεν, -δοῖμεν	ἱσταίημεν, -σταῖμεν
	τι-θείητε, -θεῖτε	ἱείητε, -εῖτε	διδοίητε, -δοῖτε	ἱσταίητε, -σταῖτε
	τι-θείησαν, -θεῖεν	ἱείησαν, -εῖεν	διδοίησαν, -δοῖεν	ἱσταίησαν, -σταῖεν
Imperative	τί-θει	ἵ-ει	δί-δου	ἵ-στη
	τι-θέ-τω	ἱ-έ-τω	δι-δό-τω	ἱ-στά-τω
	τί-θε-τε	ἵ-ε-τε	δί-δο-τε	ἵ-στᾰ-τε
	τι-θέ-ντων	ἱ-έ-ντων	δι-δό-ντων	ἱ-στά-ντων
Inf.	τι-θέ-ναι	ἱ-έ-ναι	δι-δό-ναι	ἱ-στά-ναι
Partic.	τι-θείς, -θέντος	ἱ-είς, -έντος	δι-δούς, -δόντος	ἱ-στάς, -στάντος
	τι-θεῖσα, -θείσης	ἱ-εῖσα, -είσης	δι-δοῦσα, -δούσης	ἱ-στᾶσα, -στάσης
	τι-θέν, -θέντος	ἱ-έν, -έντος	δι-δόν, -δόντος	ἱ-στάν, -στάντος

Note 1.—Occasional secondary forms are the indic. forms τιθεῖς, τιθεῖ —

VERBS IN -μι.

Reduplication in the Present Stem.

OF THE FOUR VERBS:

δίδωμι *give*,　　　pres. stem διδω-, διδο-,　　　verb st. δω-, δο-,
ἵστημι *place, set*　　　"　　"　　ἱστη-, ἱστᾰ-,　　　"　　"　　στη-, στᾰ-.

2. SECOND AORIST ACTIVE.

St.	θη- and θε-		ἡ- and ἑ-		δω- and δο-		στη- and στᾰ-	
							intransitive middle	
Indicative	—— ἔ-θη-κα		—— ἦ-κα		—— ἔ-δω-κα		ἔ-στη-ν, *stood,*	
	—— ἔ-θη-κα-ς		—— ἦ-κα-ς		—— ἔ-δω-κα-ς		ἔ-στη-ς　[*stepped*	
	—— ἔ-θη-κε(ν)		—— ἦ-κε(ν)		—— ἔ-δω-κε(ν)		ἔ-στη	
	ἔ-θε-μεν		εἷ-μεν		ἔ-δο-μεν		ἔ-στη-μεν	
	ἔ-θε-τε		εἷ-τε		ἔ-δο-τε		ἔ-στη-τε	
	ἔ-θε-σαν		εἷ-σαν		ἔ-δο-σαν		ἔ-στη-σαν	
Subjunctive	θῶ (θέ-ω)		ὦ (ἕ-ω)		δῶ (δό-ω)		στῶ (στά-ω)	
	θῇς		ᾖς		δῷς		στῇς	
	θῇ		ᾖ		δῷ		στῇ	
	θῶ-μεν		ὦ-μεν		δῶ-μεν		στῶ-μεν	
	θῆ-τε		ἦ-τε		δῶ-τε		στῆ-τε	
	θῶσι(ν)		ὦσι(ν)		δῶσι(ν)		στῶσι(ν)	
Optative	θείη-ν		εἴη-ν		δοίη-ν		σταίη-ν	
	θείη-ς		εἴη-ς		δοίη-ς		σταίη-ς	
	θείη		εἴη		δοίη		σταίη	
	θείημεν,	θεῖ-μεν	εἴημεν, εἷ-μεν		δοίημεν,	δοῖ-μεν	σταίημεν,	σταῖ-μεν
	θείητε,	θεῖ-τε	εἴητε, εἷ-τε		δοίητε,	δοῖ-τε	σταίητε,	σταῖ-τε
	θείησαν,	θεῖε-ν	εἴησαν, εἷε-ν		δοίησαν,	δοῖε-ν	σταίησαν,	σταῖε-ν
Imper.	θέ-ς		ἕ-ς		δό-ς		στῆ-θι	
	θέ-τω		ἕ-τω		δό-τω		στή-τω	
	θέ-τε		ἕ-τε		δό-τε		στῆ-τε	
	θέ-ντων		ἕ-ντων		δό-ντων		στά-ντων	
Inf.	θεῖ-ναι		εἷ-ναι		δοῦ-ναι		στῆ-ναι	
Partic.	θείς,	θέντος	εἵς, ἕντος		δούς,	δόντος	στάς,	στάντος
	θεῖσα,	θείσης	εἷσα, εἵσης		δοῦσα,	δούσης	στᾶσα,	στάσης
	θέν,	θέντος	ἕν, ἕντος		δόν,	δόντος	στάν,	στάντος

ἱείς, ἱεῖ—and the plural forms with -κα: ἔθηκαν, ἐδώκαμεν, 99, 3.

SECOND CONJUGATION :

3. PRESENT AND IMPERFECT MIDDLE AND PASSIVE.

Stems:		τι-θε-	ἱ-ε-	δι-δο-	ἱ-στᾰ-
Indicative	S. 1.	τί-θε-μαι	ἵ-ε-μαι	δί-δο-μαι	ἵ-στᾰ-μαι
	2.	τί-θε-σαι	ἵ-ε-σαι	δί-δο-σαι	ἵ-στᾰ-σαι
	3.	τί-θε-ται	ἵ-ε-ται	δί-δο-ται	ἵ-στᾰ-ται
	P. 1.	τι-θέ-μεθα	ἱ-έ-μεθα	δι-δό-μεθα	ἱ-στᾰ́-μεθα
	2.	τί-θε-σθε	ἵ-ε-σθε	δί-δο-σθε	ἵ-στα-σθε
	3.	τί-θε-νται	ἵ-ε-νται	δί-δο-νται	ἵ-στα-νται
Imperfect	S. 1.	ἐ-τι-θέ-μην	ἱ-έ-μην (ἱ!)	ἐ-δι-δό-μην	ἱ-στᾰ́-μην
	2.	ἐ-τί-θε-σο	ἵ-ε-σο	ἐ-δί-δο-σο	ἵ-στᾰ-σο
	3.	ἐ-τί-θε-το	ἵ-ε-το	ἐ-δί-δο-το	ἵ-στᾰ-το
	P. 1.	ἐ-τι-θέ-μεθα	ἱ-έ-μεθα	ἐ-δι-δό-μεθα	ἱ-στᾰ́-μεθα
	2.	ἐ-τί-θε-σθε	ἵ-ε-σθε	ἐ-δί-δο-σθε	ἵ-στα-σθε
	3.	ἐ-τί-θε-ντο	ἵ-ε-ντο	ἐ-δί-δο-ντο	ἵ-στα-ντο
Subjunctive	S. 1.	τι-θῶ-μαι	ἱ-ῶ-μαι	δι-δῶ-μαι	ἱ-στῶ-μαι
	2.	τι-θῇ	ἱ-ῇ	δι-δῷ	ἱ-στῇ
	3.	τι-θῆ-ται	ἱ-ῆ-ται	δι-δῶ-ται	ἱ-στῆ-ται
	P. 1.	τι-θώ-μεθα	ἱ-ώ-μεθα	δι-δώ-μεθα	ἱ-στώ-μεθα
	2.	τι-θῆ-σθε	ἱ-ῆ-σθε	δι-δῶ-σθε	ἱ-στῆ-σθε
	3.	τι-θῶ-νται	ἱ-ῶ-νται	δι-δῶ-νται	ἱ-στῶ-νται
Optative	S. 1.	τι-θεί-μην	ἱ-εί-μην	δι-δοί-μην	ἱ-σταί-μην
	2.	τι-θεῖ-ο	ἱ-εῖ-ο	δι-δοῖ-ο	ἱ-σταῖ-ο
	3.	τι-θεῖ-το	ἱ-εῖ-το	δι-δοῖ-το	ἱ-σταῖ-το
	P. 1.	τι-θεί-μεθα	ἱ-εί μεθα	δι-δοί-μεθα	ἱ-σταί-μεθα
	2.	τι-θεῖ-σθε	ἱ-εῖ-σθε	δι-δοῖ-σθε	ἱ-σταῖ-σθε
	3.	τι-θεῖ-ντο	ἱ-εῖ-ντο	δι-δοῖ-ντο	ἱ-σταῖ-ντο
Imper.	S. 2.	τί-θε-σο	ἵ-ε-σο	δί-δο-σο	ἵ-στᾰ-σο
	3.	τι-θέ-σθω	ἱ-έ-σθω	δι-δό-σθω	ἱ-στά-σθω
	P. 2.	τί-θε-σθε	ἵ-ε-σθε	δί-δο-σθε	ἵ-στα-σθε
	3.	τι-θέ-σθων	ἱ-έ-σθων	δι-δό-σθων	ἱ-στά-σθων
Infinitive		τί-θε-σθαι	ἵ-ε-σθαι	δί-δο-σθαι	ἵ-στα-σθαι
Participle		τι-θέ-μενος, -η, -ον	ἱ-έ-μενος, -η, -ον	δι-δό-μενος, -η, -ον	ἱ-στά-μενος, -η, -ον

Note 2. — σ in -σαι and -σο remains in the present and impf. (except subj. and hence τίθεσαι, ἐτίθεσο, τίθεσο — δίδοσαι, ἐδίδοσο.

Note 3. — Rare collat. forms are optatives with οι: τιθοῖτο, συνθοῖτο, as also subj. and optatives with irregular accentuation: τίθηται, πρόσθηται,

VERBS IN -μι. — *Concluded.*

SECOND AORIST MIDDLE.

Stems:		θε-	ἑ-	δο-	
Indicative	S. 1.	ἐ-θέ-μην	εἵ-μην	ἐ-δό-μην	
	2.	ἔ-θου	εἷ-σο	ἔ-δου	
	3.	ἔ-θε-το	εἷ-το	ἔ-δο-το	
	P. 1.	ἐ-θέ-μεθα	εἵ-μεθα	ἐ-δό-μεθα	
	2.	ἔ-θε-σθε	εἷ-σθε	ἔ-δο-σθε	
	3.	ἔ-θε-ντο	εἷ-ντο	ἔ-δο-ντο	
Subjunctive	S. 1.	θῶ-μαι	ὦ-μαι	δῶ-μαι	
	2.	θῇ	ᾗ	δῷ	
	3.	θῆ-ται	ἧ-ται	δῶ-ται	
	P. 1.	θώ-μεθα	ὥ-μεθα	δώ-μεθα	
	2.	θῆ-σθε	ἧ-σθε	δῶ-σθε	
	3.	θῶ-νται	ὧ-νται	δῶ-νται	
Optative	S. 1.	θεί-μην	εἵ-μην	δοί-μην	
	2.	θεῖ-ο	εἷ-ο	δοῖ-ο	
	3.	θεῖ-το	εἷ-το	δοῖ-το	
	P. 1.	θεί-μεθα	εἵ-μεθα	δοί-μεθα	
	2.	θεῖ-σθε	εἷ-σθε	δοῖ-σθε	
	3.	θεῖ-ντο	εἷ-ντο	δοῖ-ντο	
Imper.	S. 2.	θοῦ	οὗ	δοῦ	
	3.	θέ-σθω	ἔ-σθω	δό-σθω	
	P. 2.	θέ-σθε	ἔ-σθε	δό-σθε	
	3.	θέ-σθων	ἔ-σθων	δό-σθων	
Infinitive		θέ-σθαι	ἔ-σθαι	δό-σθαι	
Participle		θέ-μενος, -η, -ον	ἔ-μενος, -η, -ον	δό-μενος, -η, -ον	

opt.), but d i s a p p e a r s in all forms of the aorist except in the indicative εἷσο.

δίδοσο — but ἔθου, θοῦ — οὗ — ἔδου, δοῦ.

ἐπιθοίμεθα, συνεπιθοῖντο, ἐφιοῖμεν, παριοῖτε, προσιοῖεν, προοῖτο, προοῖντο.

πρόηται, ἐπίθωνται, τίθοιτο, σύνθοιτο, πρόοιντο, ἀφίοιεν (against 99, 4).

REMARKS ON THE PARADIGMS.

99. 1. In the present, imperfect and II aorist, the mood suffixes and personal endings are applied to the stem directly (*i.e.* without thematic vowel).

2. The stem vowel in the sing. of the indic. act. of the three tenses is **long**.

3. The sing. of the aor. ind. act. is always supplied by ἔθηκα, ἦκα, ἔδωκα (for ἔθην, ἦν, ἔδων). The respective plural forms (as ἔθηκαν, ἐδώκαμεν, ἧκαντο) are less frequent; for ἔστην see 102.

4. The **accent** recedes here too (72, 11. 12), in both the simple and the compound verbs, as far back as possible (*recessive accent!*), but never beyond the augment. Subjunctives always accent the contracted syllable, optatives accent the syllable containing the modal suffix.

5. Accents of the aor. imper.: ἄφες, ἀντίθες, ἐπίθες, παράθες, ἀπόδος —
ἀφοῦ, προσθοῦ (or πρόσθου), ὑπόθου.

THE REMAINING TENSES.

100. 1. Their formation is regular, except that in a few forms the stem vowel is short: δέδομαι, ἐδόθην, στἄτός; in others the stem vowel is long (irreg. formation): εἶ-μαι (from ἔ-ε-μαι).

Fut.	Act. Mid.	θή-σω θή-σομαι	ἤ-σω ἤ-σομαι	δώ-σω δώ-σομαι
Perf.	Act. Mid. Pass.	τέ-θη-κα (κεῖμαι)	εἶ-κα εἶ-μαι	δέ-δω-κα δέ-δο-μαι
Aor.	Pass. Fut. Pass.	ἐ-τέ-θην τε-θή-σομαι	εἵ-θην ἐ-θή-σομαι	ἐ-δό-θην δο-θή-σομαι
Verb.	Adject.	θε-τός, -τέος	ἐ-τός, -τέος	δο-τός, -τέος

2. Ἵστημι has, besides the intransitive second aor. ἔστην *placed myself, stepped, stood*, a transitive first aor. ἔστησα *set, placed*. The other tenses are partly transitive, partly intransitive. The following is a synopsis of

The meanings of ἵστημι *make stand, set, place.*

	TRANSITIVE			INTRANSITIVE
	Active: place, set	Middle: place for my own sake	Passive: am placed	place myself, stand
Present Future	ἵστημι στήσω	ἵσταμαι στήσομαι	ἵσταμαι σταθήσομαι	ἵσταμαι place myself, stand στήσομαι shall pl. m., shall stand
Aorist Perfect Pluperfect Fut. Perf.	ἔστησα —— —— ——	ἐστησάμην —— —— ——	ἐστάθην —— —— ——	ἔστην placed myself, stood ἕστηκα have pl. m., stand εἱστήκειν had pl. m., stood ἑστήξω shall have pl. m., shall stand

Note 1.— The intransitive forms supply the respective forms of the passive.

Note 2.— Note that the Engl. " stand, stood " etc. are used in two different senses !

VERBS INFLECTED LIKE ἵστημι.

101. The following six verbs (the last three of which are deponents without reduplication in the present stem) inflect their presents and imperfects like ἵστημι.

Present	Stem	Future	Aorist	Perfect	Remarks
1. ὀνίνημι profit, help	ὀνη ὀνᾰ	ὀνήσω ὀνήσομαι	ὤνησα ὠνήθην	—— ——	Impf. ὠφέλουν.
2. πίμπλημι fill	πλη πλᾰ	πλήσω πλησθήσομαι	ἔπλησα ἐπλήσθην	πέπληκα πέπλησμαι	πλήθω : am full.
3. πίμπρημι burn, set on fire	πρη πρᾰ	πρήσω πρησθήσομαι	ἔπρησα ἐπρήσθην	πέπρηκα πέπρησμαι	πρήθω : burn, am on fire.
4. ἄγαμαι wonder at, admire	ἀγᾰ(σ)	ἀγάσομαι	ἠγάσθην	—— ἀγαστός	
5. δύναμαι am able, can	δυνη δυνᾰ	δυνήσομαι	ἐδυνήθην ἐδυνάσθην	δεδύνημαι	
6. ἐπίσταμαι know, understand	ἐπιστη ἐπιστᾰ	ἐπιστήσομαι	ἠπιστήθην	——	

Note 1.—The aorist ἐπριάμην bought is inflected like the imperfect and present of the above deponents; inf. πρίασθαι (present: ὠνοῦμαι 112, 18).

Note 2. — Unlike ἵστημι, these deponents (also ἐπριάμην) have the recessive accent in the subjunctive and optative; hence

> subj. δύνωμαι, ἐπίστωμαι, πρίωμαι,
> opt. δύναιο, ἐπίσταιτο, πρίαισθε, ἄγαιντο.

102. PRIMITIVE or ROOT–AORISTS (ἔστην and others).

1. Ἔστην and the aorists of some other verbs in -ω are formed directly from the verb stem (the root). They all have

a long vowel in the ind., imper. (except 3. p. pl.) and inf.,
a short vowel before vowels and before -ντ.

2. The following verbs are the most important:

a) Stems with final A-sound (ā, η : ă).

1. ἀπο-διδράσκω *run away*	δρᾱ,	δρᾰ	ἀπ-έδρᾱν	110, 9.
2. βαίνω *go, step, walk*	βη,	βᾰ	ἔβην	
3. φθάνω *am beforehand*	φθη,	φθα	ἔφθην	109, 2.

b) Stems with final E-sound (η : ε).

4. ῥέω *flow, run*	ῥυη,	ῥυε	ἐρρύην

c) Stems with final O-sound (ω : ο).

5. γιγνώσκω *know*	γνω,	γνο	ἔγνων	110, 11.
6. ἁλίσκομαι *am taken*	ἁλω,	ἁλο	ἑάλων	110, 4.
7. (βιόω)ζάω *live*	βιω,	βιο	ἐβίων	112, 13.

d) Stems with final Y-sound (ῡ : ῠ).

8. δύομαι *sink*, intr.	δῡ,	δῠ	ἔδῡν	Act. 91, 6; 93.
9. φύομαι *am born*	φῡ,	φῠ	ἔφῡν	Act. φύω, *bring forth*, 93.

3. **Paradigm.**

Stems	στη-, στᾰ-	ῥυη-, ῥυε-	γνω-, γνο-	δῡ-, δῠ-
Indicative	ἔ-στη-ν *stood*,	ἐρ-ρύη-ν	ἔ-γνω-ν	ἔ-δῡ-ν
	ἔ-στη-ς [100, 2	ἐρ-ρύη-ς	ἔ-γνω-ς	ἔ-δυ-ς
	ἔ-στη	ἐρ-ρύη	ἔ-γνω	ἔ-δυ
	ἔ-στη-μεν	ἐρ-ρύη-μεν	ἔ-γνω-μεν	ἔ-δυ-μεν
	ἔ-στη-τε	ἐρ-ρύη-τε	ἔ-γνω-τε	ἔ-δυ-τε
	ἔ-στη-σαν	ἐρ-ρύη-σαν	ἔ-γνω-σαν	ἔ-δυ-σαν
Subjunctive	στῶ (from στά-ω)	ῥυῶ	γνῶ	δύω
	στῇς	ῥυῇς	γνῷς	δύῃς
	στῇ	ῥυῇ	γνῷ	δύῃ
	στῶ-μεν	ῥυῶμεν	γνῶμεν	δύωμεν
	etc. see p. 77	etc. like θῶμεν, p. 77	etc. like δῶμεν, p. 77	etc.

Paradigm. — Concluded.

Stems	στη-, στᾰ-	ῥυη-, ῥυε-	γνω-, γνο-	δῡ-, δῠ-
Optative	σταίη-ν σταίη-ς σταίη σταῖ-μεν [1] etc. see p. 77	ῥυείη-ν ῥυείη-ς ῥυείη ῥυεῖ-μεν [2] etc. like θεῖμεν, p. 77	γνοίη-ν γνοίη-ς γνοίη γνοῖ-μεν [3] etc. like δοῖμεν, p. 77	
Imperative	στῆ-θι στή-τω στῆ-τε στά-ντων		γνῶ-θι γνώ-τω γνῶ-τε γνό-ντων	δῦ-θι δύ-τω δῦ-τε δύ-ντων
Inf.	στῆ-ναι	ῥυῆ-ναι	γνῶ-ναι	δῦ-ναι
Partic.	στάς,　στάντος στᾶσα, στάσης στάν,　στάντος	ῥυείς,　-έντος ῥυεῖσα, -είσης ῥυέν,　-έντος	γνούς,　γνόντος γνοῦσα, γνούσης γνόν,　γνόντος	δύς,　δύντος δῦσα, δύσης δύν,　δύντος

[1] or σταίη-μεν etc.　　　[2] or ῥυείη-μεν etc.　　　[3] or γνοίη-μεν etc.

4. There is a middle future and a I perfect to all these aorists;

e.g.　a) βήσομαι,　　ἔβην,　　βέβηκα　　have gone,
　　　b) ῥυήσεται,　ἐρρύη,　ἐρρύηκε(ν)　has flowed,
　　　c) γνώσομαι,　ἔγνων,　ἔγνωκα　　have known,
　　　d) φύσομαι,　　ἔφῦν,　　πέφυκα　　am by nature.

MIXED PERFECTS (WITH AND WITHOUT -κα).

103. 1. Besides ἕστηκα *stand*, there are forms without a -κα, directly derived from the reduplicated verb stem ἑ-στᾰ; thus especially

perf. ind. ἕστᾰ-μεν, ἕστᾰ-τε, ἑστᾶσι(ν);　　plupf. ἕστᾰ-σαν.
　　inf. ἑστᾰ-ναι;　　part. ἑστώς,　　ἑστῶσα,　　ἑστώς,
　　　　　　　　　　　　　ἑστῶτος,　ἑστώσης,　ἑστῶτος.

2. Likewise τέθνηκα *am dead* (pres. 110, 7):
perf. ind. τέθνᾰ-μεν, τέθνᾰ-τε, τεθνᾶσι(ν);　　plupf. ἐτέθνᾰ-σαν.
　　inf. τεθνᾰ-ναι;　　part. τεθνεώς,　τεθνεῶσα, τεθνεός,
　　　　　　　　　　　　　　τεθνεῶτος, τεθνεώσης, τεθνεῶτος.

3. Moreover, δέδοικα *fear* (stem δει-, δῐ-, aor. ἔδεισα):
perf. ind. δέδῐα, -ας, -ε(ν), δέδῐ-μεν, δέδι-τε, δεδί-ᾱσι(ν).
　　plupf. ἐδέδι-σαν;　inf. δεδιέναι;　part. δεδι-ώς, -υῖα, -ός,
　　　　　　　　　　　　　　　　　　　　　　-ότος, -υίας.

4. Finally, a defective perfect with present meaning:

οἶδα *know, novi*

(= *have seen*, of εἰδ-, ἰδ- (ϝιδ-), *vid-eo ;* aor. εἶδον *saw*, 112, 6).

Pres. and aor. are supplied by γιγνώσκω (110, 11) *nosco.*

PERFECT (PRESENT)	PLUPERFECT (IMPERFECT)	MOODS, INFIN., PARTIC.
οἶδ-α *know, novi* οἶσθα οἶδ-ε(ν) ἴσ-μεν ἴσ-τε ἴσᾱσι(ν)	ᾔδ-η (-ειν) *knew,* ᾔδ-ησθα (-εις) *noveram* ᾔδ-ει ᾔδ-ε-μεν ᾔδ-ε-τε ᾔδ-ε-σαν	Subj. εἰδῶ, -ῇς Opt. εἰδείην Imp. ἴσ-θι, ἴστω etc. Inf. εἰδ-έ-ναι Part. εἰδ-ώς, -υῖα. -ός, -ότος, -υίας

Future εἴ-σομαι *shall know* (*novero*) and *shall know* (*learn, cognoscam*).

2. VERBS IN -μι OF A DIFFERENT FORMATION.

104. 1. φημί *say, affirm*, st. φη-, φᾰ-, Lat. *fā-ri,*

collateral form φάσκω.

PRESENT IND.	IMPERFECT	SUBJUNCTIVE	OPTATIVE	IMPERATIVE
φη-μί φής (φῄς) φη-σί(ν) φᾰ-μέν φᾰ-τέ φᾱσί(ν)	ἔ-φη-ν ἔ-φη-σθα ἔ-φη ἔ-φᾰ-μεν ἔ-φᾰ-τε ἔ-φᾰ-σαν	φῶ φῇ-ς φῇ φῶ-μεν φῆ-τε φῶσι(ν)	φαίη-ν φαίη-ς φαίη φαῖ-μεν φαῖ-τε φαῖε-ν	 φᾰ-θι φᾰ-τω φά-τε φά-ντων

Infin. φᾰ-ναι	Fut. φή-σω
Partic. (φάς) or φάσκων	Aor. ἔ-φη-σα

Note 1.— The whole of the pres. ind. except φής is enclitic. 9, 1.

Note 2.— φάναι and the impf. ἔφην have also the force of aorists.

Note 3.— φημί means a) *say, declare :* fut. ἐρῶ, λέξω, aor. εἶπον, ἔφην.

           b) *say yes, assent :* fut. φήσω, aor. ἔφησα.

οὔ φημι = *nego, say no, refuse, deny.*

2. **εἶμι** *shall go*, st. εἰ-, ἰ-, Latin *ī-re*, *ĭ-ter*.

PRESENT IND.	IMPERFECT	SUBJUNCTIVE	OPTATIVE	IMPERATIVE
εἶ-μι *shall go*	ἦ-α *went*	ἴ-ω *(that) I may go*	ἴ-οι-μι	
εἶ	ἤ-εις	ἴ-η-ς	ἴ-οι-ς	ἴ-θι
εἶ-σι(ν)	ἤ-ει	ἴ-ῃ	ἴ-οι	ἴ-τω
ἴ-μεν	ἦ-μεν	ἴ-ω-μεν	ἴ-οι-μεν	
ἴ-τε	ἦ-τε	ἴ-η-τε	ἴ-οι-τε	ἴ-τε
ἴ-ᾱσι(ν)	ἦ-σαν	ἴ-ωσι(ν)	ἴ-οιε-ν	ἰ-ό-ντων

Infin. ἰ-έναι	Part. ἰ-ών, ἰ-οῦσα, ἰ-όν G. ἰ-όντος, ἰ-ούσης	Verb. Adj. ἰ-τέον

Note 1.—The pres. ind. has always a future meaning; the opt., inf. and part. have sometimes future, sometimes present force.

Note 2.—Note the accent in compounds:

e.g. ἄπειμι, ἄπιμεν, ἄπιθι,
but ἀπῇα, ἀπῇμεν, ἀπῇσαν (99, 4).

3. **εἰμί** *am*, st. ἐσ-, Lat. *es-se*.

PRES. IND.	IMPERFECT	SUBJUNCTIVE	OPTATIVE	IMPERATIVE
εἰμί	ἦν (ἦ)	ὦ (from ἐσ-ω)	εἴη-ν (from ἐσ-ιη-ν)	
εἶ	ἦσθα	ᾖ-ς	εἴη-ς	ἴσ-θι
ἐσ-τί(ν)	ἦν	ᾖ	εἴη	ἔσ-τω
ἐσ-μέν	ἦμεν	ὦ-μεν	εἴη-μεν εἶ-μεν	
ἐσ-τέ	ἦτε (ἦσ-τε)	ἦ-τε	εἴη-τε	ἔσ-τε
εἰσί(ν)	ἦσαν	ὦσι(ν)	εἴη-σαν εἶε-ν	ἔσ-των

Infin. εἶναι (from ἐσ-ναι) Part. ὤν, οὖσα, ὄν, G. ὄντος, οὔσης.	Future ἔσομαι, ἔσῃ (ἔσει), 3. p. sing. ἔσ-ται, otherwise regular.

Note 1.—The whole present ind. (except εἶ) is enclitic when it is merely the copula, but orthotoned when it means: *to exist, to be* (in a certain state or condition).

Note 2.—In this latter case, the 3. p. sing. is: ἔστιν, as also in the meaning: *it is possible* (= ἔξεστι(ν)) and after ὡς, οὐκ, εἰ, καί, as well as after τοῦτ' and ἀλλ': ὡς ἔστιν, τοῦτ' ἔστιν, ἀλλ' ἔστιν.

Note 3.—Accentuation of the compounds:

e.g. ἄπειμι, ἄπει,　ἄπεστιν, ἄπισθι,
but ἀπῶ,　ἀπεῖμεν, ἀπῆμεν, ἀπέσται.

4. **χρή** *it is necessary, one must (ought).*

From a combination of the noun χρή (sc. ἐστίν *opus est*) and certain forms of εἰμί the following forms result :

impf. χρῆν and ἐχρῆν ;   subj. χρῇ ;   opt. χρείη ;
inf. χρῆναι :   part. τὸ χρεών (indecl.).

5. **κάθημαι** *am seated*, st. ἡσ-, καθη(σ)- ; and
6. **κεῖμαι** *lie, iaceo*, st. κει- are thus inflected :

PRESENT	IMPERFECT	IMPERATIVE	PRESENT	IMPERFECT	IMPERATIVE
κάθη-μαι	ἐ-καθή-μην		κεῖ-μαι	ἐ-κεί-μην	
κάθη-σαι	ἐ-κάθη-σο	κάθη-σο	κεῖ-σαι	ἔ-κει-σο	κεῖ-σο
κάθη-ται	ἐ-κάθη-το	καθή-σθω	κεῖ-ται	ἔ-κει-το	κεί-σθω
etc.	etc.	etc.	etc.	etc.	etc.

Inf. καθῆ-σθαι	Inf. κεῖ-σθαι
Part. καθή-μενος	Part. κεί-μενος
Fut. καθεδοῦμαι, -ῇ (112, 14).	Fut. κείσομαι, -σῃ, -σεται etc.

Note 1.—The simple ἧμαι, ἧσαι, ἧσται is poetic. Like the future, the subj. and opt. are supplied by καθέζομαι (112, 14).

Note 2.—Both the simple κεῖσθαι and its compounds serve as perf. pass. of τίθημι (100, 1) ;

e.g. ὑποτίθημι *lay under*,   — ὑπόκειται *it underlies* ;
νόμους τιθέασιν οἱ ἄρχοντες,   — οἱ νόμοι κεῖνται,
θέσθαι τὰ ὅπλα ἐκέλευσεν,   — τὰ ὅπλα ἔκειτο.

Note 3.— A list of forms of like or similar sound
of ἵημι, ἵστημι, οἶδα, εἶμι, εἰμί, κάθημαι.

παρέν, παρῆν, πάρες, πάρει 2, παρῇ, παρῇ 3, παρίῃ, παριῇ 2, παρείη 2, ἀφείη, ἀπείη, παρήει.

παρείς, παρεῖεν 2, πάρεισιν 2, παρεῖσιν, ἀφεῖσιν, ἄπεισιν 2, παριᾶσιν, παρίασιν, παρίωσιν, παριοῦσιν, παροῦσιν.

ἴθι, ἴσθι 2, ἴτε 2, ἴστε 2, ἔτε, παρῆτε 3, παρῇτε, παρεῖτε 2, παρεῖται, παρεῖτο 3, παρείητε 2, ἧτε, ἧτε, ἧτε 2, ἧστε, ἧσθε 3, ἔσθε, εἶσθε 5.

ἐστέ, ἔστε, ἔστη, ἴστη 2, ἔσται, ἔσεσθαι, εἴσεσθε 2, εἴσεσθαι, εἴσεσθαι, εἰσέσθαι, εἰσεῖσθε 5, εἰσεῖσθαι, καθέσθαι, καθεῖσθαι, καθῆσθαι, ἧσεσθαι.

ἵστασαν, ἔστασαν, ἱστᾶσαν, ἑστῶσαν, παρίεσαν, παρεῖσαν 2, ᾖσαν, ἧσαν, καθῆσον, κάθησο, κάθεσθε, κάθησθε, καθῆσθε, καθεῖσθε 5.

Which of these forms may belong to other verbs than the above-named, and to what verbs?

3. VERBS IN -νῡμι (-ννῡμι).

105. 1. They are inflected like the verbs in -μι in the present and imperfect of the active, middle and passive;

the subj. and optative always, other forms sometimes, follow the -ω
inflection ;

e.g. δεικνύει = δείκνῦσιν, ἐδείκνυε = ἐδείκνῦ etc.

2. The υ of the syllable -νῦ is lo n g in the sing. of the pres.
and impf. ind., as well as in the 2. p. sing. imper. active ; elsewhere
it is short.

3. Paradigm : δείκ-νῦμι *show*.

Verb stem δεικ-, present stem δεικ-νῦ-.

			ACTIVE	MIDDLE AND PASSIVE
Present Indic.	S.	1.	δείκ-νῦ-μι	δείκ-νῦ-μαι
		2.	δείκ-νῦ-ς	δείκ-νῦ-σαι
		3.	δείκ-νῦ-σι(ν)	δείκ-νῦ-ται
	P.	1.	δείκ-νῠ-μεν	δεικ-νῠ-μεθα
		2.	δείκ-νῠ-τε	δείκ-νῠ-σθε
		3.	δεικ-νῠ-ᾱσι(ν)	δείκ-νυ-νται
Imperfect	S.	1.	ἐ-δείκ-νῦ-ν	ἐ-δεικ-νῠ-μην
		2.	ἐ-δείκ-νῦ-ς	ἐ-δείκ-νῠ-σο
		3.	ἐ-δείκ-νῡ	ἐ-δείκ-νῠ-το
	P.	1.	ἐ-δείκ-νῠ-μεν	ἐ-δεικ-νῠ-μεθα
		2.	ἐ-δείκ-νῠ-τε	ἐ-δείκ-νῠ-σθε
		3.	ἐ-δείκ-νῠ-σαν	ἐ-δείκ-νῠ-ντο
Subjunctive	S.	1.	δεικ-νῠ-ω	δεικ-νῠ-ωμαι
		2.	δεικ-νῠ-ης	δεικ-νῠ-η
			etc.	etc.
Optative	S.	1.	δεικ-νῠ-οι-μι	δεικ-νῠ-οί-μην
		2.	δεικ-νῠ-οι-ς	δεικ-νῠ-οι-ο
			etc.	etc.
Imperative	S.	2.	δείκ-νῡ	δείκ-νῠ-σο
		3.	δεικ-νῠ-τω	δεικ-νῠ-σθω
	P.	2.	δείκ-νῠ-τε	δείκ-νυ-σθε
		3.	δεικ-νῠ-ντων	δεικ-νῠ-σθων
Infinitive			δεικ-νῠ-ναι	δείκ-νῠ-σθαι
Participle			δεικ-νῠς, -νῦσα, -νύν	δεικ-νῠ-μενος, -μένη,
			gen. -νύντος, -νύσης	-μενον
Future		Act. δείξω,	Mid. δείξομαι,	Pass. δειχθήσομαι,
Aorist		" ἔ-δειξα,	" ἐδειξάμην,	" ἐδείχθην,
Perfect		" δέ-δειχ-α,	δέ-δειγ-μαι.	

106. THE REMAINING VERBS IN -νῦμι.

a) Stems with final A-sound.

Present	Stem	Future	Aorist	Perfect
1. κεράννῡμι mix (with: τινί)	κερᾰ(ς) κρᾱ	κερῶ, -ᾷς κρᾱθήσομαι	ἐκέρᾰσα ἐκρᾱθην	—— κέκρᾱμαι
2. κρεμάννῡμι hang, tr., suspend	κρεμᾰ(σ)	κρεμῶ, -ᾷς κρεμασθήσομαι	ἐκρέμᾰσα ἐκρεμάσθην	—— [itr. κρέμαμαι hang,
3. πετάννῡμι spread out, expand	πετᾰ(σ) πτα	πετῶ, -ᾷς πετασθήσομαι	ἐπέτᾰσα ἐπετάσθην	πέπτᾰμαι
4. σκεδάννῡμι scatter, disperse	σκεδᾰ(σ)	σκεδῶ, -ᾷς σκεδασθήσομαι	ἐσκεδᾰσα ἐσκεδάσθην	—— ἐσκέδασμαι

b) Stems with final O-sound.

5. ῥώννῡμι strengthen	ῥω(σ)	ῥώσω ῥωσθήσομαι	ἔρρωσα ἐρρώσθην	—— ἔρρωμαι
6. στρώννῡμι spread out	στρω	στρώσω στρωθήσομαι	ἔστρωσα ἐστρώθην	—— ἔστρωμαι

c) Stems ending in -γ.

7. ζεύγνῡμι yoke, join together	ζευγ	ζεύξω ζευχθήσομαι	ἔζευξα ἐζεύχθην	—— ἔζευγμαι
8. μείγνῡμι mix (with: τινί)	μειγ	μείξω μειχθήσομαι	ἔμειξα ἐμείχθην	—— μέμειγμαι
9. πήγνῡμι fasten πήγνῡμαι am fastened	πηγ πᾰγ	πήξω πᾰγήσομαι	ἔπηξα ἐπάγην	πέπηγα am fixed
10. ῥήγνῡμι break, tr. ῥήγνῡμαι burst, itr.	ῥηγ ῥᾰγ	ῥήξω ῥᾰγήσομαι	ἔρρηξα ἐρρᾰγην	ἔρρωγα

d) Stems ending in a liquid.

11. ἀπ-όλλῡμι perdo, destroy, lose ἀπ-όλλῡμαι pereo, perish	ὀλ-ε	ἀπολῶ, -εῖς ἀπολοῦμαι, -ῇ	ἀπώλεσα ἀπωλόμην	ἀπολωλεκα ἀπωλωλέκειν ἀπόλωλα ἀπωλώλειν
12. ὄμνῡμι swear	ὀμ-ο	ὀμοῦμαι, -ῇ	ὤμοσα	ὀμώμοκα ὠμωμόκειν

C. IRREGULAR CONJUGATION.

Introductory Note.

107. Some of the irregular verbs have their presents enlarged or strengthened in a manner different from that described in 77, others form their tenses from several, mostly quite different, stems.

Hence we obtain five other classes of verbs, 108–112.

Fourth Class (Lengthening of Vowel in Present).

108. The verbs have in the present a lengthened vowel. In the II aorist, however, they take, as a rule, the corresponding short or weak vowel. In some of them there is a change of quality (ablaut) in the II perfect.

A similar change from strong to weak vowel (11), and the ablaut is sometimes met with in word formation :

E.g.   φεύγω *flee,*   II aor. ἔφῠγον,   ἡ φυγή, ὁ φυγάς.
    λείπω *leave,*   II perf. λέλοιπα,   λοιπός.

Note. — Here belong four verbs in -έω :

   πλέω *sail*   (fut. πλεύ-σομαι),   χέω *pour* (τὸ χεῦ-μα *gush*),
   πνέω *breathe* (τὸ πνεῦ-μα *breath*),   ῥέω *flow* (τὸ ῥεῦ-μα *stream*).

Πλεύω became first πλέϝω, then πλέω; for the forms of ῥέω, see 102, 4. b.

Present	Stem	Future	Aorist	Perfect
1. τήκω *melt,* tr.	τηκ	τήξω	ἔτηξα	———
τήκομαι *melt,* itr.	τᾰκ	τᾰκήσομαι	ἐτάκην	τέτηκα
2. πλήττω *strike*	πληγ	πλήξω	ἔπληξα	———
(112, 15) pass.		πληγήσομαι	ἐπλήγην	πέπληγμαι
ἐκ-πλήττω	πληγ	ἐκ-πλήξω	ἐξ-έπληξα	———
frighten				
ἐκ-πλήττομαι am	πλᾰγ	ἐκ-πλᾰγήσομαι	ἐξ-επλᾰγην	ἐκ-πέπληγμαι
frightened, fear				am panic-stricken
3. τρίβω *rub*	τρῑβ	τρίψω	ἔτρῐψα	τέτρῐφα
pass.	τρῐβ	τριβήσομαι	ἐτρίβην	τέτριμμαι
4. λείπω *leave*	λειπ	λείψω	ἔλῐπον	λέλοιπα
pass.	λῐπ	λειφθήσομαι	ἐλείφθην	λέλειμμαι
5. πείθω *persuade*	πειθ	regular, see 97, 8. 9.,		πέποιθα *trust,*
	πῐθ	πιστός, πίστις [except :		*rely*
6. φεύγω *flee*	φευγ	φεύξομαι	ἔφυγον	πέφευγα
	φῠγ			

Present	Stem	Future	Aorist	Perfect
7. πλέω sail	πλευ	πλεύσομαι	ἔπλευσα	πέπλευκα
8. πνέω breathe, blow	πνευ	πνεύσομαι	ἔπνευσα	πέπνευκα
9. χέω pour	χεν	χέω	ἔχεα	κέχῠκα
pass.	χῠ̆	χῠθήσομαι	ἐχῠθην	κέχῠμαι

Fifth or Nasal Class.

109. The present is lengthened by a **nasal.**

a) Present in -νω.

1. τῐνω pay, suffer τῐνομαι punish	τῐ τει	τείσω τείσομαι	ἔτεισα ἐτεισάμην	τέτεικα τέτεισμαι
2. φθᾰνω am before-hand (with τινὰ ποιῶν τι), antici-pate	φθᾰ φθη	φθήσομαι	ἔφθην and ἔφθᾰσα	—— ἔφθᾰκα
3. κάμνω am weary. become tired (πο-ρευόμενος of march-ing)	κᾰμ κμη	καμοῦμαι, -ῇ	ἔκαμον	κέκμηκα
4. τέμνω cut	τεμ τμη	τεμῶ, -εῖς τμηθήσομαι	ἔτεμον ἐτμήθην	τέτμηκα τέτμημαι
5. ἐλαύνω drive, set in motion; intr. march, ride etc.	ἐλαυ ἐλᾰ	ἐλῶ, -ᾷς ἐλαθήσομαι	ἤλᾰσα ἠλᾰθην	ἐλήλᾰκα ἐλήλᾰμαι

b) Present in -νέο-μαι.

6. ἱκ-νέο-μαι come to, usu. ἀφ- arrive at	ἱκ	ἀφίξομαι	ἀφῑκόμην	ἀφῑγμαι

c) Present in -άνω.

7. αἰσθάνομαι per-ceive, hear (τινός and τὶ), observe	αἰσθ-η	αἰσθήσομαι	ἠσθόμην (αἰσθέσθαι)	ᾔσθημαι (ᾐσθῆσθαι)
8. ἁμαρτάνω sin (τὶ); miss (τινός)	ἁμαρτ-η	ἁμαρτήσομαι ἁμαρτηθήσεται	ἥμαρτον ἡμαρτήθην	ἡμάρτηκα ἡμάρτημαι
9. αὐξάνω, αὔξω in-crease, tr.	αὐξ-η	αὐξήσω αὐξήσομαι	ηὔξησα ηὐξήθην	ηὔξηκα ηὔξημαι

d) Present in -άνω with a nasal in the stem syllable.

PRESENT	STEM	FUTURE	AORIST	PERFECT
10. λαγχάνω obtain (by lot, something	λἄχ, λήχ τινός)	λήξομαι	ἔλᾰχον	εἴληχα
11. λαμβάνω take, receive, get, obtain	λᾰβ ληβ	λήψομαι ληφθήσομαι	ἔλᾰβον ἐλήφθην	εἴληφα εἴλημμαι
12. λανθάνω escape the notice (of τινά), am hidden from ἐπιλανθάνομαι forget (something	λᾰθ ληθ τινός)	λήσω ἐπιλήσομαι	ἔλᾰθον ἐπελᾰθόμην	λέληθα ἐπιλέλησμαι
13. μανθάνω learn	μᾰθ-η	μαθήσομαι	ἔμᾰθον	μεμάθηκα
14. πυνθάνομαι inquire, learn, hear (τινός τι)	πῠθ πευθ	πεύσομαι	ἐπυθόμην	πέπυσμαι
15. τυγχάνω hit (something τινός), obtain (something from τινός τινος)	τῠχ-η τευχ	τεύξομαι	ἔτῠχον	τετύχηκα

Sixth Class : Inchoative Verbs.

110. The present is enlarged by -σκο, -σκε (-ισκο, -ισκε).

a) Without Reduplication in the Present.

1. γηράσκω grow old	γηρᾱ	γηράσομαι	ἐγήρᾱσα	γεγήρᾱκα
2. ἡβάσκω, ἡβάω grow to, am at man's estate	ἡβα ἡβη	ἡβήσω	ἤβησα came to man's estate, reached manhood	ἤβηκα have been young!
3. ἀρέσκω please	ἀρε	ἀρέσω	ἤρεσα	————
4. ἀλίσκομαι am taken	ἀλ-ω	ἀλώσομαι	ἑάλων ἥλων	ἑάλωκα ἥλωκα
5. ἀνᾱλίσκω, ἀνᾱλόω spend, use up	ἀν-ᾱλ-ω	ἀνᾱλώσω ἀνᾱλωθήσομαι	ἀνήλωσα ἀνηλώθην	ἀνήλωκα ἀνήλωμαι
6. εὑρίσκω find	εὑρ-η εὑρ-ε	εὑρήσω εὑρεθήσομαι	ηὗρον ηὑρέθην	ηὕρηκα ηὕρημαι

Present	Stem	Future	Aorist	Perfect
7. ἀπο-θνήσκω *die off*	θάν θνη	ἀπο-θανοῦμαι, [-ῇ]	ἀπ-έθανον fut. pf.	τέθνηκα *am dead* τεθνήξω *shall be dead*
8. διδάσκω *teach* pass. Mid. *take lessons, have myself taught*	διδᾰχ	διδάξω διδαχθήσομαι διδάξομαι	ἐδίδαξα ἐδιδάχθην ἐδιδαξάμην	δεδίδᾰχα δεδίδαγμαι διδακτός

b) With Reduplication in the Present.

9. ἀπο-διδράσκω *run away*	δρᾱ	ἀπο-δράσομαι	ἀπ-έδρᾱν	ἀπο-δέδρᾱκα
10. μιμνήσκω *remind* (usu. ἀνα-, ὑπο-) (τινά τι *one of*) μιμνήσκομαι *remember, am mindful; mention* (τινός)	μνη μνη(σ)	ἀνα-μνήσω μνησθήσομαι	ἀν-έμνησα ἐμνήσθην	—— μέμνημαι *memini* μεμνήσομαι *meminero*
11. γιγνώσκω *know, learn to know*	γνω(σ)	γνώσομαι γνωσθήσομαι	ἔγνων ἐγνώσθην	ἔγνωκα ἔγνωσμαι γνωστός
12. τιτρώσκω *wound*	τρω	τρώσω τρωθήσομαι	ἔτρωσα ἐτρώθην	τέτρωκα τέτρωμαι τρωτός

Seventh or E-Class.

111. The verb stem is enlarged by an E-sound, either in the present or in the other tenses only.

a) Verbs with an enlarged present stem:

1. γαμέω *marry (a woman γυναῖκα)* γαμοῦμαι *marry (a man ἀνδρί,*	γαμ-ε γαμ-η *nubo)*	γαμῶ, -εῖς γαμοῦμαι, -ῇ	ἔγημα ἐγημάμην	γεγάμηκα γεγάμημαι
2. δοκέω *seem, am looked upon as; believe, think* δοκεῖ *videtur, it seems good, best,*	δοκ-ε *advisable*	δόξω δόξει	ἔδοξα ἔδοξε(ν)	—— δέδοκται *it has been decreed*

Verbs with an enlarged present stem. — *Concluded.*

PRESENT	STEM	FUTURE	AORIST	PERFECT
3. ὠθέω *push* (impf. ἐώθουν, 89, 1. note)	ὠθ-ε	ὤσω ὠσθήσομαι	ἔωσα ἐώσθην	ἔωκα ἔωσμαι
b) Verbs with a short present stem :				
4. ἐθέλω (θέλω) *am willing*	ἐθελ-η	ἐθελήσω	ἠθέλησα	ἠθέληκα
5. μέλλω *am about, intend ; am expected* or *destined ; hesitate*	μελλ-η	μελλήσω	ἐμέλλησα	
6. ἐρ- (ἐρωτάω) *ask*	ἐρ-η	ἐρωτήσω and ἐρήσομαι	ἠρώτησα and ἠρόμην	ἠρώτηκα
7. γίγνομαι *fio, am born, happen,*	γεν-η become	γενήσομαι	ἐγενόμην	γεγένημαι II pf. γέγονα
8. ἄχθομαι *am displeased, vexed, angry* (at [ἐπί] τινί)	ἀχθ-εσ	ἀχθέσομαι	ἠχθέσθην	
9. βούλομαι *wish, desire*	βουλ-η	βουλήσομαι	ἐβουλήθην	βεβούλημαι
10. δεῖ *it is necessary, one must, ought*	δε-η	δεήσει	ἐδέησε	δεδέηκε
11. δέομαι *need, want* (τινός); *ask, beg*	δε-η (τινός τι)	δεήσομαι	ἐδεήθην	δεδέημαι
12. μέλει μοι (τινός *something*) *is an object of care to me*	μελ-η	μελήσει	ἐμέλησε	μεμέληκε
13. ἐπι-μέλομαι, -μελοῦμαι *take care* (of τινός, *that* ὅπως)	μελ-η	ἐπιμελήσομαι	ἐπεμελήθην	ἐπιμεμέλημαι
14. οἴομαι (οἶμαι) *think, believe*	οἰ-η	οἰήσομαι	ᾠήθην	
15. μάχομαι *fight* (*against, with* τινί)	μαχ-ε(σ) μαχ-η	μαχοῦμαι,-ῇ	ἐμαχεσάμην	μεμάχημαι

Eighth or Mixed Class.

112. Contains Verbs with several altogether different stems.

Present	Stem	Future	Aorist	Perfect
1. αἱρέω *take, capture*	αἱρη	αἱρήσω	εἷλον	ᾕρηκα
Mid. *take for myself; choose*	ἑλ	αἱρήσομαι	εἱλόμην	ᾕρημαι
Pass. (to Act. and Mid.)	αἱρε	αἱρεθήσομαι	ᾑρέθην	ᾕρημαι
2. ἔρχομαι *go, come* impf. ᾖα 104, 2	ἐρχ, εἰ, ἰ, ἐλ(υ)θ	εἶμι	ἦλθον	ἐλήλυθα ἥκω *adsum*
3. ἐσθίω (βιβρώσκω) *eat, consume*	ἐσθι, ἐδ φαγ, βρω	ἔδομαι κατα-βρωθήσομαι	ἔφαγον κατ-εβρώθην	κατα-βέβρωκα κατα-βέβρωμαι
4. ἕπομαι *sequor, follow* (impf. εἱπόμην, 89, 1)	ἑπ, σεπ, σπ	ἕψομαι	ἑ-σπόμην s. σπῶμαι-ἐπίσπωμαι o. σποῖτο-ἐπίσποιτο imp. σποῦ-ἐπίσπου	
5. ἔχω *have, hold* (coll. form: ἴσχω) impf. εἶχον 89, 1	ἐχ, σεχ σχ-η	ἕξω σχήσω	ἔσχον subj. σχῶ opt. σχοίην imp. σχ ές, σχέτω	ἔσχηκα
Middle		ἕξομαι σχήσομαι	ἐσχόμην subj. σχῶμαι opt. σχοίμην imp. σχοῦ, σχέσθω	ἔσχημαι
Compounds:				
a) παρ-έχω *furnish, supply, afford, provide*		παρ-έξω παρα-σχήσω	παρ-έσχον subj. παράσχω opt. παράσχοιμι imp. παράσχες	παρ-έσχηκα
Mid. *furnish* etc. (*from my own means*)		παρ-έξομαι παρα-σχήσομαι	παρ-εσχόμην subj. παράσχωμαι opt. παράσχοιτο imp. παράσχου	παρ έσχημαι
b) ἀν-έχομαι *endure, suffer;* impf. ἠνειχόμην 89, 7		ἀν-έξομαι	ἠν-εσχόμην subj. ἀνά-σχωμαι etc.	ἠν-εσχημαι
c) ὑπ-ισχ-νέο-μαι *promise*		ὑπο-σχήσομαι	ὑπ-εσχόμην subj. ὑπό-σχωμαι etc.	ὑπ-έσχημαι
6. ὁράω *see,* impf. ἑώρων 89, 2	ὁρα (ϝορα) ὀπ, ἰδ (ϝιδ)	ὄψομαι ὀφθήσομαι	εἶδον ὤφθην	ἑώρακα, ὄπωπα ἑώραμαι, ὦμμαι

Eighth or Mixed Class. — *Continued.*

Present	Stem	Future	Aorist	Perfect
7. πάσχω *experience, suffer*	πασχ, πᾰθ πενθ	πείσομαι	ἔπαθον	πέπονθα
8. πίνω *drink*	πῑν, πι πω, πο	πίομαι ποθήσομαι	ἔπῐον ἐπόθην	πέπωκα πέπομαι
9. πίπτω *fall*	πετ, πεσ πτω	πεσοῦμαι, -ῇ	ἔπεσον	πέπτωκα
10. τρέχω *run* [impf.] θέω (only pres. and	τρεχ δραμ-η	δραμοῦμαι, -ῇ	ἔδραμον	δεδράμηκα
11. φέρω *bear, carry* Mid. *carry (for myself)* Pass. *am borne, carried* φέρομαι *hurry, rush, fly,* etc.	φερ, οἰ, ἐνε(γ)κ	οἴσω οἴσομαι ἐνεχθήσομαι ἐνεχθήσομαι	ἤνεγκον and ἤνεγκα ἠνεγκάμην ἠνέχθην Verb. A. ἠνέχθην	ἐνήνοχα }ἐνήνεγμαι οἰστέον ἐνήνεγμαι
12. ἀγορεύω λέγω φημί *speak, say, talk; discourse, harangue, affirm, declare* Pass. Compounds; *e.g.* a) ἀπ-αγορεύω 1) *forbid,* 2) *give out* b) δια-λέγομαι *speak, converse* (with τινί) but c) λέγω *gather, collect* (with συν-, ἐκ-, κατα-)	ἀγορευ, λεγ, φη, φᾰ, ϝεπ, ϝερ, ῥη	ἐρῶ, ἐρεῖς λέξω, φήσω, 104, 1. n. ῥηθήσομαι λεχθήσομαι ἀπ-ερῶ δια-λέξομαι συλ-λέξω συλ-λεγήσομαι	εἶπον, εἰπέ and εἶπα ἔλεξα, ἔφησα ἐρρήθην ἐλέχθην ἀπ-εῖπον δι-ελέχθην συν-έλεξα συν-ελέγην	εἴρηκα εἴρημαι λέλεγμαι ἀπ-είρηκα δι-είλεγμαι συν-είλοχα συν-είλεγμαι
13. ζάω (βιόω) *live*	ζη, βιω	βιώσομαι	ἐβίων	βεβίωκα

Eighth or Mixed Class. — *Concluded.*

Present	Stem	Future	Aorist	Perfect
14. καθίζω tr. *make sit down*, intr. *sit down* καθίζομαι *sit down*	ἱδ-	καθιῶ, -εῖς	ἐκάθισα	———
καθέζομαι intr. *am seated* and *sit down*	ἑδ, ἡ(σ)	καθεδοῦμαι, -ῆ	ἐκαθεζόμην 1) *considebam* and 2) *consedi*	κάθημαι *consedi = sedeo, am seated* 104, 5
15. παίω, τύπτω | *strike,* πατάσσω, | *beat*	παι, τυπ, παταγ,	παίσω	ἔπαισα	πέπαικα
πλήττω ʃ Pass.	πληγ	πληγήσομαι	ἐπλήγην	πέπληγμαι
ἐκ-πλήττω *frighten*	πληγ	ἐκ-πλήξω	ἐξ-έπληξα	———
ἐκ-πλήττομαι *am panic-stricken*	πλᾱγ	ἐκ-πλᾰγήσομαι	ἐξ-επλάγην	ἐκ-πέπληγμαι
16. πωλέω, πιπράσκω, ἀποδίδομαι *sell* (ὀλίγου, πολλοῦ 151)	πωλη, δω, δο, πρᾱ	πωλήσω ἀποδώσομαι πρᾱθήσομαι	ἐπώλησα ἀπεδόμην ἐπράθην	πεπώληκα πέπρᾱκα πέπρᾱμαι
17. σκοπέω and -έομαι, σκέπτομαι *look,* *view, consider,*	σκοπε, σκεπ *examine*	σκέψομαι	ἐσκεψάμην	ἔσκεμμαι
18. ὠνέομαι *buy* (*for* τινός : ὀλίγου, πολλοῦ 151)	ὠνη, πρια	ὠνήσομαι ὠνηθήσομαι	ἐπριάμην ἐωνήθην	ἐώνημαι ἐώνημαι

113. Certain Occasional Irregularities
Occurring with Attic Writers in the Inflection of Verbs.

For Reference.

ἄγνυμι *break,* tr.; (ϝαγ-): κατ-άξω, κατ-έαξα; augm. 89, 1. n.

ἄγνυμαι *break,* intr.: pf. κατ-έᾱγα *have been (am) broken;* aor. p. ἐάγην.

ἄγω: 97, 16; aor. a. also ἦξα.

αἰνέω: 91, 5; f. also ἐπαινέσω and παραινέσομαι; pf. p. ᾔνημαι.

ἀκροάομαι *hear;* ἀκροάσομαι, ἠκροασάμην; cf. βοήσομαι and 80.

ἀλαλάζω *raise the war-cry;* aor. ἠλάλαξα: 77, 3, b. n.

ἀλείφω *anoint;* pf. p. ἐξ-αλήλιμμαι w. Attic redupl.: 89, 5.

ἀλέξω *ward off* (chiefly poetic); (ἀλεκ-, ἡ ἀλκ-ή): f. ἀλεξήσω.

    Mid. ἀλέξομαι, f. ἀλεξήσομαι and ἀλέξομαι. a. ἠλεξάμην.

ἀλέω *grind;* pf. p. ἀλήλε(σ)μαι, see 89, 5 and 91, 4.

ἅλλομαι *leap;* f. ἁλοῦμαι, I a. ἡλάμην, ἅλασθαι (like ἆραι 90, 3 for ἥλασθαι according to 84, 2), II a. ἡλόμην, ἁλέσθαι.

ἀπ-αμείβομαι *reply* (chiefly poet.) D. M. 72, 3; rarely ἀπημείφθη.

ἀμφιγνοέω *am in doubt;* augm. ἠμφιγν. or ἠμφεγν. 89, 6 and 7.

ἀμφισβητέω *dispute;* augm. ἠμφισβ. or ἠμφεσβ. 89, 7.

ἀναλίσκω: 110, 5; also (incorrectly) ἀνάλισκον etc. without augm.

ἀνδάνω *please;* (ἀδ-, σϝαδ-, ἡδύς): f. ἁδήσω; a. ἕαδον, ἁδεῖν; pf. ἕᾱδα.

ἀνύτω besides ἀνύω (ἀνύω) *accomplish:* ἀνύσω, ἤνῠσα, ἤνῠκα, ἤνυσμαι, ἠνύσθην, ἄνυστός, see 77, 2. n.; 83, 1; 91, 4.

ἀποδημέω *am abroad;* augm. ἀπεδήμησα, redupl. ἀποδεδήμηκα (agt. 75, 3, from ἀπόδημος).

ἀραρίσκω *join, fit;* (ἀρ-, see 110, b.): aor. ἤρᾰρον; pf. ἄρᾱρα *fit well.*

αὐαίνω *dry;* sometimes drops the augm.: αὐαίνετο (besides ηὐαίνετο).

βαίνω: 102, 4. a.; pf. p. (ξυμ-, παρα-) -βέβᾱμαι; aor. -εβάθην.

βιόω: 112, 13; aor. opt. also βιῴη besides βιοίη, part. also βιώσας besides βιούς.

βιώσκομαι, ἀνα-: *bring (and come) to life again;* aor. -βιώσασθαι.

βλαστάνω *sprout;* (βλαστ-η, 109, c.): βλαστήσω, ἔβλαστον, βεβλάστηκα.

βλώσκω *go;* (μολ-, μλω-, 15): μολοῦμαι, ἔμολον; cf. ὁ αὐτόμολος.

βούλομαι: 111, 9; sometimes augm. η- (ἠβουλόμην, ἠβουλήθην).

γηθέω *rejoice;* pf. γέγηθα, with present force.

γηράσκω: 110, 1; poetic aor. also ἐγήραν, γηρᾶναι, according to 102, 2. a.

δάκνω *bite;* (δηκ-: δᾰκ-, 109, a.): δήξομαι, ἔδακον, δέδηγμαι, ἐδήχθην.

δαρθάνω *sleep;* (δαρθ-η 109, c.): κατ-έδαρθον, κατα-δεδάρθηκα.

δει-, δῐ-: 103, 3; plupf. 3. pl. also ἐδεδίεσαν.

διαιτάομαι *live, diet;* augm. διῃτώμην, διῃτήθην and redupl. ἐδεδιητητο.

δίδημι, collat. with δέω *bind;* 3. p. plur. pres. διδέασιν.

διψάω *thirst;* contr. like ζάω 91, 2: διψῆς, διψῇ, ἐδίψη, διψῆν.

δράω *do;* pf. pass. δέδραμαι. Aor. p. ἐδράσθην; v. adj. δραστέος.

δύναμαι: sometimes augm. η- (ἠδυνάμην, ἠδυνήθην) and in the impf. also ἐδύνω (ἠδ.) for ἐδύνασο.

δύω: 91, 6; pf. ἀπο-δέδυκα is very rarely also trans.: πολλούς.

ἐγγυάω *pledge;* augm. and redupl. ἠγγ. (or ἐνεγύων, ἐγγεγύηκα).

ἐγείρω *awaken;* fut. ἐγερῶ, -εῖς. Aor. ἤγειρα. Aor. pass. ἠγέρθην *was awakened* and *awoke.*

ἐγείρομαι *awake,* intr. Aor. ἠγρόμην (14), according to 86; pf. ἐγρήγορα, plup. ἐγρηγόρειν (no augm.) *am, was awake,* cf. 89, 5.

ἐγκωμιάζω *extol, eulogize;* fut. -άσω and -άσομαι; impf. ἐνεκωμ.; pf. ἐγκεκωμ.

εἰμί: 104, 3; verb. adj. συν-εστέον (impf. ἤμην).

εἶμι: 104, 2; collat. impf. sing. 1. ᾖειν, 2. ᾔεισθα, 3. ᾔειν, plur. 3. ᾖεσαν. Opt. also ἰοίην. Imper. 3. pl. also ἴτων; v. adj. also ἰτητέον (from ἰτάω, not used in Attic dial.).

ἐκκλησιάζω *vote;* augm. ἐξεκλησίαζ ν or ἠκκλησ. etc.

ἐλέγχω *convict;* reg., only perf. with Attic redupl., 89, 5: ἐλήλεγκται, plup.
ἐλήλεγκτο (no augm.).

ἐλίσσω *roll;* besides εἰλίσσω, augm. εἴλισσον, εἴλιγμαι etc., according to 89, 1;
all the forms are also found with the smooth breathing: ἐλίττω etc.

ἐναντιόομαι: 89, 6; also ἐν-ηντιούμην, ἐν-ηντιώθην, ἐν-ηντίωμαι.

ἕννυμι, ἀμφι-, *clothe,* ἀμφιῶ, -εῖς, ἠμφίεσα, ἠμφίεσμαι.

ἐνοχλέω *annoy;* augm. ἠνώχλουν, -ησα, -ημαι, according to 89, 7.

ἐπιορκέω *swear falsely;* augm. ἐπιώρκουν, ἐπιώρκησα.

ἐπίσταμαι: 101, 6; has also ἐπίστω for ἐπίστασο; ἠπίστω for ἠπίστασο.

ἐργάζομαι *work;* augm. εἰργ. (89, 1) and ἠργ., redupl. εἰργ.

ἕρπω and ἑρπύζω *creep, serpo;* augm. εἷρπον, εἵρπυσα, according to 89, 1.

ἔρχομαι: 112, 2; fut. ἐλεύσομαι (chiefly poetic and Ionic); aor. imper. ἐλθέ
like εἰπέ 72, 12. d.

ἐσθίω: 112, 3; pf. ἐδήδοκα, ἐδήδεσμαι (comp. 89, 5); v. adj. ἐδεστέον.

ἑστιάω *entertain;* augm. εἱστίων, εἱστίασα, εἱστίακα etc. 89, 1.

εὕδω *sleep,* usu. καθ-; see below καθεύδω.

εὐεργετέω *do good;* augm. εὐεργ. or εὐηργ.

ἐχθάνομαι, usu. ἀπ-, *incur hatred;* (ἐχθ-η, according to 109, c.): ἀπ-εχθήσομαι,
ἀπ-ηχθόμην, ἀπ-ήχθημαι.

ἔχω: 112, 5; ἀμπ-έχω and -ίσχω *envelop;* impf. ἤμπισχον; ἀμπέχομαι *have
(something) wrapped about me;* augm. ἠμπειχόμην, according to 112, 5. b.

ἕψω *cook;* fut. ἑψήσω; aor. act. ἥψησα, verb. adj. ἑψητός and ἑφθός.

ζώννυμι *gird,* according to 106, b.: ζώσω, ἔζωσα, ἔζω(σ)μαι.

ἧμαι, κάθημαι: 104, 5. Impf. also καθήμην, καθῆσο, καθῆστο etc., subj. καθώμεθα,
opt. καθήμην or καθοίμην.

ἠμί *say,* impf. ἦν δ' ἐγώ and ἦ δ' ὅς *said I, said he,* cf. 104, 1.

θέω *run,* pres. and impf. 91, 3; (from θεύω, θέϝω, like πλέω 108, note); fut.
θεύσομαι according to 108, note.

θιγγάνω *touch;* (θιγ-, 109, d.): θίξομαι, ἔθιγον.

θνήσκω, ἀπο-: 110, 7; properly θνη-ίσκω; wrongly θνήσκω; pf. opt. τεθναίην,
imper. 3. sg. τεθνάτω.

θρύπτω *crush, enervate;* pf. pass. τέθρυμμαι of τρύφ-, according to 21, 2.

ἱδρόω *sweat,* reg.; besides ἱδροῦντι also ἱδρῶντι τῷ ἵππῳ.

ἵζω, see καθίζω.

ἵημι: 98–100; ἀφίημι: impf. also ἠφίειν, augm. according to 89, 7.

ἱλάσκομαι *appease;* st. ἱλα(σ): ἱλάσομαι, ἱλασάμην.

ἵστημι: besides τὸ ἑστώς (103, 1) also τὸ ἑστός, τὸ καθεστός.

καθεύδω: 89, 6; augm. besides ἐκάθευδον sometimes καθηῦδον; f. καθευδήσω.

καθίζω: 112, 14; augm. besides ἐκάθισα (89, 6) also καθῖσα.

καίνω: 86, 3; pf. κατα-κέκονα, according to 88, 3.

καίω: 92, 2, compare 77, 3. d. n.; aor. act. also (ἔκηα), ἔκεα (poetic); aor. pass.
also ἐκάη (poet. and Ionic).

καλέω: 92, 5; opt. pf. pass. κεκλῇο (no periphrasis).

κεῖμαι: 104, 6; subj. κέηται, κέωνται; opt. κέοιτο, κέοιντο.

κεράννυμι: 106, 1; pass. perf. κεκέρασμαι; aor. ἐκεράσθην.

κερδαίνω gain; aor. besides ἐκέρδηνα also ἐκέρδᾱνα, against 84, 2.

κλάω break; (κλᾰ(σ)-): κλάσω, ἔκλασα, κέκλασμαι, ἐκλάσθην, according to 91, 4.

κλέπτω steal; κλέψομαι and κλέψω, ἔκλεψα, κέκλοφα (88, 3. d.), κέκλεμμαι, ἐκλάπην (87, 3), κλεπτός and κλεπτέος.

κλίνω: 97, 49; pass. also ἐκλίνην (and ἐκλίνθην), κλινήσομαι.

κνάω scrape; mid. κνῆται, κνῆσθαι, contr. like ζῆν etc., 91, 2.

κορέννυμι satiate; (κορεσ-): κορέσω, ἐκόρεσα, κεκόρεσμαι, ἐκορέσθην.

κρούω knock, strike: κέκρουμαι, ἐκρούσθην, κρουστός, like κλείω 91, 7.

κτάομαι acquire, reg.; pf. opt. κεκτῴμεθα (without periphrasis).

κτίννυμι, ἀπο-, kill; coll. with ἀπο-κτείνω (κτείνυμι).

λαμβάνω: 109, 11; II aor. imp. λαβέ (like εἰπέ 72, 12. d.).

λέγω collect, gather in ἐκ-, κατα-, συλ-λέγω: 112, 12. c.; pf. p. also -λέλεγμαι; aor. συν-ελέχθην (chiefly Ionic).

λεύω, gen. κατα-, stone; aor. p. κατελεύσθην, see 91, 7.

λούω wash, bathe (λόϝω lavo), reg.; besides also λοῦται, ἐλοῦτο, ἐλοῦντο, λοῦσθαι and other contracted forms.

μείγνυμι: 106, 8 (see μίγνυμι); aor. p. ἐμίγην (μειγ: μῖγ, 11, 1).

μεθύσκω make drunk, μεθύσκομαι and μεθύω am drunk: ἐμεθύσθην.

μέλλω: 111, 5; sometimes ἠ- as augm. (ἤμελλον, ἠμέλλησα).

μένω remain, halt; f. and a. reg.; pf. μεμένηκα; v. a. μενετός, -τέον.

μερ- allot (τὸ μέρος, μερίζω — μόρος, μοῖρα): pf. pass. εἵμαρται it is allotted, fated; ἡ εἱμαρμένη lot, fate, destiny.

μίγνυμι, μίξω etc., late and improper spelling for μείγνυμι, μείξω etc.: 106, 8.

μιμνήσκω: 110, 10; (also μιμνήσκω and ἐμνήσθην); pf. pass. without periphrasis: subj. μεμνώμεθα, opt. μεμνῇο, μεμνῇτο, μεμνήμεθα (or μεμνῷο, μεμνῴμεθα).

μνημονεύω remember; redupl. ἀπ-εμνημόνευκα, cf. 74, 2. 3.

νέμω distribute, deal out; fut. and aor. regular; but then νενέμηκα, νενέμημαι, ἐνεμήθην, according to 111, b.

νέω swim, see 108, note, like πλέω 108, 7: νεύσομαι, ἔνευσα, νένευκα.

οἴγω, ἀν-: 89, 2; also ἤνοιγεν, ἤνοιξεν; f. pf. p. ἀνεῴξεται.

οἶδα: 103, 4; οἶδας collat. with οἶσθα; 2. p. sg. impf. ᾔδης and ᾔδεισθα, in the plur. (poet.) ᾖσμεν, ᾖστε, ᾖσαν; f. εἰδήσω; v. adj. ἰστέον one must ascertain.

οἰκτείρω pity, reg.; better οἰκτίρω (77, 3. d.), οἰκτιρῶ, ᾤκτιρα.

οἴχομαι, go away, am gone away: f. οἰχήσομαι; pf. οἴχωκα (ᾤχωκα and ᾤχημαι).

ὄμνυμι: 106, 12; pf. ὀμώμο(σ)ται, ὠμό(σ)θησαν — ἀπώμοτος.

ὀνίνημι: 101, 1; besides (poet.) aor. mid. ὠνήμην (ὠνάμην), opt. ὄναιτο, inf. ὄνασθαι to reap profit.

ὁράω: 112, 6; aor. imp. act. also ἰδέ (like εἰπέ 72, 12. d.); aor. also middle: εἰδόμην, imp. ἰδοῦ, when exclamation: ἰδού, behold, lo! ecce!

ὀφείλω owe: ὤφελον 86, 3; ὀφειλήσω, ὠφείλησα, ὀφειληθείς.

ὀφλισκάνω: incur (a penalty); (ὀφλ-η): ὀφλήσω, ὤφλον (improperly accented ὄφλειν and ὄφλων) and ὤφλητα, ὤφληκα.

πάομαι (Doric) = κτάομαι and πέπαμαι = κέκτημαι.

παρανομέω act contrary to law; παρενόμουν, παρανενόμηκα.

παροινέω act insultingly; augm. ἐπαρῴνησα, like 89, 7.

παύω cause to stop, reg., except παυστέον, ἄπαυστος with σ. Herodotus has also ἐπαύσθην. — παύομαι stop, cease: παύσομαι, ἐπαυσάμην, πέπαυμαι.

πείθω: 97, 8. 9; II pf. πέποιθα 108, 5; aor. mid. ἐπιθόμην.

πεινάω hunger; is contracted like ζάω 91, 2: πεινῇς, πεινῇ, ἐπείνη, πεινῆν. πειράομαι, Μ. Ρ. 95, 3; but also aor. mid. ἐπειρασάμην.

πέτομαι fly; fut. πτήσομαι; aor. ἐπτόμην (according to 86) or ἐπτάμην (according to 100) or ἔπτην (according to 102, 2. a.).

πήγνυμι: 106, 9; opt. pres. πηγνῦτο (for πηγνῦιτο).

πίμπλημι and πίμπρημι may lose their μ, when preceded by ἐμ: ἐμπίπλημι, ἐμπίπρημι, ἐμπιπρᾶσιν etc., but always ἐνεπίμπλην etc., ἐνεπίμπρων collat. with ἐνεπίμπρασαν.

πλέκω plait: πλέξω, ἔπλεξα, πέπλεγμαι, ἐπλάκην, 87, 3.

πλέω: 108, 7; fut. also πλευσοῦμαι (the so-called Doric future); also πεπλευσμένος navigated, ἄπλευστος not yet navigated, and πλευστέον.

πλήττω: 108, 2; 111, 15; πεπληγέναι doubtful for πεπλῆχθαι.

πνίγω choke, tr.; strangle (like τρίβω 11, 1 and 108, 3): πνίξω, ἔπνιξα; mid.-pass. choke, intr.; am drowned: πνῖγήσομαι, ἐπνίγην, πέπνιγμαι.

ποθέω long for, desire, reg.; sometimes also ποθέσομαι, ἐπόθεσα.

πορ- procure, bring about (πορίζω, πορσύνω): II aor. ἔπορον gave; pf. p. πέπρωται it is fated; ἡ πεπρωμένη and τὸ πεπρωμένον fatum.

πράττω: 97, 13; besides πέπρᾱγα have fared, am (in a state or condition).

ῥιγόω am cold, shiver, reg.; besides also subj. ῥιγῷ, inf. ῥιγῶν, part. ῥιγώντων.

σαλπίζω sound the trumpet; (σαλπιγγ- 77, 3. b. note): ἐσάλπιγξεν (ὁ σαλπιγκτής).

σβέννυμι quench; (ἀπο-, κατα-): σβέσω, ἔσβεσα, ἔσβεσμαι, ἐσβέσθην. σβέννυμαι am quenched: σβήσομαι, ἔσβην, ἔσβηκα, see 102, 4.

σείω shake; p. with σ: σέσεισμαι, ἐσείσθην, σειστός; 91, 7.

σήπω rot, tr. ἀπο-, κατασήπομαι, intr. rot, become rotten (like τήκομαι 108, 1): σάπήσομαι, ἐσάπην, ἀπο-σεσηπώς rotten.

στάζω drop (σταγ- stagnum): στάξω, ἔσταξα, ἐν-έστακται, 77, 3. b. n.

στηρίζω prop (στηριγ-): ἐστήριξα, ἐστήρικτο, στηριχθείς, 77, 3. b. n.

στίζω prick (στιγ-): στίξω, ἔστιξα, ἔστιγμαι, στικτός 77, 3. b. n.

τάττω: 97, 14; occasionally τετάχαται and ἐτετάχατο (against 83, 2 without periphrasis, after the Ionic manner).

τίθημι: 98–100; pf. τέθεικα late (Hellenistic) form.

τίνω: 109, 1; incorrect τίσω, ἔτισα, etc. (τει: τῖ-, 109, 1; 11, 1).

τιτράω (τετραίνω) bore: ἔτρησα, τέτρημαι.

τλη: τλά sustain, endure, defective stem, wanting in the present; forms τλήσομαι, ἔτλην, τέτληκα, according to 102, 3. 4.

τρέω tremble; aor. ἔτρεσα, according to 91, 4.

τρίβω *rub;* (τρῖβ-; τρῐβ-, 11, 1): τρίψω, ἔτρῑψα, τέτρῐφα, τέτρῑμμαι, ἐτρίφθην and ἐτρῐβην, 108, 3.

ὑποπτεύω *am suspicious, apprehend,* augm. ὑπώπτευον, ὑπώπτευσα.

φεύγω: 108, 6; fut. also φευξοῦμαι (so-called Doric future).

φημί: 104, 1; ἔφης collat. form with ἔφησθα, φαθί with φάθι.

φθείρω, usu. δια-; reg. like σπείρω 97, 33; there is also a II pf. act. διέφθορα, tr. and intr.; perf. p. 3. p. plur. also ἐφθάραται, like τετάχαται, without periphrasis after the Ionic manner.

φρέω (only in composition) *let:* δια-φρήσω, εἰσ-φρήσομαι *to let in;* inf. aor. m. ἐπ-εισ-φρέσθαι *to let in besides;* compare θέσθαι.

χαίρω *rejoice:* χαιρήσω, ἐχάρην, κεχάρηκα, according to 102, 2. b.

χαλάω *let loose:* χαλάσω, ἐχάλασα, ἐχαλάσθην, according to 91, 4.

χόω *heap up, erect:* κέχωσμαι, ἐχώσθην, χωστός, according to 91, 7.

χράω *give oracles:* χρήσω, ἔχρησα; mid. *consult the oracle:* χρήσομαι, ἐχρησάμην, pass. κέχρησται, ἐχρήσθη *the oracle was given.*

χράω *lend, supply;* contr. χρῇς, χρῇ, χρῆν (91, 2); and forms (91, 1) ἔχρησα, *lent,* ἐχρήσατο *he had something lent to him, borrowed.*

(Likewise ἀπο-, ἐκ-, καταχράω *suffice.*)

Moreover ἀποχρῇ (wrongly ἀπόχρη) *it is enough,* impf. ἀπέχρη.

ψεύδω *deceive;* 97, 10: fut. 3. sg. ψευσεῖ (Doric future; compare 112, 9 and in 113 the verbs πλέω, φεύγω).

PART III. : SYNTAX.

I. AGREEMENT.

SUBJECT AND PREDICATE

114. 1. A neuter plural subject generally takes a **singular** verb.

> Καλὰ ἦν τὰ σφάγια *the omens were favorable.*
>
> Τὰ μεγάλα δῶρα τῆς τύχης ἔχει φόβον.

2. Two subjects or a **dual** subject have their predicate sometimes in the dual, sometimes in the plural.

> Δύο καλώ τε κἀγαθὼ ἄνδρε τέθνατον or τεθνᾶσιν.
>
> Κριτίας καὶ ᾿Αλκιβιάδης ἐδυνάσθην τῶν ἐπιθυμιῶν κρατεῖν.

3. Observe the idiomatic agreement between the Greek and the English in cases where a **collective** noun in the singular *may* take a plural verb.

> Μέρος τι ἀνθρώπων οὐχ ἡγοῦνται θεούς.
>
> ᾿Αθηναίων τὸ πλῆθος οἴονται ῞Ιππαρχον τύραννον ὄντα ἀποθανεῖν.

4. A masculine or feminine subject often takes for its predicate the **neuter** singular of an adjective, which is then used as a noun. Compare *Turpe senex miles.*[1]

> ᾿Αθάνατον ἡ ψυχή *the soul is (an) immortal (being).*
>
> Πονηρὸν ὁ συκοφάντης *a sycophant is a scoundrel.*
>
> Δεινὸν οἱ πολλοί *the mob is a terror.*

5. The gender and number of a **pronominal** subject or object agree with the predicate noun. Compare *ea firma amicitia est.*

> Αὕτη ἄλλη πρόφασις ἦν.   Οὗτοι νόμοι εἰσίν.
>
> Καὶ οἶμαι, ἔφη, ἐμὴν ταύτην πατρίδα εἶναι.

But sometimes also: ῎Εγωγέ φημι ταῦτα φλυαρίας εἶναι.

Note.—Definitions require the **neuter** of the pronoun, which is then the predicate, and not the subject, of the sentence.

> Τί φῂς ἀρετὴν εἶναι; *Quid dicis virtutem esse?*

ADJECTIVE. COMPARISON.

115. 1. Adverbial phrases which signify **place**, **situation**, **time**, **manner**, **succession**, or **a state of mind**, are expressed

---

[1] Note the frequent omission of the copula in short statements.

in Greek by adjectives agreeing with the word (subj. or obj.) to which they relate. Compare

Socrates primus hoc docuit. Socrates venenum laetus hausit.
Σκηνοῦμεν ὑπαίθριοι ἐν τῇ τάξει *in the open air.*
Τριταῖοι ἐκ Σπάρτης ἐγένοντο ἐν τῇ Ἀττικῇ *on the third day.*
Ἐπύαξα προτέρα Κύρου εἰς Ταρσοὺς ἀφίκετο *before Cyrus.*
Ἑκοῦσαι αἱ πόλεις χρήματα συνεβάλλοντο *willingly.*
Κατέβαινον εἰς τὰς κώμας ἤδη σκοταῖοι *it was already dark when . . .*

2. To denote the highest possible degree of anything, ὡς, ὅτι, ᾗ or οἷος may be added to the superlative. *E.g.* ὡς τάχιστα *quam celerrime, as quickly (soon) as possible ;* ἄνδρας ὅτι πλείστους *as many men as possible;* χωρίον οἷον χαλεπώτατον *almost impregnable.*

Δεῖ ὅτι μάλιστα εὐμαθεῖς εἶναι τοὺς νέους.

II. THE ARTICLE.

116. The originally (Homer!) demonstrative force of the article ὁ, ἡ, τό *the* is still apparent

1. in ὁ μέν — ὁ δέ *(the) one — the other* (through all cases);
in τὸ μέν — τὸ δέ } adverbially: *partly — partly,*
τὰ μέν — τὰ δέ } *sometimes — sometimes.*
in πρὸ τοῦ *before this, erenow, formerly.*
2. in ὁ δέ, ἡ δέ, τὸ δέ *but (and) he, but (and) she,* etc.
in the acc. with inf. τὸν δέ, τὴν δέ, τοὺς δέ *but (and) he, she,* etc.
and καὶ τόν, καὶ τήν, καὶ τούς *and he, and she, and they* (nom. καὶ ὅς 129, 1. note 3).
Οἱ μὲν ἐτόξευον, οἱ δ' ἐσφενδόνων.
Ἐπορεύθησαν τὰ μέν τι μαχόμενοι, τὰ δὲ καὶ ἀναπαυόμενοι.
Κῦρος δίδωσι Κλεάρχῳ μυρίους δαρεικούς· ὁ δὲ λαβὼν τὸ χρυσίον στράτευμα συνέλεξεν.
Τὸν δὲ γελάσαι *whereupon (it is said) he laughed.*

Note 1. — The article in the above meaning has of late begun to be orthotoned: ὅ, ἥ, οἵ, αἵ.

Note 2. — For other proofs of the dem. force of the art., see 117, 1; 119, notes 1 and 2.

USE OF THE ARTICLE.

117. The Greek article sometimes corresponds to the English, sometimes differs from it. Thus it may have

1. an **individualizing** force, when it points to one particular person or thing in order to distinguish it from others (*limited signification*):

Τῶν ἑπτὰ σοφῶν σοφώτατος ἦν Σόλων.

'Ο σοφὸς ἐν αὑτῷ περιφέρει τὴν οὐσίαν his property.

Τὴν δίκην ἐπιθεῖναί τινι to inflict due, condign punishment upon.

Ξέρξης ἡττηθεὶς τῇ μάχῃ ἐκ τῆς Ἑλλάδος ἀπεχώρει in the well-known battle.

Κῦρος ὑπισχνεῖτο δώσειν τρία ἡμιδαρεικὰ τοῦ μηνὸς τῷ στρατιώτῃ (distributive force: singulis militibus singulis mensibus: a (each) soldier a (per) month).

2. a **generic** force, when it points to a particular person or thing in order to make it the r e p r e s e n t a t i v e of a w h o l e c l a s s.　Here the English often prefers the indefinite article.

Ἀλλ' εὖ φέρειν χρὴ συμφορὰς τὸν εὐγενῆ (a [the] noble-minded man).

Δεῖ τὸν στρατιώτην φοβεῖσθαι μᾶλλον τὸν ἄρχοντα ἢ τοὺς πολεμίους (a soldier ought to fear his commander).

Νικᾷ ὁ μείων τὸν μέγαν δίκαι' ἔχων.

Note 1.—There is therefore a difference between

πολλοί many,　and οἱ πολλοί the most, most people (the majority, multitude),

ὀλίγοι (a) few,　" οἱ ὀλίγοι (**the** few =) the oligarchs,

πλείονες (still) more, a greater number,

　　　　　　　　and οἱ πλείονες the majority, generality,

πλεῖστοι very many,　" οἱ πλεῖστοι the greatest number, most.

ἄλλοι alii,　　　　" οἱ ἄλλοι ceteri,

ἐμὸς φίλος a (some) friend of mine, and ὁ ἐμὸς φίλος (this) my friend,

τοιοῦτος ἀνήρ such a man = a (some) man of such qualities,

ὁ τοιοῦτος ἀνήρ such a man = the (this, that) man of such qualities.

Note 2. — ὁ βουλόμενος whoso will, any person who wishes,

　　　ὁ τυχών " the first one meets," a chance comer, any one,

　　　ὁ τολμήσων such a one as will, or as is able to, venture (Quality !).

118. The article is **used** in the following cases, in which it refers to a definite object.　Here the English o f t e n omits it.

1. With the a p p o s i t i o n a f t e r t h e p e r s o n a l p r o n o u n (expressed or understood):

ἡμεῖς οἱ Ἕλληνες we Greeks. ἐγὼ ὁ τλήμων 1 wretched man.

Εἰ βούλεσθέ μοι οἵ τε στρατηγοὶ καὶ οἱ λοχαγοὶ ἐλθεῖν, λέξω.

2. With c a r d i n a l n u m b e r s, esp. when they denote a definite portion of a whole number which is either expressed or otherwise known, hence also with fractions.

Τὰ δύο μέρη two thirds.

Ἀπῆσαν τῶν λόχων δώδεκα ὄντων οἱ τρεῖς three twelfths.

3. With ἄμφω, ἀμφότερος and ἑκάτερος (*uterque*), often also with ἕκαστος :

τὼ παῖδε ἀμφοτέρω *both* (*the*) *sons*, ἐπὶ τῶν πλευρῶν ἑκατέρων, ἕκαστον (τὸ) ἔθνος, ἑκάστης (τῆς) ἡμέρας, ἑκάστου ἔτους.

4. With the possessive genitives οὗ, ἧς, ὧν *whose, of whom, of which:*

Ἀπέθανεν ὁ φίλος, οὗ τὸν υἱὸν παιδεύω *whose son*.
Αἰσχύνθητε Δία, ἐν οὗ τῷ ἱερῷ ἐσμεν.

Likewise with the posses. pron. 64 ; 126 ; with the demonstr. 65 ; 128 ; with πᾶς, 123.

5. N o t e. — P o e t s frequently omit the article where it cannot be dispensed with in prose.

119. The article is **omitted** in the following cases — though referring to a definite object. Its omission partly agrees with, and is partly contrary to, English usage.

1. With the predicate noun or adjective :

Ἀεὶ κράτιστόν ἐστι τἀληθῆ λέγειν.
Αἱ δεύτεραί πως φροντίδες σοφώτεραι.
Κάλλιστόν ἐστι κτῆμα παιδεία βροτοῖς.
Χαιρεφῶν ἐμὸς ἑταῖρος ἦν ἐκ νέου.

2. With words that denote persons (as θεός, ἄνθρωπος, στρατηγός, etc.), when they are used as appellatives in a generic sense, 117, 2.

Πάντων μέτρον ἄνθρωπός ἐστιν *man* (in general).

3. With certain appellatives, which are then used almost with the force of proper names :

βασιλεύς *the king of Persia*, μέγας βασιλεύς *the Great King*,
ἐν ἄστει *in the city* (*of Athens*), ἐπὶ θάνατον *to execution*, ἥλιος, οὐρανός, etc.
Ἦν ἥλιος ἐπὶ δυσμαῖς. Ἦν ἤδη ἀμφὶ ἡλίου δυσμάς.

N o t e 1. — The uses of the article may thus be illustrated in the word ἄνθρωπος :

ὁ ἄνθρωπος = a) *the* (i.e. *this particular*) *man, the man* (*mentioned before*) ; *each man* (117, 1). — b) *man* (in general, with all the constituent elements of human nature, *mankind, the human race*), e.g. θνητός ἐστιν (= οἱ ἄνθρωποι θνητοί εἰσιν) (117, 2).

ἄνθρωπος = a) *a man* (*some man, any one individual of the human race*), e.g. ἔλεξεν αὐτῷ *told him* (117, note 1). — b) *man* (in general, one man serving as the representative of mankind), e.g. πάντων μέτρον ἄνθρωπός ἐστιν (119, 2).

N o t e 2. — However, the predicate noun takes the article, whenever it is to be emphasized as quite definite, as previously mentioned or generally known, hence esp. with participles that are used as nouns, with ὁ αὐτός *the same*, τοὐναντίον, θάτερον (= τὸ ἕτερον), etc.

Αὐτὴ ἡ πολιτεία ἔκειτο τὰ ἆθλα the prize (belonging to a contest).

Οὗτός ἐστιν ὁ σώφρων, οὗτος ὁ ἀνδρεῖος the truly wise man, the very type of a wise man.

Οἱ ἄνδρες εἰσὶν οἱ ποιοῦντες, ὅ, τι ἂν ἐν ταῖς μάχαις γίγνηται are precisely those, who perform.

Ἐγὼ μὲν ὁ αὐτός εἰμι, ὑμεῖς δὲ μεταβάλλετε.

Note 3.—Proper names do not require the article. When the person spoken of is to be marked as identical with one that has been previously mentioned, or as one that is well known, the article is generally added to the person's name or to its apposition, if there be one.

E.g.   ὁ Σωκράτης or Σωκράτης ὁ Ἀθηναῖος.
        the (well-known) Athenian Socrates.

Note 4.—Names of countries, originally adjectives, as a rule, take the article.

ἡ Ἀσία, ἡ Εὐρώπη, ἡ Ἑλλάς, ἡ Ἀττική (sc. γῆ).

Note 5.—Names of rivers stand between the article and ποταμός; e.g. ὁ Εὐφράτης ποταμός the (river) Euphrates. Other geographical names also have the attributive position (120), if their gender coincides with that of their respective appellatives (ὄρος, πόλις), as τὸ Πήλιον ὄρος, but ἡ Αἴτνη τὸ ὄρος.

Note 6.— Words that signify parts of the body, virtues, vices, faculties, arts, size, descent, length, width, name, etc., are more frequently without than with the article.

The article is also omitted in very many familiar expressions : κατὰ γῆν καὶ κατὰ θάλατταν, ἐκ νέου, ἐκ παιδός (παίδων), κατ᾽ ἀγρούς ruri, ἐν δεξιᾷ, etc. etc.

120. A word has the **attributive position**, when it stands between the article and the noun, or after the noun with the article repeated.

ὁ ἀγαθὸς ἀνήρ the good man,

or ὁ ἀνὴρ ὁ ἀγαθός the man (and more particularly) the good man.

Thus ἡ τῶν Περσῶν ἀρχή, ὁ δῆμος ὁ τῶν Ἀθηναίων,

ὁ παρὼν καιρός, κατὰ τοὺς νόμους τοὺς κειμένους.

Δέδοικα μὴ ἐπιλαθώμεθα τῆς οἴκαδε ὁδοῦ.

Ὁ τόπος οὗτος ἐκαλεῖτο Ἀρμενία ἡ πρὸς ἑσπέραν.

By means of the attributive position adverbs and adverbial phrases are used as adjectives. E.g.

τὴν ἄνω ὁδόν (cf. " the above remark "), οἱ τότε ἄνθρωποι (cf. " the then president "), ἡ οἴκαδε ὁδός, ἡ πρόσθεν φιλία, —

τοὺς οἴκοι στασιώτας — τὸ ἐν Πλαταιαῖς ἔργον.

Note. — Dependent genitives (for partitives, see 145, 1) are not confined to the attributive position. Thus besides ἡ τῶν Περσῶν ἀρχή, τῶν Περσῶν ἡ ἀρχή and ἡ ἀρχὴ τῶν Περσῶν are equally good.

121. A word has the **predicate position**, when it stands b e f o r e the article, or follows the noun without an additional article. See 145, 1.

ἀγαθὸς ὁ ἀνήρ or ὁ ἀνὴρ ἀγαθός (*sc.* ἐστίν or ὤν),
the man is good or *the man, who (when, etc. . . . he) is good.*
Εἶχον πάντες τὰς ἀσπίδας ἐκκεκαλυμμένας.

Note.—Compare in English: The law makes a difference between things stolen and things found.

122. A change of position sometimes changes the meaning. Hence :

1. ὁ αὐτὸς βασιλεύς *the same king, idem rex,*
ὁ βασιλεὺς αὐτός ⎫
αὐτὸς ὁ βασιλεύς ⎬ *the king himself, rex ipse ;* 127.

2. ἡ μέση πόλις *the middle city* (between two others),
ἡ πόλις μέση ⎫
μέση ἡ πόλις ⎬ *the middle (center) of the city.*

3. τὸ ἄκρον ὄρος *the high, peaked mountain,*
τὸ ὄρος ἄκρον ⎫
ἄκρον τὸ ὄρος ⎬ *the top, brow of the mountain.*

4. ἡ ἐσχάτη νῆσος *the farthest, most distant of several islands,*
ἡ νῆσος ἐσχάτη ⎫
ἐσχάτη ἡ νῆσος ⎬ *the end, extremity, edge of the island.*

123. Πᾶς (**ἄπας, σύμπας, ὅλος**) mean :

1. when qualifying a noun **with the article** — in which case a d e f i n i t e object is referred to —

a) in p r e d i c a t e position : *all.*
πᾶσα ἡ πόλις ⎫
ἡ πόλις πᾶσα ⎬ *all the city, the (this) whole city.*
πᾶσαι αἱ πόλεις ⎫
αἱ πόλεις πᾶσαι ⎬ *all the (these) cities (individually, severally).*

b) in a t t r i b u t i v e position : *whole, entire, total, complete.*
ὁ πᾶς ἀριθμός *the sum total, the whole number.*
ἡ πᾶσα πόλις *the entire city, the whole of the city (the city in its totality,* opp. *the various parts of the city).*
αἱ πᾶσαι πόλεις *the union (confederation) of cities, the United Cities (all the cities collectively),*
hence οἱ πάντες, τὰ σύμπαντα (with numbers): *in all, all told.*

2. when qualifying a noun **without the article** — here an i n d e f i nite object is referred to —
every, any, all, whole, nothing but, extreme, absolute, utter, sheer.

πᾶσα πόλις ⎱ *a whole city; every (any) city.*
πόλις πᾶσα ⎰

πᾶσαι πόλεις *whole cities; any (number of) cities imaginable,
all the cities imaginable.*

Πᾶσαν ὑμῖν τὴν ἀλήθειαν ἐρῶ. — Οὐδὲ οἱ πάντες ἄνθρωποι.

Εἰς πάντας τοὺς θεοὺς καὶ εἰς ἅπασαν τὴν πόλιν ἡμαρτήκασιν.

Εἴ που διακοπείη ἡμῶν ἡ φάλαγξ, τῇ ὅλῃ φάλαγγι κακὸν ἔσται.

Ναῦς διέφθειραν τὰς πάσας ἐς διακοσίας *in all.*

Τῷ γὰρ καλῶς πράσσοντι πᾶσα γῆ πατρίς. See An. 2, 5, 9.

Πάσῃ τέχνῃ καὶ μηχανῇ *by every means and device.*

παντὶ σθένει *with all might, at full speed.*

πάντες ἄνθρωποι *"everything human," everybody, all the world.*

πᾶν ἀγαθόν *nothing but what is good.*

ἐν πάσῃ ἀπορίᾳ *in sheer want of everything, in utter want.*

124. By **prefixing the article** any word (adj., part., adv., inf.),
even parts of sentences or entire sentences can be used as nouns.
Thus the neuter of an adjective may supply an abstract noun.

τὸ ἀγαθόν, οἱ πολλοί, οἱ πλείονες, οἱ παρόντες,

οἱ νῦν,   οἱ πάλαι, τὸ ὅπως,   τὸ γνῶθι σαυτόν,

τὸ δίκαιον *justice,* τἀληθῆ *truth,* τὸ ἀναγκαῖον *what is (was,*
etc.) *necessary.*

Νέοις τὸ σιγᾶν κρεῖττόν ἐστι τοῦ λαλεῖν.

Note. — Here belong expressions like the following:

τὰ οἴκοι *the state of affairs at home, in one's country; home life.*

τὰ τῶν φίλων κοινά *the property of friends is common.*

τὰ πρὸς τὸν πόλεμον *what belongs to war; military matters.*

οἱ περὶ Κῦρον, οἱ ἀμφὶ Ἀριαῖον *Cyrus, Ariaeus and his men, followers, etc.*

τὸ τοῦ Δημοσθένους, illud Demosthenis, *that (word) saying of Dem.*

III. PRONOUNS.

125. 1. The **reflexive pronouns** (62) are used

a) **directly,** when they refer to the subject of that sentence
(or clause) in which they stand [*Direct Reflexives*],
as in : — γνῶθι σαυτόν *know thyself.*

Δίδωμί σοι ἐμαυτὸν δοῦλον καὶ σύμμαχον.

Ὁ σοφὸς ἐν αὑτῷ περιφέρει τὴν οὐσίαν.

b) **indirectly,** when they stand in subordinate (dependent)
clauses and refer to the subject of the principal
sentence (or clause) [*Indirect Reflexives*], as in :

Ὀρέστης φεύγων ἔπεισεν Ἀθηναίους ἑαυτὸν κατάγειν *to restore him.*

2. Instead of the **indirect** reflexive of the third person,

a) either the oblique cases of αὐτός may be used, in
which case the statement is taken objectively from the
point of view of the writer:

Λέγουσι Ξενοφῶντι, ὅτι μεταμέλοι αὐτοῖς (*se paenitere*).

b) or the forms οἷ (encl. οἱ) and σφίσιν (rarely σφῶν,
σφᾶς) are employed:

Κῦρος ἠξίου ἀδελφὸς ὢν βασιλέως δοθῆναι οἷ (*sibi*) ταύτας τὰς
πόλεις. — (ἐρίζοντά οἱ : An. 1, 2, 8).

126. Possessive pronouns. — The relation of property may be
expressed by the individualizing article (see 117, 1). But more
frequently this is done by means of the possessive pronouns and
the possessive genitive of the personal pronouns. See 64, 3.

Σοὶ τοῦτο δίδωμι, ὅτι μου τὴν μητέρα τιμᾷς.

Καὶ ὑμεῖς ἅπαντες τοὺς ὑμετέρους παῖδας ἀγαπᾶτε.

Κἀπὶ τοῖς σαυτῆς κακοῖσι κἀπὶ τοῖς ἐμοῖς γελᾷς.

Ἀστυάγης τὴν ἑαυτοῦ θυγατέρα μετεπέμψατο καὶ τὸν παῖδα αὐτῆς.

Μᾶλλον πιστεύετε τοῖς ὑμετέροις αὐτῶν ὀφθαλμοῖς ἢ τοῖς τούτου
λόγοις (cf. *vestra ipsorum opera*).

127. The **intensive pronoun** αὐτός admits of a variety of uses :

1. **self**, *ipse*, e.g. ὁ υἱὸς αὐτός *filius ipse, the son himself.*

2. in the oblique cases : *of him, of her, of it*, etc., *eius*, etc. It
never heads a sentence. ὁ υἱὸς αὐτοῦ *filius eius, his son;* στέργω
αὐτόν *I love him.* See 61. 63.

3. with the article : *the same, idem,* ὁ αὐτὸς υἱός.

4. καὶ αὐτός (*et ipse*) means : *himself, himself too, likewise, in
turn.*

Σοφοῖς ὁμιλῶν καὐτὸς ἐκβήσῃ σοφός.

5. with ordinal numbers αὐτός assigns to a person a prominent
place among others :

τρίτος αὐτός *himself the third* = *he with two others.*

Στρατηγὸς ἦν Ξενοκλείδης πέμπτος αὐτός.

6. for αὐτοῖς ἀνδράσιν and ὁ αὐτός τινι see 158, 3.

128. Demonstrative pronouns (see 65).

1. Ὅδε *this one* (*here* or *there*), points ahead to what is present,
what is before and connected with one's self, or to what
follows.

Οὗτος *this, that, the said,* points back to what has been previously mentioned, to what precedes.

Ἐκεῖνος that, yonder, that — yonder, that — over there, points to things absent or remote in reality or only in thought.

ἥδε ἡ ἡμέρα this (the present) day, τόδε τὸ ὄρος the m. before me (or us). ἥδε ἡ χείρ (this) my hand, this hand of mine.

Τεκμήριον δὲ τούτου (i.e. of what was said) καὶ τόδε (the following). Ταῦτα μὲν δὴ σὺ λέγεις, παρ᾽ ἡμῶν δὲ ἀπάγγελλε τάδε.

Τοιόσδε and τοιοῦτος, τοσόσδε and τοσοῦτος, ὧδε and οὕτως etc. are to be distinguished as ὅδε and οὗτος.

Κλέαρχος μὲν τοσαῦτα εἶπε· Τισσαφέρνης δὲ ὧδε ἀπεκρίνατο.

2. Observe that ὅδε (like hic) points to what concerns and is near (in place, time or thought) the person speaking, οὗτος (like iste) to what concerns the person spoken to, ἐκεῖνος (like ille) to what is remote in some way or other with respect to the person speaking. Moreover, these pronouns must often be rendered by adverbs.

ὅδε ἕστηκα here I am (stand). — Ἡρόμην, ὅπου αὐτὸς εἴη. Οὗτος, ἔφη, ὄπισθεν προσέρχεται there he comes behind you. Νῆες ἐκεῖναι ἐπιπλέουσι ships are coming yonder. (Note the omission of the article in cases such as this.)

Note 1. — "He who," "that which" are expressed by οὗτος ὅς, as in: οὗτος ὃς λέγει, or ὁ with the participle (201), as in: ὁ λέγων.

Αἱρεῖσθε τὸν ἐροῦντα him, the person, who is to speak.

Note 2. — καὶ οὗτος is sometimes used in the sense of καὶ αὐτός et ipse, ipse quoque (127, 4); so also, though less frequently, καὶ ἐκεῖνος: too, likewise.

Ἀγίας καὶ Σωκράτης καὶ τούτω ἀπεθανέτην A. and S. too.

Note 3. — καὶ οὗτος (= et is, atque is) introduces an additional qualification to a noun previously mentioned, καὶ ταῦτα (= idque) adds a supplementary remark to a previous statement: and that too, and besides, and yet, although.

Ἀπόρων ἐστὶ καὶ ἀμηχάνων, καὶ τούτων πονηρῶν, . . . and that too, besides.
Μένωνα οὐκ ἐζήτει, καὶ ταῦτα παρ᾽ Ἀριαίου ὢν τοῦ Μένωνος ξένου although.

129. Relative pronouns and adverbs (66. 68. 69).

1. ὅς who, that, which, what, and the other simple relatives (οἷος, ὅσος, οὗ, ὅτε, ὡς) point to some **definite** object (individualizing force: limited signification).

ὅστις whoever, whichever, whatever, and the other compound relatives (ὁπ. . . . .) point either to some **quality** of a person (or thing) or to a whole **class** (generic force: unlimited signification).

Ἔστιν Δίκης ὀφθαλμός, ὃς τὰ πάνθ᾽ ὁρᾷ.

Μακάριος, ὅστις οὐσίαν καὶ νοῦν ἔχει.

Note 1. — Therefore ὅστις (not ὅς) is always used after negatives:
οὐκ ἔστιν ὅστις, οὐδείς ἐστιν ὅστις, τίς ἐστιν ὅστις; likewise πᾶς ὅστις any person who (plur. πάντες ὅσοι as many as).

Note 2. — Note the following idiomatic expressions:

ἔστιν ὅστις	some, ἔστιν ὅτε sometimes ἔστιν οὗ somewhere, here and there,
ἔστιν ᾧ	to some, ἔστιν οἱ and εἰσὶν οἱ some, sunt qui, nonnulli.

Ἔστιν ὅτε καὶ οἷς βέλτιον τεθνάναι ἢ ζῆν *sometimes and for some death is better than life.*

Note 3.— ὅς has demonstrative force (116) in καὶ ὅς (*and*) *he,* ἦ δ' ὅς *said he.*
Οὐδεὶς ἀντέλεγε, καὶ ὃς ἡγεῖτο . . . *no one contradicted; whereupon he advanced.*
ὅσπερ points to things that are k n o w n : *qui quidem.* An. 3, 2, 10. (See 66, 2.)
ὅσγε adds at once a r e a s o n : *quippe qui.* An. 1, 6, 5.

2. A relative pronoun, whose antecedent is in the g e n i t i v e or d a t i v e case, is often put in the s a m e case instead of in the a c c u s a - t i v e.   This is called **assimilation** or attraction of the r e l a t i v e p r o - n o u n.   If the antecedent is a d e m o n s t r a t i v e, it is dropped; if a n o u n, it is usually placed, w i t h o u t the article, at the e n d of the relative clause.   For example : οὐδὲν ὧν = οὐδὲν τούτων ἅ.

Ἄξιοι ἔσεσθε τῆς ἐλευθερίας, ἧς κέκτησθε *of the liberty you enjoy.*
Οἱ χρησμῳδοὶ ἴσασιν οὐδὲν ὧν λέγουσιν *nothing of what they say.*
Νῦν ἐπαινῶ σε ἐφ' οἷς λέγεις τε καὶ πράττεις *for what you say.*
Τούτους ἄρχοντας ἐποίει ἧς κατεστρέφετο χώρας *rulers of whatever land he conquered.*
Ἡριππίδας ἐπορεύετο σὺν ᾗ εἶχε δυνάμει *with what force he had.*

Note. — The antecedent (a noun or a pronoun) is sometimes assimilated to the relative.   This is called *inverted assimilation.*
Ἀνεῖλεν αὐτῷ ὁ Ἀπόλλων θεοῖς οἷς ἔδει θύειν.

3. When two (or several) relative clauses follow in succession, and the case of the second relative pronoun differs from that of the first, it is either dropped or replaced by αὐτός (less frequently by οὗτος or ἐκεῖνος) or a personal pronoun is used.

Ἀριαῖος, ὃν ἡμεῖς ἠθέλομεν βασιλέα καθιστάναι, καὶ (*sc.* ᾧ) ἐδώκα-
μεν καὶ (*sc.* παρ' οὗ) ἐλάβομεν πιστά, ἡμᾶς κακῶς ποιεῖν πειρᾶται.
Ποῦ δὴ ἐκεῖνός ἐστιν ὁ ἀνήρ, ὃς συνεθήρα ἡμῖν, καὶ σὺ μάλα ἐθαύμα-
ζες αὐτόν;
Καὶ νῦν τί χρὴ δρᾶν; ὅστις ἐμφανῶς θεοῖς ἐχθαίρομαι, μισεῖ δέ μ'
Ἑλλήνων στρατός.

130. Interrogative pronouns and adverbs (67 ; 69).
τίς, ποῖος, πόσος, ποῦ, πότε, πῶς are used directly and indi- rectly.
ὅστις, ὁποῖος, ὁπόσος, ὅπου, ὁπότε, ὅπως are used in indirect questions only.
Τίς τε καὶ πόθεν πάρει ;
Μάθε πρῶτον, τίνες εἰσίν.   Οὐκ ἴστε ὅ,τι ποιεῖτε.

Note. — Ὅς, ἥ, ὅ may take the place of the indirect interrogative pronoun. Ἀκούσατε, ᾧ τρόπῳ ὑμῖν ἡ δημοκρατία κατελύθη. — Compare 179, 1.

IV. THE CASES.

131. The Greek, like other kindred languages, originally had eight cases, but in course of time lost three of them: the ablative (*whence?*), the locative (*where? when?*) and the instrumental (*whereby? wherewith?*). The lost cases are made up for partly by the genitive, partly by the dative.

A. THE ACCUSATIVE.

132. The accusative is the case of the so-called direct or nearer object, which is either external to, and merely affected by, the action (ἐνίκησαν τοὺς πολεμίους), or internal to, and already implied in the meaning of, the action (τίνα νίκην ἐνίκησας;).

1. ACCUSATIVE OF EXTERNAL OBJECT.

133. Verbs that regularly take an external object in the accusative are called transitive, all others intransitive verbs. For verbs which are transitive in Greek, see the Lexicon.

Attention is here called to:

> do good (*harm*) to one εὖ (κακῶς) ποιῶ τινα,
> speak well (*ill*) of one εὖ (κακῶς) λέγω τινά,
> escape the notice of λανθάνω τινά (*secretly, unawares!*),
> swear, swear falsely by ὄμνυμι, ἐπιορκέω τινά.

Hence νὴ Δία yes, by Zeus; οὐ μὰ τοὺς θεούς no, by the gods.

am on my guard against, beware of φυλάττομαί τινα.

Οὐδεὶς ποιῶν πονηρὰ λανθάνει θεόν.

134. Even (originally) intransitive verbs, esp. such as express motion and are compounded with a preposition, are employed as transitives. *E.g.*

μένω wait, stay, remain,	τινά, τὶ wait for, am in store for, expect,
σπουδάζω⎫ am eager, in earnest,	τινά⎫ promote, further,
σπεύδω ⎭ press on, hasten,	τὶ ⎭ urge on, push,
πλέω sail, go by sea,	τὴν θάλατταν sail (*over*) the sea.

In like manner (cp. the English *to under-go dangers*):

> διαβαίνω ποταμόν, ὑφίσταμαι κινδύνους, ὑπερβαίνω ὄρος.
> παραβαίνει τοὺς νόμους, διέρχομαι τὴν χώραν, παραπλέω νῆσον etc.

135. Verbs that signify *to name, make, appoint* and the like take **two accusatives**, one of the **external object**, the other a **predicate** accusative. In the passive both accusatives become nominatives.

Δαρεῖος Κῦρον σατράπην ἐποίησε. Κῦρος στρατηγὸς ἀπεδείχθη.

136. The following verbs take **two accusatives** of the external object, one of the **person**, the other of the **thing** affected.

remind of, ask, question   (ἀνα-)μιμνήσκω, ἐρωτάω ⎫
demand from, ask for, exact   αἰτέω, ἀπαιτέω, πράττομαί ⎬ τινά τι.
deprive of, rob of   ἀφαιρέομαι, ἀποστερέω ⎭

Ἀναμνήσω ὑμᾶς τοὺς τῶν προγόνων κινδύνους.

Κῦρον αἰτήσομεν πλοῖα καὶ ἡγεμόνα.

Τὸν πάντα δ᾽ ὄλβον ἦμαρ ἕν μ᾽ ἀφείλετο.

Note 1.— In the **passive**, the acc. of the person becomes the subject nominative, that of the thing remains unchanged: Αἰάκης ἀπεστέρητο τὴν ἀρχήν.

Note 2. — For ἀποστερέω τινά τινος and ἀφαιρέομαί τινός τι see 147, 2. with note 2.

2. ACCUSATIVE OF INTERNAL OBJECT.

137. Sometimes a transitive or an intransitive verb takes an accusative of the internal object (**accusative of content** or **cognate accusative**). The object may be

1. a **noun** of k i n d r e d **etymology** or **meaning**. It is nearly always m o d i f i e d by an a t t r i b u t e (or a relative clause). The cognate accusative is more frequent in Greek than in English. (*Figura etymologica.* Compare: *vitam iucundam vivere, to live a pleasant life.*)

ταύτην τὴν στρατηγίαν στρατηγεῖν — κάλλιστον ἔργον ἐργάζεσθαι — δουλείας δουλεύειν, οἵας οὐδ᾽ ἂν δοῦλος οὐδείς —

Μέγιστα καὶ ἀνοσιώτατα ἁμαρτήματα ἁμαρτάνουσιν.

κινδυνεύω τὸν ἔσχατον κίνδυνον — τὸν ἱερὸν πόλεμον στρατεῦσαι — ἄπιμεν, ἥνπερ ἤλθομεν, ἢ ἄλλην τινὰ ὁδόν ;

Ζήσεις βίον κράτιστον, ἢν θυμοῦ κρατῇς.

Note. — The modifyin̨g attribute may be wanting in certain idiomatic phrases with pregnant meaning, as in φυλακὰς φυλάττειν to keep watch and ward, φόρον φέρειν to pay tribute, and some others.

2. or an **attribute** (sometimes a noun, sometimes the neuter of an adjective or pronoun) relating to a noun that is understood.

Ὀλύμπια νικᾶν = Ὀλυμπικὴν νίκην νικᾶν,

ἡδὺ γελᾶν to laugh heartily — δεινὰ ὑβρίζειν to commit an outrageous insult, πάντα νικᾶν, οὐδὲν φροντίζειν, τὰ ἄλλα ἐπιμελεῖσθαι etc.

Οὐκ ἔστιν ὅστις πάντ᾽ ἀνὴρ εὐδαιμονεῖ.

138. Many transitive verbs take **two accusatives**, one a c o g n a t e accusative, the other of the e x t e r n a l object. See 133.

Βασιλεὺς ἡμᾶς τὰ ἔσχατα αἰκίζεται.

Λακεδαιμόνιοι πολλὰ τὴν πόλιν ἡμῶν ἠδικήκασι καὶ μεγάλα.

ɪ

Note.— In the passive the acc. of the external object becomes the subject nominative, the cognate acc. is retained:

ἄλλην εὐεργεσίαν εὐεργετηθείς — οὐδὲν ἀδικούμενος.

3. GREEK ACCUSATIVE — ACCUSATIVE OF EXTENT — ADVERBIAL ACCUSATIVE.

139. The accusative is sometimes somewhat loosely used after verbs that express a state or condition, as well as after adjectives, in order to limit their application. (Accus. of limitation; **Greek Accus.** Compare: *os humerosque deo similis.*)

κάμνω τὴν κεφαλήν *suffer from my head, have a headache;*
κάμνω τοὺς ὀφθαλμούς *suffer from my eyes, have sore eyes.*

(τὸ) ὄνομα, γένος, εἶδος *by name, by birth — race, in appearance, in form.*

(τὸ) εὖρος, ὕψος, βάθος, πλῆθος, κάλλος *in breadth, . . . (its) breadth being . . .*

Βέλτιόν ἐστι σῶμά γ᾽ ἢ ψυχὴν νοσεῖν.
Τυφλὸς τά τ᾽ ὦτα τόν τε νοῦν τά τ᾽ ὄμματ᾽ εἶ.

140. The **accusative of extent** (of space and time) answers the questions: *how far?* (*for*) *how long?*

Τῆς Ἑλλάδος οὐ μεῖον ἢ μύρια στάδια ἀπεῖχον.
Ψευδόμενος οὐδεὶς λανθάνει πολὺν χρόνον.

Note 1.— τριάκοντα ἔτη γεγονώς *triginta annos natus 30 years old.*
    and: ἐνάτην ἡμέραν (*this being the ninth day* =) *eight days ago* (*before*).

Note 2.— The terminal accusative without a preposition (*whither?*) is found only in poetry.
In prose a preposition must be used; hence only εἰς Ἀθήνας *Athenas.*

141. Very many accusatives of content, of restriction and of extent have by frequent use become adverbs or adverbial phrases (**Adverbial Acc.**).

Οὐδέν *in no respect, not at all,*
τί *in what respect? why?*
πολύ *much, by far, multo,*
(τὰ) πάντα *in all respects, in every way, in all,*
(τὸ) πρῶτον ⎫ *in the first place,*
(τὴν) πρώτην ⎭ *at first,*
μακράν *far, a long way,*
τὶ *in any (some) respect, to some extent, at all,*

τἆλλα *in other respects, for the rest,*
τίνα τρόπον; — τοῦτον τὸν τρόπον, *in what manner? in this manner, thus,*
τὸ πρίν, τὸ νῦν *formerly; nowadays, at present,*
πολλά *in many respects, often,*
τὰ πολλά *for the most part, generally,*

ἀρχήν at all, at first, from the beginning,
τὸ λοιπόν for the rest, for the (in) future,
τὴν ταχίστην (ὁδόν) as soon as possible,

τὸ κατ' ἐμέ, τὸ κατὰ τοῦτον as far as depends on me (him), as far as I am (he is) concerned. 199, 5.
πρόφασιν professedly, pretendedly, ostensibly.

Note.— For the acc. absolute see 203, 4.

B. THE GENITIVE.

142. The Greek Genitive is partly **genitive proper** and partly represents the original **ablative** (*whence-case*) which denotes the source of an action. This can be either material (*separation — comparison — matter*) or mental (*cause*).

1. THE GENITIVE PROPER.

143. The **possessive genitive** with nouns and adjectives, as also after εἶναι, γίγνεσθαι (*to belong to, be owned by; to be the part, characteristic, in the power of; to betoken, give evidence of* etc.) denotes the owner or author.

ἡ Κύρου στρατιά — τὸ τοῦ Σόλωνος τὰ τῶν Ἑλλήνων etc.
ἱερὸς ὁ χῶρος τῆς Ἀρτέμιδος — Κίμων Μιλτιάδου, Περικλῆς ὁ Ξανθίππου. — ἀπόρων ἐστὶ καὶ ἀμηχάνων.
ἐν Ἅιδου (sc. τῇ οἰκίᾳ), εἰς Ἅιδου. Compare: *at my brother's.*
Πενίαν φέρειν οὐ παντός, ἀλλ' ἀνδρὸς σοφοῦ — but ἐμόν ἐστιν.

Compare : *cuiusvis hominis est errare* — but *meum est.*

144. The **objective genitive**, which denotes the object of an action or feeling, is used

1. with nouns which denote an action (compare *cupiditas gloriae*):
ἡ τῆς πατρίδος σωτηρία — ἡ ἐπιθυμία ἡδονῶν,
τὸ μῖσος Παυσανίου the hatred of (*felt against*) P. (subj. *hatred of* [*felt by*] *Paus.*),
βίᾳ τῶν πολιτῶν *against the will of the citizens,*
δι' αἰσχύνην ἀλλήλων καὶ Κύρου *from a sense of shame before.*

2. with judicial verbs, nouns and adjectives that denote a charge or crime. *E.g.*
to accuse of, charge with αἰτιάομαι, γράφομαί τινά τινος.
to convict, detect one doing, catch in αἱρέω τινά τινος — ἁλίσκομαί τινος.
guilty of αἴτιος, ἀναίτιός τινος.
Ἐάν τις ἁλῷ τῆς κακώσεως τῶν γονέων, δεδέσθω.

3. with verbs and adjectives expressing the following notions (and their opposites):

desire : ἐπιθυμέω, ἐράω, ἐφίεμαι, ὀρέγομαί τινος.

knowledge : ἔμπειρος, ἄπειρος, ἐπιστήμων τινός.

memory : μέμνημαι, μνήμων — ἐπιλανθάνομαί τινος.

concern : ἐπιμέλομαι, φροντίζω — ἀμελέω τινός,

    μέλει μοί τινος — ἐπιμελής, ἀμελής τινος.

participation : κοινωνέω, μετέχω — μεταδίδωμί τινος.

power : ἄρχω, βασιλεύω — κύριος, ἐγκρατής τινος, see 148, 2.

plenty : ἐμπίμπλημι, πληρόω — πλήρης, μεστός, κενός τινος.

  Ὁ γραμμάτων ἄπειρος οὐ βλέπει βλέπων.

  Ἄνθρωπος ὢν μέμνησο τῆς κοινῆς τύχης.

4. after verbs that signify :

to seize, grasp, touch : λαμβάνομαι, ἅπτομαί τινος.

to cling : ἔχομαι, — *hit, find :* τυγχάνω τινός.

to obtain : λαγχάνω, — *miss, lose :* ἁμαρτάνω τινός.

to be mistaken, disappointed : ψεύδομαι, *experience :* πειράομαί τινος.

  Ἐλάβετο τῆς χειρὸς αὐτοῦ.

  Ἐσφάλημεν τῆς δόξης. Πολλῶν κακῶν πεπειράμεθα.

Note. — With many of the verbs that belong to 3 and 4, the objective genitive is at the same time partitive.

145. 1. The **partitive genitive** is the genitive of the **whole** of which a part is taken. It has nearly always the predicate position (121). It is more frequent in Greek than in Latin, and may be used wherever there is an expressed or implied relation of whole to part.

  τῶν ἀνθρώπων οἱ σοφοί — (but only οἱ θνητοὶ ἄνθρωποι) —

  ὁ ἄριστος ἁπάντων — τίς ἡμῶν — οὐδεὶς αὐτῶν —

  Θῆβαι τῆς Βοιωτίας — ποῦ γῆς ; *ubi terrarum?* —

  ὀψὲ τῆς ἡμέρας — εἰς τοῦθ᾽ ὕβρεως (*eo vecordiae*).

  Ἀριστεὺς ἤθελε καὶ αὐτὸς τῶν μενόντων εἶναι.

2. Accordingly, the partitive genitive may be dependent upon any verb, if its action affects only a part and not the whole of the object. It follows, therefore, especially

a) verbs that signify *to eat, to drink, to take, to taste,* if only part of the food etc. is taken.

  Τῶν κηρίων ὅσοι ἔφαγον, πάντες ἄφρονες ἐγίγνοντο.

  Ὀλίγοι σίτου ἐγεύσαντο. — but : Σωκράτης τὸ φάρμακον ἔπιεν.

b) verbs and adjectives that signify participation or fulness. See 144, 3.

Note 1. — καινόν τι (*aliquid novi*) [not: καινοῦ τι],

  οὐδὲν ἀγαθόν (*nihil boni*) [not: οὐδὲν ἀγαθοῦ].

Note 2. — When a partitive genitive depends on a numeral adjective, the latter agrees in gender with the genitive:

ὁ λοιπὸς τοῦ χρόνου — τῆς γῆς τὴν πολλήν — τοῦ σίτου τὸν ἥμισυν.

146. The **genitive of quality** is used almost exclusively with definite numbers to express size or age. An. 1, 2, 8.

Τριῶν ἡμερῶν ὁδόν — τεῖχος εὖρος εἴκοσι ποδῶν, ὕψος δὲ ἑκατόν — Πρόξενος ἦν, ὅτε ἀπέθνῃσκεν, ἐτῶν ὡς τριάκοντα.

Note. — In other instances, quality is expressed by the Greek accusative. 139 sq.

2. THE GENITIVE WITH ABLATIVE FORCE.

147. The genitive of separation is used with verbs (and adjectives of kindred meaning) that signify

1. *to separate, remove, free* and the like.

Here belongs: φείδομαί τινος *I spare.*

Ἀπέχει ἡ Πλάταια τῶν Θηβῶν σταδίους ἑβδομήκοντα.

2. *to deprive, be in want of, need* and the like.

Note in particular: δεῖ μοί τινος *I need something.*

Ὁ μηδὲν ἀδικῶν οὐδενὸς δεῖται νόμου.

Note 1. — "*I ask something of some one*" means δέομαί τινός τι, if the thing asked for is expressed by a neuter adjective or pronoun. Otherwise, αἰτῶ with two accusatives is generally used.

E.g. Ὑμῶν δεόμεθα ταῦτα, but: Κῦρον ᾔτησαν μισθόν.

Note 2. See 136. — Ἀφαιρέομαι takes also τινός τι.

3. *to begin* and *to cease :*

ἄρχω *I begin* (what *others* continue): τοῦ λόγου *open the discussion.*
ἄρχομαι (*I begin* what I *myself* continue): τοῦ λόγου *my speech.*
ἄρχομαι ἀπό, ἔκ τινος *from, with, at :* ἀπὸ or ἐκ τῶν θεῶν.
παύω *cause to stop,* τινά τινος *restrain, prevent ; depose, divest* (ἀρχῆς).
παύομαι, λήγω τινός *quit, cease, desist from* (ὀργῆς).

Πειρᾶσθε σὺν τοῖς θεοῖς ἄρχεσθαι παντὸς ἔργου.
Ἔπαυσαν οἱ Ἀθηναῖοι Τιμόθεον τῆς στρατηγίας.

4. *to perceive, hear* etc., to denote the **person** who is heard :

ἀκούω,, μανθάνω, αἰσθάνομαι, πυνθάνομαι.

Ἀκούσεσθε ἐμοῦ πᾶσαν τὴν ἀλήθειαν.

Note. — The **thing** that is heard etc. is generally put in the **accusative.** There is, however, a difference between

ἀκούω, αἰσθάνομαί τι *I hear, learn, notice, perceive* something ; and
ἀκούω, αἰσθάνομαί τινος (persons or things) : *listen, harken, give heed, attend to, obey.*

Ἀκούσαντες τὸν θόρυβον οὐχ ὑπέμειναν.
Ἄκουε πάντων, ἐκλέγου δ᾿ ἃ συμφέρει.
Νέος ὢν ἀκούειν τῶν γεραιτέρων θέλε.

148. The **genitive of comparison** is used

1. with comparatives. It is equivalent to ἤ with a nom., acc., (gen.) or dat.

Σιγή ποτ᾿ ἐστὶν αἱρετωτέρα λόγου — cf. luce clarius.

Φιλεῖ δ᾿ ἑαυτοῦ πλεῖον οὐδεὶς οὐδένα.

Τοῦτο δ᾿ ἔξεστιν ἡμῖν μᾶλλον ἑτέρων.

2. with verbs and adjectives involving comparison, i.e. such as denote

superiority : περιγίγνομαι, στρατηγέω, ἡγέομαι (cf. 144, 3) etc. ;
inferiority : ἡττάομαι — ὑστερέω etc., am (come) later than (too late for).

῎Ανθρωπος ξυνέσει ὑπερέχει τῶν ἄλλων. — Οὐδενὸς ὕστερος.

Παυσανίας εἰς ῾Αλίαρτον ὑστέρησεν Λυσάνδρου.

Note. — κρατέω τινός: lord it over, am master of : κρατοῦσι πάντων οἱ θεοί
but κρατέω τινά: conquer, vinco : ἐκρατήσαμεν μάχαις Συρακοσίους.
ἡγέομαί τινος: am leader (head) of, command : στρατεύματος.
ἡγέομαί τινι: lead = guide, show the way to : ναυσίν.

149. The **genitive of material** denotes the material of which anything consists or is made, or the contents of anything. The Latin has here ex aliqua re.

παράδεισος παντοίων δένδρων, γέρρα δασειῶν βοῶν (β. here ox-hides).

Οἱ στέφανοι οὐκ ἴων ἢ ῥόδων ἦσαν, ἀλλὰ χρυσίου.

150. The **genitive of cause**, after verbs and adjectives denoting mental states, designates the person or thing that causes an emotion. (Comp. 159, 2.)   Also : οἴμοι ταλαίνης o te miseram.

εὐδαιμονίζω, μακαρίζω τινά τινος count one happy for,
χαλεπαίνω, ὀργίζομαί τινί τινος am angry with one on account of.

Εὐδαιμονίζω ὑμᾶς τῆς ἐλευθερίας, ἧς κέκτησθε.

151. The **genitive of price** denotes the price after verbs (and adjectives) that signify :

to buy : ὠνέομαι — to sell : πωλέω, ἀποδίδομαί τί τινος,
to value, to think worthy : τιμάω, ἀξιόω — ἄξιος, ἀνάξιος.

Τῶν πόνων πωλοῦσιν ἡμῖν πάντα τἀγάθ᾿ οἱ θεοί.

᾿Ιητρὸς γὰρ ἀνὴρ πολλῶν ἀντάξιος ἄλλων worth as much as.

Thus : πολλοῦ magno, dear — ὀλίγου, μικροῦ parvo, cheap, πλείονος, ἐλαχίστου etc. — μισθοῦ mercede, for money, for a salary. — τιμᾶσθαί τι πολλοῦ magno aestimare.

Note especially the phrase   περὶ πολλοῦ (πλείονος, πλείστου, παντός, οὐδενὸς) ποιεῖσθαι magni, pluris, etc., facere, to make much of, etc., to value highly, etc.

152. The **genitive of time** stands

1. *without an attribute*, in answer to the question : *at what time ?* (*General* statements of time !)

νυκτὸς καὶ ἡμέρας — θέρους aestate, χειμῶνος hieme,
τοῦ ἐνιαυτοῦ quotannis — τοῦ μηνός every month (117, 1. extr.).

2. *with an attribute*, in answer to the question : *since or within what time?*

πολλοῦ, πλείστου χρόνου for a long, very long time.
πέντε, δέκα ἡμερῶν within five, ten days.

153. The **genitive** is used with many verbs, one of whose component parts is a **preposition** that requires the genitive (162, 3). So especially with :

ἀπό : ἀποτρέπω τινός turn away from,　ἀπογιγνώσκω τινός despair of,
147　ἀφίστημί τινος cause to revolt from, ἀφίσταμαί τινος revolt from,
ἐκ, ἐξ : ἐκβάλλω τινά τινος banish,　ἐκπίπτω τινός am banished,
147　ἐξίστημί τινά τινος remove,　ἐξίσταμαί τινος depart, retire,

κατά meaning " *down upon, against,*" in a hostile sense :

καταγελάω τινός laugh at,　καταφρονέω τινός despise,
κατηγορέω " speak agt." = accuse,　καταψηφίζομαι "vote agt.," condemn,
πρό :　προαιρέομαί τινος prefer,　προκρίνω τινός praefero alicui,
148　προτίθημί τινος antepono alicui,　προΐστημί τινος praeficio alicui etc.

Πολλῶν κατέγνωσαν θάνατον (κατεγνώσθη θάνατος) μηδισμοῦ.

C. THE DATIVE.

154. The Greek dative has **two functions**, one of its own (**the dative proper**), the other representing the Latin ablative (**the dative of accompaniment, of means or instrument, the locative dative**).

1. THE DATIVE PROPER or OF INDIRECT OBJECT.

155. Very many (transitive as well as intransitive) verbs and adjectives[1] take **a dative of the person** (or thing) **to whom** anything is done. Most of the verbs of this kind govern other cases in English.

Ἡ μωρία δίδωσιν ἀνθρώποις κακά.
Νόμοις ἕπεσθαι τοῖς ἐπιχωρίοις καλόν.
Οὐκ ἔστιν οὐδείς, ὅστις οὐχ αὑτῷ φίλος.

Note. — εὔχομαί τινί τι wish one something : ὑμῖν ἀγαθά.
　　　εὔχομαι θεοῖς τι promise the gods : σωτήρια, δεκάτην,

[1] esp. βοηθέω τινί help,　　　δουλεύω serve,
ἕπομαι, ἀκολουθέω follow,　πείθομαι obey,
πιστεύω, πέποιθα trust,　ἀρκέω suffice, help,
ἀπειλέω threaten,　　πρέπει, προσήκει it becomes,
ὀργίζομαι am angry with (at),　συμφέρει it is of advantage.

or *implore the g. for, implore something from the g.*: σωτηρίαν, σώζειν.
φθονέω τινί τινος *begrudge one something* (150).

156. The **dative of advantage** (or disadvantage) designates the
person (or thing) for whose sake, benefit or a d v a n t a g e (disadvantage) anything is done or exists, at whose disposal it is etc.   So
especially with εἶναι and γίγνεσθαι. Εἰσὶν ἐμοί *sunt mihi, I have.*

Ἐνταῦθα Κύρῳ βασίλεια ἦν καὶ παράδεισος.

Ἕκαστος οὐχὶ τῷ πατρὶ καὶ τῇ μητρὶ μόνον γεγένηται, ἀλλὰ καὶ
τῇ πατρίδι.

157. Closely akin are the following varieties :

1. The **ethical dative** denotes in general the person who is m o r-
ally or mentally interested in an action.   In particular it
designates

a) the person who **desires** the performance of an action.

Τί σοι μαθήσομαι; *what do you want me to learn? — tell me, what . . .?*
Μή μοι θορυβήσητε *pray, do not raise an uproar.*
Τούτῳ πάνυ μοι προσέχετε τὸν νοῦν *I beg you to pay close attention to this.*

b) the person whose **feelings** (*joy, surprise, distress, impatience*) are awakened
by an action [often untranslatable].

Πῶς ἡμῖν ἔχεις; *how is our darling?* comp. *quid mihi Celsus agit? =* " *How
fares my Celsus?* "
Ὦ τέκνον, ἦ βέβηκεν ἡμῖν ὁ ξένος; *O daughter, is the stranger gone at length?*

c) the person with whose **mind** or **view** anything accords.

Οὗτως ἔχει σοι ταῦτα *such is the case — you understand?*
Ἡμῖν δ᾽ Ἀχιλλεὺς ἄξιος τιμῆς *in our opinion.*

2. The **dative of agent** denotes the p e r s o n a l a g e n t or author
of an action.   This dative :

is a l w a y s used with the verb. adj. in -τέος : ἡμῖν ποιητέον *nobis
faciendum est,* and
often with the passive, esp. the perf. pass. (instead of ὑπό with
the genit.):

τὰ ὑμῖν πεπραγμένα *your achievements — your policy.*
Ἐὰν ἐκεῖ νικῶμεν, πάνθ᾽ ἡμῖν πεποίηται.

3. The **dative of reference** : "*judging from the point of view of one
who,*" "*with respect to one (doing),*" "*when or as one* [*you*] . . .*"
Compare : *in universum aestimanti.*

Διαβάντι, εἰσπλέοντι (*as you sail in*), προϊοῦσιν.   An. 3, 5, 15 ; 6, 4, 1 ;
(Ὡς) συνελόντι εἰπεῖν.   [3, 2, 22.
Τῷ γὰρ καλῶς πράσσοντι πᾶσα γῆ πατρίς.

Likewise γίγνεταί μοι βουλομένῳ,　　　ἡδομένῳ,　　　ἀχθομένῳ,
I am pleased with it,　　　*glad of it,*　　　*vexed at it.*
Ἐπανέλθωμεν, εἴ σοι ἡδομένῳ ἐστίν *if you please.*

Note.—In the phrase ὄνομά μοί ἐστι (*mihi nomen est*), the name is always put in the same case as ὄνομα: Ἐμοὶ δ' ὄνομα κλυτὸν Αἴθων.

2. THE DATIVE OF UNION.

158. The dative of **union** and **accompaniment** denotes union, approach or concurrence, in both a friendly and a hostile sense. Here the English generally uses the preposition *with*.

1. It follows verbs, adjectives and adverbs to denote the person (or thing) with whom any sort of **union** (or its opposite) is entered into; thus esp.

διαλέγομαι *speak, converse,*　　　ὁμιλέω *associate, mingle,*
μάχομαι, πολεμέω *fight, make war,*　　σπένδομαι *make a treaty,*
ὁμολογέω, ὁμονοέω *agree,*　　　κεράννυμι, μείγνυμι *mix,*
κοινωνέω, μετέχω, μεταδίδωμι 144, 3.　　ἅμα, ὁμοῦ *together with,*

　χράομαί τινι *utor aliquo familiariter, am intimate with.*

　　Σοφοῖς ὁμιλῶν καὐτὸς ἐκβήσῃ σοφός.　"Αμα τῇ ἡμέρᾳ.
　　Θεῷ μάχεσθαι δεινόν ἐστι καὶ τύχῃ.

Note.—Πολεμεῖν and μάχεσθαι σύν τινι or μετά τινος mean:
　to fight with = *in alliance with one, as one's ally.*

2. It denotes **accompaniment** of military forces (mostly without σύν):
　　ὀλίγῳ στρατεύματι ἐφέπεσθαι *parva manu.*
　　δισχιλίοις ὁπλίταις στρατεύειν.

3. It stands with αὐτός "*together with,*" — "*even inclusive of,*" and: ὁ αὐτός τινι, "*the same as:*"
Μίαν ναῦν λαμβάνουσιν αὐτοῖς ἀνδράσιν *with all the crew—men and all.*
Ἐν ταὐτῷ ἦσθα τούτοις *at the same place as these.*

4. It is often qualified by σύν (163, 27): σὺν τοῖς θεοῖς.

3. THE INSTRUMENTAL USES OF THE DATIVE.

159. The dative (as instrumental case) is used like the **ablative** in Latin.

1. The **dative of instrument** denotes the means or instrument by which anything is accomplished. So especially with χράομαι: *use, employ; treat, deal with; have as.*

　　Οὐδεὶς ἔπαινον ἡδοναῖς ἐκτήσατο.
　　Χρῆται ἡμῖν βασιλεὺς ὅ,τι βούλεται.

2. The **dative of cause** denotes the m o t i v e or c a u s e.   So esp. with verbs denoting emotion.   See 150.

εὐνοίᾳ, ὕβρει, φθόνῳ, φόβῳ ποιεῖν τι *out of kindness* etc.

Ἀβουλίᾳ τὰ πολλὰ βλάπτονται βροτοί *suffer harm because of.*

Χαλεπῶς ἔφερον οἱ στρατιῶται τοῖς παροῦσι πράγμασιν.

N o t e.—Ἐπί is often added to this dative in connection with verbs denoting emotion.   θαυμάζειν ἐπὶ ποιήσει, μέγα φρονεῖν ἐπ' ἀρετῇ etc.

Χαίρειν ἐπ' αἰσχραῖς ἡδοναῖς οὐ χρή ποτε.

3. The **dative of manner** denotes m a n n e r or a t t e n d a n t cir-cumstances.   It is generally accompanied by an attribute.

τούτῳ τῷ τρόπῳ, οὐδενὶ τρόπῳ *in this way, in no wise,*

τῇδε, ταύτῃ, δρόμῳ, βίᾳ, κραυγῇ, σιγῇ,

δημοσίᾳ *publice,* ἰδίᾳ *privatim,* κοινῇ *jointly,*

τῷ ὄντι, ἔργῳ *in deed, in fact, really,*

λόγῳ, προφάσει *avowedly, professedly, pretendedly* (141),

παντὶ σθένει *with all one's might,* πάσῃ τέχνῃ καὶ μηχανῇ *by every means and device.*

Οἱ Λακεδαιμόνιοι κρίνουσι βοῇ καὶ οὐ ψήφῳ.

4. The **dative of degree of difference** with comparative expressions denotes m e a s u r e or d e g r e e of difference: *by how much . . .*

πολλῷ (μακρῷ) κρεῖττον *much* or *by far better,* ὀλίγῳ ἐλάττους τρια-κοσίων,

πολλοῖς ἔτεσιν ὕστερον *many years later,* πόλει λογίμῃ ἀσθενέστερος.

ὅσῳ — τοσούτῳ: *quo — eo, the — the.*

N o t e. — Besides πολλῷ etc., the adverbial accusative (141) is often used: πολὺ χεῖρον, ὀλίγον πρότερον, as always οὐδέν, τί and τὶ (never οὐδενί etc.).

4. THE LOCATIVE DATIVE.

160. The dative (as locative case), which corresponds to the Latin ablative of place and time, is used

1. as **dative of place** in answer to the question: " where? "   In prose a prepo-sition (ἐν, παρά, ὑπό) is always added — except in the adverbial expressions τῇδε, ταυτῃ, ᾗ — κύκλῳ — and in the locatives Μαραθῶνι, Ἀθήνησιν (51).

2. as **dative of time** in answer to the question : " when? "

a) w i t h o u t ἐν (dates or names of festivals!):

ταύτῃ τῇ ἡμέρᾳ, τῇ ὑστεραίᾳ, τετάρτῳ ἔτει,

τῷ ἐπιόντι μηνί, Παναθηναίοις, —

b) with ἐν (= *during, within the space of, in the course of,* see 152, 2):

Ἐν ἔτεσιν ἑβδομήκοντα ἐξῆν σοι ἀπιέναι.

Ἐν νυκτὶ βουλὴ τοῖς σοφοῖσι γίγνεται.

Note.— To be distinguished: τὴν ἡμέραν (140), ἡμέρας (152), τῆς ἡμέρας (152), τῇ ἡμέρᾳ and ἐν τῇ ἡμέρᾳ.

161. The dative is used with verbs one of whose component parts is a preposition that requires the dative:

σύν : σύνειμι *am together with,*	συμμαχέω *fight in alliance with,*
158 : συμπονέω *toil together with,*	συμπράττω *work with, concur, help,*
ἐν : ἔνειμι *am in, at,*	ἐμμένω *abide by,*
160 : ἐμπίπτω *fall into,*	ἐντυγχάνω *come upon, find,*
ἐπί : ἐπιβουλεύω *plot against,*	ἐπιδίδωμι *give in addition,*
158 : ἐπιτίθεμαι *attack,*	ἐπιτρέπω *give up, commit ;*

less frequently after verbs compounded with παρά, ὑπό: πάρειμι, ὑπόκειμαι.

V. PREPOSITIONS.

162. 1. All prepositions were originally adverbs. Homer, Herodotus and the Attic poets still regard them as such, whilst in standard prose only πρός (*besides, in addition,* in : πρὸς δέ and πρὸς δὲ καί) is used adverbially.

2. As adverbial locative particles, the prepositions are frequently joined to the oblique cases in order to bring out more clearly, and define more plainly, their local meaning. Broadly speaking, prepositions

with the genitive ⎫　　　　　　　　⎧ whence? whereof?
with the dative ⎬ answer the question ⎨ where? wherewith?
with the accusative ⎭　　　　　　　　⎩ whither? how far?

3. In many cases, however, the Greeks took a different view of things from ours and, in consequence, expressed the same thought by means of different prepositions. Compare : στράτευμα συνέλεξεν ἀπὸ τούτων τῶν χρημάτων *with this money —* δεῖν ἐκ δένδρων *to tie up to trees —* ἐξ ἀριστερᾶς *on the left.*

4. USES AND MEANINGS OF THE PREPOSITIONS.

		GENITIVE	DATIVE	ACCUSATIVE
with one case	ἀντί	*instead of, for*		
	ἀπό	*from, away (down) from*		
	ἐκ, ἐξ	*out of, from, in consequence of*		
	πρό	*before, in behalf of*		
	ἐν		*in, at, during*	
	σύν		*together with*	
	εἰς			*to, into, against*
	ἀνά			*up along, over, through*

USES AND MEANINGS OF THE PREPOSITIONS. — *Concluded.*

		GENITIVE	DATIVE	ACCUSATIVE
with two cases	διά	through		owing to, thanks to, on account of
	κατά	down from; down upon, against		down along, over, according to
	μετά	with		after, post
	ὑπέρ	above, super, for, pro		beyond
with three cases	ἀμφί	about, de	about, on account of	about
	ἐπί	upon	upon, because of, for the purpose of	up to, against, towards, in quest of
	παρά	from beside, on the part of	by the side, near, at	alongside of, by and beyond, against, during
	περί	on, concerning, de	about, around	about
	πρός	by, from, on the part of	at, near, besides	towards, against
	ὑπό	from beneath, under, by (agent !), through	under, sub w. abl.	to a place and under, sub w. acc.

5. The **prepositional adverbs** take the genitive :

ἄνευ	without,	sine,	ἄχρι and μέχρι as far as, until,
ἐκτός	outside,	extra,	ἔξω out of, without,
ἐντός	inside,	intra,	εἴσω into, within,
μεταξύ	between,	inter,	ἐγγύς and πλησίον near, prope,
πλήν	except,	praeter,	πόρρω and πρόσω far from,
πέραν	on the other side,	trans,	πέρᾱ beyond, ultra,
ἔμπροσθεν	in front of, before,		ἕνεκα (ἕνεκεν) for the sake of, causā,
ὄπισθεν	behind, after,		ἐναντίον opposite, in presence of, coram,

ἑκατέρωθεν, ἀμφοτέρωθεν, ἔνθεν καὶ ἔνθεν from both sides, etc.

163. USES AND MEANINGS OF THE PREPOSITIONS.

1. **'Αμφί** with the ACCUSATIVE (Gen., Dat.) =περί with the acc., **about.**
   a) of PLACE: οἱ ἀμφὶ 'Αριαῖον, 124 note.
   b) of TIME: ἀμφὶ μέσας νύκτας *about midnight.*
   c) FIGURATIVELY : ἀμφὶ τὰ πεντήκοντα ἔτη *about, circiter.*

2. **'Ανά** with the ACCUSATIVE: **up, up along, over** (opp. to κατά).
   a) of PLACE: ἀνὰ τὸν ποταμόν, ῥοῦν *up the river.*
      ἀνὰ τὸ πεδίον, τὰ ὄρη *over, through, upon.*
   b) of TIME: ἀνὰ πᾶσαν τὴν ἡμέραν *all day long.*
   c) FIGURATIVELY : ἀνὰ κράτος *to the extent of one's power,* ἀνὰ λόγον *in due proportion.*
   d) DISTRIBUTIVELY : ἀνὰ πέντε *five each,* ἀνὰ πᾶσαν ἡμέραν *every day.*

3. 'Αντί with the GENITIVE: instead of, for, in return for.

αἱρεῖσθαι τὸ χεῖρον ἀντὶ τοῦ βελτίονος.

τιμωρώμεθα τοὺς ἄνδρας ἀνθ᾽ ὧν ὑβρίσθημεν.

4. 'Από with the GENITIVE: from, away from, off from.

a) of PLACE: ἀφ᾽ ἵππου *from the horse, on horseback,* ἀπὸ Σάρδεων.

b) of TIME: ἀπὸ τούτου τοῦ χρόνου *from (ever since) this time.*

c) FIGURATIVELY: καλεῖσθαι ἀπό τινος *to be named after one.*

means: στράτευμα συλλέγειν ἀπὸ τῶν χρημάτων *with.*

cause: ἀπὸ τούτου τοῦ τολμήματος *for, in consequence of.*

5. Διά with the GENITIVE: through (the midst of).

a) of PLACE: *per,* διὰ μέσης τῆς πόλεως *through the center of the city.*

inter, διὰ χειρῶν ἔχειν *in hand, to be working at.*

b) of INTERVAL: διὰ πέντε σταδίων *at a distance of.*

διὰ πολλοῦ (ὀλίγου) *longo interiecto tempore.*

c) of MEDIUM: *per,* δι᾽ ἑρμηνέως *through (the medium of) an interpreter.*

6. Διά with the ACCUSATIVE: on account of, owing to, by the help of.

mostly of CAUSE and AGENCY: διὰ ταῦτα *on this account, for this reason,* διὰ προδοσίαν, διὰ ἡμᾶς *owing to us* (whether merit or demerit).

7. Εἰς (ἐς) with the ACCUSATIVE: into, against = *in* c. acc.

a) of PLACE: εἰς τὴν πόλιν *into the city,* εἰς πολεμίους ἰέναι *against.*

b) of TIME, limit: εἰς τὴν ἑσπέραν *"into eventide"* = *until (on, at, for, toward) the evening.*

or extension: εἰς τὸ λοιπόν *for (in) the future.*

c) FIGURATIVELY, purpose: διδόναι, χρῆσθαι εἴς τι *for.*

w. numerals: εἰς (τοὺς) ἑκατόν *about (to the number of) a hundred.*

8. 'Εκ, ἐξ with the GENITIVE: out of, from within, *ex* (opp. to εἰς).

a) of PLACE: ἐκ τῆς πόλεως φεύγειν, ἐκ τῆς γῆς φύεσθαι.

b) of TIME: ἐκ παίδων *from childhood,* ἐκ παλαιοῦ *from ancient times.*

ἐκ τούτου *from (after) that time, thereupon,* ἐξ οὗ *ex quo, since.*

c) FIGURATIVELY, congruity: ἐκ τῶν παρόντων *as the state of things would require.*

consequence: ἐκ τούτων *in consequence of this.*

manner: ἐκ παντὸς τρόπου *in every possible manner.*

9. 'Εν with the DATIVE: in, within, at, on, *in* c. abl.

a) of PLACE: ἐν Ἀθήναις, ἐν τοῖς Ἕλλησιν *among.* πεφευγέναι ἐν τοῖς ὀχυροῖς.

ἄτιμος ἐν τοῖς στρατιώταις, ἐν τῷ Εὐξείνῳ Πόντῳ, *on (by) the shore of.*

b) of TIME: ἐν νυκτί, ἐν ταῖς σπονδαῖς *during,* 160, 2.

c) FIGURATIVELY: ἐν φόβῳ εἶναι, ἐλπίδας ἔχειν ἔν τινι.

10. 'Επί with the GENITIVE: upon.

a) of PLACE, where?: ἐφ᾽ ἅρματος ὀχεῖσθαι, — ἐπὶ τοῦ ὄρους *on top of.*

whither?: ἐπὶ Ἰωνίας, ἐπ᾽ οἴκου ἀπιέναι *in the direction of, towards.*

b) of Time: ἐπὶ Κροίσου βασιλεύοντος *during (in) the reign*.

ἐπ' ἐμοῦ *me vivente*, οἱ ἐφ' ἡμῶν *our contemporaries*.

c) Figuratively: ἐφ' ἑαυτοῦ *by himself, alone*, ἐπὶ καιροῦ *as circumstances suggested*.

d) Distributively: ἐπὶ τεττάρων πορεύεσθαι *four men deep*.

11. **Ἐπί** with the Dative: **upon.**

a) of Place, where?: ἐπὶ ναυσίν, πόλις ἐπὶ τῇ θαλάττῃ οἰκουμένη *situated by the seaside*.

b) of Time, " *immediately after* " : ἐπὶ τῷ τρίτῳ σημείῳ, ἐπὶ τούτοις.

c) Figuratively, charge: οἱ ἐπὶ τῷ στρατεύματι, οἱ ἐπὶ τῇ πόλει.

dependency: ἐφ' ὑμῖν ἐστι *penes vos*, ἐπὶ βασιλεῖ γίγνεσθαι *to fall into the hands of*.

cause (with verbs denoting emotion 159, 2): χαίρειν ἐπ' αἰσχραῖς ἡδοναῖς.

condition: ἐπὶ τούτοις *on such terms*, ἐφ' ᾧ τε *on condition that*, 180, 2. d.

object: ἐπὶ θανάτῳ ἄγειν, ἐπὶ βλάβῃ, ἐπὶ τῷ κερδαίνειν *with a view to*.

in honor of: ἐπὶ Πατρόκλῳ, ἐπὶ Λεωνίδᾳ.

12. **Ἐπί** with the Accusative: **towards, against.**

a) of Place: ἐφ' ἵππον ἀναβαίνειν, ὁδὸς ἐπὶ Σοῦσα φέρουσα, ἰέναι, πορεύεσθαι ἐπί τινα, in both a friendly and a hostile sense.

b) of Time: ἐπὶ τρεῖς ἡμέρας, ἐπὶ πολὺν χρόνον *for the space of*.

c) Figuratively: object (*in quest of*): ἐπὶ λείαν (*praedatum*) ἐξιέναι, ἐφ' ὕδωρ πέμπειν *to fetch*.

13. **Κατά** with the Genitive: **down from, down upon = against.**

a) of Place: κατ' οὐρανοῦ, κατὰ τῶν ὀρῶν, τειχῶν ῥίπτεσθαι — οἰκεῖν κατὰ γῆς *beneath* (where?), δῦναι κατὰ γῆς *beneath* (whither?).

b) Figuratively: *down upon = against*: λέγειν κατά τινος, cf. 153.

14. **Κατά** with the Accusative: **down along, over** (extension), **according.**

a) of Place: κατὰ τὸν ποταμόν *down the river*, κατ' ἀγρούς *ruri*, κατὰ γῆν καὶ κατὰ θάλατταν. τοὺς καθ' αὐτούς *opposite*.

b) of Time: κατ' ἐκεῖνον τὸν χρόνον *in (at, during) that time*.

c) Figuratively, reference: τὰ κατὰ τὸν πόλεμον.

congruity: κατὰ δύναμιν *to the extent of one's power;* κατὰ τοὺς νόμους *according*.

manner: κατὰ τάχος — καθ' ἡσυχίαν *at leisure*.

κατὰ μικρόν *little by little, into small pieces*.

with numbers: ἀπέθανον κατὰ ἑξακισχιλίους ἄνδρας *about*.

d) Distributively, by: καθ' ἕνα *one at a time*, κατ' ἄνδρα *viritim*, καθ' ἡμέραν *day by day*, κατ' ἔτος, κατ' ἐνιαυτόν *every year*.

15. **Μετά** with the Genitive: (in company) **with, amid.**

attendance, company, alliance: εἶναι μετά τινος *to side with*, μάχεσθαι μετά τινος *in alliance with*, οἱ μετὰ Κύρου *C. and his followers*.

manner, attendant circumstances: μετὰ δακρύων, κινδύνων *amid tears, dangers*.

16. **Μετά** with the ACCUSATIVE: **after, next to,** *post, secundum.*
    a) of TIME: μετὰ τὴν μάχην, μετὰ ταῦτα, μεθ' ἡμέραν *at daybreak.*
    b) of RANK, SUCCESSION: θειότατον μετὰ θεοὺς ἡ ψυχή.

17. **Παρά** with the GENITIVE: **from (beside).**
    of PLACE: ἥκειν παρὰ βασιλέως, αἰτεῖν, μανθάνειν παρὰ φίλων.

18. **Παρά** with the DATIVE: **by (the side of), with.**
    of PLACE, esp. with names of persons: παρὰ Κλεάρχῳ εἶναι, παρὰ τοῖς
    Μήδοις καὶ ἐν τοῖς Πέρσαις.—παρὰ τῇ πόλει ὁρμίζεσθαι, παρὰ τῷ βωμῷ
    θύειν.

19. **Παρά** with the ACCUSATIVE: **to or towards, alongside.**
    a) of PLACE: πέμπειν πρέσβεις παρὰ Φίλιππον.
       παρὰ τὴν θάλατταν πορεύεσθαι, οἰκεῖν *alongside, on the shore of.*
    b) of TIME: παρ' ὅλον τὸν βίον *per totam vitam.*
    c) FIGURATIVELY:
       going by and beyond: παρὰ τοὺς νόμους, ὅρκους (opp. κατά) *against.*
       difference, *by:* παρὰ πολύ *by far,* παρὰ τοσοῦτον, παρ' ὀλίγον.
       compared with: παρὰ τοὺς ἄλλους εὔτακτος.
       in proportion to: παρὰ τὴν ἑαυτοῦ ῥώμην *on account of.*

20. **Περί** with the GENITIVE: **about, on, concerning,** *de.*
    λέγειν περὶ τῆς εἰρήνης, ἐρίζειν, φοβεῖσθαι περὶ τῆς ἀρχῆς.
    περὶ πολλοῦ, οὐδενός, παντὸς ποιεῖσθαι: 151.

21. **Περί** with the DATIVE: **about** (rare in prose).
    a) of PLACE: στρεπτοὺς περὶ τοῖς τραχήλοις ἔχειν.
    b) FIGURATIVELY: δεδιέναι περὶ πάσῃ τῇ πόλει *for.*

22. **Περί**: with the ACCUSATIVE: **about, around, near.**
    a) of PLACE: οἱ περὶ Κῦρον, περὶ τὰ ὅρια, περὶ τὴν πόλιν.
    b) of TIME: περὶ μέσας νύκτας, περὶ πλήθουσαν ἀγοράν.
    c) FIGURATIVELY: *in respect to, against:* ἁμαρτάνουσι περὶ ἡμᾶς.

23. **Πρό** with the GENITIVE: **before,** *ante,* and **for, in behalf of,** *pro.*
    a) of PLACE: πρὸ τῶν πυλῶν, τὰ πρὸ ποδῶν.
    b) of TIME: πρὸ τῆς μάχης, πρὸ ἡμέρας, οἱ πρὸ ἡμῶν.
    c) FIGURATIVELY, preference: πρὸ πολλῶν αἱρεῖσθαι, τιμᾶσθαι.
       in defence of: πρὸ τῆς πατρίδος μάχεσθαι *for* (see ὑπέρ).

24. **Πρός** with the GENITIVE: **from, on the part of.**
    a) of PLACE: ἔπαινον πρὸς ὑμῶν ἔχω, τὸ πρὸς ἑσπέρας τεῖχος,
       ἑστάναι πρὸς τοῦ ποταμοῦ *so as to face the river.*
    b) FIGURATIVELY: πρός τινος εἶναι *to side with* (*stare ab aliquo*), see 15.
       in swearing: ὀμνύναι πρὸς θεῶν *by the gods,* see 133.

25. **Πρός** with the DATIVE: **at, by, near.**
    a) of PLACE: πρὸς Βαβυλῶνι, πρὸς ταῖς πηγαῖς, τῇ ἀγορᾷ *at Babylon,* etc.
    b) FIGURATIVELY: *besides, in addition to* (cf. 162, 1): πρὸς τῷ ὑπάρχοντι
       πόνῳ, πρὸς τούτοις *besides this.*

26. **Πρός** with the ACCUSATIVE: **towards, against.**

a) of PLACE: πρὸς μεσημβρίαν, ἰέναι πρὸς βασιλέα as friend or as enemy.
σπονδὰς ποιεῖσθαι πρός τινα *with.*

b) of TIME: πρὸς ἑσπέραν *towards evening.*

c) FIGURATIVELY: *in regard to:* ἄθυμος πρὸς τὴν ἀνάβασιν, πρὸς ταῦτα
εἶπε *by way of answer.*
compared with: οὐδὲν τὰ χρήματα πρὸς τὴν σοφίαν *nihil ad.*
end, purpose: παιδεύεσθαι πρὸς ἀρετήν, λέγειν πρὸς χάριν.

27 **Σύν, ξύν** with the DATIVE: **with, cum.**

union, accompaniment $\left\{\begin{array}{l} \text{οἱ σὺν Φαλίνῳ } the \ followers \ of \ Ph., \ σὺν \ τοῖς \\ \text{ὅπλοις.} \\ \text{σὺν κραυγῇ — σὺν τῷ δικαίῳ.} \end{array}\right.$
attendant circumstances

aid: σὺν τοῖς θεοῖς *with the help, by the blessing of.*

28. **Ὑπέρ** with the GENITIVE: **over,** *super,* **in behalf of,** *pro.*

a) of PLACE: ὑπὲρ τῆς γῆς, γήλοφος ὑπὲρ τῆς κώμης ἦν.

b) FIGURATIVELY, *in behalf of:* στρατηγεῖν ὑπὲρ Φιλίππου.
in defence of: μάχεσθαι ὑπὲρ τῆς πατρίδος.
cause: ὀργίζεσθαι ὑπὲρ τῶν γεγενημένων.
(In the sense of περί with the GENITIVE only since Demosthenes.)

29. **Ὑπέρ** with the ACCUSATIVE: **beyond,** *supra, ultra.*

a) of PLACE: ὑπὲρ τὸν Ἑλλήσποντον οἰκεῖν.

b) of TIME: ὑπὲρ τὰ πεντήκοντα ἔτη γεγονώς *amplius annos 50 natus.*

c) FIGURATIVELY: ὑπὲρ δύναμιν *supra vires.*

30. **Ὑπό** with the GENITIVE: **under, beneath.**

a) of PLACE, *from beneath:* ὑπὸ γῆς ἦλθεν εἰς φῶς.
under: ὑπὸ γῆς οἰκεῖν, οὔτ' ἐπὶ γῆς οὔθ' ὑπὸ γῆς.

b) FIGURATIVELY ("*under the influence of*"), *in consequence, on account
of:* = *ab* with the passive: νικᾶσθαι ὑπὸ τῶν Ἑλλήνων, ἀποθνήσκειν
ὑπὸ φονέως *at the hand of,* κακὰ πάσχειν ὑφ' ὧν οὐκ ἔδει.
cause: ὑπὸ λύπης *through grief,* ὑπὸ λιμοῦ ἀπόλλυσθαι *to die of hunger.*
accompaniment: ὑπὸ σάλπιγγος *to the sound of trumpet.*

31. **Ὑπό** with the DATIVE: **under,** *sub* with the ABL.

a) of PLACE: ὑπὸ τῷ οὐρανῷ, ὑπὸ τῇ ἀκροπόλει *at the base of.*

b) FIGURATIVELY: ὑπὸ τυράννοις εἶναι, γίγνεσθαι *in the power of.*
ὑφ' ἑαυτῷ ποιεῖσθαι *to bring under one's control.*

32. **Ὑπό** with the ACCUSATIVE: **to a place and under,** *sub* with the Acc.

a) of PLACE: ὑπὸ τὰ δένδρα ἀπῆλθον, ὑπὸ τὸν λόφον *sub collem.*

b) of TIME: ὑπὸ νύκτα *sub noctem,* ὑπὸ τοὺς αὐτοὺς χρόνους.

33. **Ὡς** with the ACCUSATIVE: **to, towards** (with *personal* objects).

πρέσβεις ὡς βασιλέα πέπομφεν.

VI. THE VOICES OF THE VERB.

ACTIVE VOICE.

164. 1. Some verbs are both transitive and intransitive:

E.g.

ἄγειν	lead,	intr.	*march,*
αἴρειν	*lift up,*	"	*set out, set sail,*
ἐλαύνειν	*drive,*	"	*drive, march,*
καταλύειν	*unyoke,*	"	*halt, take up quarters,*
ὁρμᾶν	*urge on,*	"	*set out,*
τελευτᾶν	*bring to an end,*	"	*die,*
εἰς-, ἐμβάλλειν	*throw into,*	"	*invade : empty,*
ἐξιέναι (-ιέναι)	*send out,*	"	*empty, have an outlet,*
διαφέρειν	*carry across,*	"	*differ,*
ἔχειν	*have, hold,*	with adv.:	*be* (in a certain condition),
πράττειν	*do,*	" "	*be, do, fare.*

Note. — For transitive and intransitive tenses of the same verb, see 93.

2. Some active verbs serve as passives of other verbs.

E.g.

ἀποκτείνειν to kill :	ἀποθνῄσκειν (ὑπό τινος) to be killed,
ἑλεῖν or λαβεῖν take :	ἁλῶναι to be taken,
ἐκβάλλειν banish :	ἐκπίπτειν or φεύγειν to be banished,
εὖ λέγειν speak well of :	εὖ ἀκούειν to enjoy a good repute,
εὖ, κακῶς ποιεῖν τινα	εὖ, κακῶς πάσχειν (ὑπό τινος)
to treat well, etc.	to be treated well.

3. The active voice sometimes has a **c a u s a t i v e** meaning:

Κῦρος ἐξέκοψε τὸν παράδεισον καὶ τὰ βασίλεια κατέκαυσεν

Cyrus had the park cut down and the palace burnt.   Comp. *Caesar pontem fecit.*

MIDDLE VOICE.

165. 1. The middle voice denotes that the agent is acting **with reference to himself.** As this reference may have either an accusative — or a dative — or a dynamic signification, there are three kinds of the middle voice :

a) **the accusative middle**: the agent acts o n h i m s e l f, being at once the subject and the direct (*i.e.* accusative) object of the action. The Direct (Reflexive) Middle :

λούω wash,	λούομαι wash myself, take a bath,
γυμνάζω train,	γυμνάζομαι train myself,
ἐνδύω clothe,	ἐνδύομαι clothe myself, etc.

к

Some direct middles assume an intransitive meaning;

e.g. ἵστημι *place,* ἵσταμαι *place myself = stand,*
παύω *stop,*   παύομαι *stop myself = cease,*
φαίνω *show,*   φαίνομαι *show myself = appear.*

For the so-called Middle-Passives (M. P.), see 95, 3.

b) **the dative middle**: the agent acts for himself, for his own sake, his own advantage. The Indirect Middle or the Middle of Advantage. See 156.

αἱροῦμαι *take for myself, make my choice, choose,*
ἀμύνομαί τινα *ward one off to my own adv., defend myself agt.,*
μεταπέμπομαι *send for one sc. to come to me, summon to my presence,*
φυλάττομαι *watch one sc. lest he should harm me, am on my guard agt.,*
παρέχομαι μάρτυρας *sc. to give evidence in my own favor,*
λυώμεθα μώνυχας ἵππους *let us unyoke our horses,*
ἄρχω *begin* what others continue, ἄρχομαι *begin* my own work.
Ὁ νομοθέτης νόμους τίθησιν, ὁ δῆμος νόμους τίθεται *the people make their own laws.*

c) **the dynamic middle**: the agent effects some result by his own means (δυνάμει). Here the action involves some exertion, activity, effort on the part of the agent.

παρέχομαι *supply from my own means, furnish what is my own,*
σκοποῦμαι *look at closely, examine, search,*
πολιτεύω *am a citizen;* πολιτεύομαι *take part in the government,*
πόλεμον ποιῶ *bring about a war, bellum moveo,* but
 ποιοῦμαι *make, wage war, bellum gero,*
ἐπαγγέλλομαι *announce something done by myself, offer, profess.*

2. The middle too has often a **causative** meaning:

δανείζομαι *cause one to lend to myself,* borrow,
μισθοῦμαι *cause to be let to myself,* hire, bribe,
ποιοῦμαι ὅπλα *have arms made for myself,*
παρατίθεμαι δεῖπνον *have a meal served to myself,*
δικάζομαι *have my case tried,* go to law.

Note. — One verb may, of course, at the same time express several of the relations which belong to the middle voice.

PASSIVE VOICE.

166. 1. Also intransitive verbs form a personal passive.

E.g. ἄρχω τινός *rule (over) one,* ἄρχομαι *am ruled (over),*
κταφρονέω τινός *despise,* καταφρονοῦμαι *am despised,*
ἐπιβουλεύω τινί *plot against,* ἐπιβουλεύομαι *am plotted against,*

πιστεύω τινί *trust*,   πιστεύομαι *am trusted*,
φθονέω τινί *invideo alicui*,   φθονοῦμαι *mihi invidetur*.

Note. — The only impersonal passive of an intransitive verb (compare *itur, perventum est*) is δέδοκται *visum est, it has been agreed upon*.

2. With the passive, the agent is put in the genitive with ὑπό = *ab* c. abl., 163, 30. b.

Note. — Occasionally ἀπό, ἐκ, παρά and πρός with the gen. are used instead of ὑπό. For the dative of the agent in connection with the verbal adjective or the perf. passive, see 157, 2.

VII.   THE TENSES OF THE VERB.
THE TENSES IN GENERAL.

167. 1. The forms of the Greek verb simultaneously denote an action

a) as either past, present or future:
they express the **period of the action** ;
b) as either momentary, continuous or completed:
they express the **stage of the action**.

2. Every form of the verb is capable of denoting the **stage of the action.**   An action is therefore described by the forms

a) of the aorist stem :
as simply taking place (*no qualification being implied*), as commencing (*entrance upon a state*), as being (*successfully*) accomplished, in a word as **attained.**

b) of the present stem :
as going on and (*still, as yet*) in progress, as stopping short before its accomplishment (*the conative tenses!*), as repeated or customary, as qualified (*modality!*), as **continued.**

c) of the perfect stem :
as fully accomplished and resulting in a certain state, as still felt in its consequences, as lasting in its result, as **completed.**

φυγ- (*e.g.* εἶν): *to flee* [169, 4 *to have fled*] as a simple occurrence — *to take to flight* [inceptive] — *to flee* [successfully] = *escape;* Xen. An. 1, 3, 20.

φευγ- (*e.g.* ειν): *to flee = to be* [still, as yet] *fleeing* — *to attempt* etc. *fleeing* — *to flee* [repeatedly] — *to be under accusation; to be a fugitive, live in exile.*   An. 3, 2, 19.

πεφευγ- (*e.g.* έναι): *to have fled = to have* [already and fully] *accomplished the flight;* — *to be in safety, out of reach.*   An. 1, 4, 8.

Thus ἀποθνῆσκειν *to be dying,*   θαυμάζειν *to be wondering,*
ἀποθανεῖν *to die,*   θαυμάσαι *to (be struck with) wonder,*
τεθνάναι *to be dead.*   τεθαυμακέναι *to be full of wonder.*

κτᾶσθαι *to be acquiring,*   πίπτειν *to be (in the act of) falling,*
κτήσασθαι *to obtain possession of,* πεσεῖν *to fall, commence falling,*
κεκτῆσθαι *to be in possession of, own.* πεπτωκέναι *to have fallen, iacēre.*

3. The **period of the action** is expressed solely by the **indicatives:**
the present by the present and perfect,
the past by the aor., impf. and plupf. (**augment!** 73, 1),
the future by the future and fut. perfect.

Note. — For the infinitive and the dependent moods (subj., opt., imper.), see
169; for the participle, see 170.

4. Table in Illustration of the Meanings of the Tenses:

STAGE OF ACTION	PERIOD OF ACTION			STEMS
	Past	Present	Future	
Attainment	Indic. Aor.	——	Future	**Aorist** Stem
a) simple occurrence				(including the
(*histor.* sense)	ἀπέθανεν		ἀποθανεῖται	future and
b) entrance upon state				inchoative
(*ingress.* sense)	ἐβασίλευσεν	γηράσκει	βασιλεύσει	verbs)
Continuance	Imperfect	Present	Future	**Present** Stem
progress of action				(including the
(*durative* sense)	ἀπέθνησκεν	ἀποθνήσκει	βασιλεύσει	future)
Completion	Pluperfect	Perfect	Fut. Perfect	**Perfect** Stem
lasting results				
(*perfect* sense)	ἐτεθνήκει	τέθνηκεν	τεθνήξει	

Note. — There is no sequence of tenses in Greek, because the tense
of the leading verb never affects that of the dependent verb.

THE INDICATIVES.

168. 1. The **present indicative** and the **imperfect,** which represent
action as going on (**Durative Present — Durative Imperfect**),

 a) **describe** conditions, situations, customs, manners, characters,
  express repeated or customary action, denote general truths,
  detail attendant circumstances.

Πλοῖον ἐς Δῆλον ὡΆθηναῖοι πέμπουσιν (*every year*).

Ξενίας ὁ ὅΑρκὰς τὰ Λύκαια ἔθυσε καὶ ἀγῶνα ἔθηκεν · ἐθεώρει δὲ τὸν
ἀγῶνα καὶ Κῦρος.

 b) denote action that is prepared, intended, expected, attempted,
started, but not accomplished (**Conative Present — Conative Imperfect**).

ὅΕπειθον αὐτούς, καὶ οὃς ἔπεισα, τούτους ἔχων ἐπορευόμην *tried to p.*

Note 1. — There is, also, an Historical Present for lively narration

Ἐπεὶ ἐτελεύτησε Δαρεῖος, Τισσαφέρνης διαβάλλει τὸν Κῦρον.

Note 2. — A number of present tenses, besides denoting an action, at once involve persistence of result, and may in consequence be rendered by the perfect, and their imperfects by the pluperfect. Examples are

νικῶ conquer $\begin{cases} have\ conquered = \\ am\ victorious. \end{cases}$ ἡττῶμαι am conquered $\begin{cases} have\ been\ c. = \\ am\ inferior. \end{cases}$

ἀδικῶ do wrong $\begin{cases} have\ done\ wrong = \\ am\ to\ blame. \end{cases}$ μανθάνω learn $\begin{cases} have\ learned = \\ know\ (novi). \end{cases}$

Note 3. — The indicative of ἥκω am come, here and of οἴχομαι am gone, off has always perfect force, the other moods have perfect as well as aorist force.

2. The **aorist indicative** presents the following peculiarities (167).

a) **Historical Aorist.** — Being the tense of narration, it merely chronicles events that once came to pass.   It corresponds to the historical perfect in Latin.

Ἦλθον, εἶδον, ἐνίκησα veni, vidi, vici.

b) **Gnomic Aorist.** — It denotes a general truth gathered from experience.

Οὐδεὶς ἔπαινον ἡδοναῖς ἐκτήσατο.

Compare *Omne tulit punctum, qui miscuit utile dulci.*

c) The **Pluperfect Aorist** denotes an action as prior to another past action, especially in temporal and relative clauses.   It is therefore rendered by a pluperfect.

Ἐπεὶ ἐσάλπιγξε, προβαλόμενοι τὰ ὅπλα ἐπῇσαν.

Δαρεῖος Κῦρον μεταπέμπεται ἀπὸ τῆς ἀρχῆς, ἧς αὐτὸν σατράπην ἐποίησεν.

Note. — Sometimes the imperfect is thus used. It then brings out more forcibly continued or repeated action.

Κῦρος εἶδε τὰς σκηνάς, οὗ οἱ Κίλικες ἐφύλαττον had been watching.

Οἵπερ πρόσθεν προσεκύνουν, καὶ τότε προσεκύνησαν.

d) The **Ingressive Aorist** expresses the entrance upon a state or condition.

E.g.   ἐβασίλευσα became king,   ἠράσθην took a fancy to,
         ἐνόσησα fell sick, was taken ill,   ἐθάρσησα took heart,
         ἐδάκρυσα burst into tears,   ἐσίγησα became silent.

Διὰ μικρὸν ἐπολεμήσατε started a war.

Πεισιστράτου τελευτήσαντος Ἱππίας ἔσχε τὴν ἀρχήν.

Note. — All these aorists may, of course, be used also in the historical (2. a) sense:

ἐβασίλευσα was (once) king,   ἐνόσησα was (once) sick.

3. The **future indicative** denotes both the attainment (ingressive sense) and the continuance (durative sense) of a future action. Hence ἄρξω means both : *I shall obtain power* (ingress.), and : *I shall have power* (durat.).

Σκεπτέον μοι δοκεῖ εἶναι, ὅπως τὰ ἐπιτήδεια ἕξομεν.

Ὁ δίκαιος ἀνὴρ εὖ βιώσεται, κακῶς δὲ ὁ ἄδικος.

Note.—Μέλλω with the fut., pres. or aor. inf. means (see 111, 5):

a) *am about, willing to:*   μέλλω ὑμᾶς διδάξειν.

b) *am likely, expected to:*   ἀγορὰν οὐδεὶς ἔτι παρέξειν ἔμελλεν.

4. The **perfect, pluperfect** and **future perfect indicative** express action already completed, as well as the state resulting from it.

In the Present	Past	Future
ἕστηκα *stand* (100, 2),	εἱστήκειν *stood*,	ἑστήξω *shall stand*.
τέθνηκα *am dead*,	ἐτεθνήκειν *was dead*,	τεθνήξω *shall be dead*.
μέμνημαι *am mindful*,	ἐμεμνήμην *was m.*	μεμνήσομαι *shall be m.*

Ἀπολελοίπασιν (*are gone*) ἡμᾶς Ξενίας καὶ Πασίων, ἀλλ᾽ οὐκ ἀποπεφεύγασιν (*out of reach*).   Φράζε καὶ πεπράξεται.

Οὐ βουλεύεσθαι ἔτι ὥρα, ἀλλὰ βεβουλεῦσθαι (*plans should be ready*).

Note. — In Greek, therefore, the perfect is never historical perfect; the pluperfect does not describe an action merely as prior to another past action, 2 c ; the future perfect corresponds to the fut. perfect in Latin in independent sentences only ; for the dependent clauses, see 187, 2, I.

INFINITIVES AND DEPENDENT MOODS (Subj., Opt., Imp.).

169. 1. According to 167, 3, these forms of the verb do not imply the period of an action. They merely describe the stage of action, as explained in 167, 2. Thus, εἴπωμεν ἢ σιγῶμεν; means almost as much as : *shall we break, or continue in, our silence?*

2. The time of the action in this case is expressed by the tense of the principal verb : *e.g.*

λέγω ταῦτα }
εἶπον ταῦτα } ἵνα πεισθῆτε
ἐρῶ ταῦτα }
{ *in order that you may now obey,*
{ *in order that you might (at that time) obey,*
{ *in order that you may obey at some future time.*

3. Accordingly, the imperative of the

aorist: expresses one single instance of a command to be obeyed then and there ;

present: expresses either one single command — which is then viewed in its continuance — or a command to be obeyed continually or at least repeatedly ; hence also general rules and maxims of life.

Μεῖνον παρ' ἡμῖν καὶ συνέστιος γενοῦ.

Τοὺς μὲν θεοὺς φοβοῦ (*make it a rule ever to fear*), τοὺς δὲ γονέας τίμα, τοῖς δὲ νόμοις πείθου.

4. It is only in indirect discourse that the opt. and the infin. express the period of the action, as they then represent the corresponding indicatives of the direct discourse. In indirect discourse, therefore

> the aor. opt. and inf. denote a past action,
> the fut. opt. and inf. denote a future action,
> the pres. opt. and inf. denote either a present or
> (accdg. to 177, note) a past action.

ἔλεγον, ὅτι δοίη (αὐτὸν δοῦναι)   *that he had given* (ἔδωκε),
ἔλεγον, ὅτι δώσοι (αὐτὸν δώσειν) *that he would give* (δώσει),
ἔλεγον, ὅτι διδοίη (αὐτὸν διδόναι) *that he gave* (δίδωσιν), or
  that he had given (ἐδίδου).

Note.— The fut. opt. is never found except in indirect discourse and, consequently, always has a future meaning.

THE PARTICIPLES.

170. 1. The participles denote "relative time," *i.e.* they represent the secondary action as either contemporaneous with or antecedent or subsequent to the principal action expressed by the leading finite verb.   Accordingly, the secondary action is marked by

a) the **present** as contemporaneous with the principal action.

> Σοφοῖς ὁμιλῶν καὐτὸς ἐκβήσῃ σοφός.

b) the **aorist** as prior to the principal action.

> Δίκαια δράσας συμμάχους ἕξεις θεούς.

c) the **perfect** as finished and still lasting in its results at the time when the principal action takes place.

> Διαβεβηκόσι τοῖς Ἕλλησι (*the Greeks had already reached the other bank of the river, when*) φαίνεται ὁ Μιθραδάτης.
>
> Ἐσκεμμένα καὶ παρεσκευασμένα πάντα λέγω.

d) the **future** as subsequent to the principal action.

> Ὁ βάρβαρος ἐπὶ τὴν Ἑλλάδα δουλωσόμενος ἦλθεν (*in order*) *to subjugate it.*

2. The participles depend, therefore, for their time on the principal finite verb;

e.g. ταῦτα λέγων ἀκούει *while saying* (*while he says*) *this, he hears,*
ταῦτα λέγων ἤκουσεν *while saying* (*while he said*) *this, he heard,*
ταῦτα λέγων ἀκούσεται *while saying* (*while he shall be saying*) *this, he will hear,*

or   ταῦτ' εἰπὼν ἀποβαίνει (ἀπέβη, ἀποβήσεται).

VIII. THE MOODS OF THE VERB.

Introductory Notes.

171. 1. There are two main divisions of sentences:

a) such as contain a simple **statement** or assertion: (neg. *οὐ*).

b) such as express a **wish**, desire, command: (neg. *μή*).

2. The modal particle **ἄν**, which is often approximately rendered by: "*possibly, perhaps, if the opportunity should present itself*" (see 174, 2), is of frequent occurrence in statements, but rarely found in sentences of the second kind.

Note. — Position of *ἄν*. Ἄν is, as a rule, placed after its verb. Often, however, it is attached to some prominent word in the sentence, esp. to interrogatives, negatives, and adverbs. In relative and conjunctional clauses which require the verb to be in the subjunctive *ἄν* stands next to the relative or to the conjunction, with which it often forms one word (*ἐάν, ὅταν, ἐπάν, ἐπειδάν*).

A. MOODS IN INDEPENDENT SENTENCES.

172. The **indicative** mood expresses in general the relation of **reality** and, in consequence, has its proper place in declaratory sentences. In this the Greek is not at variance with our idiom. However, there are some uses of the indicative peculiar to Greek.

1. The **imperfect without ἄν** stands in certain impersonal expressions which imply ability, possibility, necessity, duty, propriety. In English we employ, as a rule, a different mood.

ἔδει, ἐχρῆν, προσῆκεν oportet, decet or oportebat, decebat,

it would be necessary etc.; you (one) should or ought —

it would have been necessary etc.; you (one) should or ought to have —

ἐξῆν, εἰκός, δίκαιον, ἀναγκαῖον ἦν aequum est, erat,

it would be possible, proper — it would have been proper —

you (one) might, you (one) might have —

προαιρετέον, παιδευτέον ἦν praeferendum est, erat,

you (one) ought to educate — you (one) ought to have educated.

The thought implied here (not so in 172, 3!) is this:

you ought etc. to do, but you do not,

you ought to have done, but you did not.

Τί σιγᾷς; οὐκ ἐχρῆν σιγᾶν, τέκνον *you ought not.*

Αἰσχρῶς κακὰ εἰργάσω τούτους, οὓς ἥκιστα ἔδει.

Note. — Ἔδει etc. may, of course, also denote reality (*it was necessary*). It has, therefore, three meanings: *it was necessary, it would be n., it would have been n.*

To denote a true case of unreality, ἄν must be added, according to 172, 3: ἔδει ἄν *it would be* or *would have been necessary*.

2. The **indicative of the historical tenses without ἄν** expresses an unattainable wish. It is preceded by εἴθε, εἰ γάρ, ὡς. The negative is μή.

a) The imperfect refers to the present.

b) The aorist refers to the past.

Εἴθε ἦσθα δυνατὸς δρᾶν, ὅσον πρόθυμος εἶ *O that you were able.*

Εἴθ᾽ εὕρομέν σ᾽ Ἄδμητε μὴ λυπούμενον *Would that we had found you.*

Note. — A hopeless wish may also be expressed by ὤφελον, -ες, -εν etc. with the present or aorist infinitive.

᾽Αλλ᾽ ὤφελε μὲν Κῦρος ζῆν *Would that Cyrus were alive.*

῾Ως ὤφελον πάροιθεν ἐκλιπεῖν βίον *O that I had departed life before.*

3. The **indicative of the historical tenses with ἄν** may express unreality. The negative is μή.

a) The imperfect with ἄν refers to the present:

ἔλεγον ἄν *dicerem I should say* (but now I do not say).

b) The aorist with ἄν refers to the past:

ἔλεξα ἄν ⎫ *dixissem I should have said*
εἶπον ἄν ⎭ (but I did not say).

Examples are given in 185.

4. Again, the **indicative of the historical tenses with ἄν** may express past potentiality. "**The Potential Indicative.**"

ἔλεγεν (εἶπεν) ἄν τις *diceres one (you) might have said;*

θᾶττον ἢ ὡς τις ἂν ᾤετο *faster than you would have believed.*

Εἴ τις Κλεάρχῳ δοκοίη βλακεύειν, ἔπαισεν ἄν *he would sometimes apply the cane:* iterative ἄν.

Note. — Accordingly, the indicatives of the historical tenses are capable of expressing three different relations:

        a) past reality, 167, 3;
        b) unreality, 172, 3;
        c) past potentiality, 172, 4.

173. The **subjunctive** is the mood of anticipation, inasmuch as it expresses that the speaker anticipates something to happen or to be done.

1. The **hortatory** subjunctive is used in exhortations. It is almost confined to the 1. person plural. The negative is μή.

῎Ιωμεν *eamus let us go.*   Καὶ δὴ λέγωμεν.

῝Α ψέγομεν ἡμεῖς μὴ μιμώμεθα.

Note. — To the 2. and 3. persons commands are given in the imperative, 175.

2. The **deliberative** subjunctive is used in questions of appeal. It stands almost only in the 1. person. The negative is μή.

Τί ποιῶμεν; *quid faciamus? what shall we do?*
Εἴπωμεν ἢ σιγῶμεν ; ἢ τί δράσομεν; see 169, 1.
Πότερον βίαν φῶμεν ἢ μὴ φῶμεν εἶναι ;

3. The **prohibitive** subjunctive is used in prohibitions. The 2. and 3. persons of the aor. subj. are used instead of the neg. aor. imperative. The negative is μή.

Μὴ ποιήσῃς *ne feceris: do not do!*
Μηδὲν ἀθυμήσητε ἕνεκα τῶν γεγενημένων.

174. The **optative** is the mood of thought or supposition, inasmuch as it expresses that the speaker fancies something to be possible. It is used

1. **without ἄν** to denote an attainable wish. It may take in addition the particles :

εἴθε, εἰ γάρ, ὡς *O that, O if, Would that.* The negative is μή.

Ὦ παῖ, γένοιο πατρὸς εὐτυχέστερος.
Μή μοι γένοιθ' ἃ βούλομ', ἀλλ' ἃ συμφέρει.

Note. — For the method of expressing a hopeless wish, see 172, 2.

2. **with ἄν** to express *possibility (may might, can could, will shall, possibly, perhaps, peradventure).* It is apt to render a command less imperative or a statement less positive. The negative is οὐ. **The Potential Optative.**

Ἴσως ἄν τις εἴποι *forsitan dixerit quispiam, perhaps somebody may say.*
Ὥρα ἄν εἴη συσκευάζεσθαι *it may be time, — I believe, it is time.*

Ὦ παῖ, γένοιο πατρὸς εὐτυχέστερος,
τὰ δ' ἄλλ' ὅμοιος, καὶ γένοι' ἂν οὐ κακός.

Note. — For the potential indicative (past potentiality), see 172, 4. Notice the difference

between εἴποι (λέγοι) ἄν τις *dixerit quispiam*
and εἶπεν (ἔλεγεν) ἄν τις *diceres.*

175. The **imperative** denotes a positive demand. The negative is μή. See the examples in 169, 3.

A prohibition is expressed by the present imperative or aorist subjunctive with μή :

μὴ ποίει or μὴ ποιήσῃς,
μὴ ποιείτω or μὴ ποιήσῃ,

in the third person more frequently μὴ ποιησάτω.

B. MOODS IN DEPENDENT SENTENCES.

SEQUENCE OF MOOD.

176. 1. Greek has no sequence of tenses, but a **sequence of mood**, which presupposes the distinction of principal and historical tenses.

2. **Principal tenses** are all such verbal forms as refer either to the present or to the future : the present, perfect, and future tenses of the indicative ; the potential optative ; all subjunctives and imperatives.

3. **Historical tenses** are all such verbal forms as refer to the past : the aorist indicative, the imperfect, the pluperfect, the historical present, the potential indicative.

4. The construction of dependent sentences varies, of course, and accordingly the verb is sometimes required to be in the indicative, sometimes in the subjunctive, and sometimes in the optative. Now the **sequence of mood** briefly stated is this : When the construction of a sentence would require the verb to be in the subjunctive with or without ἄν, or in the indicative without ἄν, the writer may employ the optative without ἄν (called the Indirect Optative from its frequent occurrence in the Indirect Discourse ; see 177, 193). However, these subjunctives or indicatives can be changed to the optative only when they depend upon an historical tense. On the contrary, the indicative with ἄν (172, 3 unreality, or 172, 4 past potentiality), or the optative with ἄν (174, 2 present potentiality) are never changed to the Indirect Optative; but remain unaltered.

5. The **subject** of a dependent sentence is often "anticipated," *i.e.* placed for emphasis in the principal sentence, and made the object of the principal verb (Anticipation or **prolepsis**). For example :

Οἶνον ἔφρασεν ἔνθα ἦν κατορωρυγμένος.

Ἐξήγγειλε τοῖς φίλοις τὴν κρίσιν τοῦ Ὀρόντα ὡς ἐγένετο.

SIMPLE SENTENCES IN INDIR. DISCOURSE.

177. They are introduced by ὅτι, ὡς *that*, and take

after a **princ.** tense the **indic.** (potent., unreal.[1]),

after an **hist.** tense the **opt.** (potent., unreal.), rarely the indicative.

For other cases of indirect discourse, see 193, 1 and 202, 2, n. 1.

The negative is οὐ.

Λέγει ὁ κατήγορος, ὡς ὑβριστής εἰμι καὶ βίαιος.

Κῦρος ἔλεγεν, ὅτι ἡ ὁδὸς ἔσοιτο πρὸς βασιλέα μέγαν.

Ἔλεγον, ὅτι Κῦρος μὲν τέθνηκεν, Ἀριαῖος δὲ πεφευγὼς ἐν τῷ σταθμῷ εἴη.

Note. — The sentence ἔλεγεν, ὅτι ἀδικοίην (*present* opt.) may mean :

both : he said [that] I was doing wrong (direct : ἀδικεῖς),

and : he said [that] I had been doing wrong (direct : ἠδίκεις), 169, 4.

---

[1] (potent., unreal.) = " unless the expression of potentiality or unreality should require a different mood." See 176, 4.

DEPENDENT CAUSAL CLAUSES.

178. They are introduced by

ὅτι, διότι, ὡς *because, as, quod,*
ἐπεί *since, because,* ἐπειδή *inasmuch as, quoniam,*
ὅτε, ὁπότε *since then, quando,*

and take after a **princ.** tense the **indic.** } (potent.
    after an **hist.** tense the **indic.** (point of view of *writer*) } or
        or the **opt.** (view of *leading subject*) } unreal.)

The negative is οὐ.

Ἀθηναῖοι ἐνόμισαν ἡττᾶσθαι ὅτι οὐ πολὺ ἐνίκων
                     (reason assigned by writer).

Οἱ Ἀθηναῖοι Περικλέα ἐκάκιζον, ὅτι στρατηγὸς ὢν οὐκ ἐπεξάγοι
                     (reason ass. by the κακίζοντες).

Ἐθαύμαζον οἱ Ἕλληνες, ὅτι οὐδαμοῦ Κῦρος φαίνοιτο οὐδ᾽ ἄλλος ἀπ᾽
αὐτοῦ οὐδεὶς παρείη.

Δέομαί σου παραμεῖναι ἡμῖν, ὡς ἐγὼ οὐδ᾽ ἂν ἑνὸς ἥδιον ἀκούσαιμι ἢ σοῦ.

DEPENDENT OR INDIRECT QUESTIONS.

179. 1. They are introduced by **interrogative** or **relative** pro
nouns and adverbs (130), or by the interrogative **particles**:

    εἰ *if, whether, num,*

    πότερον — ἤ, εἰ — ἤ } *whether — or,*
    πότερα — ἤ, εἴτε — εἴτε } *utrum — an.*

They take after a **princ.** tense the **indic.** } (pot. or
    after an **hist.** tense the **opt.** (rarely the indic.) } unreal.)

The negative is οὐ.

Συμβουλευόμεθά σοι, τί χρὴ ποιεῖν.

Ἐπήρετο τὸν Μηδοσάδην, εἰ ἀληθῆ ταῦτ᾽ εἴη.

Οἵων ἂν ἐλπίδων ἐμαυτὸν στερήσαιμι, ταῦτα λέξω.

Ξενοφῶν οὐ τοῦτο πρῶτον ἠρώτα, πότερον λῷον εἴη αὐτῷ πορεύεσθαι ἢ
μένειν, ἀλλὰ τοῦτ᾽ ἐπυνθάνετο, ὅπως ἂν κάλλιστα πορευθείη.

Note 1. — Observe that εἰ has not the same limitations as *si* in Latin.

Note 2. — Ordinarily the negative is οὐ. But μή is not unfrequently found,
esp. in the second part of alternative indirect questions.

2. Dependent questions implying **doubt** (173, 2) take

    after a **princ.** tense the **subjunctive,**
    after an **hist.** tense the **optative** or **subjunctive.**

The negative is always μή.

Ὁρῶ σε ἀποροῦντα, ποίαν ὁδὸν ἐπὶ τὸν βίον τράπῃ *which road to take.*

Ὁ Θηβαῖος ἠπόρει, ὅ,τι χρήσαιτο ᾡ πράγματι *what to make of it.*

CONSECUTIVE CLAUSES.

180. 1. They are introduced by ὥστε (ὡς) *so that, so (such . . .) as.*
An **actual** result (histor. fact) requires ὥστε with the **indic.** (pot.,
unreal.), neg. **οὐ,**
a merely **conceivable** (expected, possible) result or **tendency** shad-
ing over into **purpose** requires ὥστε (ὡς) with the **inf.**, neg. **μή.**

Ἦν ψῦχος δεινόν, ὥστε τὸ ὕδωρ ἐπήγνυτο.
Ἔχω τριήρεις ὥστε ἑλεῖν τὸ ἐκείνων πλοῖον *so as to be able.*
Κραυγὴν πολλὴν ἐποίουν οἱ στρατιῶται καλοῦντες ἀλλήλους, ὥστε καὶ
τοὺς πολεμίους ἀκούειν *could hear* or *could not help hearing it.*

2. The **infinitive** is regularly used in the following cases :
　　a) to denote an **intended** result :
Πᾶν ποιοῦσιν ὥστε δίκην μὴ διδόναι.
Πάντας οὕτω διατιθεὶς ἀπεπέμπετο ὥστε αὐτῷ μᾶλλον φίλους εἶναι ἢ
βασιλεῖ.

　　b) after such expressions as : *to be able, qualified; to bring about,
effect; to be such as; e.g.*
　　　　Τὸ θεῖον τοιοῦτόν ἐστιν ὥστε πανταχοῦ παρεῖναι.
　　　　Τίς οὕτω δεινός ἐστι λέγειν ὥστε σε πεῖσαι ;

　　c) after a **comparative with** ἤ, or after a **negative**;
e.g.　Βραχύτερα ἠκόντιζον ἢ ὡς ἐξικνεῖσθαι ἡμῶν.
　　　　Ταῦτα οὐ πάλαι ἐστὶ γεγενημένα, ὥστε ἀγνοεῖν ὑμᾶς.

　　d) when ὥστε means *on condition that* (= *provided that, dummodo*) **and**
takes the place of the more frequent ἐφ' ᾧ, ἐφ' ᾧτε with inf. (or fut. indic. 191, 3. c).

Πολλὰ Τιμασίωνι οἱ Ἡρακλεῶται ὑπισχνοῦντο ὥστε ἐκπλεῖν.
Ἔφασαν ἀποδώσειν τοὺς νεκρούς, ἐφ' ᾧ μὴ κάειν τὰς οἰκίας.

Note 1.—Ὥστε, with the force *wherefore, consequently, itaque,* sometimes introduces independent clauses.

Εἰς τὴν ὑστεραίαν οὐχ ἧκε Τισσαφέρνης · ὥσθ' οἱ Ἕλληνες ἐφρόντιζον.

Note 2.—For the s u b j e c t (nom. or acc.) of the infinitive, see 197.

FINAL CLAUSES.

181. 1. Final clauses are introduced by
　　　　ἵνα, ὡς, ὅπως, *ut, in order that,*
　　negatived ἵνα μή, ὡς μή ⎫
　　　　ὅπως μή or μή ⎬ *ne, lest, in order that — not.*

After a　**princ.** tense they always　take the **subj.** (pres. or aor.),
after an **hist.** tense they generally take the **opt.** (pres. or aor.),
　　　　　　　　　　　　　　　　less frequently the subjunctive.

Μὴ φθόνει τοῖς εὐτυχοῦσι, μὴ δοκῇς εἶναι κακός.

Ταῦτ᾽ εἰπὼν εὐθὺς ἀνέστη, ἵνα περαίνοιτο τὰ δέοντα.

Τὰ πλοῖα ᾽Αβροκόμας κατέκαυσεν, ἵνα μὴ Κῦρος διαβῇ.

2. In like manner, final object clauses after **verbs of fearing** and other expressions that imply *apprehension, anxiety, alarm,*

introduced by **μή**, *ne, that, lest,*

negatived **μὴ οὐ**, *ne non, that — not,*

always take after a princ. tense the **subj.**,

after an **hist.** tense the **opt.**,

less frequently the subjunctive.

Δέδοικα, μὴ ἐπιλαθώμεθα τῆς οἴκαδε ὁδοῦ.

᾽Εφοβεῖτο, μὴ οὐ δύναιτο ἐκ τῆς χώρας ἐξελθεῖν.

Note. — When these verbs signify : *to scruple, hesitate, be reluctant, shrink from,* like *vereor, metuo, dubito* in Latin, they require the infinitive. See An. 1, 3, 17.

3. Final object clauses after **verbs of caring** and other expressions that imply *care, anxiety, concern, endeavor,*

as ἐπιμέλομαι, φροντίζω *take care, am concerned,*

σκοπῶ, σκοποῦμαι *see, consider,*

μέλει μοι *it is an object of care, thought to me, I mind,*

σκεπτέον (ἐστίν) *(you, we) must see to it that, — examine,*

βουλεύομαι *deliberate,* παρασκευάζομαι *get ready, prepare myself,*

introduced by **ὅπως, ὡς** *how, that,*

negatived **ὅπως μή, ὡς μή** *that — not, how — not,*

take either the **subj.** or the **opt.** (see 181, 1) or

generally the **future indicative** (according to 191, 3, c).

῞Οπως in this case is a relative and the clauses are final rel. clauses.

Σκεπτέον μοι δοκεῖ, ὅπως ὡς ἀσφαλέστατα μενοῦμεν.

Κῦρος βουλεύεται, ὅπως μήποτε ἔσται ἐπὶ τῷ ἀδελφῷ.

Compare An. 3, 1, 38 with 3, 1, 13. 16 ; 4, 6, 10 (bis) with 1, 3, 11.

Note 1. — In independent sentences expressing apprehension, warning, a cautious or ironical assertion,

μή or **ὅπως μή** with the subj. means : *I wish that — not ; I am afraid that,*

μὴ οὐ with the subj. means : *I rather think that — not ; not . . . I dare say,*

οὐ μή with the aor. subj. or fut. indic. means : *hardly, very improbably, not at all likely, surely not.*

Μὴ λίαν πικρὸν εἰπεῖν ᾖ. ῞Οπως μὴ ποιήσητε, ὃ πολλάκις ὑμᾶς ἔβλαψεν.

᾽Αλλὰ μὴ οὐ τοῦτ᾽ ᾖ χαλεπόν, θάνατον ἐκφυγεῖν, ἀλλὰ πονηρίαν.

Τὸν ἄνδρ᾽ ἐκεῖνον οὔ τι μὴ λίπω ποτέ.

Τοὺς πονηροὺς οὐ μή ποτε βελτίους ποιήσετε.

Note 2. — Μή with the indicative after verbs of fearing or caring has interrogative force (*if not, whether not*), and often represents the thing feared as positively
taking or having taken place :

Φοβούμεθα, μὴ ἅμα ἀμφοτέρων ἡμαρτήκαμεν *we fear we have missed.*

"Ορα μή with the ind.: (*see if not*) *perhaps, beware lest* ; *e.g.* ὅρα μὴ σκῆψιν οὐκ οὖσαν τίθῃς.
  with the subj.: *take care not to, beware lest :* μὴ πῆμα νῦν σαυτῇ τιθῇς.

HYPOTHETICAL PROPOSITIONS.

182. 1. Hypothetical propositions are introduced by

εἰ, ἐάν (= εἰ ἄν, also ἄν, ἤν) *if, in case that, if perchance.*

2. The negative of the condition is always μή; that of the
conclusion either οὐ or μή, according to its character as a statement
or a wish. See 171, 1.

Note. — The condition is also called protasis, the conclusion apodosis.

Classification.

183. 1. There are four types of hypothetical sentences :

I. **The First Type** (*expressing conditioned reality*) :
  Asserts merely the nexus between protasis and apodosis.

II. **The Second Type** (*expressing unreality*) :
  Represents the unreality of both protasis and apodosis.

III. **The Third Type** (*expressing potentiality*) :
  Represents both protasis and apodosis as conceivable.

IV. **The Fourth Type** (*expressing a single future or repeated occurrence*) :
  Represents the protasis as possible or even as expected in
a certain contingency.

Note. — The choice of any one of the four forms depends on the point
of view of the writer, which is, of course, somewhat free to shift.

2. The conditional clauses admit of the following variety of
construction :

	In the Protasis.	In the Apodosis.
I. **First Type:**	εἰ with ind.,	indicative ;
II. **Second Type:**	εἰ with hist. tense ind.,	ἄν with hist. tense ind. ;
a) *present:*	εἰ with impf.,	ἄν with impf. ;
b) *past:*	εἰ with aor. ind.,	ἄν with aor. ind. ;
	(plup.)	(plup.)
III. **Third Type:**	εἰ with opt.,	ἄν with opt. ;
IV. **Fourth Type:**		
a) *fut., pres.:*	ἐάν with subj.,	princ. tense ind. ;
b) *past:*	εἰ with opt.,	hist. tense ind.
The negative is	μή,	οὐ, μή (182, 2).

Conditional Sentences of the First Type.

184. This form merely sets forth the nexus between the conclusion and the condition; in other words: it sets forth the conclusion as real, if the condition be real—but implies nothing as to the latter.

Εἰ with **ind.** of **any** tense — **indic.** of **any** tense.

Εἰ βούλει — δύνασαι.

If you wish, you can : Si vis, potes.

Εἰ θεοί τι δρῶσιν αἰσχρόν, οὐκ εἰσὶν θεοί.
Εἰ δείν' ἔδρασας, δεινὰ καὶ παθεῖν σὲ χρή.
Εἰ μὴ καθέξεις γλῶσσαν, ἔσται σοι κακά.

Conditional Sentences of the Second Type.

185. Both the condition and the conclusion are represented as unreal or contrary to fact.

Εἰ w. **hist.** tense **indic.**,   ἄν w. **hist.** tense **indic.** ;

for the present: impf.,   ἄν w. impf.,
for the past: aor. (plupft.),   ἄν w. aor. (plupft.).

a) **Present time :**

Εἰ ἐβούλου, ἐδύνασο ἄν.
Si velles, posses (sed non vis).
If you wished, you could (but you do not wish).

Φῶς εἰ μὴ εἴχομεν, ὅμοιοι τοῖς τυφλοῖς ἂν ἦμεν.
Εἰ μὴ γὰρ ἦν Χρύσιππος, οὐκ ἂν ἦν στοά.

b) **Past time :**

Εἰ ἐβουλήθης, ἐδυνήθης ἄν.
Si voluisses, potuisses (sed non voluisti),
If you had wished, you could have (but you did not wish).

Οὐκ ἂν ἐποίησεν Ἀγασίας, εἰ μὴ ἐγὼ ἐκέλευσα.
Εἰ τριάκοντα μόναι μετέπεσον τῶν ψήφων, ἀπεπεφεύγη ἄν.

c) **Mixed Forms :**

Εἰ μὴ ὑμεῖς ἤλθετε, ἐπορευόμεθα ἂν ἐπὶ βασιλέα.
Εἰ γὰρ σὺ μὲν παῖς ἦσθ', ἐγὼ δὲ σὸς πατήρ,
ἔκτεινά τοί σ' ἂν κοὐ φυγαῖς ἐζημίουν.

Note. — In conditional sentences of the second type, the imperfect occasionally expresses continuance of a past, and the aor. ind. instantaneous occurrence of a present, action.

Οὐκ ἂν Ἀγαμέμνων νήσων ἠπειρώτης ὢν ἐκράτει, εἰ μή τι καὶ ναυτικὸν εἶχεν. *A. would not have been master, had he not had.* . . . . Εἰ μὴ πατὴρ ἦσθα, εἶπον ἄν σ' οὐκ εὖ φρονεῖν.

Conditional Sentences of the Third Type.

186. Both the condition and the conclusion are set forth as purely imaginable, or as mere thoughts or suppositions that are gratuitously assumed by the speaker.

Εἰ with optative — ἄν with optative.

Εἰ βούλοιο, δύναιο ἄν : *Si velis, possis.*

If you should wish (= *Suppose you were to wish*), *you would be able.*

Εἴ τις ξυνελὼν ταῦτα φαίη, ὀρθῶς ἂν εἴποι.

Εἰ ἀναγκαῖον εἴη ἀδικεῖν ἢ ἀδικεῖσθαι, ἑλοίμην ἄν. μᾶλλον ἀδικεῖσθαι ἢ ἀδικεῖν.

Note. — Suppositions that are contrary to fact may evidently also be expressed by the speaker, if he chooses, in this potential form. See 183, 1. note.

Καὶ ἔγωγ' ἄν, εἰ σὺ εἴην (which is contrary to fact !), ἔνορκον ἂν ποιησαίμην ὥσπερ Ἀργεῖοι.

Conditional Sentences of the Fourth Type.

187. 1. The condition is represented as objectively possible, or even as anticipated under certain circumstances. The conclusion is set forth as positively certain. This form of hypothetical proposition is especially employed to express thoughts or truths of universal application and is, therefore, of constant occurrence in legal phraseology.

2. Sentences of this type admit of a double construction.

I. The condition refers to a **single future occurrence** (*if*).

᾿Εάν with subj. (pres. or aor.) — fut. indic. or imperative.

᾿Εὰν βούλῃ (βουληθῇς), δυνήσῃ.

Si voles (*volueris*), *poteris. If you wish, you will be able.*

῞Ηξω παρὰ σὲ αὔριον, ἐὰν θεὸς ἐθέλῃ.

Νέος ἂν πονήσῃς, γῆρας ἕξεις εὐθαλές.

᾿Εὰν δ' ἔχωμεν χρήμαθ', ἕξομεν φίλους.

Compare *Donec eris felix, multos numerabis amicos.*

Here the pres. subj. stands in the sense of the Latin future,
the aor. subj. stands in the sense of the Latin fut. perfect.

II. The condition implies **repeated occurrence** (*as often as*).

a) in the **present** :

᾿Εάν with subj. (pres. or aor.) — present indicative.

᾿Εὰν βούλῃ (βουληθῇς), δύνασαι.

Cum vis (*voluisti*), *potes. If* (= *whenever*) *you wish, you* (*always*) *can.*

῞Απας λόγος, ἂν ἀπῇ τὰ πράγματα, μάταιος φαίνεται.

᾿Αν ἐγγὺς ἔλθῃ θάνατος, οὐδεὶς βούλεται θνήσκειν.

L

b) in the **past**:

Εἰ with **opt**. (pres. or aor.) — **hist**. tense **ind**. (esp. impf.).

Εἰ βούλοιο (βουληθείης), ἐδύνασο.

Cum volebas (volueras), poteras.

If (= as often as) you (had) wished, you (always) could.

Ξενοφῶν εἴ πού τι ὁρῴη βρωτόν, διεδίδου.

Εἴ τίς γέ τι Κύρῳ προστάξαντι καλῶς ὑπηρετήσειεν, οὐδενὶ πώποτε ἀχάριστον εἴασε τὴν προθυμίαν. — (See Anab. 2, 3, 11 ; 1, 9, 19. cf. 172, 4.)

Here the **pres**. opt. stands in the sense of the Lat. imperfect,
the **aor**. opt. stands in the sense of the Lat. pluperfect.

Note. — These hypothetical forms account for the construction of those temporal and relative clauses (190, 3. and 4. b ; 191, 4. d) in which

ὅταν, ἕως ἄν, πρὶν ἄν—ὃς ἄν, ὅπως ἄν, ᾗ ἄν take the subj. after a princ. tense,

or ὅτε, ἕως, πρίν — ὅς, ὅπως, ᾗ take the opt. after an hist. tense.

All these clauses are equivalent in meaning to hypothetical propositions.

188. 1. The protasis of one type is sometimes followed by the apodosis of another. In particular, a potential apodosis (as a more polite and less peremptory mode of expression, 174, 2) is often joined to a protasis of the first or the fourth type.

Δείξαιμι ἂν ταῦτα, εἴ μοί τινα βούλεσθε συμπέμψαι.

Οὐδέ, ἂν πολλαὶ γέφυραι ὦσιν, ἔχοιμεν ἄν, ὅποι σωθῶμεν.

2. Besides the simple particles εἰ and ἐάν, the following combinations are worthy of note:

a) **εἰ μή** after a negative means (like *nisi*): *save, except, unless.*

b) **εἰ δὲ μή**, when used without a verb after εἰ μὲν (μή), ἐὰν μὲν (μή), is the regular expression for the English: *otherwise, or else.*

c) **εἴπερ** with the indic. means: *si quidem, if indeed, if really, if it be true that.* Sometimes it is equivalent to: *since indeed,* etc.

d) **εἰ μὴ ἄρα** with the indic. is (like *nisi forte, nisi vero*) used chiefly in irony: *unless perhaps, unless indeed, unless of course, unless forsooth.*

e) **ὥσπερ ἂν εἰ** with the opt. (denoting potentiality) } *(just) as if, as*
or with hist. tense ind. (denoting unreality) } *though.*

CONCESSIVE AND ADVERSATIVE CLAUSES.

189. Being introduced by **εἰ καί, ἐὰν καί** *granting that, although,*
καὶ εἰ (κεἰ), καὶ ἐάν (κἄν) *even if, even*
supposing, even though, although,

they perfectly agree in construction with conditional sentences. Their negative is μή.

Κεἰ μὴ πέποιθα, τοὔργον ἔστ᾽ ἐργαστέον.

Γελᾷ δ᾽ ὁ μωρός, κἄν τι μὴ γελοῖον ᾖ.

Note. — Sentences introduced by "*although, even though,*" may also be expressed by the participle with καί or καίπερ prefixed, the negative being οὐ. See 203, 3. e.

TEMPORAL CLAUSES.

190. 1. They are introduced by the temporal particles

ὅτε, ὁπότε, ἡνίκα, ὡς *when, cum* with the indic.,

ἐπεί, ἐπειδή *when, after, cum* with the subj.,

ἐπεὶ (ἐπειδὴ) πρῶτον (τάχιστα) *as soon as, no sooner* . . . *than, cum*

ἀφ' οὗ, ἐξ οὗ *from the time that, since, ex quo,* [*primum,*

ἐν ᾧ *during the time that, while, dum,*

ἕως, ἔστε, μέχρι (οὗ) *while, so long as, until, dum, quoad,*

πρίν *before, until, priusquam.*

2. An **actual** (present or past) event is referred to by the **indicative**. The neg. is οὐ.

Ἐπεὶ πάντες συνῆλθον, ἐκαθέζοντο· ὅτε δὲ ταῦτα ἦν, ἦσαν μέσαι νύκτες.

3. An event may, however, be represented as **possible** only or as **anticipated** (and occasionally as intended). And here too, as in hypothetical clauses (187 with note), it may be referred to as occurring only once at some future time or as one that may repeatedly take place. Then

　　a) the **subjunctive** with ἄν (neg. μή) must be used after a princ. tense,

　　b) the **optative** without ἄν (neg. μή) is generally used after an **hist.** tense. For assimilation of mood in temporal clauses, see 192.

Note. — Ἄν (171, 2. note) attaches itself to the temporal particle, with which, if possible, it forms one word.

　　　　　Τάφος δὲ ποῖος δέξεταί μ', ὅταν θάνω ;
　　　　　Ἐπειδὰν ἄπαντα ἀκούσητε, κρίνατε.
　　　　　Μαινόμεθα πάντες, ὁπόταν ὀργιζώμεθα.

Κῦρος ἐν τῷ παραδείσῳ ἐθήρευεν, ὁπότε γυμνάσαι βούλοιτο ἑαυτόν τε καὶ τοὺς ἵππους *whenever.*

Μὴ ἀναμείνωμεν, ἕως ἂν (*until*) πλείους ἡμῶν οἱ πολέμιοι γένωνται, ἀλλ' ἴωμεν, ἕως (*while*) ἔτι οἰόμεθα εὐπετῶς ἂν (204) αὐτῶν κρατῆσαι.

4. Πρίν may always be followed by the **infinitive** (nom. or acc. with inf.: 197). Generally, however, it takes

　　a) After an **affirmative** principal sentence : the infinitive.

Διέβησαν πρὶν τοὺς ἄλλους ἀποκρίνασθαι.

Πολλοὶ ἄνθρωποι ἀποθνήσκουσι πρὶν δῆλοι (197, 3) γίγνεσθαι, οἷοι ἦσαν.

　　b) After a **negative** principal sentence :

the **indicative**, if an (historical) **fact** is referred to :

Οὐκ ἀπέπλευσαν, πρὶν ἐξεπολιόρκησαν τὴν πόλιν.

the subjunctive with ἄν, if an expected (or intended) event is referred to:

Μὴ ἀπέλθητε, πρὶν ἂν ἀκούσητε τὸ πρᾶγμα.

Οὐκ ἤθελον συμπλεῖν οἱ Κορίνθιοι, πρὶν ἂν τὰ Ἴσθμια ἑορτάσωσιν.

Note. — Πρίν never takes the optative except in indirect discourse (193, 2. b) or by way of mood assimilation (192).

RELATIVE CLAUSES.

191. 1. They are introduced by relative pronouns or adverbs.

2. **Explanatory** relative clauses, which merely serve to explain some single word, retain the mood and the negative of the corresponding independent sentences.

Πρᾶγμα, ὃ οὐκ ἐγένετο — ὃ οὐ γενήσεται —

ὃ οὐκ ἂν γένοιτο — ὃ οὐκ ἂν ἐγένετο —

ὃ μὴ γένοιτο — ὃ μήποτε ποιῶμεν —

ὃ μὴ ποιεῖτε (ποιήσητε).

3. Contrary to Latin usage, we find in Greek

a) in **causal** rel.-clauses the indicative (neg. οὐ).

Θαυμαστὸν ποιεῖς, ὃς (ὅτι) ἡμῖν οὐδὲν δίδως *qui des.*

b) in **consecutive** rel.-clauses the indicative, mostly the future (neg. οὐ).

Παῖδές μοι οὔπω εἰσίν, οἵ με θεραπεύσουσιν *qui me colant: to take care.* Τίς οὕτω μαίνεται, ὅστις οὐ βούλεταί σοι φίλος εἶναι; *as not to desire.* Οὐκ ἔστιν ὅπως ἥβην κτήσῃ πάλιν αὖθις.

c) in **final** rel.-clauses regularly (even after a leading histor. tense) the fut. indic. (neg. μή).

Ἡγεμόνα αἰτήσομεν Κῦρον, ὅστις ἡμᾶς ἀπάξει *qui abducat.* Ἔδοξε τῷ δήμῳ τριάκοντα ἄνδρας ἑλέσθαι, οἳ τοὺς πατρίους νόμους συγγράψουσι, καθ' οὓς πολιτεύσουσιν *conscriberent, viverent.*

4. **Hypothetical** rel.-clauses, *i.e.* such as are equivalent to (and may be resolved into) hypothetical ones, require the moods of the hypothetical protases: 183 (neg. μή). See however 192.

ὅς (ὅστις) = εἴ τις,   ὃς ἂν (ὅστις ἄν) = ἐάν τις.

a) First Type (184):   Ἃ μὴ οἶδα, οὐδὲ οἴομαι εἰδέναι.

Ἃ μὴ προσήκει, μήτ' ἄκουε μήθ' ὅρα.

b) Second Type (185):   Οὐκ ἂν ἐπεχειροῦμεν πράττειν ἃ (εἴ τινα) μὴ ἠπιστάμεθα.

c) Third Type (186):   Ἐγὼ μὲν ὀκνοίην ἂν εἰς τὰ πλοῖα ἐμβαίνειν, ἃ ἡμῖν Κῦρος δοίη (εἴ τινα δοίη).

d) Fourth Type (187):

A single future occurrence : Ἀπόκριναι ὅ,τι ἄν σε ἐρωτῶ.

Τῷ ἀνδρί, ὃν ἄν ἔλησθε, πείσομαι.

Repeated occurrence, pres.: Νέος δ' ἀπόλλυθ', ὅντιν' ἄν φιλῇ θεός.

past: Οὐ ἅψαιτο Μίδας, ἐγίγνετο χρυσός.

Note. — Here belongs: Ἥξω ἔχων ἱππέας ὡς ἄν δύνωμαι πλείστους.   187, n.

192. The verbs of final, temporal and relative clauses are occasionally " *assimilated to* " (made to agree in mood with) that of the main sentence.   This assimilation of mood is of two kinds :

1. An optative without ἄν may follow an opt. with or without ἄν :

Εἴθε ἥκοις, ἵνα γνοίης. Ἔρδοι τις, ἦν ἕκαστος εἰδείη τέχνην.

Οὐκ ἄν ἐπὶ πᾶν ἔλθοι βασιλεύς, ὡς πᾶσι φόβον παράσχοι ;

2. The indicative of some hist. tense without ἄν may be used after an expression of unreality (172, 2. 3, whether statement or wish) in the main sentence.

Εἰ γὰρ ὤφελον οἷοί τ' εἶναι οἱ πολλοὶ τὰ μέγιστα κακὰ ἐργάζεσθαι, ἵνα οἷοί τ' ἦσαν καὶ ἀγαθὰ τὰ μέγιστα.

Εἰ τῷ ὄντι ξένος ἐτύγχανον ὤν, ξυνεγιγνώσκετε ἄν μοι, εἰ ἐν ἐκείνῃ τῇ φωνῇ τε καὶ τῷ τρόπῳ ἔλεγον, ἐν οἷσπερ ἐτεθράμμην.

A Summary of the Rules for Indirect Discourse.

193. 1. When **independent** sentences, whether statements or wishes, are indirectly quoted, *i.e.* are made to depend upon a verb of saying or thinking,

a) **statements** require the infinitive (for whose subject, see 197), or the participle (202, 2, n. 1) or a finite verb with ὡς or ὅτι.

E.g. Directly quoted : Σωκράτης ἔλεγεν · " οἱ θεοὶ πάντα ἴσασιν."

Indirectly : Σωκράτης ἔλεγεν ὅτι οἱ θεοὶ πάντα ἴσασιν or εἰδεῖεν, or τοὺς θεοὺς πάντα εἰδέναι.

b) **wishes** require the infinitive (for whose subject, see 197).

E.g.   Directly : Μὴ παραχωρεῖτε (παραχωρήσητε) τῆς τάξεως.

Indirectly : Ἀξιῶ ὑμᾶς μὴ παραχωρεῖν (-ρῆσαι) τῆς τάξεως.

2. When **dependent** sentences are to be quoted indirectly :

a) After a principal tense, both the mood and the tense of the direct discourse remain unchanged.

b) After an historical tense, the potential and the unreal moods remain unchanged, while indicatives, as well as subjunctives with or without ἄν, may be retained or changed to the indirect optative without ἄν.   (See 176, 4.)

3. Not unfrequently the indirect turns abruptly into the direct discourse.   See An. 1, 3, 14. 16. 20 ; 1, 9, 25.

4. Indirect discourse, introduced by ὅτι or ὡς, is occasionally changed to an infinitive construction; an indirect quotation with ὅτι (ὡς) or in the infinitive is sometimes continued by the indirect optative.

SUMMING UP OF THE USES OF THE PARTICLE ἄν.

194. The modal particle ἄν can be used only:

1. With the indicative of the hist. tenses to denote unreality, 172, 3.

2. With the indicative of the hist. tenses to denote past potentiality (including the ἄν iterativum), 172, 4.

3. With the subjunctive in hypothetical clauses of the fourth type (both in the purely hypothetical and in the hyp.-temporal or hyp.-relative clauses), 187; 190, 3. 4; 191, 4.

4. With the optative to denote potentiality, 174, 2.

5. With the infinitive and the participle to denote potentiality or unreality, 204.

6. Rarely with the final particles ὡς, ὅπως (never with the final ἵνα; ἵν' ἄν is always relative = ubicunque). Ὡς ἄν μάθῃς ἀντάκουσον.

Note.—Ἄν sometimes occurs twice (πῶς ἂν οὐκ ἂν πάσχοιμεν;), or it is occasionally omitted (by the poets, Thucydides and Herodotus) where the above rules would require it. For the position of ἄν, see 171, note.

THE VERBAL NOUNS AND ADJECTIVES.

PRELIMINARY NOTE.

195. Infinitives and participles may be inflected by means of the article; they are therefore used as nouns. However, they do not hereby lose their character as verbs. For a) they are qualified by adverbs, not by adjectives; b) they take their objects in the same cases respectively as the other forms of the verb (τὸ ἀκριβῶς τοῖς νόμοις πείθεσθαι); c) they have the properties of voice and express the stage of action (see 167: λιπεῖν, λιπέσθαι, λειφθῆναι — φυγεῖν, φεύγειν, πεφευγέναι); d) they may be modified by ἄν.

A. THE INFINITIVE.

196. The infinitive is originally a verbal noun with a dative (locative) meaning: ἰέναι to the going, to go, λῦσαι to loose.

SUBJECT AND PREDICATE OF INFINITIVE.

197. 1. The subject of the infinitive is omitted when it is the same as that of the leading verb:

Ἀδικεῖσθαι ὑφ' ἡμῶν νομίζει Κῦρος : se esse injuria affectum.

Ὁμολογῶ ἁμαρτεῖν confiteor me peccasse.

2. The subject of the infinitive is put in the accusative when it is not the same as the subject of the leading verb and not already contained in a genitive or dative depending on the main verb. There is therefore an *Accusative-with-Infinitive construction* in Greek, as well as in English. *E.g.* Σωκράτης ἡγεῖτο θεοὺς πάντα εἰδέναι.

Note.— The indefinite subject "*one, a person,* [*we, you*]" (= τινά, τινάς) is omitted: Γράμματα μαθεῖν δεῖ καὶ μαθόντα νοῦν ἔχειν.

3. Predicate qualifications (nouns or adjectives) agree with the word (whether expressed or understood) to which they relate.

'Ερωτώμενος, ποδαπὸς εἴη, Πέρσης ἔφη εἶναι.

Νομίζω ὑμᾶς ἐμοὶ εἶναι καὶ φίλους καὶ συμμάχους.

Δίκαιον εὖ πράττοντα μεμνῆσθαι θεοῦ (*sc.* τινά).

"Εξεστιν ὑμῖν εὐδαίμοσι γενέσθαι, or (ὑμᾶς) εὐδαίμονας γενέσθαι.

'Ωρέγοντο τοῦ (198) πρῶτος ἕκαστος γίγνεσθαι.

Κῦρος παραγγέλλει Ξενίᾳ ἥκειν λαβόντι τοὺς ἄλλους,

or (αὐτὸν) ἥκειν λαβόντα τοὺς ἄλλους.

INFINITIVE WITH THE ARTICLE.

198. 1. By prefixing the article, the infinitive becomes a noun (124) or is used substantively without losing its character as a verb. See 195.

2. The infinitive **may** take the article when it is the subject or the object accusative. It **must** have the article when it is in the genitive or the dative, or when it depends on a preposition.

Νέοις τὸ σιγᾶν κρεῖττόν ἐστι τοῦ λαλεῖν *silence . . . prating.*

Νίκησον ὀργὴν τῷ λογίζεσθαι καλῶς *by sound reasoning.*

'Εκ τοῦ πρότερος (197, 3) λέγειν ὁ διώκων ἰσχύει *because he speaks first.*

Τὸ πολλὰ τολμᾶν πόλλ' ἁμαρτάνειν ποιεῖ *daring . . . blundering.*

INFINITIVE WITHOUT THE ARTICLE.

199. 1. The **supplementary** infinitive (or acc. with inf.) is used to complete the idea

a) conveyed by **impersonal** verbs and expressions, such as:

δεῖ, χρή, δοκεῖ, ἔξεστιν, οἷόν τέ ἐστιν, προσήκει, συμβαίνει, ἄξιον, δίκαιον, δυνατόν, καλόν — ὥρα, καιρός, νόμος ἐστίν.

'Αλλὰ γὰρ ἤδη ὥρα ἀπιέναι.

'Αγαθοῖς ὑμῖν προσήκει εἶναι. An. 3, 2, 11.

Note.—Some of the above expressions are often used **personally.**

E.g. δοκῶ *videor, it seems that I, I seem,* ἄξιός εἰμι, δίκαιός εἰμι *I have a right, am entitled to, it is right that I, it is right for me (to do).*

b) of verbs that signify:

to say and to declare, to believe and to hope,
to desire and to wish, to forbid and to hinder
to teach and to learn, to understand and to know

ἱΠρωταγόρας ἔλεγε πάντων χρημάτων μέτρον εἶναι ἄνθρωπον.

Ὅ,τι ἂν ποιῇς, νόμιζ᾽ ὁρᾶν θεούς τινας.

Ἔλπιζε τιμῶν τὸν θεὸν πράξειν καλῶς.

Καλῶς ἀκούειν μᾶλλον ἢ πλουτεῖν θέλε.

Τί κωλύσει αὐτὸν βαδίζειν ὅποι βούλεται ;

Τὴν τῶν κρατούντων μάθε φέρειν ἐξουσίαν.

Εἴκειν δ᾽ οὐκ ἐπίσταται κακοῖς.

2. The **limiting** (or *epexegetic*) infinitive (generally in the **active** voice) is used to limit the application of such adjectives as: *able, capable, worthy, clever, skilled, easy, agreeable* and their opposites. *E.g.*

χαλεπὸς εὑρεῖν *difficilis inventu,*	ἄξιος ἐπαινέσαι *dignus qui laudetur,*
ἱκανοὶ φυλάττειν *sufficient to* —,	οἷος ἄρχειν *fit for ruling* —,
δεινὸς λέγειν *clever at speaking,*	οἷος ζῆν *enough to live upon,*
ἀμήχανος εἰσελθεῖν *difficult to* —,	οἷός τέ εἰμι *am able.*

Ῥᾴδια πάντα θεῷ τελέσαι *easy to accomplish.*

Γνῶναι πάντων ὑμεῖς ὀξύτατοι τὰ ῥηθέντα.

Κῦρος πάντων ἦν ἄρχειν ἀξιώτατος.

3. The **final** infinitive denotes a **purpose** with verbs that signify *to give, deliver, allow ; to choose, appoint* and the like.

Τὰς κώμας διαρπάσαι τοῖς Ἕλλησιν ἐπέτρεψεν . . . *diripiendas tradidit!*

Εἵλοντο Δρακόντιον δρόμου ἐπιμεληθῆναι.

4. An **infinitive absolute** (with or without the article) is used in:

ὀλίγου, μικροῦ δεῖν " *little being wanting* " = *almost.*

ὡς (ἔπος) εἰπεῖν *so to speak ; ἑκὼν εἶναι willing(ly), voluntarily.*

ὡς συνελόντι εἰπεῖν *to be brief, in short, to sum up.* See 157. 3.

ὡς ἐμοὶ δοκεῖν *as it seems to me ; τὸ νῦν εἶναι at present, just now.*

τὸ κατὰ τοῦτον (ἐπὶ τούτῳ) εἶναι *so far as he is concerned.*

Μικροῦ δεῖν ὅμοιόν ἐστι τῷ ὀνειδίζειν.

Ἀληθές γε ὡς ἔπος εἰπεῖν οὐδὲν εἰρήκασιν.

Τὸ ἐπ᾽ ἐκείνοις εἶναι ἀπολώλατε.

B. THE PARTICIPLE.

INTRODUCTORY NOTE.

200. The participle is a **verbal adjective** and is, therefore, used as an **adjective**. Its double character as adjective and as verb is explained in 195.

The Participle as Attribute and Substantive.

201. As an attribute the participle is like an adjective.

Οἱ παρόντες ἡγεμόνες — οἱ νῦν ὄντες ἄνθρωποι *the present generation* — ἡ Μίδου καλουμένη κρήνη *the so-called fountain of Midas* —

τοῖς Θρᾳξὶ τοῖς ὑπὲρ Ἑλλήσποντον οἰκοῦσι to those Thracians who —
(128, note 1).

As a substantive with the article (117, 1. 2) it has two uses :

individualizing (οὐ): ὁ γραψάμενος τὸν Σωκράτη the accuser of,
or generalizing (μή): ὁ τυχών, ὁ βουλόμενος any one who wishes,
ὁ μὴ πιστεύων si quis non credit (203, 3, d).

The Participle as Predicate.

202. It completes the action of the finite verb.

1. It belongs to the **subject** of the verb, when it is used with verbs

a) that express some particular mode of being (in such or such a state). *E.g.*

τυγχάνω am by chance, happen or chance (to be) — adv. by chance.
λανθάνω am hidden, escape notice — secretly, without (his) knowing.
διάγω, διατελῶ, διαγίγνομαι continue (doing) — constantly.
δῆλος, φανερός εἰμι, φαίνομαι it is evident that I — evidently.
φθάνω anticipate, am beforehand — before, sooner, first.
οἴχομαι am gone — adv. away, off.

Ἡ ψυχὴ ἀθάνατος φαίνεται οὖσα. Ἔτυχον παραγενόμενος ἵππον ἔχων.
Ἑπτὰ ἡμέρας πάσας μαχόμενοι διετέλεσαν. Ἔλαθον ἐξελθόντες.
Ἔφθησαν τοὺς Πέρσας ἀφικόμενοι εἰς τὴν πόλιν.

b) that signify to begin and to cease, to persevere and to grow weary.

E.g. ἄρχομαι begin (by), at first; παύομαι, λήγω cease (from).
ἀνέχομαι endure, can bear; ἀπαγορεύω, κάμνω grow weary (of).
Οὔποτε ἐπαυόμην ὑμᾶς οἰκτίρων.　Οὐκ ἀνέξομαι ζῶσα.
Μὴ κάμῃς φίλον ἄνδρα εὐεργετῶν.　Παῦσαι λέγων.
Παύω τοὺς ἐχθροὺς γελῶντας I make the enemy stop laughing.

c) that signify to be right and to do wrong, to be superior and to be inferior to one, e.g.

καλῶς ποιῶ do well (to or in) — ἀδικῶ do wrong (to or in) —
χαρίζομαί τινι, χάριν φέρω τινί do one a favor, oblige one (by) —
νικῶ, κρατῶ outdo (in) — ἡττῶμαι, λείπομαι am inferior (in); wanting (in) —
Καλῶς ἐποίησας προειπών.　Ἔστε νικῶη ἀλεξόμενος.
Ἀδικεῖτε πολέμου ἄρχοντες καὶ σπονδὰς λύοντες.
Μῆδον καταλιπὼν Κυαξάρῃ ἐχαρίσατο.

d) that denote **mental states**, as

χαίρω, ἥδομαι *delight* (*in*), *am delighted* (*to*) —
ἄχθομαι, ἀγανακτῶ *am displeased, vexed, angry* (*at*) —
αἰσχύνομαι *am ashamed* (*to do*), (*do*) *with a sense of shame* —
μεταμέλομαι *repent* (*of*), *am sorry* (*for*).

Ἥδομαι ἀκούων σου φρονίμους λόγους.   Τιμώμενοι χαίρουσιν.
Οὐκ ἂν ἀχθοίμην μανθάνων.   Τοῦτο οὐκ αἰσχύνομαι λέγων.

2. It belongs either to the **subject** or the **object** of the verb,
when it is used with verbs

a) that signify a (mental or sensitive) **perception**.   *E.g.*

ὁρῶ, περιορῶ (*overlook, allow*), ἀκούω, αἰσθάνομαι, καταλαμβάνω,
οἶδα, ἐπίσταμαι, μέμνημαι, γιγνώσκω, εὑρίσκω and the like.

Compare: *Catonem vidi sedentem, Socratem audio dicentem.*

Ὁρῶμεν πάντα ἀληθῆ ὄντα, ἃ λέγετε *omnia vera esse.*
Οὐκ ἤδεσαν αὐτὸν τεθνηκότα.   Ἐὰν ἁλῷς τοῦτο πράττων, ἀποθανεῖ.
Μείζω τὸν ἄνθρωπον γιγνόμενον περιορῶμεν.

b) that denote the **cause** or **occasion** of such a perception.

E.g.   δείκνυμι, δηλόω, (ἀπο)φαίνω, ἀγγέλλω, (ἐξ)ελέγχω.

Κῦρον ἐπιστρατεύοντα πρῶτος ἤγγειλα.
Πάνθ᾽ ἕνεκα ἑαυτοῦ ποιῶν Φίλιππος ἐξελεγχθήσεται.

Note 1. — The above mentioned verbs expressive of thought or
emotion may also take ὅτι with a finite form of the verb.

Note 2. — Observe the difference of idiom in:

ἴσθι (μέμνησο) θνητὸς ὤν *scito te esse mortalem.*
Ὁρῶμεν ἡμεῖς ἀδύνατοι ὄντες περιγενέσθαι.

Note 3. — Σύνοιδα ἐμαυτῷ *am conscious of* takes the participle now in the
nominative, now in the dative, — μεταμέλει μοι *repent, am sorry* takes it only
in the dative.   Ἐγὼ οὐ ξύνοιδα ἐμαυτῷ σοφὸς ὤν or σοφῷ ὄντι.

Note 4. — Ἀκούω, αἰσθάνομαι and πυνθάνομαι are construed as follows:
ἀκούω w. gen. part.: *hear* [myself, in person] *that* — (see 147, 4, note).
ἀκούω w. acc. part.: *hear* [through others] (as a fact) *that* — =ὅτι.
ἀκούω w. acc. and inf.: *hear* (as a rumor) *that* —.

Note 5. — In like manner several of the above verbs take sometimes the participle, sometimes the infinitive, in order to imply a different shade of meaning.

E.g.	with the Participle	with the Infinitive
ἄρχομαι	{ *am at the beginning* (of an action), *begin by* (doing something), *at first.*	*begin, undertake, set* or *go about* (*doing*), *proceed* (*to do*).
φαίνομαι	*it is evident that I, I am evidently, apparet.*	*it seems that I, videor.*
αἰδέομαι αἰσχύνομαι	} *am ashamed if* (*doing*), i.e. *do with a sense of shame,*	*am ashamed to* (*do*), i.e. *omit* (*doing*) *from shame.*

γιγνώσκω	(learn to) know,		determine, resolve	
ἐπίσταμαι	understand,	that	understand, know how	to do
οἶδα, μανθάνω	know, learn,	(follows an	know, learn how	some-
ἐπιλανθάνομαι	forget,	assertion)	forget	thing.
μέμνημαι	remember,	(ὅτι, ὡς)	am careful, remember	199, 1. b.

μέμνημαι (οἶδα, ἀκούω), ὅτε with indic. memini cum, remember (the time) when.

Note 6.—Accordingly:

    μεμνήσθω ἀνὴρ ἀγαθὸς εἶναι let him remember to be a brave soldier,
but: μεμνήσθω ἄνθρωπος ὢν let him remember that he is a man.

The Circumstantial Participle.

203. 1. The circumstantial participle is equivalent to a variety of conjunctional clauses. In English we sometimes retain the participle, sometimes employ a subordinate clause. This participle is either appositive or absolute.

a) An **appositive** participle may be used only when its subject occurs in some case or other in the main sentence.

b) An **absolute** participle may be used only when its subject does not occur in any form in the main sentence.

2. The Greek has a genitive absolute corresponding to the ablative absolute in Latin.

    Θεοῦ διδόντος οὐδὲν ἰσχύει φθόνος,
    καὶ μὴ διδόντος οὐδὲν ἰσχύει πόνος.

Note.— Differently from the Latin, the Greek

a) allows the participle to be without a subject whenever the latter is easily understood from the context: οὕτως ἐχόντων quae cum ita sint.

b) does not allow the participle to be replaced by either a noun or an adjective (Cicerone consule, Hannibale vivo!), but ὢν must always be added. Therefore, Pericle duce = Περικλέους ἡγεμόνος ὄντος. — Ἑκών and ἄκων are considered as participles: me invito = ἐμοῦ οὐχ ἑκόντος.

3. Either participial construction may correspond

    a) to a **causal** clause, which, for greater clearness, often commences with

ἅτε, οἷον, οἷα (the author's reason): since, as, because, inasmuch as.
ὡς (reason of the subject of the leading verb): since, as though, on the ground, plea, under the pretence, saying, thinking that, as if to signify etc. See 178.

    Λέγω δὲ τοῦδ᾽ ἕνεκα, βουλόμενος δόξαι σοι ὅπερ ἐμοί.
    ῞Ατε ἐξαίφνης ἐπιπεσόντες πολλὰ ἀνδράποδα ἔλαβον.
    Ἀνεθορύβησαν ὡς εὖ εἰπόντος τοῦ Ἀγασίου.

b) to a **final** clause. The part. must be in the future and is often preceded by ὡς : *in order to, with the intention, avowed object of* (neg. μή).

Ὁ ἡγησόμενος οὐδεὶς ἔσται.

Οἱ Ἀθηναῖοι παρεσκευάζοντο ὡς πολεμήσοντες.

c) to a **temporal** clause. The part. is often emphasized by such adverbs as

ἅμα *while,* αὐτίκα, εὐθύς *immediately, forthwith,* μεταξύ *while,* etc.

ἅμα πορευόμενοι *during (on) their march,* or : *while marching,* εὐθὺς παῖδες ὄντες *a pueris, from (earliest, their very) boyhood.*

Πολλαχοῦ με ἐπέσχε λέγοντα μεταξύ.

Ταῦτ' ἐπράχθη Κόνωνος στρατηγοῦντος.

d) to a **conditional** clause (neg. μή).

Δίκαια δράσας συμμάχους ἕξεις θεούς.

Γευόμενος καὶ σὺ γνώσει ὅτι ἡδέα ἐστίν *if you taste, you will find* . . .

Οὐκ ἂν δύναιο μὴ καμὼν εὐδαιμονεῖν.

e) to a **concessive** or **adversative** clause. For the purpose of clearness, καί or καίπερ (neg. οὐ) may be added. See 189, note.

Ἔρχεται τἀληθὲς εἰς φῶς ἐνίοτ' οὐ ζητούμενον.

Εἰσήλθετε ὑμεῖς καίπερ οὐ διδόντος τοῦ νόμου.

4. The **participle** (often with ὡς, ὥσπερ) **is used absolutely** (**Accusative Absolute**) with such impersonal expressions as :

δέον, προσῆκον *since (when, although) it is* or *was necessary, proper,*

ὄν, ἐξόν, παρόν *since (when, although) it is* or *was possible,*

δόξαν, δεδογμένον *since (if, although) it is* or *was resolved,*

ἄδηλον ὄν, αἰσχρὸν ὄν *since (if, although) it is* or *was unknown, shameful.*

Κατακείμεθα, ὥσπερ ἐξὸν ἡσυχίαν ἄγειν.

Οἱ δ' οὐ βοηθήσαντες δέον ὑγιεῖς ἀπῆλθον ;

Βουλῆς ἀξιοῖ τυχεῖν Φίλων, οὐ μετὸν αὐτῷ.

Infinitive or Participle with ἄν.

204. Both the infinitive and the participle require the modal suffix ἄν, if the finite verb for which they stand would be

either the optative with ἄν,

or the ind. of an historical tense with ἄν.

Consequently, infinitives or participles with ἄν always denote either potentiality or unreality.

Σὺν ὑμῖν ἂν οἶμαι τίμιος εἶναι, ὅπου ἂν ὦ.

Ἀρίστιππος αἰτεῖ Κῦρον εἰς δισχιλίους ξένους καὶ μισθόν, ὡς οὕτως περιγενόμενος ἂν τῶν ἀντιστασιωτῶν.

Note.—Aorist infinitives or participles that stand for optatives never denote past time. Compare 169. 170.

C. THE VERBAL ADJECTIVES.

205. 1. Verbal adjectives in -τός, -τή, -τόν denote (79, 9) either what **has been** done : λυτός (*that has been*) *loosed,* ἄκρατος *unmixed,* or what **may be** done : βρωτός *that may be eaten, eatable,* ἀόρατος *invisible.*

2. Verbal adjectives in -τέος, -τέα, -τέον denote **necessity.**

E.g. λυτέος *solvendus,* πειστέον *oboediendum,* ἰτέον *it is necessary to go, one must go.*

The personal construction emphasizes the person (or thing) that must be acted upon.

The impersonal construction emphasizes the kind of action that is to be done.

The person who must do something is put in the dative (157, 2).

Οἱ συμμαχεῖν ἐθέλοντες εὖ ποιητέοι.

Οἰστέον πᾶσι τὴν τύχην. Τῷ ἀδικοῦντι δοτέον δίκην.

3. In -τικος denote aptness, ability

X. THE PARTICLES.

THE NEGATIVE PARTICLES.

206. 1. There are two negative adverbs : οὐ and μή.

By οὐ (οὔτε, etc.) we **deny** (the truth of) a statement, by μή (μήτε, etc.) we **desire** that something feared may not happen.

Ἐγὼ θρασὺς καὶ ἀναιδὴς οὔτ᾽ εἰμὶ μήτε γενοίμην.

2. Accordingly, οὐ stands in all **statements,**

i.e. in independent and dependent declarations, in questions and causal sentences, as well as in ordinary relative and temporal clauses.

Οὐ δυνατόν ἐστιν — ἔλεγεν, ὅτι οὐ δυνατὸν εἴη — τί οὐκ ἤλθετε ; — ἐπεὶ ταῦτ᾽ οὐκ ἐγένετο — ὅθεν οὐκ ἔστιν ἐξελθεῖν.

3. μή is required in all sentences that express a **desire,**

i.e. in independent and dependent wishes and prohibitions, as well as in dependent final clauses.

Μή μοι γένοιθ᾽ ἃ βούλομ᾽ ἀλλ᾽ ἃ συμφέρει.

Μὴ φθόνει τοῖς εὐτυχοῦσι, μὴ δοκῇς εἶναι κακός.

Δέδοικα, μὴ ἐπιλαθώμεθα τῆς οἴκαδε ὁδοῦ.

4. Again, μή is used

a) in conditions and in all such phrases or clauses as are equivalent in sense to a condition.

Εἰ μὴ καθέξεις γλῶσσαν, ἔσται σοι κακά.

ᾺA μὴ οἶδα, οὐδὲ οἴομαι εἰδέναι.

Ὁ μὴ δαρεὶς ἄνθρωπος οὐ παιδεύεται.

b) with the infinitive, with which, however, after verbs of saying οὐ may also be used:

Ὑπισχνοῦντο μηδὲν χαλεπὸν αὐτοὺς πείσεσθαι.

Τολμῶσι λέγειν οὐδεμίαν μάχην γεγονέναι.

Note 1. — After the verbs of controverting, denying, doubting, and the like, which convey a negative idea, the dependent assertion receives an additional οὐ, which must not be rendered in English.

Οὐκ ἂν ἀρνηθεῖεν ἔνιοι, ὡς οὐκ εἰσὶ τοιοῦτοι.

Note 2. — In like manner, after verbs of hindering, refraining, avoiding, refusing, declining, denying, escaping, and the like, μή is often added to the infinitive, or μὴ οὐ, when the main verb itself is negatived (also τὸ μή and τὸ μὴ οὐ respectively).

Μικρὸν ἐξέφυγε μὴ καταπετρωθῆναι *narrowly escaped being stoned.*

Ὁ φόβος τὸν νοῦν ἀπείργει μὴ λέγειν, ἃ βούλεται *hinders from saying.*

Οὐδεὶς πώποτε ἀντεῖπε μὴ οὐ καλῶς ἔχειν τοὺς νόμους *denied that the laws are good.*

Καὶ φημὶ δρᾶσαι κοὐκ ἀπαρνοῦμαι τὸ μὴ οὐ *I do not deny it.*

Μή is always added after verbs of forbidding:

e.g. Ἀπηγόρευε μηδένα βάλλειν πρὶν Κῦρος ἐμπλησθείη θηρῶν.

5. **Accumulation of Negatives** of the same kind. A negative or several negatives following another negative of the same kind emphasize the negation, if they are compounded, but neutralize it, if they are simple.

Οὐκ ἐρεῖ οὐδεὶς οὐδέν *no one will say anything.*

Οὐδεὶς οὐκ ἀποθανεῖται *every one will die.*

6. **Combination of Negatives** of a different kind.

a) **οὐ μή** with the aor. subj. or fut. indic. is used in cautious or ironical assertions: "*hardly, not likely, certainly not*" (181, 3. note 1).

Τοὺς πονηροὺς οὐ μή ποτε βελτίους ποιήσετε.

b) **μὴ οὐ** with the subj. (or indirect optat. 193, 2, b) after verbs of fearing means: *ne non, that not* (181, 2; compare 3, note 1, "*perhaps not, I rather think . . . not*").

Ἐφοβεῖτο μὴ οὐ δύναιτο ἐκ τῆς χώρας ἐξελθεῖν.

c) **μὴ οὐ** with the inf. after a negative main verb (or after negative expressions) = *not to* (206, 4. note 2).

Οὐχ ὅσιόν σοί ἐστι μὴ οὐ βοηθεῖν δικαιοσύνῃ.

Πᾶσιν αἰσχύνη ἦν μὴ οὐ συσπουδάζειν.

THE INTERROGATIVE PARTICLES.

207. In independent questions, the Greeks expressed

1. the Latin *-ně :*   by ἦ and ἆρα,
2. the Latin *nonne :*   by οὐ, ἆρ᾽ οὐ — οὐκοῦν *nonne igitur ?*

                             ἦ γάρ and ἄλλο τι ἤ *does* or *is he* (*she, it*) *not ?*
3. the Latin *num :*   by μή, ἆρα μή ⎱ *" indeed?"* implying a

                             μῶν (= μὴ οὖν) ⎰ neg. answer.
4. the Latin *utrum — an :* by πότερον (πότερα) — ἤ,

   the Latin *— an :*   by —— ἤ.

N o t e. — For dependent questions, see 179.

THE REMAINING PARTICLES.

Their Most Common Meanings and Usages.

208. N o t e 1. — Such particles as cannot begin a sentence are called p o s t-
p o s i t i v e. In the subjoined list, they are marked by an asterisk. The references
are to Xenophon's Anabasis.

N o t e 2. — It should be remembered that the meanings of the Greek particles
which are given below are in many instances merely approximate. The Greeks were
able by them to express the finest shades of meaning. In English, the stress of the
voice, a change of tone, or even a gesture, will sometimes serve the same purpose.

1. ᾽Αλλά adversative: *on the other hand, but, yet, still, however, on the
   contrary, rather, sed, at ;* especially after negatives.

   with imper. and subjunctives: *well then, come now, come then.*
   in replies: *well, well but, but mind, for my own part.*
   in transitions to some new topic: *but enough of this, be this as it
   may.*

   ἀλλ᾽ οὐ, ἀλλὰ μή : *ac non, not, and not, but not, instead of ;* = καὶ οὐ. 2, 1, 10.
   ἀλλ᾽ οὖν (γε) : *yet certainly, yet at least, yet at any rate.*
   εἰ μὴ — ἀλλά γε : *si non — at tamen.*
   οὐ μὴν (μέντοι) ἀλλά : *verum tamen, however, still.*

2. ἄλλως : *in another way, otherwise, differently ; at random.*

   ἄλλως τε καί : (*both in other respects and*) = *especially, above all, particularly.*
   τὴν ἄλλως : *to no purpose, fruitlessly, in vain, idly* (cf. τὴν ταχίστην 141).

3. ἅμα : *at the same time, together with, at once.*
   With dat. 158, 1.   With part. 203, 3. c.

   ἅμα μέν — ἅμα δέ : — *and at the same time, at once — and, both — and ; partly —
   partly.*
   ἅμα (τε) — καί : *both — and* (καὶ ἅμα : *and at the same time*), *as soon as —
   at once, scarce — when, no sooner — than.*

4. **ἄρα** inferential : *therefore, then, consequently, accordingly.*

   intimating that, what is said, is obvious, a matter of course:
   *obviously, evidently, naturally, apparently, as one may con-
   clude, as may be expected, as is known, videlicet.*

   sometimes epexegetic : *to wit, namely.*

   introducing something that follows: *next, immediately, forthwith.*

   εἰ ἄρα, ἐὰν ἄρα : *if perhaps; to wit, if: if indeed, if forsooth.*

   εἰ μὴ ἄρα with the indic. : *that is to say, if not; unless perhaps, unless forsooth,
   nisi forte, nisi vero.* 188, 2. d.

   ὡς (ὅτι) ἄρα : *to wit, that ; namely, that.*

   οὐκ ἄρα : *consequently not ; then after all not* (with imperfect).

5. **ἆρα**; interrogative = *-ně?* ἆρ' οὐ; = *nonne ?* — ἆρα μή; = *num?*
   207, 2. 3.

6. **ἀτάρ** (Homer **αὐτάρ**) adversative : *but, yet, but yet, on the other hand.*
   implying emphasis and gradation : *but above all, but especially, vero.*

7. **αὖ** adversative : *in turn, on the contrary, on the other hand ; likewise, too, again.* 1, 6, 7 ; 1, 10, 11 ; 1, 1, 7.

8. **γάρ** stating a reason, cause or motive: *for, enim ;* — often account-
   ing for a thought which is to be supplied.

   explaining and specifying: *namely, to wit,* — often introducing
   an announced (or an expected) explanation.

   in animated questions, denoting impatience, surprise, like *nam*
   in *quisnam ?* τίς γάρ; *"why, who . . ."* or *"who, pray, . . ."*
   or *"who then."*

   ἀλλὰ γάρ : *at enim, but* (a thought to be supplied) *for = but of course ; however;
   but since, since however; but alas !*

   καὶ γάρ : *etenim, and* (*I may well say so*) *for, for truly, and to be sure.
   nam etiam, for also, for even.
   nam et, for both* (*. . . et, and*).

   For εἰ γάρ, see 172, 2 ; 174, 1.

9. **γέ** (encl.), like *quidem,* emphatic and restrictive : *indeed, certainly,
   at all events, at least.*

   ἐπείγε : *quandoquidem, since indeed ;* ἀλλὰ — γέ : *yet certainly, yet at least, yet
   at any rate.*

   For ἔγωγε etc., see 61, 2 ; for ὅσγε, 129, 1. note 3.

10. **γοῦν** (from γὲ οὖν), emphatic: *at least, at any rate, at all events,
    certe.*

11. **δέ** adversative : *but, however, autem, atqui* (by far less emphatic
    than ἀλλά). See καί and μέν; in replies often: *to be sure, certainly.*

    δέ very frequently simply *connects* clauses: *and, thereupon,* etc., or
    it is not translated at all. *But not, and not =* ἀλλ' οὐ or οὐ μέντοι.

    For οὐδέ, see below 31.

12. ***δή** temporal: *already, presently, now, just now, immediately, iam ;*
νῦν δή : *just now, even now, now at once.*
inferential: *then, therefore, accordingly.*
marking as a matter of course: *evidently, as is known, scilicet, of course, you know.* καὶ δὴ καί *and of course (and therefore) also;* see below 19.
with an imperative, strongly urging: λέγε δή *now then, go on to say!; pray, tell me!*
emphatic and serving to call attention to something: as in ἔνθα δή *tum vero, at this juncture, at that crisis, it was then that, on this very occasion,* or merely an emphatic *then,* ὅτε δή *just at the time when.* τί δή ; *what in the world? quid tandem?*

εἰ δή *namely if, if indeed, if really.*
ὃς δή *he who, the very person who, who therefore, who in fact.*
ὅστις δή *whosoever (I do not know who), nescio quis, some one.*

13. **δῆθεν** implying gradation: *above all, especially so* (introduces an *a fortiori*). — *as it seems, to all appearances.*
restrictive: *of course, apparently, as is pretended.*

14. ***δήπου** (less emphatic than δή): expresses confidence that a statement will not be doubted: *profecto, of course, you know, surely;* often ironically like *opinor, credo.*

15. ***δῆτα** (more emphatic than δή): *indeed, certainly, to be sure.*
οὐ δῆτα : *no! indeed not, of course not.* τί δῆτα : *what then?*

16. **εἴτε — εἴτε** (*sive — sive*): *be it that — or that; whether — or* (i.e. in both cases).
In dependent questions: *whether — or; if — or if;* 179.

17. **ἦ** in asseverations: *truly, of a surety, really, verily;* still more emphatic is ἦ μήν, see below 25.
For the interrogative particle ἦ, see 207.
ἦ που *surely.*

18. **ἤ** disjunctive: *or;* often doubled ἤ — ἤ, *aut — aut.*
comparative: *than,* after comparatives and comparative expressions (such as ἄλλος, ἕτερος, ἐναντίος).
ἄλλο τι ἤ: *is it not so? nonne?* 207, 2.
ἤτοι (γε) — ἤ (or ἤ — ἤτοι) : *aut — aut.*
ἀλλ' ἤ after a negative particle or a question : *nisi, but, except.*

Note. — With numerals and measures, ἤ is often omitted after the adverbial comparatives πλέον (coll. form πλεῖν), ἔλαττον, μεῖον, as well as after the corresponding adjectives; *e.g.* πέμπει οὐκ ἔλαττον δέκα ἄνδρας *non minus decem;* ἔτη γεγονὼς πλείω ἑβδομήκοντα *annos natus amplius septuaginta.*

19. **καί** copulative: *and, also, too;* emphatic: *even ;* sometimes inferential: *and consequently* (= *itáque*); with comparatives: *still, yet.*

Where more than two words are to be joined, the Greek repeats καί with
each one of them (polysyndeton).

καί — καί, *both — and*, joins things of equal importance. See below 39.

καί after expressions of **sameness** or **likeness**: *as;* ὅμοιος, ὁμοίως, ὁ
αὐτὸς καί = *similis, similiter, idem atque.*

δὲ καί: *moreover, also, besides; likewise, (and) — too;* 1, 4, 17.

καὶ δέ: *(but, and) also, (but, and) even; moreover;* here δέ connects, καί
emphasizes. 2, 6, 8.

καὶ δὴ καί: *and (therefore) evidently also, and especially also.*

οὐ μόνον — ἀλλὰ καί: *not only — but also.*

ἤδη — καί: *iam — cum, already — when* (cf. *cum inversum*).

οὔπω — καί: *nondum — cum, not yet — when.*

20. **καίτοι** concessive: *and yet, still, though, however.*
    but, atqui (in the minor of a syllogism). See 40.

21. **μά** in asseveration; followed by the acc. of the god or thing called
    upon as witness (see 133).

    μὰ τοὺς θεούς : *by the gods !* ναὶ μὰ Δία: *yes, by Zeus.*

    οὐ μὰ Δία: *no, by Zeus.*

22. *****μέν**, a weak form of μήν. It is used

    a) in asseveration: *certainly, truly, indeed, in truth.*

    καὶ (ἀλλὰ) μὲν δή *and (but) certainly, and in fact; even — indeed.*

    οὐ μὲν δή *certainly not, indeed not.* Compare 32 extr.

    b) μέν — δέ are used in general to call attention to *any* kind of
    correlation (not only antithetical relations!) of those words (or even parts
    of sentences) which they follow and which the author wishes to be
    viewed *conjointly*, and not singly.

    μέν is then mostly *not* translated, but only marked by the tone; see 1, 1, 1;
    so in πρῶτον μέν — ἔπειτα δέ *in the first place — in the second place.*

    μέν — δέ are frequently used in forming *periods*, (Dem. 16, 30) ; also in the
    figure *anaphora* 1, 3, 16: *"showing in the first place — in the second place — in the
    third place";* sometimes to be rendered by: *as — so.* See ὁ μέν — ὁ δέ 116.

    μέν — δέ are often *adversative: — but, however, on the contrary, whilst, whereas*
    sometimes *concessive: indeed — but; it is true — but.*

23. *****μέντοι** emphatic: *indeed, really, certainly, in truth.*

    adversative (often after μέν): *but, yet, however; — for all
    that, nevertheless, all the same.*

    in questions: οὐ μέντοι —; *is it not so? nonne?*

    For οὐ μέντοι ἀλλά, see 1.

24. **μή**: *not*, the negative adverb in expressions of desire. 206, 3;
    apparently heading an independent sentence, 181, 3, note 1;
    in questions = *num*, 207, 3.

    οὐ μή and μὴ οὐ 206, 6 ; μηδέ, see οὐδέ below 31.

    μὴ ὅτι (= μὴ εἴπω, εἴπῃς, ὑπολάβῃς, ὅτι) : *not only.*

    μὴ ὅτι and μὴ ὅπως (like οὐχ ὅπως) : *not only not.*   [*less (more).*

    μὴ ὅτι and μὴ τί γε δή (sc. εἴπῃς) : *not to mention, to say nothing of, much*

    ὅτι μή (like εἰ μή 188, 2. a) : *except, but, nisi.*

25. ***μήν**, in asseveration: *vero, verily, in truth, certainly*, often preceded by ἦ : *upon my sacred honor* (see above 17).

adversative: *but, however, nevertheless, yet, for all that.*

ἀλλὰ μήν : *at vero, but certainly, but still.*

καὶ μήν : *et vero, and yet, and in fact.*

Both ἀλλὰ μήν and καὶ μήν are also used in transitions to some *new* (and more important) topic: *furthermore;* also in the *minor* of a syllogism: *but, now, but now.* For οὐ μὴν ἀλλά, see 1.

26. **μῶν**, interrogative = **μὴ οὖν**: *num . . . ?* implying a negative answer. 207, 3.

27. **ναί**, in replies: *yes.* ναὶ μὰ Δία: *yes, by Zeus;* compare 21.

28. **νή**, in asseveration; **νὴ Δία**: *yes, by Zeus.* 133.

29. ***νύν** (encl.), illative: *then, therefore.* See 40.

30. **οὐ**: *not*, the negative adverb in statements. 206, 2.

In direct questions: ἆρ' οὐ, οὐκοῦν: *nonne*, 207, 2.

οὔ τι : *not a whit, not at all, by no means, not in the least.*

οὐχ ὅτι (οὐκ ἐρῶ ὅτι); *not only;* also: *although.*

οὐ μόνον ὅτι and οὐχ ὅτι μόνον : *not only.*

οὐχ ὅπως (οὐκ ἐρῶ ὅπως) : — ἀλλὰ καί (οὐδὲ) : *not only not — but even (not even)* ; after negative expressions : *not to mention, much less.*

μόνον οὐ (οὐχί), ὅσον οὐ: *tantum non, almost, all but.* Dem. 1, 2.

ὅσον οὔπω, ὅσον οὐκ ἤδη : *almost already.*

31. **οὐδέ (μηδέ)**, copulative: a) *and not, nor, neque* where some n e g a-t i v e particle precedes (otherwise *and not* = καὶ οὐ).

b) *also not, likewise not, neither; not even, ne — quidem.*

οὐδ' εἰ : *not even if.* Compare 189.

οὐδέ — οὐδέ : *not even — nor.*

οὐδέ — δέ : *but . . . neither (likewise not), nor yet.*

32. ***οὖν**, confirmative: *indeed, certainly, the fact is, at any rate.*

inferential : *then, therefore, consequently, accordingly.*

It also introduces a promised or expected explanation, *e.g.* in the transition from the exordium to the subject-matter of a speech: *then* often not translated.

ἆρ' οὖν; (affirmative inference) : *really? indeed?*

ἀλλ' οὖν (γε) : *yet surely, yet certainly, yet at least, but at any rate.*

δ' οὖν: *now, but now* (in the m i n o r of a syllogism); *but certain it is that, yet at any rate, but at all events.*

καὶ γὰρ οὖν : *wherefore then, and consequently also, and on that account, for at any rate, for the fact is.*

μὲν οὖν : a) confirmative: (πάνυ, κομιδῆ, οὐ) μὲν οὖν *to be sure, certainly.*

  b) introducing a correction: *nay rather, immo vero.*

  c) when corresponding to a following δέ, each particle has its original force.

joined to relatives: **ὁστισοῦν** (ὁντιναοῦν, ἡστινοσοῦν etc.) : *quicunque, whosoever.*

33. **οὐκοῦν** (a strengthened οὖν) is:
   a) inferential and confirmative : *therefore, then, accordingly;*
   b) interrogative : = *nonne igitur?*　207, 2.

34. **οὔκουν** (a strengthened οὐκ) is:
   a) inferential and confirmative : *therefore not, at any rate not.*
   b) interrogative : *therefore not? so then not?*

35. **οὔτε — οὔτε** (**μήτε — μήτε**) : *neque — neque, neither — nor.*
   οὔτε (**μήτε**) **— τέ** : *neque — et, on the one hand not — and (but) on the other hand, not only not — but even.*
   οὔτε — οὐ (poet.) : = **οὔτε — οὔτε**.
   οὔτε — οὐδέ : *neither — nor even ; neque — et ne — quidem.*

36. ***πέρ** (encl., from πέρι) : *just, even, indeed, very, very much;* w. part.
   often = καίπερ. Compare Homer Od. α 6 with α 315.
   ὅσπερ *the very person who ;* **ἐπείπερ** *seeing that, because precisely.*
   ὥσπερ *just as, even as ;* **ὅτεπερ** *just (at the very time, even) when ;* **εἴπερ** *if indeed,* 188, 2. c.

37. **πλήν** : *except, save, but,* is :
   a) a prepositional adverb with genit., 162, 5.
   b) a conjunction : *except that, save that, only ;*
      it stands with the indic. or with the verb understood.

38. ***πώ** (encl.) *yet, as yet ;* mostly joined to negatives :
   οὔπω *nondum, not yet* (**οὐκέτι** *iam non, no longer !*)

39. ***τέ** (encl., Lat. = -que), copulative : *and;* in prose
   τέ — τέ : *both — and* (= καί — καί) generally connects sentences of equal importance, whereas
   τέ — καί : *as well as, not only — but also,* connects single words that supplement each other and of which the second is of greater importance.

40. ***τοί** (encl.) in asseveration : *verily, in truth, surely.* In this sense it is often joined to other particles :
   καίτοι above 20 ; **μέντοι** above 23 ; **οὔτοι** *indeed not.*
   τοίγαρ inferential : *therefore, then, consequently, accordingly ;* strengthened forms are **τοιγαροῦν** and **τοιγάρτοι** : *for this very reason, precisely on that account.*
   τοίνυν : inferential (esp. in the conclusion of a syllogism) : *therefore, consequently ;* introducing a m i n o r proposition : *but, atqui ;*
   sometimes synonymous with δέ : *besides, moreover, again, furthermore* (esp. **ἔτι τοίνυν**).

HOMERIC DIALECT.

ON THE SOUNDS.

209. 1. Vowels : η for α: φιλίη, νεηνίης, πρήσσω — ἀληθείη.
ει for ε : ξεῖνος, εἵνεκα, χρύσειος.
ου for ο : μοῦνος, οὔνομα, πουλύς etc.

2. Metathesis : κάρτος, καρτερός, ἔδρακον, ἔπραθον.
θρῴσκω : ἔθορον — βλώσκω : ἔμολον.

3. Metathesis of Quantity : 'Ατρείδεω and 'Ατρείδᾱο.
στέωμεν and στήομεν. ἔως, τέως and ἧος, τῆος.

4. Contraction : γήραος, τέραα, τεράων, τεράεσσι, μένεα,
τέγεος, φίλεον, ἀοιδιάει, ἀοιδιάουσα etc.
'Ερμῆς, ἠοῦς, ἠῶ, σέλᾳ, τιμᾷ, ἐφορμᾶται —
εο and εου to ευ : θέρευς, φιλεῦντες, σεῦ — νεικεῦσι.
εεα to εια or εα : εὐκλείας, δυσκλέα.
εεαι to ειαι or εαι : μυθεῖαι or μυθέαι.

5. Synizesis : Πηληιάδεω 'Αχιλῆος — ἀλλ' ὅτε δὴ ἕβδομον ἦμαρ.
χρυσέοισιν ἐπὶ κλισμοῖσι — εἰλαπίνη ἦε γάμος.
ἀλλ' ἑῶμέν μιν πρῶτα — ἦ οὐκ ἀίεις etc.

6. Apocope : in ἄρ (for ἄρα), in ἄν (for ἀνά), κάτ, πάρ, ἄπ, ὕπ ;
with assimilation : κάλ-λιπε, κάβ-βαλε, κάτ-θεμεν, κατ-θέμεν,
κὰρ ῥόον, κὰπ πεδίον, κὰκ κεφαλῆς, κὰδ δὲ παρειῶν, ἀλ-λέξαι,
ἀμ-μείξας, ἀμ-πνεῦσαι, ἀγ-κρεμάσας, ἀν-στήσας, ἂμ πεδίον.

7. A digamma was originally in the following words :

ϝέαρ *vēr*	ϝίς *vīs*	ϝέλ-δομαι *vel-le*
ϝεσθής *vestis*	ϝοῖκος *vīcus*	ϝερ- *ver-bum*
ϝέσπερος *vesper*	ϝοῖνος *vīnum*	ϝιδ-, ἔ-ϝιδον ⎫
ϝείκοσι *viginti*	ϝέπος, ϝόψ *vōx*	ϝοῖδα, ϝεῖδος ⎭ *vid-ēre*

ϝῶνος, ὁ (hence ἐ-ωνούμην 89, 1.
note)

ϝαλίσκομαι hence (ἑάλων, ἑά-
λωκα)

ϝοράω (hence ἐ-ώρων 89, 2)

ϝεκών (hence ἀέκων, i.e. ἀϝέκων)

ϝέλπομαι (hence ἔολπα, i.e. ϝέ-
ϝολπα)

ϝεργάζομαι (hence ϝέϝοργα and
εἴργ.)

8. There was an initial σϝ in ὅς (σϝός)= *suus*, ἔ = *sē*, ἑκυρός =
socer, ἀνδάνω, aor. εὔαδον (= ἔσϝαδον), ἡδύς (*suāvis*) etc.

165

9. Doubling of Consonants:

ποσσίν, δικάσσατε—ἔσσομαι, ἐτέλεσσα.

ὅττι, ὅππως, ὁππότε — ἔδδεισεν, ἀδδήσειεν.

τόσσος, ἔμμορε, ἔννεον, ἔλλαβε, ἔσσυτο.

10. Auxiliary Consonants (ἀνδρός, γαμβρός, μεσημβρία):

ἤμβροτον of ἁμαρτάνω, μέμβλεται of μέλει.

μέμβλωκα of ἔμολον, βλώσκω — ἄμβροτος.

INFLECTION OF NOUNS.

210. 1. A-Decl.: ἱππότᾰ. Ἀτρείδαο, Ἀτρείδεω, ἐυμμελίω.

δῖα θεάων, πυλέων ἐξέσσυτο, κὰδ δὲ παρειῶν.

ἀθανάτῃσι θεῆς — ἀκταῖς, πάσαις.

2. O-Decl.: ἀργυρέοιο βιοῖο — ὅο κράτος, Αἰόλοο κλυτὰ δώματα.

θεοῖσιν ἐπουρανίοισιν — τοῖιν ὤμοιιν.

3. Conson. Decl.: ποσ-σί, ποσί, πόδ-εσσι — βέλες-σι, βέλεσι, βελέ-εσσιν.

ἔριν and ἔριδα.   γούνατος and γουνός.

οὔατος, οὔασιν and ὠσίν.

πατέρος and πατρός, θυγατέρα and θύγατρα.

ἀνέρος and ἀνδρός, ἄνδρεσσι and ἀνδράσιν.

γήραος, οὔδεος, μένεος, θέρευς, μένεα.

κλέα, ἀγακλεές (see 209, 4). — Ἡρακλῆος, -κλῆι, -κλῆα.

ἠώς, -οῦς, -οῖ, -ῶ. — σπείους, σπῆι, σπέσσι, σπήεσσι.

πόλις: πόλιος and πόληος, πόλει and πόληι.

ἡδύς: εὐρύν and εὐρέα.   ὠκέα Ἶρις, βαθέης ὕλης.

βασιλῆος etc., βασιλεῦσι.   Ὀδυσ(σ)ῆος and -σ(σ)έος.

4. Irreg. nouns: Ἀίδης: Ἀίδαο and Ἀίδεω and Ἄιδος.

Ἄρης: Ἄρηος and Ἄρεος, voc. Ἄρες and Ἄρες.

Ζεύς: Διός and Ζηνός, Ζῆνα and Ζῆν.

κάρη, τό: καρήατος, κάρητος, κράατος and κρᾱτός, κράτων, κρᾱσίν. — κάρηνα, καρήνων.

νηῦς: νηός and νεός, νήεσσι, νέεσσι and νηυσίν.

υἱός: υἱέος and υἱος.

ἀλκή: ἀλκῇ and ἀλκί.   μάστιγι, μάστιγα and μάστι, μάστιν.

5. Suffixes. -φι: ἐξ εὐνῆφι — κρατερῆφι βίηφι (sing.), διὰ στήθεσφιν — σὺν ὄχεσφιν (plur.).

-θεν and -θι: ἐξ ἁλόθεν, ἐμέθεν — ἠῶθι πρό.

6. Adjectives: ἰφθίμους ψυχάς, ἀθανάτη ψυχή.

πο(υ)λύς, πολυ, G. πολέος, A. πο(υ)λύν (masc. and fem.).

Plur. πολέες, πολέων, πολέεσσι, πολέσσι and πολέσι,

and πολλός, πολλή, πολλόν reg.

7. Comparison : γλυκίων, φιλίων — ὤκιστος — πλέες(= πλέονες),
Comp. ἀρείων, βέλτερος, φέρτερος, λώϊον, λωΐτερον,
       κακώτερος, χειρότερος, χερείων, χερειότερος —
       μάσσων, ἆσσον.
Sup. κάρτιστος, φέριστος, φέρτατος — μήκιστος, ἄγχιστα.

PRONOUNS.

211. 1. Personal : ἐγών, ἐμεῖο, ἐμέο, ἐμεῦ, ἐμέθεν. ἄμμες, ἄμμι, ἄμμε.
       τύνη, σεῖο, σέο, σεῦ, σέθεν — τεΐν.   ὕμμες, ὕμμι, ὕμμε.
       εἷο, ἕο, εὗ, ἕθεν — ἑοῖ — ἑέ, ἕ, μίν.
       σφεῖς, σφείων, σφίσιν and σφίν, σφέας, σφάς and σφέ.
Dual : νῶι, νῶιν — σφῶι, σφῶιν — σφωέ, σφωῖν.
    2. Possess. : ἐμός, τεός, ἑός and ὅς.   ἀμός, ὑμός, σφός and σφέτερος.
Dual : νωΐτερος.   σφωΐτερος.
    3. Demonst. : the article with τοί, ταί besides οἱ, αἱ,
                  and ὅς or ὅ (both masc. : he who), ἥ, ὅ (116, note).
    4. Relative : ὅ = ὅς and ἕης = ἧς, as also those forms of ὁ, ἡ, τό,
                  which begin with τ.
    5. Interrog. : τέο and τεῦ, τέῳ and τῷ, τέων, τέοισι ;
                   the same, when used as indefinite pronouns, are
                   enclitic.
    6. Generalizing Relatives : ὅτις besides ὅστις, ὅττεο and ὅτ(τ)ευ,
                                 ὅτεῳ,
                                 ὅτινα besides ὅντινα, — ὅτινας, ἄσσα.

CONJUGATION.

212. 1. Modal suffixes, subj. : ἐγείρ-ο-μεν, ποιήσ-ε-ται, εὔξεαι, ἴομεν.
            opt. : δύη (for δυίη), φθίμην, φθῖτο, δῦμεν,
                   δαινῦτο, δαινύατο, λῦτο, λελῦτο.
    2. Augment : ἔλυσε and λῦσε, ἔβη and βῆ, ἔχεν — κάθεμεν, ἄνεσαν.
    3. Personal endings : ἐθέλωμι, ἐθέλησθα, ἐθέλησι — τίθησθα.
       πεποίθεα, -εας, -εεν, — φόβηθεν, ἴεν, ἔφαν, βάν.
       ὀδύρεαι, ἐλύσαο — βέβληαι — φραζώμεσθα.
       βεβλήαται, -ατο, ἰδοίατο — δίδωθι, ὄμνυθι.
    4. Infinitive : ἀμύνειν, ἀμυνέμεν and ἀμυνέμεναι — ἰδέ-ειν.
    5. Contract Verbs in -άω, uncontr. : ἀοιδιάει, πεινάων, μενοίνεον.
assimilated γελόωντες and γελώοντες, ὁράᾳς.
    contr. : τιμᾷ, τιμῶσι, τιμῶν, ἐφορμᾶται.
    in -έω : φιλέεις, φίλεον, φιλέωμεν, φιλεῦντες.
    in -όω : ἀρόωσι, ὑπνώοντας, δηιόφεν, χολοῦνται.

6. Verbs in -μι : τιθεῖ, τιθεῖσι, διδοῖσθα, διδοῖ, διδοῦσιν.

θήω (θείω), θή-ῃς, θήομεν (θείομεν), θέ-ω-μεν.
γνώ-ω, γνώ-ῃς, δώ-ο-μεν, βήω (βείω),
στή-ο-μεν (στείομεν), στέωμεν, στή-ε-τε, στήωσι.
δαμή-ω (δαμείω), δαήω, μιγήῃς, φανήῃ,
τραπήομεν (from ἐτάρπην), δαμήετε, μιγέωσι.

εἶμι : εἶσθα, ἤια, ἴσαν, ἴμεν(αι), εἴσομαι, εἴσατο.
εἰμί : ἔασι, ἔα and ἔον, ἦην, ἔ(μ)μεν(αι), ἔσεται, ἐσσεῖται.
οἶδα : ἠείδης, εἴδομεν, ἰδέω, ἴδμεν(αι), ἰδυῖα, εἰδήσω.

7. Like forms (of different verbs):. ἴσαν (εἶμι, οἶδα), εἴσομαι
(εἶμι, οἶδα, εἴδομαι), εἰσάμην (εἶμι, εἴδομαι).

8. Presents with the force of futures : καλέω, τελέω, ἀνύω, ἐρύω,
ἀντιόω, δήω, κείω, κακκείοντες, νέομαι, βείομαι.

9. Aorists without σ : ἔκηα, ἔσσευα, ἔχευα, ἠλεύατο and ἀλέασθαι.

10. Aorists of Liquids with σ : ἔκελσα, ἄρσα, ἔκερσα, ὦρσα.

11. Mixed Aorists : ἷξον, δύσετο, βήσετο, λέξεο, ὄρσεο, οἰσέμεν(αι).

12. Reduplicated Second Aorists :

ἤραρον, ὤρορον, ἐπέφραδε, τεταρπώμεσθα, ἀμπεπαλών.
πεπιθεῖν, πεφιδέσθαι (fut. πεπιθήσω, πεφιδήσεται).
ἐπέπληγον, πεπλήγοντο, κέκλυθι, ἐνένιπε and ἠνίπαπον.
With syncope : κέκλετο, ἔτετμε, ἔπεφνε, ἄλαλκε.
In a causative sense : λελάχωσι, ἐκλέλαθον.

13. Primitive or Root-Aorists Act. and Mid.

(the aor. mid. mostly in an intr. or pass. sense) :

ἐγήρα, ἔκταν (1. p. sg. and 3. p. pl.), κτάμεναι, κτάς,
ἔκτατο, κτάσθαι, βλῆτο, λύντο, ἔφθιτο, φθίμενος,
Subj. κτέωμεν, βλήεται, φθίεται, φθιόμεσθα.
Opt. βλῇο (βλεῖο), φθίμην, φθῖτο 212, 1.
ἐδέγμην, δέξο, δέκτο, μεῖκτο, ἄλτο, πάλτο, πέρθαι, ἄρμενος.
λέκτο (of λέγω and λεχ-), πλῆτο (of πελάζω and πίμπλημι)

14. Aorists of different formation :

ἄειρα and ἀέρθην (of ἀείρω, αἴρω),
ἠράμην and ἀρόμην, ἀρέσθαι of ἄρνυμαι.
ἦρσα, ἤραρον, ἄρμενος, ἄρθην of ἀραρίσκω.
of ὄρνυμι : ὦρσα (212, 10) ; ὤρορον (212, 12).
       ὤρετο (with ὄρηται, ὄροιτο 86).
       ὦρτο (with ὄρσαι, ὄρθαι, ὄρμενος, 212, 13).
       and ὄρσευ, ὄρσευ (accdg. to 212, 11).

15. Perf. and Plupft. : κεκοπώς, πεφύασι, τεθνηώς.

With Attic redupl. : ἄρηρα, ὄρωρα, ἀλάλημαι, ἐρέριπτο.

With change of vowel : λέλασται (besides λήθομαι), ἔοικα and ἔικτον, εἰδώς and ἰδυῖα, πέφευγα and πεφυγμένος, τετεύχατο and τέτυκτο, τετύχθαι, τετυγμένος — ἄωρτο of ἀείρω.

With irreg. accent : ἀκάχησθαι, ἀκαχήμενος, ἐσσύμενος, ἀλάλησθαι, ἀλαλήμενος.

16. Iterative forms : ἔχεσκον, ἔλεσκε, μνησασκετο. στάσκον, κέ-σκετο.

ON SYNTAX.

Cases and Prepositions.

213. 1. The cases without a preposition are used in a local sense (cf. 162, 2).

Accus.: whither: ἔρχεσθον κλισίην.

Gen.: { where : ἔρχονται πεδίοιο —
{ whence: ἀνέδυ πολιῆς ἁλός — πίθων ἠφύσσετο οἶνος.

Dat.: { where : αἰθέρι ναίων — ἀκροτάτῃ κορυφῇ.
{ whither: χεὶρ πεδίῳ πέσε — θαλάσσῃ ἔλσαι Ἀχαιούς.

2. Prepositions : εἰνί, ἐνί and εἰν, παραί and ὑπαί, προτί and ποτί, ἀμφίς and ὑπείρ.

3. Prep. as adverbs : ἐν δέ, σὺν δέ, πρὸς δέ, μετὰ δέ, περὶ δέ.

περὶ μὲν θείειν ταχύς, περὶ δ' ἱρὰ θεοῖσιν ἔδωκε

4. Tmesis : ἐκ δ' ἔβαν αὐτοί — ἐξ ἔρον ἔντο — ἐπὶ κνέφας ἦλθε.

νήπιοι, οἳ κατὰ βοῦς Ὑπερίονος ἠελίοιο ἤσθιον.

5. Anastrophe : Κικόνων ὕπο δῃωθέντες — φυγὼν ὕπο νηλεὲς ἦμαρ.

6. Ἀνά w. the dat. : upon : χρυσέῳ ἀνὰ σκήπτρῳ.

7. Μετά w. the dat. : among : μετὰ τοῖσιν ἀνέστη.

between, in, with : e.g. μετὰ χερσὶν ἔχειν.

8. Ἔνι (for ἔνεστιν, ἔνεισιν), ἔπι, μέτα, πάρα — ἄνα.

Moods. — Infinitive.

214. 1. In independent sentences, the subjunctive (with or without ἄν), being the mood of anticipation, borders on the meaning of the future indicative.

Καί ποτέ τις εἴπῃσιν, cf. ὥς ποτέ τις ἐρέει.

Οὐ γάρ πω τοίους ἴδον ἀνέρας οὐδὲ ἴδωμαι.

2. Ἄν (κέ(ν)) may be used (contrary to Attic usage, 194) :

with the fut. ind. : Καί κέ τις ὧδ' ἐρέει.

in the protasis of conditional sentences of the third type :

Εἰ τούτω κε λάβοιμεν ἀροίμεθά κε κλέος ἐσθλόν.

frequently in final clauses :

'Αλλ' ἴθι, μή μ' ἐρέθιζε, σαώτερος ὥς κε νεηαι
rarely with the optative in wishes: ὥς κέ οἱ αὖθι | γαῖα χάνοι.

3. Ἄν (κέ(ν)) may be **omitted**, contrary to Attic usage,
with the potential optative :

'Ρεῖα θεός γ' ἐθέλων καὶ τηλόθεν ἄνδρα σαῶσαι.

with the iterative hypothetical subjunctive in conditional, as
well as hypoth.-relative and -temporal sentences:

Εἰ δ' αὖ τις ῥαίῃσι θεῶν ἐνὶ οἴνοπι πόντῳ, | τλήσομαι.
Ζεὺς | ἀνθρώπους ἐφορᾷ καὶ τίνυται, ὅς τις ἁμάρτῃ.
Ὦ φίλοι, οὐ γάρ πω καταδυσόμεθ' ἀχνύμενοί περ
εἰς 'Αΐδαο δόμους, πρὶν μόρσιμον ἦμαρ ἐπέλθῃ.

frequently also in comparisons :

Ὡς δ' ὅτε καπνὸς ἰὼν ἐξ ἄστεος αἰθέρ' ἵκηται
τηλόθεν ἐκ νήσου, τὴν δήιοι ἀμφιμάχωνται,
ὡς ἀπ' 'Αχιλλῆος κεφαλῆς σέλας αἰθέρ' ἵκανεν.
with the indicative implying unreality:
ἔνθα με κῦμ' ἀπόερσε *might have swept away.*

4. The infinitive with the force of an optative :
Ζεῦ ἄνα, Τηλέμαχόν μοι ἐν ἀνδράσιν ὄλβιον εἶναι,
καί οἱ πάντα γένοιτο, ὅσα φρεσὶν ᾗσι μενοινᾷ.

5. The infinitive with the force of an imperative :
Νοστήσας δὴ ἔπειτα φίλην ἐς πατρίδα γαῖαν
σῆμά τέ οἱ χεῦαι καὶ ἐπὶ κτέρεα κτερεΐξαι
πολλὰ μάλ', ὅσσα ἔοικε, καὶ ἀνέρι μητέρα δοῦναι.

215. THE MOST COMMON GRECIAN MEASURES, WEIGHTS AND COINS.

1. MEASURES OF LENGTH.

στάδιον	πλέθρα	ὀργυιαί	πήχεις	πόδες	EQUIVALENTS	
stadia	plethra	fathoms	cubits	feet	meters	feet
1	5	100	333⅓	500	164	540
	1 πλέθρον	20	66⅔	100	32.8	108
		1 ὀργυιά	3⅓	5	1.64	5.4
			1 πῆχυς	1½	.492	1.6
				1 πούς	.328	1.08

The above stadium was the itinerary stadium which was somewhat shorter than other stadia.

The Olympic stadium = 600 ft., reckoning .32 m to the foot,
= 192 m = 629 ft.

The Greek-Roman stadium = 600 ft., reckoning .29 m to the foot,
= 1 '8 m = 584 ft.

Parasang = 30 stadia = 4.92 km = 3.05 miles = an hour's march.

2. MEASURES OF CAPACITY.

DRY MEASURES				LIQUID MEASURES				
μέδιμνος	χοίνικες	Approximate		μετρητής	χόες	κοτύλαι	Approximate	
		gallons	pints				gallons	pints
1	48	12		1	12	144	9	
	1 χοῖνιξ		2		1 χοῦς	12		6
						1 κοτύλη		$\frac{1}{2}$

3. WEIGHTS AND COINS.

τάλαντο / (talent)	μναῖ (mina)	δραχμαί (drachma)	ὀβολοί (obol)	APPROXIMATE EQUIVALENTS			
				grammes	grains	dollars	cents
1	60	6000	36,000	26,400 =	405,000	1080	
	1 μνᾶ	100	600	440 =	6750	18	
		1 δραχμή	6	4.40 =	67.5		18
			1 ὀβολός	.73 =	11.2		3

The ratio of gold to silver was 10 or (in commerce) 12 to 1.

The Persian Δαρεικός (στατήρ) was exactly one Attic gold stater
= about $5.40.

Besides the above weights and coins of the Solonian coinage, the
ancient Aeginetan commercial weights were in vogue still at the
early Roman period. Of the latter, a talent = 36,156 grammes, a
mina = 602.6 gr., a drachma = 6.03 gr.

INDEXES.

In these Indexes the references are to the *Sections* of the Grammar. The *Prepositions* and *Particles* which are mentioned in alphabetical order in 163 and 208 are generally not included in the Greek Index. Nor is any reference made to the *Homeric Dialect.*

I. ENGLISH INDEX.

Ablative use of gen. 147 ff.

Ablaut 11, 2. See 88, 3. 108.

Absolute: acc. 203, 4. gen. 203, 2. 3.

Accent 3, 3. 4. gener. princ. 6–10. recessive 6, 6. in decl. 25, 5. 6. of monosyll. 36, 6. 7. in conjug. 72, 11. 12. of verbs in -μι 99, 4.

Accusative case: synt. 131–141. abs. 203, 4. w. inf. 197, 2. 199, 1.

Action, time or stage of 167, 1–4. 169, 1–4.

Active voice 164.

Adjectives: classif. 52–55. irreg. 55.

Adverbs 59; correl. 69. w. gen. 162, 5.

Adversative clauses 189. partic. in 203, 3. e.

Agreement, synt. 114. 115.

Alphabet 1. used as numerals 70.

Anastrophe 213, 5.

Anticipation or prolepsis 176, 5.

Aorist 72, 4. 79, 3. 8. second 86. 87. primitive or root 102. synt. 167, 2. 3. 168, 2. — 212, 9–14.

Apocope 209, 6.

Apposition: w. person. pron. 118, 1. w. names of persons 119, n. 3.

Article 26. in dual 71. synt. 116–124.

Assimilation 19. of rel. to case of antec. 129, 2. inverted 129, 2. n. of mood 192.

Atonics 8.

Attic: decl. 35. redupl. 89, 5. fut. 90, 1.

Attraction of rel. 129, 2. w. n.

Attributive position of art. 120.

Augment 73. in compounds 75. in plupf. 79, 5. peculiarities of 89.

Augmented tenses 72, 6. — 176, 3.

Barytones 7.

Breathings 3.

Caring, vbs. of 181.

Case-endings, locative 51.

Cases: synt. 131–161. of infin. 198, 2.

Causal sentences, depend. 178. caus. rel. claus. 191, 3. a.

Caution, vbs. of 181.

Coins 215, 3.

Comparison: of adj. 56–58. of adv. 59, 3.

Compensative lengthening 13.

Compound words : accent of 6, 6. augm. and redupl. of 75. comp. verbs trans. 134.

Concessive clauses 189. partic. in 203, 3. e.

Conditional sentences 182–188.

Conjugation 72–113. of pure verbs 78–81. of mute verbs 82. 83. of liquid verbs 84. 85. of verbs in -ω 97. of verbs in -μι 98–106. irregul. 107–113.

Consecutive clauses 180. rel. 191, 3. b.

Consonants: final 23. movable 24. euphonic changes in 19.

Contraction 16. of nouns: 1st and 2d decl. 30. 33. of verbs 81. 91, 1 ff. accent of contr. syll. 16, 2.

Copula 114, 4. foot-note. 104, 3. n. 1.

Coronis 18, 1.

Correlative: pron. 68. adv. 69.

Crasis 18. 63, 1. n. 68, 2. n.

Danger, vbs. of 181, 1. 2. w. notes 1. 2.

Dative case, synt. 154–161.

Declension 25 ff.

Demonstrative pron. 65. — 128.

Dependent sentences 176 ff.

Deponent verbs 72, 3. passive, middle dep. 95, 1. 2.

Digamma 1, 2. n. 1. omission of 89, 1.

Diminutives all neut. 25, 2.

Diphthongs 2, 2. 3. 3, 4.

Division of syllables 5.

Doric: gen. 29, 3. fut. 113, *s.v.* πλέω, φεύγω, ψεύδω.

Dual: in decl. 71. in conj. 96. synt. 114, 2.

Dubitative: subj. 173, 2. quest. 179, 2.

Durative present, imperf. 168, 1.

E-class of verbs 111.

Elision 17.

Enclitics 9. w. accent if emphatic 10.

Final clauses 181. final rel. cl. 191, 3. c.

Final consonants 23. movable 24.

Time: of action 167. relative 170. acc. of 140. gen. of 152. dat. of 160, 2.
Transitive and intr. verbs 164, 1. 93. 133.

Verb stem 72, 7.
Verbal nouns and adjectives 72, 1. 12. c. 79, 9. 195–205.
Verbs: in -ω 76–97. contract 81 ff. in

-μι 98 ff. in -ννμι 105 ff. irregular 107–112.
Vocative case 25, 4. 36, 5.
Vowels, change of 11 ff.

Weights 215, 3.
Wishes: attainable 174, 1. hopeless 172, 2.

II. GREEK INDEX.

ἀγαθός 58, 1. 59, 2.— 199, 2.

ἀγάλλομαι 159, 2. w. n., 202, 1 d.

ἄγαμαι 95, 2. 101, 4.— 150.

ἀγανακτέω 159, 2. w. n., 202, 1 d. 2. n. 1.

ἀγγέλλω 85, 2. 97, 30.— 202, 2. b. & n. 1.

ἀγῆναι & ἄγνυμι 113.

ἀγορεύω 112, 12.

ἄγω 97, 16. 94, 3. 113. — 164.

ἀδεῖν, ἀδήσω 113, s.v. ἀνδάνω.

ἀδελφός 60.

ἄδηλον ὄν 203, 4.

ἀδικέω 75, 3. 94, 2 (& 3).— 133. 168, 1. n. 2. 202, 1. c.

ᾄδω, see 94, 1.

Ἀθήναζε, -ηθεν 51.

Ἀθήνησι 51.— 160, 1.

ἀθρόος, a, ον 60.

ἀθυμέω 75, 3.

αἰδέομαι 91, 4.— 133. 202, 2. n. 5.

Ἀιδου, ἐν & εἰς 143.

αἰδώς 44, 3.

αἰνέω 91, 5. 113.

αἱρέομαι 112, 1. — 135. 199, 3.

αἱρέω 112, 1. — 144, 2. 164, 2. 165, 1. b.

αἴρω 90, 3. 97, 47.— 164, 1.

αἰσθάνομαι 109, 7.— 147, 4. w. n. 202, 2. n. 4.

αἰσχρόν ὄν 203, 4.

αἰσχρός 57, 2.— 199, 2. 206, 4. n. 2.

αἰσχύνομαι 95, 3.— 133. 159, 2. 202, 2. n. 5.

αἰτέω 136. 199, 1.

αἰτιάομαι 95, 1. — 144, 2.

αἴτιος 144, 2.

ἀκούω 89, 5. 94, 1. 97, 41.— 147, 4. w. n. 202, 2. n. 1 & 4.

ἀκρατής 144, 3.

ἀκροάομαι 113.— 147, 4.

ἄκρος w. art. 122, 3.

ἄκων 115, 1. 203, 2. n. b.

ἀλαλάζω 113.

ἀλγεινός, ἀλγίων 60.

ἀλείφω 113.

ἀλέξω 113.

ἀλέω 113.

ἀλήλε(σ)μαι 113, s.v. ἀλέω.

ἀλήλιμμαι 113, s.v. ἀλείφω.

ἁλίσκομαι 110, 4. — 144, 2. 164, 2. 202, 2.

ἀλλάττω 87, 3.

ἀλλήλων 63, 3.

ἄλλοθεν, -θι, -σε 51.

ἅλλομαι 113.

ἄλλο τι ἤ 207, 2.

ἅμα 158, 1. 203, 3. c.

ἁμαρτάνω 109, 8.— 144, 4. 202, 1. c.

ἀμείβομαι, ἀπ- 113.

ἀμελέω, ἀμελής 144, 3.

ἀμνημονεύω, ἀμνήμων 144, 3.

ἄμοιρος 144, 3.

ἀμπέχω and -ίσχω 113, s.v. ἔχω.

ἀμύνομαι 133. 165, 1. b.

ἀμύνω 165, 1. b.

ἀμφιγνοέω 113.

ἀμφιέννυμι 113, s.v. ἕνν.— 136.

ἀμφισβητέω 113.

ἀμφιῶ,-εῖς 113, s.v. ἕννυμι.

ἀμφότερος 118, 3.

ἀμφοτέρωθεν 162, 5.

ἄμφω 70, 1.— 118, 3.

ἄν 194, see 171, 2. w. n.; see ἐάν.

ἀναγκαῖον ἦν 172, 1.

ἀναίτιος 32, 4.— 144, 2.

ἀνακράζω 86, 3.

ἀναλίσκω, ἀναλόω 110, 5. 113.

ἀναμιμνήσκω 136.

ἀνάξιος 32, 4.— 151.

ἀνδάνω 113.

ἄνευ 162, 5.

ἀνέχομαι 89, 7. 112, 5. b. — 202, 1. b.

ἀνήρ 42.

ἀνιάω, -άομαι 95, 3.

ἀνοίγω 89, 2.

ἀντέχω μὴ οὐ 206, 4. n. 2.
ἀντιλέγω 206, 4. w. n. 1. 2.
ἀντιποιέομαι 158. 144, 3.
ἀνύτω, ἀνύω 77, 2. n. 113.
ἄξιος 151. 199, 1.
ἀξιόω 136. 151. 199, 1.
ἀπαγορεύω 112, 12. a.—
202, 1. b. 206, 4. n. 2.
ἀπαλλάττω 95, 3. 147, 1.
ἀπαμείβομοι 113.
ἀπαντάω 94, 1.
ἀπείργω 147, 1.
ἄπειρος 144, 3.
ἀπεχθάνομαι 113, s.v. ἐχθ.
ἀπέχομαι 147, 1.
ἀπέχρη 113, s.v. χράω.
ἀπέχω 147, 1. 199, 1.
ἀπημείφθη 113, s.v. ἀπαμείβομαι.
ἀπιστέω 75, 3. 206, 4.
w. n. 1. 2.
ἄπλους 60.
ἁπλοῦς 34. 56, 4. b.
ἀπογιγνώσκω 153.
ἀποδείκνυμι 135. 202, 2. b.
ἀποδημέω 113.
ἀποδίδομαι 112, 16.—151.
ἀποδιδράσκω 102, 2. 110,
9.—133.
ἀποδύω, see 93. 113, s.v.
δύω.—136.
ἀποθνῄσκω 110, 7. 113;
pf. 103, 2.—164, 2.
167, 2.
ἀποκρίνομαι 95, 1.
ἀποκρύπτω & mid. 136.
ἀποκτείνω 97, 34.—164, 2.
ἀπολαύω 94, 1.—144, 3.
145, 2.
ἀπόλλυμαι, -μι 106, 11.
Ἀπόλλων 60.
ἀπονοέομαι 95, 2.
ἀπορέω 147, 2.
ἀποστερέω 94, 3.—136.
147, 2.

ἀποστερίσκω, see -στερέω.
ἀποσυλάω 136.
ἀποτρέπω 153.
ἀποτυγχάνω 144, 4.
ἀποφαίνομαι (τὴν) γνώμην
165, 1. c.
ἀποφεύγω 133. 144, 2.
ἀποχράω suffice, and
ἀπόχρη 113, s.v. 2. χράω.
ἅπτομαι 144, 4.
ἆρα, ἆρα μή, ἆρ' οὐ 207.
ἀρᾰρεῖν, ἀρᾱρέναι of
ἀραρίσκω 113.
ἀρέσκω 110, 3.
Ἄρης 60.
ἀρκέω 91, 4.—155.
ἁρμόζω, ἁρμόττω 77, 3. a.
n. 82, 3. 97, 7.
ἀρνέομαι 95, 2.—206, 4.
n. 1.
ἀρχήν 141.
ἄρχομαι begin 147, 3. 165,
1. b. 199, 1. b. 202,
1. b. 2. n. 5.
ἄρχω 97, 15; 94, 3. rule
144, 3. 166, 1. 168, 3;
begin 147, 3. 199, 1. b.
202, 1. b.
ἄσμενος 115, 1.
ἄστυ 47, 2. 60.—119, 3.
ἄτε 203, 3. a.
ἅτερος 68, 2. n.
ἄττα and ἅττα 67, 4. n. 1.
αὐξάνω 09, 8.
αὐτίκα 203, 3. c.
αὐτός 63. 61.—122, 1.
125, 2. a. 127. 158, 3
(bis).
ἀφαιρέομαι 136. 147, 2.
n. 2.
ἀφειδέω, ἀφειδής 147, 1.
ἄφθονος 60.
ἀφικνέομαι 109, 6.
ἀφίστημι, ἀφίσταμαι 153.
ἄχθομαι 111, 8.—155.

157. 3. 159, 2. 202, 1.
d. 2. n. 1.
ἄχρι (ἄχρις) 162, 5.

βαίνω 102, 2. a. 4. a. 113.
βάλλω 92, 4. 97, 51.
βασιλεύς 119, 3.
βασιλεύω 144, 3. 167, 4.
168, 2. d.
βέβᾰμαι 113, s.v. βαίνω.
βιάζομαι 95, 1.
βιβάζω 90, 1.
βιβρώσκω 112, 3.
βιόω 112, 13. 113.
βιῴην, βιώσας, βιώσκομαι,
βιώσασθαι 113.
βλακίστατος, βλάξ 60.
βλάπτω 77, 2. 97, 20.
94, 2.—133.
βλαστάνω 113.
βλώσκω 113.
βοάω 94, 1.
βοηθέω 155.
βορέας, βορρᾶς 60.
βουλεύομαι ὅπως 181, 3.
βούλομαι 111, 9. 113.
ὁ βουλόμενος 117, 2. n. 2.
βουλομένῳ μοι γίγνεται
157, 3.
βοῦς 48, 4.

γαμέω 111, 1.— mid. 156.
γελάω 91, 4. 94, 1.
γέμω, γεμίζω 144, 3.
γεραιός 56, 3.
γέρας 60.
γεύομαι, γεύω 145, 2. cf.
165, 1.
γηθέω 113.
γηράσκω 110, 1. 113.
γίγνομαι 111, 7.—156.
157, 3.
γιγνώσκω 110, 11. 102.—
202, 2. n. 1. & 5.
γόνυ 39, 3.

εἰσπράττω & mid. 136.
εἴσω 162, 5.
εἴτε — εἴτε 179. 208, 16.
εἴωθα 89, 4.
ἐκ, ἐξ 24, 2. — 162, 3.
163, 8. 166, 2. a.
ἕκαστος 118, 3.
ἑκάτερος 118, 3.
ἑκατέρωθεν 162, 5.
ἐκβάλλω 153. 164, 2.
ἐκδύω (91, 6), see 93. —
136. [129, 3.
ἐκεῖνος 65. 64, 3, a. 128.
ἐκκλησιάζω 113.
ἐκλέγω 112, 12. c. 113.
ἐκπίπτω 153, see 164, 2.
ἔκπλεως, τὰ ἔκπλεω 60.
ἐκπλήττομαι, -ττω 108, 2.
112, 15. — 133.
ἐκτός 162, 5.
ἐκφεύγω 133.
ἑκών 115, 1. 203, 2. n. b.
ἑκὼν εἶναι 199, 4.
ἐλαττόομαι 148, 2.
ἐλάττων 58, 4. 5.
ἐλαύνω 109, 5. — 164, 1.
ἐλέγχω 113. — 202, 2. b.
ἐλεύθερος 147, 1.
ἐλευθερόω 147, 1.
ἐλεύσομαι 113, s.v. ἔρχομαι.
ἐλήλεγμαι 113, s.v. ἐλέγχω.
ἐλίσσω 113.
ἐλπίζω 199, 1. b.
ἑλκύω, ἕλκω 89, 1. 92, 1.
ἐμβάλλω 164, 1.
ἐμοὶ δοκεῖν 199, 4.
ἐμός 64; ἐμόν ἐστι 143.
ἔμπειρος 144, 3.
ἐμπίμπλημι 101, 2. 113.
— 144, 3.
ἐμπίμπρημι 101, 3. 113.
ἐμπίμπλημι ⎱
ἐμπίμπρημι ⎰ 113, s.v. πίμπ.
ἐμπίπτω 161.
ἔμπλεως 144, 3.

N

ἔμπροσθεν 162, 5.
ἐναντιοομαι 89, 6. 95, 2.
113.
ἐναντίον 162, 5.
ἐναντίος 32, 3.
ἐνδεής 45, 1. — 147, 2.
ἐνδύω (91, 6). 93. —
136.
ἕνεκα 162, 5.
ἐνεπίμπρων 113, s.v. πίμ-
πρημι.
ἐνηντιούμην etc. 113, s.v.
ἐναντιόομαι.
ἔνθα, ἔνθεν 69, w. n. ἔνθεν
καὶ ἔνθεν 162, 5.
ἐνθυμέομαι 95, 2.
ἔνι 213, 8.
ἐννοέομαι 95, 2.
ἔννυμι 113.
ἐνοχλέω 113. — 161.
ἐντέλλομαι 95, 1.
ἐντός 162, 5.
ἐντρέπομαι 144, 3.
ἐντυγχάνω 161.
ἐν ᾧ 190, 1.
ἐξ, see ἐκ.
ἐξελέγχω 113. — 202, 2. b.
ἔξεστιν 197, 3. 199, 1. a.
ἐξῆν 172, 1.
ἐξίημι 164, 1.
ἐξικνέομαι 144, 4.
ἐξίσταμαι, ἐξίστημι 153.
ἐξόν 203, 4.
ἐξ οὗ 190, 1.
ἔξω 162, 5.
ἔοικα 89, 3. — 155. 202, 2.
n. 2.
ἐπαγγέλλομαι 165, 1. c.
ἐπαινέω 91, 5. 113.
ἐπάν (ἐπεὶ ἄν) 171, 2. n.
190, 3. n.
ἐπεί causal 178. temporal
190, 1.
ἐπείγομαι 95, 3.
ἐπειδάν 171, 2. a. 190, 3.

ἐπειδή quoniam 178. post-
quam 190, 1.
ἐπήν (ἐπεὶ ἄν) 190, 3.
ἐπιβουλεύω 161. 164, 1.
ἐπιδημέω 113, s.v. ἀποδ.
ἐπιδείκνυμι 202, 2. b.
ἐπιδίδωμι 161.
ἐπιθυμέω 144, 3. 199, 1. b.
ἐπιλαμβάνομαι 144, 4.
ἐπιλανθάνομαι 109, 12. —
144, 3.
ἐπιλείπω 133.
ἐπιμελέομαι, ἐπιμέλομαι
111, 13. — 144, 3. 181, 3.
ἐπιμελής 144, 3.
ἐπιορκέω 113. — 133.
ἐπιπεδέστερος, ἐπίπεδος 60.
ἐπίσταμαι 101, 6. — 199,
1. b. 202, 2. n. 1 & 5.
ἐπιστήμων 144, 3. [b.
ἐπιτάττω 155. 161. 199,1.
ἐπιτήδειος 199, 2.
ἐπιτίθεμαι 161.
ἐπιτιμάω 161.
ἐπιτρέπω 161. 199, 3.
ἐπιτυγχάνω 161. 144, 4.
ἐπίχαρις 39, 4.
ἕπομαι 89, 1. 112, 4. —
155.
ἐπτάμην, ἔπτην, ἐπτόμην
113, s.v. πέτομαι.
ἐρ-, see ἐρωτάω and λέγω.
ἐράω, ἔραμαι 95, 2. —
144, 3. 168, 2. d.
ἐργάζομαι 89, 1. 95, 1.
ἔργῳ 159, 3.
ἔρημος 32, 4. — 144, 3.
ἐρίζω 155.
ἑρπύζω, ἕρπω 113.
ἐρρωμένος 56, 4. c. 106, 5.
ἔρχομαι 112, 2.
ἐρωτάω 111, 6. — 136.
ἐσθίω 112, 3. 113. — 145,
2. a.
ἔστε, ἔστ' ἄν 190, 1. 3.

οἴομαι 95, 2. 111, 14.—
199, 1. b. [199, 2.
οἶος 68.— w. sup. 115, 2.
οἷόν τέ ἐστι 199, 1. a.
οἷός τέ εἰμι 199, 3.
οἷς 60.
οἴχομαι 113.— 168, 1. n. 3.
202, 1. a.
ὀκνέω 181, 2. w. n.
ὀλίγον 141. 159, 4. n.
ὀλίγος 58, 5; (οἱ) ὀλίγοι
117, 2. n. 1.
ὀλίγου parvo 141.
ὀλίγου δεῖν 199, 4.
ὀλίγῳ 159, 4.
ὀλιγωρέω 144, 3.
ὄλλυμι, see ἀπόλλυμι.
Ὀλύμπια νικᾶν 137, 2.
ὁ μέν— ὁ δέ 116, 1.
ὁμιλέω 158, 1.
ὄμνυμι 106, 12. 113.—
133. 199, 1. b.
ὅμοιος, ὁμοιόω 158.
ὁμολογέω 158, 1. 199, 1. b.
ὁμονοέω 158, 1.
ὁμοῦ 158, 1.
ὀμώμο(σ)ται etc. 113, s.v.
ὄμνυμι.
ὄναρ, ὄνειρος 50, 6.
ὄνασθαι etc. 113, s.v. ὀνίνημι.
ὀνίναμαι 101, 1.—145, 2. a.
ὀνίνημι 101, 1.— 133.
ὄνομά ἐστί μοι 157. n.
ὀνομάζω 135.
ὀξύς 199, 2.
ὄπισθεν 162, 5.
ὁπόταν 171, 2. n. 190, 3.
ὁπότε 69. — 130. 178.
190, 1.
ὁπότερος 68. — 130.
ὅπως 69.— 130.
ὅπως(μή)181,1–3. & 3. n. 1.
ὁράω 112, 6.—202, 2. a.
w. n. 1. 2. 5. 181, 3. n. 2.

ὀργίζομαι 95, 3. — 155.
150.
ὀρέγομαι 144, 3.
ὄρθριος 115, 1.
ὁρμάομαι, ὁρμάω 95, 3.
ὁρμάω 164, 1.
ὀρώρυγμαιof ὀρύττω 89, 5.
ὅς relat. 66.—129,1. (poss.
211, 2.) demonstr. 129,
1. n. 2. for τίς or ὅστις
130. n.
ὅς ἄν 191, 4.
ὅσγε 129, 1. n. 3.
ὅσον οὔπω, οὐκ ἤδη 208, 30.
ὅσπερ 66. — 129, 1. n. 3.
ὅστις 66, 2. 67, 3.— 129, 1.
ὅστις ἄν 191, 4.
ὀσφραίνομαι 147, 4.
ὅσῳ — τοσούτῳ 159, 4.
ὅταν 190, 3.
ὅτε 178. 190, 1.
ὅτεπερ 208, 36. [2.
ὅτι 177. 193, 1. 178. 115,
ὅ,τι 67, n. 2.
ὅτι μή 208, 24.
ὅτου, ὅτῳ etc. 67, note 1.
ὅτων, ὅτοις 60.
οὐ, οὐκ, οὐχ 24, 3. —206,
1. 2. 207, 2.
οὗ 8, 2. b. 24, 3. n.
οὐδ᾽ εἰ (ἐάν) 189.
οὐδείς 70, 1. — 206, 1.
οὐδέν 141. cf. 145, 2. n. 1.
& 159, 4. n.
οὐδ᾽ ὡς (ὥς) 69, n. 2.
οὐκ, see οὐ.
οὐ μὰ τοὺς θεούς 133.
οὐ μή 181, 3. n. 1. 206,
6. a.
οὔπω καί 208, 19.
οὖς 39, 3. 36, 7. c.
οὗτος 65. — 128. 129, 3.
οὕτω, οὕτως 24, 2.
οὔ φημι 104, 1. n. 3.
οὐχ ὅπως, οὐχ ὅτι 208, 30.

ὀφείλω 113. ὤφελον 86,
3. — 172, 2. n.
ὀφλήσω. ὀφλεῖν etc. of
ὀφλισκάνω 113.
ὄψιος 60.
ὀψοφάγος 60.

παιδευτέον ἦν 172, 1.
παιδεύω 78.— 136.
παῖς 39. 36, 7. c.
παίω 112, 15.
παλαιός, παλαίτερος 60.
παντὶ σθένει 123, 2. 159, 3.
πάντοθεν 51.
πάομαι 113.
παραγγέλλω 155. 199, 3.
παραδίδωμι 199, 3.
παραινέω 91, 5. 113, s.v.
αἰνέω. — 155.
παρακελεύομαι 155.
παρανομέω 113.
παραπλέω νῆσον 134.
παρασκευάζομαι 181, 3.
παρατίθεμαι 165, 2.
παρέχω 112, 5. — 165, 1. c.
199, 3.
παροινέω 113.
παρόν 203, 4.
πᾶς 41, 3. 36, 7. b. —
123.
πάσῃ τέχνῃ καὶ μηχανῇ
123, 2. 159, 3.
πάσχω 112, 7.
πατάσσω 112, 15.
πατήρ 42, 1.
πατρίς 54, n.
παύομαι, παύω 113. — 147,
3. 202, 1. b.
παύω 113. 147, 1. 202, 1. b.
πείθομαι 97, 9. 108, 5. 113.
πείθω 97, 8. 108, 5. 113.
πεινάω, πεινῆν 113.
πειράομαι 95, 3. 113.—
144, 4.
πέλεκυς 60.

πέμπω 97, 17. 83, 5. 88, 3. d.
πενέστερος 60, s.v. πένης.
πένης 54. 60.
πέπαμαι 113, s.v. πάομαι.
πέπληγα 113, s.v. πλήττω.
πέποιθα 108, 5. — 155.
πέπραγα 113, s.v. πράττω.
πέπρωται 113, s.v. πορ-.
πέρ 208, 36. 9, 2. e.
πέρα, πέρᾳ 60. — 162, 5.
περαιτέρω 60, s.v. πέρα.
πέραν 162, 5.
πέρας 60.
περιγίγνομαι 148, 2.
περίειμι 148, 2.
περιοράω 202, 2. a.
περιττεύω 148, 2.
πετάννυμι 106, 3.
πέτομαι 113.
πήγνυμι 106, 9.
πῆχυς and adj. in -π. 60.
πιθ.σθαι 113, s.v. πείθω.
πίμπλημι 101, 2. 113.—
144, 3.
πίμπρημι 101, 3. 113.
πίνω 112, 8. — 145, 2.
πιπράσκω 112, 16. — 151.
πίπτω 112, 9. — 167, 2.
πιστεύω 155.
πλακῆναι 113, s.v. πλέκω.
πλανάομαι 95, 3.
πλάττω 77, 3. a. n.
πλεῖν (ἤ) 208, 18. n.
πλείονες and οἱ πλ. 117,
2. n. 1.
πλέκω 113.
πλεονεκτέω 148, 2.
πλεονέκτης 60.
πλευσοῦμαι, πλευστέον
113, s.v. πλέω.
πλέω 108, 8. 113.
πλέως 35. 60. — 144, 3.
πλήθω 101, 2. — 144, 3.
πλήν 162, 5. 208, 37.
πλήρης 144, 3.

πληρόω 144, 3.
πλησίον 60. — 162, 5. 155.
πλήττω 108, 2. 112, 15.
πνέω 108, 8. [113.
πνίγω 113.
Πνύξ 60.
ποδήρης, -ῆρες 45, 2. n.
ποθέω 113.
ποιέομαι aestimo 151.
ποιέω 80. 97, 4. — 135.
165, 2. 181, 3. 199, 1. b.
πολεμέω 94, 2. & 3. 158,
1. w. n.
πόλεμον ποιῶ, -οῦμαι 165,
1. c.
πολιορκέω 94, 2.
πολιτεύω and mid. 165,
1. c.
πολλά, τὰ π. 141.
πολλοί, οἱ π. 117, 2. n. 1.
πολλοῦ 151. π. χρόνου
152, 2.
πολλῷ 159, 4.
πολύ 59, 2. — 141. 159,
4. n.
πολύς 55. 58, 6.
πονηρός, πονήρως 60.
πορεύομαι 95, 3.
πορ-ίζω, -σύνω 113.
πόρρω 59, 5. — 162, 5.
Ποσειδῶν 60.
πότερον (-α) — ἤ 179.
207, 4.
πούς 39, 3.; adj. in π. 60.
πρᾷος 32, 3, see πραΰς.
πράττομαι 136. 181, 3.
πράττω 97, 13. 83, 3. 88,
3. 113. — 136. 164, 1.
181, 3.
πραΰς, πραέων 60.
πρέπει 155.
πρεσβευτής 50, 7.
πρέσβυς 56, 1, see 50, 7.
πρίασθαι 101, n. 1. 2. 112,
18. — 151.

πρίν or πρὶν ἄν 190, 4.
w. n.
πρὸ τοῦ 116, 1.
προαιρέομαι 153. 199, 1. b.
προαιρετέον ἦν 172, 1.
προθυμέομαι 95, 2. 181, 3.
προΐστημι 153.
προκρίνω 153.
προνοέομαι 95, 2.
προσῆκεν 172, 1. 155
προσῆκον 203, 4.
προσκυνέω 133.
προσφέρομαι 158.
πρόσω 162, 5.
πρότερος 58, note.— 115, 1.
προτίθημι 153.
προτρέπω 199, 1. b.
προύργου 60.
προφάσει 159, 3.
πρόφασιν 141.
πρωΐ, πρῴ, πρῴτερον etc.
60.
(τὴν) πρώτην, (τὸ) πρῶ-
τον 141.
πρῶτος 58. n. — 115, 1.
πτάσθαι, πτέσθαι, πτῆναι,
πτήσομαι 113, s.v. πέτο-
μαι.
πυνθάνομαι 109, 14.— 147,
4. (163, 17). 202, 2. n.
1. 4.
πῦρ 50, 8.
πώ 208, 38. 9, 1. e.
πωλέω 112, 16. 151.

ῥᾴδιος, ῥᾷστος, ῥᾴων 58, 7.
— 199, 2.
ῥέω 102, 2. b.
ῥήγνυμι 106, 10.
ῥιγόω 113.
(ῥιπτέω) ῥίπτω 97, 22.
ῥώννυμι 106, 5.

σαλπίζω 113.
σαπῆναι etc. 113, s.v. σήπω.

TABLES FOR REPETITION

APPENDIX

CONTAINING

A LIST OF VERBS

AND

THE CHIEF RULES OF SYNTAX

Meaning	Present	Stem	Future
1. admire, wonder at	ἄγᾰμαι	ἀγᾰ́(σ)	ἀγάσομαι
2. lead; *intr.* march *med.* lead for myself *pass.* am led set sail land, *intr.*	ἄγω ἄγομαι ἀν-άγομαι κατ-άγομαι	ἄγ	ἄξω { ἄξομαι { ἀχθήσομαι ἀν-άξομαι κατ-άξομαι
3. sing	ᾄδω *pass.*	dental	ᾄσομαι ᾀσθήσομαι
4. feel shame; respect; fear; look upon with awe	αἰδέομαι	αἰδες	αἰδέσομαι
5. praise encourage, exhort, recommend	αἰνέω, usu. ἐπ- *pass.* παρ-αινέω *pass.*		ἐπ-αινέσομαι ἐπ-αινεθήσομαι παρ-αινέσω παρ-αινεθήσομαι
6. take, capture *med.* take for myself, choose *pass.* (to *med.* and *act.*)	αἱρέω αἱροῦμαι	αἱρη { ἑλ { { αἱρε	αἱρήσω αἱρήσομαι αἱρεθήσομαι
7. raise, lift; *intr.* set out, get under way *med.* raise for myself *pass.* am raised	αἴρω αἴρομαι	ἀρ, (ἀερ)	ἀρῶ, -εῖς { ἀροῦμαι, -ῃ { { ἀρθήσομαι
8. perceive, esp. by hearing, observe, become aware of	αἰσθάνομαι	αἰσθ-η	αἰσθήσομαι
9. disgrace, shame *med.* am (feel) ashamed (before one τινά)	αἰσχῦ́νω αἰσχύνομαι	αἰσχῠν	αἰσχῠνῶ, -εῖς αἰσχῠνοῦμαι, -ῇ
10. blame, find fault with, charge, accuse	αἰτιᾰ́ομαι *pass.*		αἰτιᾱ́σομαι αἰτιᾱθήσομαι

Aorist	Perfect (Nouns)	Syntax
ἠγάσθην admired	—— ἀγαστός	**ἄγαμαι**: τὶ, τινά τινος — ὅτι or *part.* μῦθον — Γοργίαν τῆς σοφίας — σοῦ, ὅτι προείλου = σοῦ προελομένου.
ἤγαγον ἠγαγόμην ἤχθην }	ἦχα ἦγμαι ἀκτός	**ἀγανακτέω** am irritated, vexed: τὶ — τινί: τοῦτο — τῷ ἐρωτήματι, w. *part.* ἀπεστερημένος.
ἀν-ηγαγόμην κατ-ηγαγόμην	ἀν-ῆγμαι κατ-ῆγμαι	**ἀγγέλλω**: Κῦρον ἐπιστρατεύοντα or ὅτι ἐπιστρατεύει (*fact*)
ἦσα ἤσθην	—— ἦσμαι τὸ ἆσμα	or Κῦρον ἐπιστρατεύειν (*rumor*). παραγγέλλω command: τῷ Κλεάρχῳ.
ἠδέσθην	ἤδεσμαι	**ἀδικέω** do wrong to: οὓς ἥκιστα ἔδει. ἀδικεῖτε πολέμου ἄρχοντες.
		αἰδοῦμαι before: τοὺς πρεσβυτέρους.
ἐπ-ῄνεσα ἐπ-ῃνέθην	ἐπ-ῄνεκα	οὐκ αἰδεῖται κακὸς εἶναι. οὐκ αἰδεῖται κακὸς ὤν.
παρ-ῄνεσα παρ-ῃνέθην	παρ-ῄνεκα	**ἐπαινῶ**: ὑμᾶς τῶν λόγων — ὑμᾶς, ἐφ' οἷς λέγετε.
εἷλον εἱλόμην ἡρέθην }	ἥρηκα ᾕρημαι αἱρετός ἡ αἵρεσις	παραινῶ: ὑμῖν μὴ ἀναχωρεῖν. **αἱρῶ**: πόλιν—convict: αὐτὸν κλοπῆς or αὐτὸν κλέπτοντα. *pass.* ἁλίσκομαι: κλοπῆς or κλέπτων. αἱροῦμαι: Κίμωνα στρατηγόν (*pass.?!*).
ἦρα, ἄρω	ἦρκα	ἀφαιροῦμαι: τοὺς ἄλλους χρήματα, or τῶν ἄλλων χρήματα.
ἠράμην, ἄρωμαι ἤρθην }	ἦρμαι	προαιροῦμαι: τὰ σώσοντα τῶν ἡδίστων.
ᾐσθόμην	ᾔσθημαι αἰσθητός ἡ αἴσθησις	**αἰσθάνομαι**, constr. like ἀκούω: τὶ, τινός and τινός τι, w. *gen.* and acc. *part.*, or w. *inf.*
ᾔσχῡνα ᾐσχύνθην	—— —— ἡ αἰσχύνη	**αἰσχύνομαι**: θεοὺς καὶ ἀνθρώπους. λέγων (ὅτι, εἰ λέγω) λέγειν vereor dicere } Gr. 202, note 5. μὴ οὐ συσπουδάζειν not to. **αἰτέω**: Κῦρον μισθόν. Κῦρον διδόναι ἡγεμόνα.
ᾐτιᾱσάμην ᾐτιάθην }	ᾐτίαμαι	**αἰτιῶμαι**: αὐτὸν ἀσεβείας, or ὅτι ἀσεβεῖ.

Meaning	Present	Stem	Future
11. hear	ἀκούω		ἀκούσομαι
12. am taken, caught	ἀλίσκομαι (*ipf.* ἠλισκόμην)	ἀλ-ω	ἀλώσομαι
13. change *med.* exchange, barter *pass.* (to *act.* and *mid.*)	ἀλλάττω ἀλλάττομαι ἀλλάττομαι esp. ἀπ-, δι-, κατ-, συν-.	ἀλλᾰγ	ἀλλάξω ἀλλάξομαι ἀλλαγήσομαι -αλλάξομαι -αλλαγήσομαι
14. miss (the mark τινός), fail, sin (τὶ)	ἁμαρτάνω *pass.*	ἁμαρτ-η	ἁμαρτήσομαι ἁμαρτηθήσεται
15. race, contend	ἁμιλλάομαι		ἁμιλλήσομαι
16. ward off, assist *med.* ward off from myself =defend myself (against τινά)	ἀμύνω ἀμύνομαι	ἀμῠν	ἀμῠνῶ, -εῖς ἀμῠνοῦμαι, -ῇ
17. force, compel	ἀναγκάζω not compounded; regular.		
18. use up, spend, expend; consume, waste	ἀνᾱλίσκω ⎱ ἀνᾱλόω ⎰ *pass.*	ἀν-ᾱλ-ω	ἀνᾱλώσω ἀνᾱλωθήσομαι
19. grieve, distress *med.* am grieved, distressed	ἀνῑάω ἀνιάομαι		ἀνιάσω ἀνιάσομαι
	ἀν-οίγω, see οἴγω		
20. finish, accomplish	ἀνύω and ἀνύτω (ἀνύω, ἀνύτω)	ἀνυ	ἀνύσω ἀνυσθήσομαι
21. forbid; give out	ἀπ-αγορεύω	(see λέγω)	ἀπ-ερῶ, -ερεῖς
22. (go to) meet	ἀπ-αντάω		ἀπ-αντησομαι

Aorist	Perfect (Nouns)	Syntax
ἤκουσα	ἀκήκοα (ἠκηκόειν) ἀκουστός	**ἀκολουθέω**: τινί or σύν τινι. **ἀκούσεσθε** ἐμοῦ τὴν ἀλήθειαν. ἀκούω τὸν θόρυβον hear the noise,
⌈ἑάλων ⌊ἥλων	ἑάλωκα ἥλωκα αἰχμάλωτος	τοῦ θορύβου listen, give heed, hearken to. ἀκούω σοῦ λέγοντος I myself hear you say,
ἤλλαξα ἠλλαξάμην ⌉ ⌋ ἠλλάγην ⌋	ἤλλαχα ἤλλαγμαι	σὲ λέγοντα ⌉ hear through others = ὅτι λέγεις ⌋ that . . . (fact). σὲ λέγειν hear that you say (rumor). ἀκούω τινός (ὑπήκοος): am subject to, obey.
-ηλλάγην	-ἤλλαγμαι	**ἁλίσκομαι**: κλοπῆς or κλέπτων, see αἱρέω.
ἥμαρτον ἡμαρτήθην	ἡμάρτηκα ἡμάρτημαι τὸ ἁμάρτημα	**ἀπ-αλλάττω** tr. set free, release: σὲ δεσμῶν. intr. get off free: ἀπὸ δεσμῶν.
ἡμιλλήθην	ἡμίλλημαι	ἀπαλλάττομαι rid myself, get rid. intr. go away, depart: πόλεως.
ἤμῡνα ἠμῡνάμην	——	**ἁμαρτάνω**: μέγιστα εἰς, περὶ ὑμᾶς. miss: σκοποῦ, οὐδεὶς ἡμάρτανεν ἀνδρός. lose: τῆς Βοιωτίας, ἐσθλῆς γυναικός. do wrong to: ἁμαρτάνετε διώκοντες.
ἀνήλωσα ἀνηλώθην	ἀνήλωκα ἀνήλωμαι	**ἀμύνω**: παισὶν ὄλεθρον — νόμῳ. ἀμύνομαι: τὸν ἐπιόντα πολέμιον.
ἠνίᾱσα ἠνιάθην	ἠνίᾱκα ἠνίᾱμαι	**ἀνιᾷς** με τὰς φρένας γελῶν. ἀνιῶμαι: τοῦτο — (ἐπὶ) ταῖς τῶν ἄλλων εὐπραξίαις — ἐχθρῷ παρόντι. **ἀξιόω** deem worthy (ἄξιός τινος): ἐμαυτὸν τῶν καλλίστων — ἠξίου οἷ δοθῆναι τὰς πόλεις. ἰητρὸς ἀνὴρ πολλῶν ἀντάξιος ἄλλων.
ἤνῡσα ἠνύσθην	ἤνυκα ἤνῡσμαι ἀνυστός	**ἀπαγορεύω**:
ἀπ-εῖπον	ἀπ-είρηκα [den ἀπόρρητος forbid-	forbid: ὑμῖν μὴ ἀπιέναι. become exhausted: τρέχων. **ἀπαντάω** encounter: τινί.
ἀπ-ήντησα	ἀπ-ήντηκα	ἀπήντησαν αὐτοῖς Χάλυβες.

Meaning	Present	Stem	Future
23. deceive threaten distrust am at a loss, doubt	ἀπατάω ἀπειλέω ἀπιστέω ἀπορέω	are *no*	compounds
24. incur the hatred (of τινί)	ἀπ-εχθάνομαι	ἐχθ-η	ἀπ-εχθήσομαι
25. enjoy	ἀπο-λαύω		ἀπο-λαύσομαι
26. say in my own defence	ἀπο-λογέομαι		ἀπο-λογήσομαι
27. fasten; kindle *med.* touch, lay hold of	ἅπτω *pass.* ἅπτομαι	ἀφ	ἅψω ἀφθήσομαι ἅψομαι
28. please; gratify	ἀρέσκω	ἀρες	ἀρέσω
29. am sufficient; aid, assist	ἀρκέω	ἀρκες	ἀρκέσω
30. fit (together), join	ἁρμόττω (ἁρμόζω) *pass.*	ἁρμοτ	ἁρμόσω ἁρμοσθήσομαι
31. deny, disown	ἀρνέομαι		ἀρνήσομαι
32. grasp hastily, seize, plunder, carry away	ἁρπάζω *pass.*	dental	ἁρπάσομαι ἁρπασθήσομαι
33. rule; begin *med.* begin *pass.* am ruled	ἄρχω ἄρχομαι	ἀρχ	ἄρξω ἄρξομαι
34. pass the night in the open air, bivouac	αὐλίζομαι	dental	αὐλιοῦμαι, -ῇ
35. increase, *trans.* *pass.* am increased, grow, increase, *intr.*	αὔξω, αὐξάνω	αὐξ-η	αὐξήσω αὐξήσομαι

Aorist	Perfect (Nouns)	Syntax
		ἀπορῶ am in want : τῶν ἐπιτηδείων. at a loss : τῷ πράγματι (τοῦτο). in doubt : ὅποι τράπωμαι — ὅ,τι δεῖ ποιεῖν. unable : κρῖναι —
ἀπ-ηχθόμην	ἀπ-ήχθημαι	οὐκ ἀπορῶ πολλὰ λέγειν. **ἀπολαύω** : τῶν ἐμῶν κτημάτων.
ἀπ-έλαυσα	ἀπο-λέλαυκα	**ἅπτω** fasten, tie : βρόχον.
ἀπ-ελογησάμην	ἀπο-λελόγημαι	light, kindle, set on fire : λύχνον, νεών, ἱερά.
ἦψα, ἅψαι		**ἅπτομαι** : θανόντων οὐδὲν ἄλγος ἅπτεται.
ἤφθην	ἧμμαι	**ἀρέσκω** : ἄρεσκε μὴ σαυτῷ μόνῳ.
ἠψάμην	ἧμμαι	pass. am satisfied, pleased with : τοῖς σοῖς λόγοις.
ἤρεσα		**ἀρκῶ** : ἀρκεῖ ἡμῖν μέτριος βίος.
	ἀρεστός	aid, ward off : ξένοις ὄλεθρον.
ἤρκεσα		it is enough that I ἀρκῶ πράττων ταῦτα.
		ἀρνοῦμαι : τὸ πρᾶγμα,
ἥρμοσα	ἥρμοκα	ὡς οὐ δέδρακα, or
ἡρμόσθην	ἥρμοσμαι	μὴ δεδρακέναι.
	ἁρμοστός	οὐκ ἀρνοῦμαι } μὴ οὐ δεδρακέναι. τίς ἀρνεῖται
ἠρνήθην	ἥρνημαι	**ἄρχω** rule : τῶν Περσῶν — (pass.?!)
ἥρπᾰσα	ἥρπᾰκα	**ἄρχω** begin :
ἡρπάσθην	ἥρπασμαι	τοῦ λόγου (others continue), λέγειν am the first to speak.
ἦρξα, ἄρξαι	ἦρχα	**ἄρχομαι** begin : τοῦ λόγου (my own speech, I continue),
{ ἠρξάμην { ἤρχθην }	ἦργμαι	ἀπὸ τῶν θεῶν παντὸς ἔργου.
	ἀρκτός ruled	**ἄρχομαι** λέγων begin to speak = am at the beginning of my speech,
	ἀρκτέος regendus and incipiendus	or: begin by speaking.
		λέγειν begin, undertake, proceed to speak, set about speaking.
ηὐλῖσάμην and ηὐλίσθην	ηὔλῖσμαι	
ηὔξησα	ηὔξηκα	
ηὐξήθην	ηὔξημαι	

Meaning	Present	Stem	Future
36. am displeased, vexed, angry	ἄχθομαι	ἀχθ-ες	ἀχθέσομαι
37. go, walk	βαδίζω	dental	βαδιοῦμαι, -ῇ
38. go, walk, step	βαίνω	βη, βᾰ	βήσομαι
39. throw *med.* throw for myself. *pass.* am thrown	βάλλω βάλλομαι	βᾰλ, βλη	βᾰλῶ, -εῖς βαλοῦμαι, -ῇ βληθήσομαι
40. force	βιάζομαι *pass.*	dental	βιᾰσομαι βιασθήσομαι
41. cause to go, bring	βιβάζω	βα, dental	βιβῶ, -ᾷς
42. injure, harm, damage, hurt	βλάπτω βλάπτομαι	βλᾰβ	βλάψω βλᾰβήσομαι
43. shout, call	βοάω		βοήσομαι
44. wish, desire	βούλομαι	βουλ-η	βουλήσομαι
45. marry (a woman) *med.* marry (a man)	γαμέω γαμέομαι	γαμ-ε γαμ-η	γαμῶ, -εῖς γαμοῦμαι, -ῇ
46. laugh	γελάω *pass.*		γελᾰσομαι γελασθήσομαι
47. give a taste *med.* taste, eat, enjoy	γεύω, usu. γεύομαι		γεύσομαι
48. grow old	γηράσκω, γηράω	γηρᾱ	γηράσομαι
49. am born; become; happen	γίγνομαι	γεν-η	γενήσομαι
50. learn to know, perceive, know; decide upon	γιγνώσκω *pass.*	γνω(σ)	γνώσομαι γνωσθήσομαι

AORIST	PERFECT	(NOUNS)	SYNTAX
ἠχθέσθην	——		ἄχθομαι : τοῖς γεγενημένοις — τοῖς πρέσβεσιν, ὅτι ἁμαρτάνει,
ἐβάδισα	βεβάδικα		μανθάνων do not like, hate.
ἔβην	βέβηκα	βᾰτός	
ἔβᾰλον ἐβαλόμην ⎫	βέβληκα, βλητός		εἰσ(ἐμ)βάλλω tr. throw into, intr. empty (of rivers), invade (of
⎬ βέβλημαι			armies).
ἐβλήθην ⎭			ἐκβάλλω banish; pass. ἐκπίπτω.
fut. pf.	βεβλήσομαι		ὑπερβάλλω go etc. over, across : τὰ ὄρη, τὰ τείχη ; surpass προγόνους
ἐβιᾰσάμην	βεβίασμαι		εὐκλείᾳ.
ἐβιάσθην	βεβίασμαι		βασιλεύω : τινός — pass. βασιλεύομαι.
ἐβίβᾰσα	——		βιάζομαι τὸν ἔκπλουν force my way
ἔβλᾰψα	βέβλᾰφα		or passage out, βιάζομαι τάδε am
ἐβλᾰβην	βέβλᾰμμαι		driven to, forced to (do) this.
ἐβόησα	βεβόηκα		βοηθέω : Κόνωνι δώδεκα ναυσιν.
ἐβουλήθην	βεβούλημαι		
ἔγημα ἐγημάμην	γεγάμηκα γεγάμημαι		γαμῶ γυναῖκα, γαμοῦμαι ἀνδρί.
ἐγέλᾰσα ἐγελάσθην	γεγέλᾰκα γεγέλᾰσμαι καταγέλαστος		
ἐγευσάμην	γέγευμαι		γεύομαι : σίτου, πόνων μυρίων.
ἐγήρᾱσα	γεγήρᾱκα am old ἀγήρᾱτος never aging, undecaying		γίγνεται with (acc. and) inf.: fit, ut. διαγίγνομαι : μανθάνων. παραγίγνομαι : εἰς Σάρδεις.
ἐγενόμην	γεγένημαι γέγονα, also pf. to εἰμί		περιγίγνομαι : survive, escape from τοῦ πάθους. am superior to τῶν ἄλλων ῥώμη. γιγνώσκω perceive that something
ἔγνων ἐγνώσθην	ἔγνωκα novi ἔγνωσμαι γνωτός known γνωστός knowable		happens : ὅτι or part. ὅτι θνητός εἰμι or θνητὸς ὤν. ὅτι θνητὸς εἶ or σὲ θνητὸν ὄντα. resolve, with inf. : μὴ μάχεσθαι.

Meaning	Present	Stem	Future
51. write *med.* write (in my own interest), accuse, indict; *pass.*	γρᾰ́φω γρᾰ́φομαι	γρᾰφ	γρᾰ́ψω γρᾰ́ψομαι γρᾰφήσομαι
52. fear		δει-, δῐ-	δείσομαι
53. point, show *med.* show (what is my own), prove *pass.*	δείκνῡμι δείκνῡμαι	δεικ	δείξω δείξομαι δειχθήσομαι
54. receive	δέχομαι	δεκ	δέξομαι
55. bind *med.* bind (for myself); *pass.*	δέω δέομαι	(δες) δε	δήσω δήσομαι δεθήσομαι
56. want, lack it is necessary, one must need, ·want (τινός); beg, ask (τινός τι)	δέω δεῖ impersonal δέομαι	(δευ) (δεϝ) δε-η	δεήσω δεήσει δεήσομαι
57. teach, instruct *med.* teach myself, have myself taught, have one taught (in my own interest) *pass.*	διδάσκω διδάσκομαι	διδᾰχ	διδάξω διδάξομαι διδαχθήσομαι
58. run away	διδράσκω, usu. ἀπο-	δρᾱ	ἀπο-δράσομαι
59. give (*pres.* and *ipf.* also: offer) *med.* give what is my own, for myself *pass.*	δίδωμι δίδομαι	δω, δο	δώσω δώσομαι δοθήσομαι
60. pursue	διώκω *pass.*	guttural	διώξομαι διωχθήσομαι

Aorist	Perfect (Nouns)	Syntax
ἔγραψα ἐγραψάμην	γέγραφα	ἀπογιγνώσκω acquit: ὑμῶν προδοσίαν.
ἐγράφην	γέγραμμαι	despair of, give up the intention of doing: μάχης or τοῦ μάχεσθαι.
ἔδεισα	δέδοικα δέδια	καταγιγνώσκω τινός τι: charge: ὑμῶν δειλίαν.
ἔδειξα ἐδειξάμην	δέδειχα ———	declare guilty: τούτου φόνον. πολλῶν κατέγνωσαν θάνατον μηδισμοῦ, πολλῶν κατεγνώσθη θάνατος μηδισμοῦ.
ἐδείχθην	δέδειγμαι	συγγιγνώσκω pardon, forgive: σύγγνωθί μοι τὴν ἁμαρτίαν.
ἐδεξάμην	δέδεγμαι	γράφομαι accuse, indict:
ἔδησα ἐδησάμην	δέδεκα ———	Σωκράτη ἀσεβείας or ὅτι ἀσεβεῖ or ὡς ἀσεβοῦντα.
ἐδέθην	δέδεμαι δετός ὁ δεσμός	δέδοικα: μὴ ἐπιλαθώμεθα ne oblin. (οὐ) δέδοικα μὴ οὐκ ἔχω ne non hab.
ἐδέησα	δεδέηκα	δέδοικα διαλέγεσθαι vereor colloqui.
ἐδέησε(ν)	δεδέηκε(ν)	δείκνυμι: ἐμαυτὸν ἀγαθὸν ὄντα, or ὅτι ἀγαθός εἰμι.
ἐδεήθην	δεδέημαι	δείκνυμαι (pass.) ἀγαθὸς ὤν.
ἐδίδαξα ἐδιδαξάμην	δεδίδαχα ———	δέω πολλοῦ εἰπεῖν am far from. ὀλίγου ἐδέησα εἰπεῖν paene dixi. δεῖ μοι: πολλῆς φρονήσεως. ἔδει (three meanings!) and ἔδει ἄν.
ἐδιδάχθην	δεδίδαγμαι διδαχή, διδακτός	δέομαι need: τῆς ὑμετέρας βοηθείας. ask, beg: ὑμῶν ἐγὼ ταῦτα, but: Κῦρον ᾔτησαν μισθόν. ὑμῶν μὴ ἀπιέναι.
ἀπ-έδρᾱν	ἀπο-δέδρᾱκα	
ἔδωκα, ἔδομεν	δέδωκα	δίδωμι allow: δός μοι σῴζειν τοὺς Ἕλληνας.
ἐδόμην	δέδομαι	ἀποδίδομαι sell: τί τινος (at a price), πολλοῦ.
ἐδόθην	δοτός ἡ δόσις δῶρον δωρεά	μεταδίδωμι: μετέδοσαν ἀλλήλοις, ὧν εἶχον ἕκαστοι.
ἐδίωξα ἐδιώχθην	δεδίωχα δεδίωγμαι	διώκω accuse: τινά τινος; φεύγεις τὴν δίκην ἢ διώκεις; ὁ διώκων the accuser.

Meaning	Present	Stem	Future
61. seem, am believed or looked upon as; believe, think it seems good, best, advisable, expedient to me = *videtur mihi*, I move	δοκέω δοκεῖ μοι	δοκ-ε	δόξω δόξει
62. can, am able, strong enough, have power	δύ̆νᾰμαι	δυνη δυνᾰ	δυνήσομαι
63. am unlucky, unhappy	δυστυχέω		δυστυχήσω
64. wrap up, cause to sink or set wrap myself up, put on (clothes), sink or set, enter, *intr.*	δύ̆ω *pass.* δύ́ομαι and δύ́νω	δῦ, δῠ	δύσω δῠθήσομαι δύσομαι
65. suffer, permit, allow, let, leave	ἐάω (*ipf.* εἴων) *pass.*		ἐάσω ἐάσομαι
66. will, am willing, ready, determined	ἐθέλω, θέλω	ἐθελ-η	ἐθελήσω θελήσω
67. accustom	ἐθίζω (*ipf.* εἴθιζον) *vass.*	dental	ἐθιῶ, -εῖς ἐθισθήσομαι
68. yield, give way, withdraw	εἴκω	ϝικ, εἰκ	εἴξω
69. resemble, am similar, am like, look like	εἴκω	ϝικ, εἰκ	——
70. am	εἰμί, εἶ, ἐστίν etc. ἦν, ἦσθα, ἦν etc. ὦ, ᾖς, ᾖ — εἴην, εἴης, ἴσθι, ἔστω — εἶναι, ὤν	ἐσ	ἔσομαι, ἔσται

Aorist	Perfect (Nouns)	Syntax
ἔδοξα	——	**δοκῶ**: seem, am believed χρήσιμοι ἐδόκουν εἶναι. believe, think: βασιλέα ἀπιέναι (not ὅτι).
ἔδοξε(ν)	δέδοκται it has been resolved on, *visum est.* ἡ δόξα, τὸ δόγμα	**δοκεῖ**: δόξαν ταῦτα— (ὡς) ἐμοὶ δοκεῖν. **δουλεύω** serve, am subject to: τινί — ἡδοναῖς — τὴν κακίστην δουλείαν.
ἐδυνήθην ἐδυνάσθην	δεδύνημαι δυνατός	**δύναμαι** (δυνατόν ἐστιν): εὑρεῖν — πόλις δυνατὴ ἀρίστη γενέσθαι, ὁδὸς δυνατὴ πορεύεσθαι.
ἐδυστύχησα	δεδυστύχηκα	
ἔδυσα ἐδύθην ἔδυν	—— δέδυμαι δέδυκα τὸ ἄδυτον	**καταδύω**: ναῦν αὐτοῖς ἀνδράσιν. δύεται ὁ ἥλιος — καταδύεται ἡ ναῦς. ἐν(ἀπο)δύομαι put on, off, στολήν.
εἴασα εἰάθην	εἴακα εἴαμαι	**ἐῶ**: οὐκ εἴων ἀδικεῖν *vetabant*—.
ἠθέλησα ἐθέλησα	ἠθέληκα	**ἐθέλω**: ἀνὴρ ἀγαθὸς γενέσθαι — οὐκ ἐθέλω refuse: εἰσιέναι.
εἴθισα εἰθίσθην	εἴθικα εἴθισμαι εἴωθα, εἰώθειν am, was wont	
εἶξα	——	**εἴκω**: τοῖς γέρουσι τῆς ὁδοῦ.
——	ἔοικα look like *plpf.* ἐῴκειν ἐοικώς similar εἰκός natural; meet; probable, likely	**ἔοικα**: φιλοσόφῳ, μεθύοντι. εἰκὸς Ἕλληνας βαρβάρων ἄρχειν. ὡς τὸ εἰκός. **εἶναι**: ἀνδρὸς σοφοῦ (but ἐμόν) ἐστιν.
ἐγενόμην	γεγένημαι, γέγονα	ἔστι μοι ὄνομα Ἀγάθων (*Gaio*). ὄνομά μοι ἔθεσαν Ἀγάθωνα. ἐξῆν — δίκαιον ἦν — ἀπιτέον ἦν — ἔξεστι — τὸ νῦν εἶναι — ἐξόν, παρόν.

Meaning	Present	Stem	Future
71. shall go (the opt., inf., and part. with *fut.* and *pres.* force)	εἶμι, εἶ, εἶσιν etc. ἦα, ᾔεις, ᾔει, ᾖμεν, ᾖτε, ᾖσαν ἴω, ἴῃς —ἴοιμι, ἴοις— ἴθι, ἴτω— ἰέναι—ἰών	εἰ, ι	εἶμι
72. shut up (in, out), hem in, enclose, press	εἴργω (εἴργω, ἔργω, εἴργνυμι) *pass.*	guttural ϝεργ	εἴρξω, εἴρξω εἴρξομαι
73. *tr.* drive; *intr.* drive, ride, march, sail etc. = *feror* and *vehor*	ἐλαύνω *pass.*	ἐλαυ ἐλᾰ	ἐλῶ, -ᾷς ἐλᾰθήσομαι
74. draw, drag	ἕλκω (*ipf.* εἷλκον) *pass.*	ἑλκ ἑλκυ(σ)	ἕλξω ἑλκῠσθήσομαι
75. hinder	ἐμποδίζω	dental	ἐμποδιῶ, -εῖς
76. am against, oppose	ἐναντιόομαι (*ipf.* ἠναντιούμην)		ἐναντιώσομαι
77. lie in ambush; way-lay (τινά)	ἐνεδρεύω		ἐνεδρεύσω
78. lay to heart, con-sider well, reflect	ἐνθῡμέομαι		ἐνθῡμήσομαι
79. examine well; in-spect, review	ἐξετάζω (ϝρ,:: ἐξήταζον) *pass.*	dental	ἐξετάσω ἐξετασθήσομαι
80. urge on, press hasten, hurry, push, press on	ἐπείγω, usu. ἐπείγομαι	guttural	ἐπείξομαι
81. desire, long for, covet	ἐπιθῡμέω		ἐπιθῡμήσω
82. swear falsely, am a perjurer	ἐπιορκέω		ἐπιορκήσω
83. know, understand, am versed in, ac-quainted with	ἐπίσταμαι ἠπιστάμην, ἠπίστατο ἐπίστωμαι, ἐπίσταιτο — ἐπίστασο	ἐπιστη ἐπιστᾰ	ἐπιστήσομαι

Aorist	Perfect (Nouns)	Syntax
——	——	περίειμι (περιεῖναι) surpass : ἄλλων πολὺ ἀρετῇ.
	ἰτός, ἰτέον	
εἶρξα εἴρχθην	—— εἶργμαι	εἴργω keep off, hinder from : τὴν ψυχὴν ἐπιθυμῶν.
ἤλᾰσα ἠλάθην	ἐλήλᾰκα ἐλήλᾰμαι plpf. ἐληλάμην	ὁ φόβος τὸν νοῦν ἀπείργει μὴ λέγειν ἃ βούλεται ἐλευθερόω (ἐλεύθερος) free : τοὺς ἀναιτίους τῆς ζημίας.
εἵλκῠσα εἱλκύσθην	εἵλκῠκα εἵλκῠσμαι	ἐλπίζω expect, hope : π ρ ά ξ ε ι ν καλῶς. μηδὲν κακὸν πείσεσθαι.
ἐνεπόδῐσα	ἐμπεπόδικα	
ἠναντιώθην	ἠναντίωμαι	ἐναντιοῦμαι : τινί — ἐναντιώσομαι ὑμῖν μηδὲν ποιεῖν παρὰ τοὺς νόμους.
ἐνήδρευσα	ἐνήδρευκα	
ἐνεθῡμήθην	ἐντεθύμημαι τὸ ἐ··ύμημα	ἐνθυμοῦμαι : ταῦτα πάντα — ὅτι ἡμῖν οὐδενὸς μέτεστιν —
ἐξήτᾰσα ἐξητάσθην	ἐξήτᾰκα ἐξήτᾰσμαι	οἵων τιμῶν ἀπεστερήμεθα — μὴ οὐκ ἔχωμεν.
ἠπείχθην	ἤπειγμαι	
ἐπεθίμησα	ἐπιτεθύμηκα	ἐπιθυμῶ : πλούτου — ἄρχειν, τιμᾶσθαι.
ἐπιώρκησα	ἐπιώρκηκα	ἐπιορκῶ : τινά — Θεὸν ἐπιορκῶν μὴ δόκει λεληθέναι.
ἠπιστήθην	—— ἡ ἐπιστήμη	ἐπίσταμαι know, understand : τέχνην. know how to : εἴκειν κακοῖς. know that : θνητὸς ὤ ν (ὅτι — εἰμί). σὲ θνητὸν ὄντα (ὅτι — εἶ). ἐπιστήμων τῶν περὶ τὰς τάξεις.

MEANING	PRESENT	STEM	FUTURE
84. follow	ἕπομαι (*ipf.* εἱπόμην)	ἑπ, σεπ, (σπ)	ἕψομαι
85. love, desire ardent-ly	ἐράω, ἔραμαι	ἐρᾰ	ἐρασθήσομαι
86. work	ἐργάζομαι (*ipf.*: εἰργαζόμην) *pass.*	ϝεργ	ἐργάσομαι ἐργασθήσομαι
87. go, come	ἔρχομαι (*ipf.* ᾖα)	ἐρχ, εἰ, ἰ ἐλ(υ)θ	εἶμι
88. ask, question	ἐρωτάω *pass.*	ἐρ-η	ἐρωτήσω ἐρήσομαι ἐρωτηθήσομαι
89. eat, consume, live on	ἐσθίω, βιβρώσκω often κατα- *pass.*	ἐσθι, ἐδ, φαγ, βρω	ἔδομαι κατα-βρωθήσομαι
90. find, discover *med.* find for myself, get, procure, obtain	εὑρίσκω εὑρίσκομαι *pass.*	εὑρ-η εὑρ-ε	εὑρήσω εὑρήσομαι εὑρεθήσομαι
91. gladden *med.* rejoice	εὐφραίνω reg. εὐφραίνομαι	εὐφρᾰν	εὐφρανοῦμαι, -ῇ
92. pray; vow	εὔχομαι	guttural	εὔξομαι
93. have, hold; *intr.* am (in a certain state, —e.g. καλῶς), fare *med.* hold for myself *Compounds*, e.g. furnish, supply, afford, provide, **grant**	ἔχω (ἴσχω) (*ipf.* εἶχον) ἔχομαι (*ipf.* εἰχό- μην) παρέχω	ἐχ, σεχ σχ-η	ἕξω, σχήσω ἕξομαι, σχήσο- μαι παρέξω, παρα- σχήσω

Aorist	Perfect (Nouns)	Syntax
ἐσπόμην σπῶμαι, ἐπίσπωμαι, σποῖτο, ἐπίσποιτο, σποῦ, ἐπίσπου	——	**ἕπομαι**: ἡγεμόνι sequor ducem. νόμοις ἐπιχωρίοις. **ἔρημός** τινος: ὑμῶν ἔρημος ὤν without you.
ἠράσθην became fond	——	**ἐρῶ** μαθήματος — τοῦ ζῆν. οὐκ ἐρῶ τυχεῖν τῆς σῆς τιμῆς.
εἰργασάμην εἰργάσθην	εἴργασμαι	**ἐρίζω** rival, vie with in something: ἐρίζουσιν Ἀφροδίτῃ κάλλος.
ἦλθον	ἐλήλυθα ἥκω adsum	
ἠρώτησα ἠρόμην ἠρωτήθην	ἠρώτηκα ἠρώτημαι	**ἐρωτῶ**: ταῦθ᾽ ὑμᾶς — ἀνήρεθ᾽ ἡμᾶς τοὺς ἐν Ἰλίῳ πόνους. **ἐσθίω**: κηρίων — ἀρούρης καρπόν.
ἔφαγον κατ-εβρώθην	κατα-βέβρωκα κατα-βέβρωμαι	**εὐδαιμονίζω** account one happy because of: ὑμᾶς τῆς ἐλευθερίας. **εὐεργετῶ** (= εὖ ποιῶ): τινά do good to.
ηὗρον (εὗρον) ηὑρόμην ηὑρέθην εὑρετός-ή εὕρεσις	ηὕρηκα (εὑρ.) ηὕρημαι τὸ εὕρημα	**εὑρήσεις**, ὅτι ἀληθῆ λέγω or ἐμὲ ἀληθῆ λέγοντα. **εὑρίσκομαι** ἀληθῆ λέγων.
ηὐφράνθην	——	**εὐφραίνομαι**: (ἐπὶ) τῇ διανοίᾳ. ὁρῶν (at seeing) ὑμᾶς παρόντας.
ηὐξάμην	ηὖγμαι εὐκτός	**εὔχομαι** wish: ὑμῖν ἀγαθά. vow: θεοῖς ἑκατόμβην, θύσειν σωτήρια.
ἔσχον σχῶ, σχοίην σχές, σχέτω ἐσχόμην σχῶμαι σχοίμην σχοῦ, σχέσθω	ἔσχηκα ἔσχημαι	pray to, beseech: θεοῖς πολυκαρπίαν for, ὑμῖν δοῦναι τἀγαθά. **ἔχω**: καλῶς ἔχει τὰ ἱερά. εὐνοϊκῶς εἴχομεν ἀλλήλοιν. **ἔχομαι**: χειρός — νόμων — cling to, τῆς αὐτῆς γνώμης.
παρέσχον παράσχω παράσχοιμι παράσχες	παρέσχηκα	ἀπέχω trans.: τοὺς υἱοὺς πονηρῶν. intr.: οὐ πολὺ Βαβυλῶνος. **ἀπέχομαι**: ἐπιθυμιῶν. **μετέχω**: ἀρχῆς — τινί τινος share with.

Meaning	Present	Stem	Future
furnish etc. (what is my own)	παρέχομαι		παρέξομαι παρασχήσομαι
endure, suffer, can bear	ἀνέχομαι (ipf. ἠνειχόμην)		ἀνέξομαι
promise	ὑπισχνέομαι		ὑποσχήσομαι
94. live	ζάω, ζῆς etc., βιόω	ζη, βιω	βιώσομαι

95. yoke, join together
   med. join for myself
	ζεύγνῡμι
	ζεύγνῡμαι
	        pass.
		ζευγ	ζεύξω
			ζεύξομαι
			ζευχθήσομαι

96. grow to man's estate; am at man's estate, in the prime of youth, young	ἡβάσκω ἡβάω	ἡβα, ἡβη	ἡβήσω
97. lead (τινός — τινί); take for, regard as (τινά τι); believe	ἡγέομαι		ἡγήσομαι
98. am glad, delight	ἥδομαι	dental (σϝἄδ, ϝἄδ)	ἡσθήσομαι
99. am arrived, am come, am here (there), *adsum*	ἥκω	guttural	ἥξω
100. am seated (see ἵζω)	ἧμαι, pros. κάθημαι *ipf.* ἐκαθήμην	ἧς καθη(s)	———
101. am weaker, beaten, defeated	ἡττάομαι		ἡττήσομαι
102. bury	θάπτω *pass.*	τἄφ	θάψω τἄφήσομαι

Aorist	Perfect (Nouns)	Syntax

παρεσχόμην
παράσχωμαι
παράσχοιτο
παράσχου
ἠνεσχόμην
ἀνάσχωμαι
ὑπεσχόμην
ὑπόσχωμαι
ὑπόσχου
	παρέσχημαι
	
	ἠνέσχημαι
	
	ὑπέσχημαι
		παρέχω : ἐμαυτὸν φίλον,
		   ἐμαυτὸν ἐρωτᾶν τῷ βουλομένῳ.
		ἀνέχομαι : πήματα πάσχων πολλά,
		   Ἀριαίου βασιλεύοντος suffer A. to
		   rule.
		
		ὑπισχνοῦμαι : δώσειν μισθόν.
		   ὑμῖν, αὐτοὺς μηδὲν πείσεσθαι.

ἐβίων	βεβίωκα	

ἔζευξα
ἐζευξάμην
ἐζεύχθην }
	ἔζευγμαι
	   τὸ ζεῦγος
	   τὸ ζυγόν
		ζεύγνυμι γέφυραν (πλοίοις) build a
		   (pontoon) bridge.
		ποταμὸν (πλοίοις) span the river
		   (by a bridge).

ἤβησα came to m.	ἤβηκα have been
	   young
		ζηλόω emulate, vie with : τὸν ἐσθλὸν
		   ἄνδρα. envy : ζηλῶ σε τοῦ νοῦ.
		ζημιόω punish, fine : Περικλέα χρή-
		   μασιν.

ἡγησάμην	ἥγημαι (with pres-
	   ent force : am of
	   opinion)
	   ἡγητέον
		ἡγοῦμαι command : στρατεύματος.
		   show the way, lead : ταῖς ναυσίν (τὴν
		   ῥᾴστην ὁδόν).
		   regard as : τὸν σοφὸν εὐδαιμονέστα-
		   τον.

ἤσθην	——	believe : ἱκανὸς εἶναι διατελεῖν,
		   τὴν παρασκευὴν μείζω εἶναι.
		ἥδομαι : (ἐπὶ) δικαίοις ἔργοις —
		   ὁρῶν τὸ φῶς or
		   ὅτι ὁρῶ τὸ φῶς.

N.B. — The ipf., subj. and opt. have also the force of *aorists*.		
——	——	
ἡττήθην	ἥττημαι ἡ ἧττα	ἡττῶμαι : τῶν Ἑλλήνων μάχῃ (-ην). am inferior to, surpassed by in some- thing.
ἔθαψα ἐτάφην	τέταφα τέθαμμαι inf. τεθάφθαι ἄθαπτος, ὁ τάφος	τῶν φίλων εὐεργεσίαις or τῶν φίλων εὐεργετῶν.

Meaning	Present	Stem	Future
103. admire, wonder at	θαυμάζω *pass.*	dental	θαυμάσομαι θαυμασθήσομαι
104. behold, look on	θεάομαι		θεάσομαι
105. die off, fall (in battle)	ἀπο-θνῄσκω	θᾰν, θνη	ἀπο-θανοῦμαι, -ῇ
106. am angry	θῡμόομαι		θῡμώσομαι
107. sacrifice; *med.* sacrifice in my own interest	θῦω θύομαι *pass.*		θύσω θύσομαι τῠθήσομαι
108. heal, cure	ἰάομαι *pass.*		ἰάσομαι ἰᾱθήσομαι
109. *tr.* make sit down *intr.* sit down sit down sit down — am seated am seated	}καθίζω καθίζομαι καθέζομαι κάθημαι p. 202	ἱδ ἑδ ἡ(σ)	καθιῶ, -εῖς ——— καθεδοῦμαι, -ῇ
110. send *med.* send in my own interest; hasten, rush	ἵημι ἵεμαι *pass.*	ἡ, ἑ	ἥσω ἥσομαι ἑθήσομαι
111. come (to), arrive (at)	ἱκνέομαι, usu. ἀφ-, ἐξ-	ἱκ	ἀφ-ίξομαι
112. make stand, place *med.* place for myself *intr.* place myself	ἵστημι ἵσταμαι *pass.* ἵσταμαι	στη, στα	στήσω στήσομαι στᾰθήσομαι στήσομαι
113. cleanse, purify, purge	καθαίρω, is not compounded; reg.	καθᾰρ	καθαρῶ, -εῖς καθαρθήσομαι

AORIST	PERFECT (NOUNS)	SYNTAX
ἐθαύμᾰσα	τεθαύμᾰκα am full of wonder	**θαυμάζω**: ὑμᾶς τῆς διανοίας, Ὅμηρον ἐπὶ ποιήσει.
ἐθαυμάσθην	τεθαύμᾰσμαι θαυμαστός	τῶν στρατηγῶν, ὅτι οὐ πειρῶνται. τίσι ποτὲ λόγοις ἔπεισαν Ἀθηναίους. εἰ μὴ ἀσμένοις ὑμῖν ἀφῖγμαι.
ἐθεᾱσάμην	τεθέᾱμαι θεᾱτός	
ἀπ-έθανον *fut. pf.*	τέθνηκα am dead τεθνήξω shall be dead	**ἀποθνῇσκω**: ὑπό τινος, pass. to ἀποκτείνω. **ἐπιθῡμέω** desire, wish for: σοφίας.
ἐθυμώθην	τεθύμωμαι	πλούτου ἄρχειν, τιμᾶσθαι } p. 199.
ἔθῡσα ἐθῡσάμην ἐτύθην }	τέθῠκα τέθῠμαι }	**θυμοῦταί**: σοι τῆς θυγατρός with you on account of. **ἴδιός**: τινος (τινι) proprius alcius, alci.
ἰᾱσάμην ἰάθην }	ἴᾱμαι	**ἱερὸς**: ὁ χῶρος Ἀρτέμιδος. **ἀφίημι** send off, let depart: βέλος, δοῦλον.
ἐκάθῐσα	——	ἀφίεμαι desist from: σωτηρίας. ἐξίημι *tr.* send forth; *intr.* empty (of rivers).
——	——	
ἐκαθεζόμην with the force of *ipf.* and *aor.* (= *considebam and consedi*)	—— —— ——	ἐφίημι send upon one: Ἀργείοις πήματα. leave, allow: σοὶ πᾶν λέγειν. ἐφίεμαι seek for: κερδῶν.
ἧκα, εἷμεν	εἷκα	**ἱκανώτατος** ἀνὴρ εἰπεῖν καὶ πρᾶξαι.
εἵμην εἵθην }	εἷμαι	**ἐξ-(ἐφ-)ικνοῦμαι** reach, hit: τῶν σφενδονητῶν.
	ἑτός — ἑτέος	**ἀφίστημι**: τοὺς συμμάχους (ἀπὸ) τῶν Ἀθηναίων.
ἀφ-ῑκόμην	ἀφ-ῖγμαι ἡ ἄφιξις	ἐφίστημι bring to a stop: στρατόν. praeficio: τῷ ξενικῷ.
ἔστησα ἐστησάμην ἐστάθην ἔστην *fut. pf.*	—— —— —— ἔστηκα stand ἑστήξω shall stand	καθίστημι make, appoint; establish: Κῦρον βασιλέα. προΐστημι praeficio: τοῦ ξενικοῦ. ὑφίσταμαι subire: κινδύνους. promise: δώσειν. withstand, resist: συμφοραῖς.
ἐκάθηρα ἐκαθάρθην	κεκάθαρκα κεκάθαρμαι	**καθαίρω**: Ἄδραστον φόνου. purify A. from blood.

Meaning	Present	Stem	Future
114. kill, slay	κατα-**καίνω**	κᾰν	κατα-κᾰνῶ, -εῖς
115. kindle, light, burn, *tr.*	**καίω** (**κᾰ́ω**), in prose mostly κατα-. *pass.*	και, κᾱ, καυ	καύσω καυθήσομαι
116. call = summon, invite; and call = term, style	**καλέω** *pass.*	κᾰλ κλη	καλῶ, -εῖς κληθήσομαι I shall be called (in either sense)
117. grow weary, become tired of	**κάμνω**	κᾰμ, κμη	κᾰμοῦμαι, -ῇ
118. lie, *iaceo*	**κεῖμαι** *ipf.* ἐκείμην, ἔκεισο etc.	κει	κείσομαι
119. bid, urge, command, order, *iubeo*	**κελεύω** *pass.*	κελευ(σ)	κελεύσω κελευσθήσομαι
120. mix	**κεράννῡμι** *pass.*	κερᾰ(σ) κρᾱ	κερῶ, -ᾷς κρᾱθήσομαι
121. weep	**κλαίω** (**κλᾱ́ω**) *pass.*	κλαυ(σ) κλᾱ	κλαύσομαι κλαυσθήσομαι
122. shut	**κλείω** (**κλῄω**) *pass.*	κλει(σ)	κλείσω κλεισθήσομαι
123. incline, cause to lean, bend	**κλίνω** *pass.*	κλῐν κλῐ	κλῐνῶ, -εῖς κλῐθήσομαι
124. lay to rest *med.* go to sleep	κοιμάω κοιμάομαι		κοιμήσομαι
125. bring, convey *med.* get for myself, acquire, get back, recover *pass.* am brought etc.; travel	**κομίζω** regul. κομίζομαι	dental	κομιῶ, -εῖς κομιοῦμαι, -ῇ κομισθήσομαι

Aorist	Perfect (Nouns)	Syntax
κατ-έκᾰνον	κατα-κέκονα	
ἔκαυσα	κέκαυκα	**καίω**: ἀνακαίειν πῦρ —
		κατακαίειν τὰς κώμας.
ἐκαύθην	κέκαυμαι	**κακουργῶ** (= κακῶς ποιῶ): τινά do
	ἄκαυ(σ)τος	harm to.
ἐκάλεσα	κέκληκα	**καλῶ**: ἐπὶ δεῖπνον, εἰς δικαστήριον.
ἐκλήθην	κέκλημαι am called	**ἐγκαλῶ**: charge, blame, reproach:
	= my name is	ὑμῖν δειλίαν, or
fut. pf.	κεκλήσομαι shall	ὅτι (ὡς) δειλοί ἐστε.
	be called	
ἔκᾰμον	κέκμηκα	**κάμνω**: μὴ κάμῃς φίλον εὐεργετῶν.
———	———	**ἀνάκειται** ἀνάθημα (ἀνατίθημι).
		διάκειμαι φιλικῶς σοι (διατίθημι).
ἐκέλευσα	κεκέλευκα	ἐπίκειμαι πολεμίοις (ἐπιτίθεμαι).
ἐκελεύσθην	κεκέλευσμαι	**κενός** empty, void, without:
	κελευστός	ἅρμα κενὸν ἡνιόχων.
ἐκέρᾰσα	———	**κεράννυμι**: οἴνῳ ὕδωρ.
ἐκράθην	κέκρᾱμαι	**κινδῡνεύω**: διαφθαρῆναι am in dan-
	ἄκρᾱτος	ger of.
ἔκλαυσα	κέκλαυκα	τὸν στρατὸν ἀποβαλεῖν.
ἐκλαύ(σ)θην	κέκλαυμαι	κίνδυνός ἐστι, μὴ πολλοὶ ἀπόλωνται
	ἄκλαυ(σ)τος	= πολλοὺς ἀπολέσθαι.
		κινδυνεύει σοφὸς εἶναι haud scio an
ἔκλεισα	κέκλεικα	sap. sit.
ἐκλείσθην	κέκλειμαι	**κοινός** common to: πάντων or πᾶσιν.
ἔκλῑνα	κέκλῐκα	**κοινόω** make common: τὴν δύναμιν.
ἐκλίθην	κέκλῐμαι	**(ἀνα) κοινόομαι** communicate, con-
		sult, confer with, τῷ θεῷ —
		Σωκράτει περὶ τῆς πορείας.
ἐκοιμήθην	κεκοίμημαι	**κοινωνέω** have a share of, share:
ἐκόμῐσα	κεκόμῐκα	ἀλλήλοις πόνων καὶ κινδύνων.
ἐκομισάμην		
	κεκόμῐσμαι	
ἐκομίσθην		

MEANING	PRESENT	STEM	FUTURE
126. hew, fell, slay, cut	κόπτω *pass.*	κοπ	κόψω κοπήσομαι
127. cry out	κράζω, often ἀνα-	κρᾰγ	ἀνα-κράξομαι
128. hang, suspend	κρεμάννῡμι *pass.*	κρεμᾰ(σ)	κρεμῶ, -ᾷς κρεμασθήσομαι
129. divide, judge	κρίνω *pass.*	κρῑν κρῐ	κρῐνῶ, -εῖς κρῐθήσομαι
answer, reply	ἀπο-κρίνομαι		ἀπο-κρῐνοῦμαι, -ῇ
130. acquire	κτάομαι		κτήσομαι
131. kill	ἀπο-κτείνω	κτεν	ἀπο-κτενῶ, -εῖς
132. obtain by lot, obtain, get	λαγχάνω	λᾰχ, ληχ	λήξομαι
133. take, receive	λαμβάνω *pass.*	λᾰβ, ληβ	λήψομαι ληφθήσομαι
134. am hidden, escape the notice of *med.* forget	λανθάνω (λήθω) ἐπι-λανθάνομαι	λᾰθ, ληθ	λήσω ἐπι-λήσομαι
135. speak, say, tell, call; say yes, affirm, declare; discourse, harangue	λέγω φημί ἀγορεύω *pass.*	ἀγορευ λεγ, φη, φᾰ ϝεπ, ϝερ, ϝη	ἐρῶ, ἐρεῖς λέξω, φήσω ῥηθήσομαι λεχθήσομαι
speak, converse with for	δια-λέγομαι ἀπ-αγορεύω see n. 21		δια-λέξομαι
136. gather, collect, assemble	λέγω (ἐκ-, κατα-, συλ-) *pass.*	λεγ	συλ-λέξω συλ-λεγήσομαι

AORIST	PERFECT (NOUNS)	SYNTAX
ἔκοψα ἐκόπην *fut. pf.*	κέκοφα κέκομμαι κεκόψομαι	
ἀν-έκρᾰγον	κέκρᾱγα cry out	**κρατέω** (ἐγκρατής, ἀκρατής) :
ἐκρέμᾰσα ἐκρεμάσθην	—— κρέμᾰμαι hang, am suspended	rule, am master of, have power over, control : ὀργῆς — πάντων οἱ θεοὶ κρατοῦσιν. conquer, defeat : Συρακοσίους μά-
ἔκρῑνα ἐκρίθην ἀπ-εκρῑνάμην	κέκρῐκα κέκρῐμαι κρῐτός, κρῐτέος ἀπο-κέκρῐμαι, also *pass.*	χαις. surpass : ἄλλους πολὺ εὐεργετῶν. **κρίνω** decide, settle : νεῖκος, ἀγῶνα. consider as : τὴν ἀρετὴν μέγιστον ἀγαθόν. accuse, try : τοὺς πρέσβεις δώρων.
ἐκτησάμην *pass.* ἐκτήθην *fut. pf.*	κέκτημαι ⎰ possess, ἔκτημαι ⎱ have κεκτήσομαι shall h.	**κωλύω** hinder, prevent : τινά τινος : τοὺς ἐπιόντας τῆς παρόδου. τοῦ κάειν. τί κωλύει ἡμᾶς (μὴ) διαβαίνειν;
ἀπ-έκτεινα	ἀπ-έκτονα	**ἀποκτείνω** : *pass.* φονεύομαι
ἔλᾰχον	εἴληχα	or ἀποθνήσκω ὑπό τινος.
ἔλᾰβον ἐλήφθην	εἴληφα εἴλημμαι ληπτέος	**λαγχάνω** obtain by lot, as my share : ὄλβον, ἀρχήν. am chosen by lot: ὁ λαχὼν πολέ- μαρχος. receive a share: ἐπαίνου, τιμῆς.
ἔλᾰθον ἐπ-ελαθόμην	λέληθα ἐπι-λέλησμαι ἡ λήθη	**λαμβάνω** seize : τῆς ζώνης τὸν Ὀρόν- ταν. (κατα)λαμβάνω ὑμᾶς κλέπτοντας. **λανθάνει** τὸ στράτευμα τρεφόμενον is
εἶπον, εἰπέ εἶπα ἔλεξα, ἔφησα ἐρρήθη, ἐλέχθην εἰρήσεται and λε- λέξεται it will have been said δι-ελέχθην	εἴρηκα εἴρημαι λέλεγμαι δι-είλεγμαι	secretly maintained. οὐδεὶς ποιῶν πονηρὰ λανθάνει θεόν. λάθρᾳ τῶν στρατιωτῶν without the knowledge. ἐπιλανθάνομαι : τῆς οἴκαδε ὁδοῦ. **λέγω** : ὑμᾶς εὖ, κακῶς (*pass.* εὖ ἀκούω). ὑμᾶς προδότας. ἔλεγεν αὐτοῖς θαρρεῖν *bono animo* *essent* ; μὴ ἀποπλεῖν *ne avehe-* *rentur.* διαλέγομαι : Σωκράτει περὶ σοφίας.
συν-έλεξα συν-ελέγην	συν-είλοχα συν-είλεγμαι	**συλλέγειν** : συλλέγεσθαι εἰς πεδίον.

Meaning	Present	Stem	Future
137. leave *med.* leave what is my own (for myself, behind me) am left, remain, fall behind	λείπω λείπομαι *pass.* (ὑπο)λείπομαι	λειπ λῐπ	λείψω λείψομαι λειφθήσομαι λείψομαι λείψομαι
138. take into account, reason, consider	λογίζομαι *pass.*	dental	λογιοῦμαι, -ῇ λογισθήσομαι
139. ruin, spoil ; insult, outrage	λῡμαίνομαι *pass.*	λῠμᾰν	λυμᾰνοῦμαι, -ῇ λυμανθήσομαι
140. grieve, pain, harass *med.* am sad, grieved, pained	λῡπέω reg. λῠπέομαι		 λῡπήσομαι
141. loose, unbind *med.* loose myself or for myself	λῠ́ω λῠ́ομαι *pass.*	λῠ, λῠ	λύσω λύσομαι λῠθήσομαι
142. rage, am mad	μαίνομαι	μᾰν	μᾰνοῦμαι, -ῇ
143. learn	μανθάνω	μᾰθ-η	μᾰθήσομαι
144. fight	μάχομαι	μαχ-ε(σ),-η	μαχοῦμαι, -ῇ
145. mix	μείγνῡμι μίσγω *pass.*	μειγ	μείξω μειχθήσομαι
146. *curae mihi est*, it is a matter of interest to me, concerns me, I care for take care	μέλει μοι ἐπι-μέλομαι (ἐπι-μελέομαι)	μελ-η	μελήσει ἐπι-μελήσομαι
147. am about to, on the point of ; likely to ; am expected, destined, doomed to; intend; delay, hesitate	μέλλω	μελλ-η	μελλήσω

Aorist	Perfect (Nouns)	Syntax
ἔλῐπον	λέλοιπα	ἐπιλείπει : ὁ σῖτος τὸν στρατόν.
ἐλιπόμην		(ὑπο)λείπομαι : τινός τινι.
ἐλείφθην }	λέλειμμαι	λέλειφθε πολὺ ἡμῶν πλήθει,
fut. pf.	λελείψεται	οὐδενὸς εὐεργετοῦντες.
ἐλείφθην	λέλειμμαι	
ἐλογῐσάμην }	λελόγισμαι	λήγω leave off, cease from: ἔριδος.
ἐλογίσθην		οὐ λήξω θεραπεύων τοὺς γονέας.
ἐλυμηνάμην }	λελύμασμαι	
ἐλυμάνθην		
		λυπῶ : ὑμᾶς πολλὰ ἐλύπουν.
		λυποῦμαι : πολλὰ (ἐπὶ) τοῖς γιγνο-
ἐλυπήθην	λελύπημαι	μένοις.
		λῡσιτελέω am profitable : ὑμῖν πολλά.
ἔλῡσα	λέλῠκα	ἀπολύω acquit : ὑμᾶς προδοσίας.
ἐλῡσάμην }	λέλῠμαι, λῠτός	καταλύω _tr._ unyoke; _intr._ make a
ἐλύθην		halt.
fut. pf.	λελύσομαι	λύσω : ὑμᾶς τῶνδε τῶν πόνων.
ἐμᾰ́νην	μέμηνα	μανθάνω : τί βούλει μαθεῖν ἐμοῦ;
		learn and know how to: σωφρο-
ἔμᾰθον	μεμᾰ́θηκα	νεῖν.
	μαθητός	learn that: θνητὸς ὤν (ὅτι — εἰμί).
		σὲ θνητὸν ὄντα (ὅτι — εἶ).
ἐμαχεσάμην	μεμάχημαι	μάχομαι : Πέρσαις or ἐπί, πρὸς Π.
ἔμειξα		in alliance with μετὰ Κύρου or
ἐμείχθην	μέμειγμαι	σὺν Κύρῳ.
		μείγνυμι : οἴνῳ ὕδωρ.
ἐμέλησε(ν)	μεμέληκε(ν)	μέλει μοι : τοῦ ἐπαίνου ὑμῶν.
		ὅπως ὑμεῖς ἐπαινέσεσθε.
		μεταμέλει μοι paenitet me, repent :
		πράξεως — ὅτι ταῦτ᾽ ἔπραξα —
ἐπ-εμελήθην	ἐπι-μεμέλημαι	ταῦτα πράξαντι.
		ἐπιμέλομαι : πᾶσαν ἐπιμέλειαν.
		ἐπιμέλονται πάντων οἱ θεοί.
ἐμέλλησα		ἐπιμελώμεθα τῶν νέων, ὅπως ὡς ἄρι-
	μελλητέον	στοι ἔσονται.
		ἐπιμελὴς (ἀμελὴς, ἀμελέω) παιδείας.
		μέλλω am about : ὑμᾶς διδάξειν.
		it is to be expected that: οὐδεὶς ἔτι
		μέλλει ἀγορὰν παρέξειν.

Meaning	Present	Stem	Future
148. find fault with, blame	**μέμφομαι** *pass.*	labial	μέμψομαι μεμφθήσομαι
149. stay, remain; await, expect, *maneo*	**μένω**	μεν	μενῶ, -εῖς
150. devise, plan, contrive	**μηχανάομαι**		μηχανήσομαι
151. stain, pollute	**μιαίνω** *pass.*	μιᾰν	μιᾰνῶ, -εῖς μιανθήσομαι
152. imitate, copy	**μῑμέομαι** *pass.*		μιμήσομαι μιμηθήσομαι
153. remind remember, recall; mention	**μιμνήσκω**, (usu. ἀνα-, ὑπο-) μιμνῄσκομαι	μνη μνη(σ)	ἀνα-μνήσω μνησθήσομαι
154. deal out, allot, distribute *med.* allot to myself, occupy; graze, feed	**νέμω** νέμομαι *pass.*	νεμ	νεμῶ, -εῖς νεμοῦμαι, -ῇ νεμηθήσομαι
155. think, am minded	**νοέω** reg., oftener -νοέομαι in compos.		-νοήσομαι
156. open	**οἴγω** (ἀν-, δι-) οἴγνῡμι *pass.*	οἰγ	ἀν-οίξω ἀν-οιχθήσομαι
157. know (*novi*)	**οἶδα**, οἶσθα etc. ᾔδειν, ᾖστον — ᾖδεσαν, εἰδῶ — εἰδείην — ἴσθι, ἴστω — εἰδέναι — εἰδώς.	εἰδ, ἰδ	εἴσομαι shall know *cognoscam and novero*
158. wail, bewail, lament	**οἰμώζω**	οἰμωγ	οἰμώξομαι
159. think, imagine, believe	**οἴομαι, οἶμαι**		οἰήσομαι

Aorist	Perfect (Nouns)	Syntax
ἐμεμψάμην	——	**μέμφομαι** find fault with: τὴν γνώ-
ἐμέμφθην	ἡ μέμψις	μην.
		blame for: ὑμῖν τὴν ἐξέλασιν
ἔμεινα	μεμένηκα	or: ὑμῖν, ὅτι ἐξηλάσατε.
ἐμηχανησάμην	μεμηχάνημαι	**μηχανῶμαι**: πρᾶγμα τοιόνδε.
	also *pass.*	cast about: ὅπως ἀποφεύξεται.
ἐμίανα	μεμίαγκα	
ἐμιάνθην	μεμίασμαι	
ἀμίαντος	τὸ μίασμα	**ἀναμιμνήσκω**: ὑμᾶς τοὺς κινδύνους.
		μιμνήσκομαι (μνήμων) τινός:
ἐμιμησάμην ⎫	μεμίμημαι	μέμνησο τῆς κοινῆς τύχης.
ἐμιμήθην ⎭		μέμνημαι remember that:
ἀν-έμνησα	——	θνητὸς ὤν (ὅτι — εἰμί),
		σὲ θνητὸν ὄντα (ὅτι — εἶ),
ἐμνήσθην	μέμνημαι *memini*	purpose, remember to:
	μεμνήσομαι *memi-*	ἀνὴρ ἀγαθὸς εἶναι.
	nero	μέμνησο πλουτῶν τοὺς πένητας ὠφελεῖν.
ἀμνηστέω	μνήμη μνῆμα	**μισθόω**: τινά τινος. μισθοῦ = *mer-*
ἔνειμα	νενέμηκα	*cede*, for money.
		νομίζω consider as: ὑμᾶς φίλους —
ἐνειμάμην ⎫	νενέμημαι	believe: ὑμᾶς ἐμοὶ φίλους εἶναι.
ἐνεμήθην ⎭		believe in: οὐ νομίζει τοὺς ἀρχαίους
		θεούς.
-ἐνοήθην	-νενόημαι	**ἀπο-νοέομαι** despair of: διαμάχε-
		σθαι.
ἀν-έῳξα (ἀν-οίξω)	ἀν-έῳχα	δια-νοέομαι intend: ἀπάγειν (ἀπάξειν).
ἀν-εῴχθην	ἀν-έῳγμαι	προ-νοέομαι foresee: τὰ μέλλοντα.
	ἀν-εῴγμην	provide for: τοῦ μέλλοντος.
		οἶδα know that: θνητὸς ὤν (ὅτι —
		εἰμί).
——	——	Κῦρον πεπτωκότα (ὅτι —).
		know how to: εἴκειν θεοῖς.
		σύνοιδα ἐμαυτῷ: οὐδὲν σοφὸς ὤν
		or οὐδὲν σοφῷ ὄντι.
ὤμωξα	ὤμωγμαι	σύνοιδα ἐμαυτῷ also: I feel guilty.
		οἴομαι: ἱκανὸς εἶναι *me esse.*
ᾠήθην	——	ὑμᾶς ἱκανοὺς εἶναι.
		οἴχομαι: ᾤχετο λάθρᾳ ἀπιών.

Meaning	Present	Stem	Future
160. am gone, am away	οἴχομαι N.B. — The ipf. and the moods may		be used aoristically.
161. *perdo*, destroy *med. pereo*, perish	ἀπ-όλλῡμι ἀπ-όλλῡμαι	ὀλ-ε	ἀπ-ολῶ, -εῖς ἀπ-ολοῦμαι, -ῇ
162. swear	ὄμνῡμι	ὀμ-ο	ὀμοῦμαι, -ῇ
163. profit, benefit, help *m. & p.* derive benefit	ὀνίνημι, ὠφέλουν ὀνίναμαι	ὀνη ὀνᾰ	ὀνήσω ὀνήσομαι
164. see	ὁράω (*ipf.* ἑώρων) *pass.*	ϝορα, ὁρα, ὀπ, ϝιδ, ἰδ	ὄψομαι ὀφθήσομαι
165. make angry *med.* am angry	ὀργίζω ὀργίζομαι	dental	ὀργιῶ, -εῖς ὀργιοῦμαι, -ῇ
166. stretch out, reach *med.* desire	ὀρέγω, usually ὀρέγομαι	guttural	ὀρέξομαι
167. set in motion ; set out, get under way [off *med.* set out, start	ὁρμάω ὁρμάομαι		ὁρμήσω ὁρμήσομαι
168. lie at anchor *tr.* moor, anchor *intr.* land, come to or lie at anchor	ὁρμέω and ὁρμέομαι ὁρμίζω ὁρμίζομαι	dental	*reg.* *reg.* ὁρμιοῦμαι, -ῇ
169. owe	ὀφείλω	ὀφελ	——
170. suffer, experience	πάσχω	πασχ, πᾰθ, πενθ	πείσομαι
171. cause to cease, stop, *tr.* *pass.* *med.* cease, stop *intr.*	παύω παύομαι		παύσω παυθήσομαι παύσομαι
172. prevail upon, per- suade, induce *pass.* *med.* obey, comply with	πείθω πείθομαι	πειθ	πείσω πεισθήσομαι πείσομαι

Aorist	Perfect (Nouns)	Syntax
		ὀκνέω scruple, hesitate : ἀποκρίνασθαι. am afraid : μὴ ἀποδόξῃ ὑμῖν.
ἀπ-ώλεσα ἀπ-ωλόμην	ἀπ-ολώλεκα ἀπ-όλωλα ἀπ-ωλώλειν	ὁμιλέω associate with : σοφοῖς ὁμιλῶν καὐτὸς ἐκβήσῃ σοφός.
ὤμοσα	ὀμώμοκα ὠμωμόκειν	ὄμνυμι (ἐπιορκέω) : ὅρκον — σπονδάς. by the gods : τοὺς θεούς — νὴ Δία — οὐ μὰ τοὺς θεούς.
ὤνησα ὠνήμην, p. ὠνήθην	ἡ ὄνησις	ὀμνύασι πάντες μὴ λείψειν τὴν τάξιν. ὁρῶμεν : ἄποροι ὄντες (ὑμᾶς ὄντας), πάντα ἀληθῆ ὄντα or
εἶδον εἰδόμην ὤφθην	ἑώρακα ὄπωπα ἑώρᾱμαι ὦμμαι	ὅτι πάντα ἀληθῆ ἐστιν. ὅρα μή w. ind. (see if not) perhaps, beware lest. w. subj. beware lest, take care not to.
ὤργῑσα ὠργίσθην	ὤργῑκα ὤργῐσμαι	περιορῶ overlook, suffer to happen : πόλιν διαφθειρομένην.
ὠρέχθην	ὤρεγμαι	ὀργίζομαι : τῷ ἀδελφῷ, ὅτι ἀπέστη — or τῷ ἀδελφῷ τῆς ἀποστάσεως. ἀδικούμενος.
ὥρμησα	ὥρμηκα	ὀρέγονται : δόξης — τοιοῦτοι γενέσθαι. τοῦ πρῶτος ἕκαστος γίγνεσθαι.
ὡρμήθην	ὥρμημαι	ὀφείλω : ἀλλ᾽ ὤφελε μὲν Κῦρος ζῆν. ὡς ὤφελον πάροιθεν ἐκλιπεῖν βίον.
ὡρμῑσάμην	ὥρμισμαι	παιδεύω : τινά τι instruct, train in. μουσικὴν ὑπὸ Λάμπρου παιδευθείς.
ὤφελον utinam	——	πάσχω : εὖ, κακῶς ὑπό τινος am treated, pass. to εὖ, κακῶς ποιῶ τινα.
ἔπᾰθον	πέπονθα	παύω : ἔπαυσαν Τιμόθεον ἀρχῆς, or Τιμόθεον ἄρχοντα.
ἔπαυσα ἐπαύθην ἐπαυσάμην }	πέπαυκα πέπαυμαι ἄπαυστος	παύομαι : Τιμόθεος ἐπαύσατο ἄρχων. ἔπειτα θρήνων καὶ γόων ἐπαύσατο. πείθω persuade to do : ποιεῖν. convince you of this : ὑμᾶς ταῦτα, that : ὡς οὐκ ἀγαθοί εἰσιν.
ἔπεισα ἐπείσθην ἐπείσθην	πέπεικα πέπεισμαι πέπεισμαι [rely πέποιθα trust,	πείθομαι (ἀπειθέω) τινί : obey : ἄρχοντι, νόμοις. believe, trust : ταῦτ᾽ ἐγώ σοι. πέποιθα : ἐμαυτῷ, τῇ χειρί.

Meaning	Present	Stem	Future
173. try, attempt *med.* try (my own skill in), attempt	πειράω *reg.* πειράομαι		πειράσομαι
174. send	**πέμπω** *pass.*	πεμπ	πέμψω πεμφθήσομαι
175. spread out, expand	**πετάννῡμι** (often ἀνα-) *pass.*	πετᾰ(σ) πτᾰ	πετῶ, -ᾷς πετασθήσομαι
176. fasten, fix *pass.* am fastened, become stiff	**πήγνῡμι** πήγνῠμαι	πηγ πᾰγ	πήξω πᾰγήσομαι
177. fill, *tr.*	**πίμπλημι** (πλήθω am full)	πλη, πλᾰ	πλήσω πλησθήσομαι
178. set fire to, burn, *tr.*	**πίμπρημι** (πρήθω am on fire)	πρη πρᾰ	ἐμ-πρήσω ἐμ-πρησθήσομαι
179. drink	**πίνω** *pass.*	πῑν, πι, πω, πο	πίομαι ποθήσομαι
180. fall	**πίπτω**	πετ, πεσ, πτω	πεσοῦμαι, -ῇ
181. lead astray *med.* stray, wander	πλανάω *reg.* πλανάομαι		πλανήσομαι
182. form, mold	**πλάττω**	πλᾰτ	πλᾰσω πλᾰσθήσομαι
183. sail, go by sea	**πλέω**	πλευ	πλεύσομαι
184. strike, beat frighten, *tr.* *pass.* am frightened in like manner: καταπλήττω	**παίω, τύπτω** πατάσσω, πλήττω **ἐκ-πλήττω** ἐκ-πλήττομαι	παι, τυπ, παταγ *pass.* πληγ, πλᾰγ	παίσω πληγήσομαι ἐκ-πλήξω ἐκ-πλᾰγήσομαι
185. breathe, blow breathe again	**πνέω**, often: ἀνα-πνέω	πνευ	πνεύσομαι
186. bring *med.* march, travel	πορεύω πορεύομαι		πορεύσω πορεύσομαι

Aorist	Perfect (Nouns)	Syntax
ἐπειράθην	πεπείραμαι πειρατέον	**πειρῶμαι** (ἔμπειρος, ἄπειρος): ἔργου, τειχῶν — κακῶν — ἀπολογήσασθαι.
ἔπεμψα ἐπέμφθην	πέπομφα πέπεμμαι -μψαι	
ἐπέτἄσα ἐπετάσθην	—— πέπτᾰμαι	
ἔπηξα ἐπάγην	—— πέπηγα am fixed πηκτός	
ἔπλησα ἐπλήσθην	πέπληκα πέπλησμαι	**ἐμπίμπλημι** (πληρόω — πλήρης, πλέως): τὴν θάλατταν τριήρων.
ἐν-έπρησα ἐν-επρήσθην	ἐμ-πέπρηκα ἐμ-πέπρησμαι	**ἐμπίμπλᾰμαι** eat my fill, eat sufficient: σίτων καὶ ποτῶν.
ἔπῐον ἐπόθην	πέπωκα πέπομαι τὸ ποτόν	**πίνω**: ἡδέος οἴνου — τὸ φάρμακον. **ἐκπίπτω**: pass. to ἐκβάλλω.
ἔπεσον	πέπτωκα	**πιστεύω** have confidence in, trust: τινί. ἐπίστευον γὰρ αὐτῷ.
ἐπλανήθην	πεπλάνημαι	am confident: ἐπίστευε μηδὲν ἂν παθεῖν. pass. am trusted: ἐπιστευόμην ὑπὸ Λακεδαιμονίων.
ἔπλᾰσα ἐπλάσθην	πέπλᾰκα πέπλᾰσμαι πλαστός — πλάσμα	**πλεονεκτέω** have more than, the advantage over, get the better of: τινός τινι — στρατιωτῶν χρήμασι καὶ τιμαῖς.
ἔπλευσα	πέπλευκα	
ἔπαισα	πέπαικα	**ἐκπλήττομαι** at: τὴν δύναμιν τῶν Ἀθηναίων.
ἐπλήγην ἐξ-έπληξα ἐξ-επλάγην	πέπληγμαι —— ἐκ-πέπληγμαι am panic-stricken	on account of: ταῖς οἴκοι κακοπραγίαις. **ποιέω**: εὖ, κακῶς τοὺς πολίτας — πολλὰ καὶ ἀγαθὰ τὴν πόλιν. pass. see πάσχω.
ἔπνευσα	πέπνευκα	**ποιοῦμαι**: περὶ πολλοῦ, πλείονος, οὐδενὸς etc. ὑμᾶς σῶσαι.
ἐπόρευσα ἐπορεύθην	πεπόρευκα πεπόρευμαι	**πολεμέω** make war upon: τινί; in alliance with σύν τινι, μετά τινος.

Meaning	Present	Stem	Future
187. do, bring about med. do, exact in my own interest	πρᾱ́ττω πρᾱ́ττομαι *pass.*	πρᾱγ	πρᾱ́ξω πρᾱ́ξομαι πρᾱχθήσομαι
188. am willing, eager	προθῡ́μέομαι		προθῡμήσομαι
189. ask, inquire, learn, hear, ascertain	πυνθάνομαι	πῠθ πευθ	πεύσομαι
190. sell	πωλέω, πιπράσκω ἀποδίδομαι *pass.*	πωλη, πρᾱ, δω, δο	πωλήσω ἀποδώσομαι πρᾱθήσομαι
191. flow	ῥέω	ῥυη, ῥυε	ῥυήσομαι
192. break, tear, *tr.* break, tear, burst, *intr.*	ῥήγνῡμι ῥήγνῠμαι	ῥηγ ῥᾰγ	ῥήξω ῥᾰγήσομαι
193. throw, fling, hurl	ῥῑ́πτω, ῥῑπτέω *pass.*	ῥῑπ	ῥῑ́ψω ῥῑφθήσομαι
194. strengthen	ῥώννῡμι, esp. in comp.; *pass.*	ῥω(σ)	ῥώσω ῥώσθήσομαι
195. dig	σκάπτω (esp. κατα-) *pass.*	σκᾰφ	σκάψω σκαφήσομαι
196. disperse, scatter	σκεδάννῡμι *pass.*	σκεδᾰ(σ)	σκεδῶ, -ᾷς σκεδασθήσομαι
197. look, view, con- sider, examine	σκοπέω, usu. σκοπέομαι, σκέπτομαι	σκοπε, σκεπ	σκέψομαι
198. draw med. draw for my- self	σπάω σπάομαι *pass.*	σπα(σ)	σπάσω σπάσομαι σπασθήσομαι
199. sow, plant	σπείρω *pass.*	σπερ	σπερῶ, -εῖς σπαρήσομαι
200. pour out med. make a treaty	σπένδω σπένδομαι	σπενδ	σπείσω σπείσομαι
201 am busy, studeo	σπουδάζω	dental	σπουδάσομαι

Aorist	Perfect (Nouns)	Syntax
ἔπραξα	πέπρᾱχα	**πράττω** am, do, fare : εὖ, καλῶς, κακῶς.
ἐπραξάμην ⎫	πέπρᾱγμαι	(εἰς)πράττω, -πράττομαι exact
ἐπράχθην ⎭	πρᾱκτός	(money) from : συμμάχους φόρον.
προεθυμήθην	προτεθύμημαι	**πρέπει** (προσήκει) τινί: decet aliquem.
ἐπῠθόμην	πέπῠσμαι	**πυνθάνομαι** inquire, ascertain, learn :
	act. & pass. ἄπυστος	πάντα σαφῶς τῶν παραγενομένων.
ἐπώλησα	πεπώληκα	learn that (fact): Κῦρον παρόντα
ἀπεδόμην	πέπρᾱκα	or ὅτι Κῦρος πάρεστιν.
ἐπράθην	πέπρᾱμαι	(report) : Κῦρον παρεῖναι.
		πωλῶ : πολλοῦ magno, ὀλίγου parvo.
ἐρρύην	ἐρρύηκα	τῶν πόνων πωλοῦσιν ἡμῖν πάντα
	τὸ ῥεῦμα, περίρρυτος	τἀγάθ' οἱ θεοί.
ἔρρηξα	—	
ἐρράγην	ἔρρωγα am broken	
	ἄρρηκτος	
ἔρρῑψα	ἔρρῑφα	
ἐρρίφθην	ἔρρῑμμαι	
ἔρρωσα		
ἐρρώσθην	ἔρρωμαι	
ἄρρωστος	ἡ ῥώμη	
ἔσκαψα	ἔσκᾰφα	
ἐσκάφην	ἔσκαμμαι	
ἐσκέδᾰσα		
ἐσκεδάσθην	ἐσκέδασμαι	**παρασκευάζομαι** : take precautions
ἐσκεψάμην	ἔσκεμμαι, also pass.	lest, take measures to prevent :
	σκεπτέον	ὅπως μὴ ἀποστήσονται.
		σκοπῶ : τοῦτο σκεπτέον μοι δοκεῖ,
ἔσπᾰσα	ἔσπᾰκα	ὅπως ὡς ἀσφαλέστατα μενοῦμεν.
ἐσπᾰσάμην ⎫	ἔσπᾰσμαι	**σπένδομαι** : σπονδάς. εἰρήνην —
ἐσπάσθην ⎭		Ἀθηναίοις καὶ Λάκωσιν.
ἔσπειρα	ἔσπαρκα	**σπεύδω, σπουδάζω** : am eager, anxious,
ἔσπᾰρην	ἔσπαρμαι	λαμπρὸν ποιεῖσθαι τὸν βίον.
ἔσπεισα	ἔσπεικα	pursue, follow up zealously, am in
ἐσπεισάμην	ἔσπεισμαι	earnest about, promote, hasten :
		τὰς περὶ τὸ μανθάνειν ἡδονάς.
ἐσπούδᾰσα	ἐσπούδᾰκα, pres.	ἀσπούδαστα.

Meaning	Present	Stem	Future
202. send	στέλλω *pass.*	στελ	στελῶ, -εῖς σταλήσομαι
203. sigh, groan	στενάζω	στεναγ	στενάξω
204. deprive of, rob am without, have lost	ἀπο-στερέω (στερίσκω) *pass.* στέρομαι (only *pres.* and *impf.*)		ἀπο-στερήσω ἀπο-στερήσομαι
205. turn, twist *pass.*⎫ *med.* turn myself⎬ subject (to my rule), subdue	στρέφω στρέφομαι κατα-στρέφομαι *pass.*	στρεφ	στρέψω στραφήσομαι κατα-στρέψομαι κατα-στραφήσο- μαι
206. spread out	στρώννῦμι *pass.*	στρω	στρώσω στρωθήσομαι
207. cause to fall *med.* and *pass.* am balked, err; fail	σφάλλω σφάλλομαι	σφᾰλ	σφᾰλῶ, -εῖς σφαλήσομαι
208. slay (esp. by cutting the throat), slaugh- ter, sacrifice	σφάττω *pass.*	σφᾰγ	σφάξω σφαγήσομαι
209. save *med.* save for myself⎫ *pass.* save myself,⎬ am saved⎭	σῴζω σῴζομαι	σῳδ, σω	σώσω σώσομαι σωθήσομαι
210. disturb, trouble, throw into dis- order	ταράττω *pass.*	ταραχ	ταράξω ταράξομαι
211. arrange, place (in order) *med.* arrange for myself, place myself	τάττω τάττομαι *pass.*	τᾰγ	τάξω τάξομαι ταχθήσομαι
212. stretch, draw tight	τείνω *pass.*	τεν	τενῶ, -εῖς τᾰθήσομαι

AORIST	PERFECT (NOUNS)	SYNTAX
ἔστειλα ἐστάλην	ἔσταλκα ἔσταλμαι	
ἐστέναξα ὁ στεναγμός	— ἐστέναγμαι	
ἀπ-εστέρησα ἀπ-εστερήθην	ἀπ-εστέρηκα ἀπ-εστέρημαι	**ἀποστερῶ**: στρατιώτας μισθόν, or στρατιώτας μισθοῦ. pass. οἱ στρατιῶται ἐστερήθησαν μισθὸν or μισθοῦ.
ἔστρεψα ἐστράφην κατ-εστρεψάμην } κατ-εστράφην }	ἔστροφα ἔστραμμαι στρεπτός κατ-έστραμμαι	
ἔστρωσα ἐστρώθην	ἔστρωμαι στρῶμα στρωτός	
ἔσφηλα ἐσφάλην	ἔσφαλκα ἔσφαλμαι τὸ σφάλμα failure	**σφάλλομαι** am disappointed of : τῆς ἐλπίδος. lose, am deprived of : ἀνδρὸς τοιοῦδε.
ἔσφαξα ἐσφάγην	— ἔσφαγμαι	
ἔσωσα ἐσωσάμην ἐσώθην	σέσωκα — σέσωσμαι	
ἐτάραξα ἐταράχθην ἡ ταραχή	τετάραγμαι ὁ ταραγμός	
ἔταξα ἐταξάμην ἐτάχθην }	τέταχα τέταγμαι τακτός, ἡ τάξις	**ἐπιτάττω** } enjoin, give orders : τινί προστάττω } τι. ὑμῖν πορεύεσθαι. ἐπιτάττεσθε (= κελεύεσθε) μεῖναι. **τελευτάω** tr. finish, end, bring to an end.
ἔτεινα ἐτάθην	τέτᾰκα τέτᾰμαι	intr. die ; expire ; come off.

Meaning	Present	Stem	Future
213. finish, accomplish; pay	τελέω *pass.*	τελεσ	τελῶ, -εῖς τελεσθήσομαι

214. accomplish
   give orders, enjoin
   med. give orders
	τέλλω, poet.
	ἐπι-τέλλω
	ἐπι-τέλλομαι
		τελ	ἐπι-τελῶ, -εῖς
			ἐπι-τελοῦμαι, -ῇ

215. cut	τέμνω *pass.*	τεμ τμη	τεμῶ, -εῖς τμηθήσομαι
216. *tr.* melt, dissolve *intr.* melt, vanish	τήκω τήκομαι	τηκ τᾰκ	τήξω τακήσομαι

217. put, set, place
   med. put etc. for
   myself
	τίθημι
	τίθεμαι
	pass.
		θη, θε	θήσω
			θήσομαι
			τεθήσομαι

218. bring forth, beget	τίκτω	τεκ	τέξομαι

219. pay, pay or suffer
   for
   med. make another pay
   = punish
	τίνω
	
	τίνομαι
		τῐ, τει	τείσω
			
			τείσομαι

220. wound	τιτρώσκω *pass.*	τρω	τρώσω τρωθήσομαι

221. turn
   med. turn for my-
   self
   turn myself
	τρέπω
	τρέπομαι
	
	τρέπομαι
	pass.
		τρεπ	τρέψω
			τρέψομαι
			
			τρέψομαι
			τραπήσομαι

222. nourish, feed
   med. rear up for
   myself
	τρέφω
	τρέφομαι
	pass.
		τρεφ	θρέψω
			θρέψομαι
			θρέψομαι

223. run	τρέχω [*ipf.*) θέω (only *pres.* &	τρεχ δραμ-η	δρᾰμοῦμαι, -ῇ
224. rub	τρίβω *pass.*	τρῑβ, τρῐβ	τρίψω τρῐβήσομαι

AORIST	PERFECT (NOUNS)	SYNTAX
ἐτέλεσα ἐτελέσθην	τετέλεκα τετέλεσμαι	**διατελῶ** w. part.: am constantly, all the time, ἑπτὰ ἡμέρας μαχόμενοι διετέλεσαν.
ἐπ-έτειλα ἐπ-ετειλάμην	ἐπι-τέταλκα ἐπι-τέταλμαι, pass.	**ἐπι-τέλλω** order, poet.; in prose usu. ἐν-τέλλομαι: τινί τι — ταῖς πόλεσιν ὁδοποιεῖν.
ἔτεμον ἐτμήθην	τέτμηκα τέτμημαι	
ἔτηξα ἐτάκην	—— τέτηκα am melted	
ἔθηκα, ἔθεμεν ἐθέμην ἐτέθην	τέθηκα —— κεῖμαι	**ἐπιτίθεμαι** attack: πολεμίοις. ἐπίκειμαι press upon: διαβαίνουσιν. προτίθημι prefer: δόξαν χρημάτων.
ἔτεκον	τέτοκα	**τίκτω**: pass. γίγνομαι.
ἔτεισα	τέτεικα	**τιμᾶν**, τιμᾶσθαί τι πολλοῦ: aliquid magno aestimare.
ἐτεισάμην	τέτεισμαι	**τιμωρέω** help: τινί — ἀλλήλοις. τιμωροῦμαι take vengeance: τινά on, τινος for.
ἔτρωσα ἐτρώθην	τέτρωκα τέτρωμαι	**τίνω**: δίκην, ὕβριν — χάριν. **ἀποτρέπω** avert: ἡμῶν βλάβην.
ἔτρεψα, ἔτρᾰπον ἐτρεψάμην put to flight ἐτρᾰπόμην ἐτρᾰπην was turned and turned myself	τέτροφα τέτραμμαι (τε- τράφθαι) τρεπτός	hinder, dissuade from: ὑμᾶς ἀδικίας. ἐπιτρέπω commit, entrust to: ὑμῖν τὴν ἀρχήν. give over to: Ἕλλησι τὴν χώραν διαρπάσαι. allow, leave: μηδενὶ κακῷ (-ὸν) εἶναι. προτρέπω urge on to: τοὺς νέους εἰς ἀρετήν. persuade, exhort, encourage: τοὺς
ἔθρεψα ἐθρεψάμην ἐτράφην	τέτροφα —— τέθραμμαι (τε- θράφθαι) θρεπτός	συνόντας ἀληθεύειν.
ἔδρᾰμον	δεδρᾰμηκα	
ἔτρῑψα ἐτρίβην	τέτρῑφα τέτρῑμμαι	

Meaning	Present	Stem	Future
225. hit; obtain, attain	τυγχάνω	τῠχ-η τευχ	τεύξομαι
226. suspect, apprehend	ὑποπτεύω		ὑποπτεύσω
227. show *med.* show what is my own show myself, appear	φαίνω φαίνομαι *pass.* φαίνομαι	φᾰν	φᾰνῶ, -εῖς φανοῦμαι, -ῇ φανθήσομαι { φανοῦμαι φανήσομαι
228. spare	φείδομαι	dental	φείσομαι
229. bear, carry *med.* carry for myself } *pass.* am carried } hurry, rush, fly etc.	φέρω φέρομαι φέρομαι	φερ, οἰ, ἐνε(γ)κ	οἴσω οἴσομαι, also *pass.* ἐνεχθήσομαι ἐνεχθήσομαι
230. flee; am an (go into) exile	φεύγω	φευγ, φῠγ	φεύξομαι
231. say, speak, — say yes, (see λέγω), affirm, declare	φημί ἔφην, ἔφησθα — φῶ — φαίην — φάθι — φάναι — (φάς), φάσκων	φη, φᾰ	φήσω
232. am beforehand, anticipate, do or come etc. before	φθάνω	φθα, φθη	φθήσομαι
233. spoil, corrupt	φθείρω (mostly δια-) *pass.*	φθερ	δια-φθερῶ, -εῖς δια-φθαρήσομαι
234. frighten fear, dread	φοβέω, more common φοβέομαι		φοβήσω φοβήσομαι
235. point (out, to), tell remark, perceive; ponder, think	φραζω φρᾰζομαι	dental	φρᾰσω φρᾰσομαι
236. guard, watch *med.* watch in my own interest = am on my guard	φυλάττω φυλάττομαι *pass.*	φυλᾰκ	φυλάξω φυλάξομαι φυλάξομαι

Aorist	Perfect (Nouns)	Syntax
ἔτῡχον	τετύχηκα	τυγχάνω hit: σκοποῦ.
		(ἀποτυγχάνω miss).
ὑπώπτευσα	ὑπώπτευκα	obtain: τῆς ἀξίας τιμῆς —
		(παρὰ) τῶνδε συγγνώμης.
		τυγχάνω w. *part.* am by chance,
ἔφηνα	πέφαγκα	happen: παρὼν ἐτύγχανεν.
ἐφηνάμην	——	(ἀπο)φαίνω: ταῦτ' ἀληθῆ ὄντα,
ἐφάνθην	πέφασμαι	or ὅτι ταῦτ' ἀληθῆ ἐστιν.
ἐφάνην	πέφηνα	ἀποφαίνομαι explain, declare my
		opinion: γνώμην.
ἐφεισάμην	πέφεισμαι	φαίνομαι φθονῶν it is evident
		(*appāret*) that.
ἤνεγκον, -κα	ἐνήνοχα	φθονεῖν it seems that
ἠνεγκάμην	} ἐνήνεγμαι	(*videor*).
ἠνέχθην		
ἠνέχθην	ἐνήνεγμαι	φειδώμεθ' ἀνδρῶν εὐγενῶν.
ἔφῡγον	πέφευγα	φέρω χαλεπῶς am annoyed, take ill:
		τοῖς παροῦσι πράγμασιν.
		λοιδορούμενος (or ὅτι).
	——	διαφέρω (διάφορος) am different
ἔφησα	——	from, excel in: ἁπάντων ἀρετῇ.
		διαφέρομαι am at variance, quarrel:
		τοῖς πονηροῖς.
		συμφέρει it is of use: πᾶσι σωφρο-
		νεῖν.
ἔφθην	——	φεύγω am accused of: τινός.
ἔφθᾰσα	ἔφθᾰκα	φεύγω τὴν γραφὴν ὑπό τινος.
		φεύγεις (are you prosecuted?) τὴν
		δίκην ἢ διώκεις;
δι-έφθειρα	δι-έφθαρκα	μικρὸν ἐξέφυγε μὴ καταπετρωθῆναι
δι-εφθάρην	δι-έφθαρμαι	(*narrow* escape!) he came near
		being stoned.
ἐφόβησα	πεφόβηκα	
ἐφοβήθην	πεφόβημαι	οὔ φησι ταῦτ' ἀληθῆ εἶναι *negat.*
ἔφρᾰσα	πέφρᾰκα	φθάνω: τινὰ ποιῶν τι do sthg. before
		some one. ἔφθησαν τοὺς Πέρσας
{ ἐφρασάμην	πέφρασμαι	ἀφικόμενοι εἰς τὴν πόλιν.
{ ἐφράσθην		φθονέω grudge one sthg.: τινί τινος.
ἐφύλαξα	πεφύλαχα	φθονοῦμαι *mihi invidetur.*
ἐφυλαξάμην	} πεφύλαγμαι	φοβοῦμαι: αὐτούς, μὴ ἐπιθῶνται.
ἐφυλάχθην		ἐφοβεῖτο, μὴ οὐ δύναιτο *ne non.*
	φυλακτέον	φοβοῦμαι εἰπεῖν *vereor dicere.*

Q

Meaning	Present	Stem	Future
237. bring forth am born, come into being	φύω φύομαι	φῦ, φῠ	φύσω φύσομαι
238. subdue, overpower	χειρόομαι *pass.*		χειρώσομαι χειρωθήσομαι
239. pour *med.* pour for myself	χέω χέομαι *pass.*	χευ, χυ	χέω χέομαι χῠθήσομαι
240. use	χράομαι *pass.*		χρήσομαι χρησθήσομαι
241. it is necessary, one must	χρή ἐχρῆν and χρῆν — χρῆ — χρείη — χρῆναι — τὸ χρεών	——	——
242. anoint	χρίω *pass.*	χρι(σ)	χρίσω χρῑσθήσομαι
243. deceive *med.* tell a lie, am false, deceive *pass.* am deceived, disappointed	ψεύδω ψεύδομαι ψεύδομαι	dental	ψεύσω ψεύσομαι ψευσθήσομαι
244. push, thrust *med.* thrust myself; push (away) from myself	ὠθέω ὠθέομαι *pass.*	ὠθ-ε	ὤσω ὤσομαι ὠσθήσομαι
245. buy, purchase	ὠνέομαι *pass.*	ὠνη, πρια	ὠνήσομαι ὠνηθήσομαι

Aorist	Perfect (Nouns)		Syntax
ἔφῡσα	——		**φρονέω** : μέγα ἐπ' ἀρετῇ am proud of.
ἔφῡν	πέφῡκα am (by nature)		**καταφρονέω** despise, contemn : τοῦ κινδύνου.
ἐχειρωσάμην	κεχείρωμαι		**φροντίζω** give heed to :
ἐχειρώθην	}		τῶν ἀνθρωπίνων οὐδέν.
			take care to : ὅπως κτήσομαι.
ἔχεα	κέχῠκα		**φυλάττομαι** : κόλακας — διαβολάς.
ἐχεάμην	——		φύλαξαι, (ὅπως) μὴ πέσῃς (πεσῇ).
ἐχύθην	κέχῠμαι		(τὸ) μὴ πεσεῖν.
ἐχρησάμην	κέχρημαι		**ἐπιχειρῶ** set to work at, attempt :
ἐχρήσθην	——		ἀδυνάτοις — διώκειν.
χρηστός		τὸ χρῆμα	**χρῶμαι** : ξύλοις ἐχρῶντο τοῖς οἰστοῖς.
			τί βούλεται ἡμῖν χρῆσθαι; what — for?
			treat, deal with : οὕτως αὐτοῖς χρῆσθε ὥσπερ ἄξιον.
			χρὴ τοὺς εὖ πράττοντας τῆς εἰρήνης
ἔχρῑσα	κέχρῑκα		ἐπιθυμεῖν.
ἐχρίσθην	κέχρῑμαι		τί σιγᾷς; οὐκ ἐχρῆν σιγᾶν, τέκνον.
χριστός		τὸ χρῖμα	**ὑποχωρέω** : τινὶ ὁδοῦ get out of the
ἔψευσα	ἔψευκα		way of, make way for one.
ἐψευσάμην			**ψαύω** touch : ἤθους δικαίου φαῦλος οὐ
	ἔψευσμαι		ψαύει λόγος.
ἐψεύσθην	am mistaken		**ψεύδω** : οἱ θεοὶ ψεύδουσί σε.
			ψεύδομαι deceive : Κῦρον πάντα.
ἔωσα	ἔωκα		am mistaken in : γνώμης.
ἐωσάμην	ἔωσμαι		τοῦτο οὐκ ἐψεύσθησαν in this.
ἐώσθην	ἔωσμαι		
ἐπριάμην	ἐώνημαι		**ὠνοῦνται** οἱ Σκύθαι τὰς γυναῖκας χρη-
ἐωνήθην	ἐώνημαι		μάτων μεγάλων.

CHIEF RULES OF SYNTAX.

Agreement.

114. The subject a neuter plural:

    in the dual:

    A masc. or fem. subject with a neuter predicate adjective:

    Pronominal subj. assim. to pred. noun:

    The assimilation sometimes omitted:

115. Adjectives instead of adverbs (place, situation, time, manner, state of mind):

Καλὰ ἦν τὰ σφάγια.
Δύο ἄνδρε τέθνατον or τεθνᾶσιν.

Οὐκ ἀγαθὸν πολυκοιρανίη — triste senex miles. —
Οὗτοι νόμοι εἰσίν — αὕτη ἄλλη πρόφασις ἦν —
ταῦτα φλυαρίας εἶναι λέγω.
Σκηνοῦμεν ὑπαίθριοι — τριταῖοι ἐγένοντο —
σκοταῖοι κατέβαινον — προτέρα ἀφίκετο —
ἑκοῦσαι ἔδοσαν — primus, laetus.

The Article.

117. The article w. individualizing force:

Ὁ σοφὸς ἐν αὑτῷ περιφέρει τὴν οὐσίαν.
τρία ἡμιδαρεικὰ τοῦ μηνὸς τῷ στρατιώτῃ.
πολλοί, οἱ πολλοί — (ὁ) ἐμὸς φίλος.

    w. generic force:

Νικᾷ ὁ μείων τὸν μέγαν δίκαι᾽ ἔχων.
ὁ βουλόμενος — ὁ τυχών — ὁ τολμήσων.

118. The article to be used:

ὁ ἐμὸς πατήρ — οὗτος ὁ ἄνθρωπος — οὐ τὸ εὖρος.
ἡμεῖς οἱ Ἕλληνες — τὰ δύο μέρη.
τὼ παῖδε ἀμφοτέρω — ἕκαστον (τὸ) ἔθνος — πᾶς 123.

119.   omitted w. the predicate:

Αἱ δεύτεραί πως φροντίδες σοφώτεραι.
Κάλλιστόν ἐστι κτῆμα παιδεία βροτοῖς.
Χαιρεφῶν ἐμὸς ἑταῖρος ἦν ἐκ νέου.

    w. certain appellatives, if used as proper names:

ἐπὶ θάνατον ἄγειν — ἐν ἄστει — (μέγας) βασιλεύς.
ἐγὼ ὁ αὐτός εἰμι — δυοῖν θάτερον τὸ τεθνάναι.
Σωκράτης ὁ Ἀθηναῖος — ἡ Εὐρώπη.

Familiar expressions:

κατὰ γῆν καὶ κατὰ θάλατταν, ἐκ νέου, ἐκ παιδός (παῖδον), κατ' ἀγρούς, ἐν δεξιᾷ.

120. Attributive position:

ὁ ἀγαθὸς ἀνήρ or ὁ ἀνὴρ ὁ ἀγαθός.

possess. and refl. pronouns:
nouns in the genitive:

ἡ ἐμὴ τύχη — τὴν ἑαυτοῦ θυγατέρα —
ἡ τῶν Περσῶν ἀρχή — but also?

121. Predicate position:

ἀγαθὸς ὁ ἀνήρ or ὁ ἀνὴρ ἀγαθός (sc. ἐστιν or ὤν).

pers. and demonstr. pron.:
partit. genitives:

ὁ πατήρ μου, τὸν παῖδα αὐτῆς — οὗτος ὁ ἄνθρωπος.
οἱ πλεῖστοι τῶν πολεμίων.

122. Change of meaning with change of position:

ὁ αὐτὸς βασιλεύς idem rex, ὁ βασιλεὺς αὐτός rex ipse.
ἡ μέση πόλις — μέση ἡ πόλις the center of the city.

123. Πᾶς, ἅπας, σύμπας, ὅλος:

ἡ πόλις πᾶσα, πᾶσα ἡ πόλις all the city.
αἱ πόλεις πᾶσαι, πᾶσαι αἱ πόλεις all (the) cities.
ἡ πᾶσα πόλις the entire city, (οἱ) σύμπαντες in all, all told.
πᾶσα πόλις (πόλις πᾶσα) every city; a whole city.

124. The article w. nounizing force:

ὁ σοφός, τὸ κακόν, τἀληθῆ, οἱ νῦν, τὸ γνῶθι σαυτόν —
τὰ οἴκοι, οἱ ἀμφὶ Ἀριαῖον, τὸ Δημοσθένους.

Pronouns.

125. Direct reflexive pronouns:

κρατῶ ἐμαυτοῦ, γνῶθι σαυτόν —
Ὁ σοφὸς ἐν αὑτῷ περιφέρει τὴν οὐσίαν within him.

Indirect refl. pronouns:
Indir. reflexives may be replaced by αὐτός: οἷ, σφίσιν:

Ὀρέστης ἔπεισεν Ἀθηναίους ἑαυτὸν κατάγειν.
Λέγουσι Ξενοφῶντι, ὅτι μεταμέλει αὐτοῖς (se paenitere).
Κῦρος ἠξίου δοθῆναι οἷ (sibi) τὰς πόλεις.

126. Possessive pronouns — position:

Κἀπὶ τοῖς σαυτῆς κακοῖσι κἀπὶ τοῖς ἐμοῖς γελᾷς.
Ἀστυάγης τὴν ἑαυτοῦ θυγατέρα μετεπέμψατο καὶ τὸν παῖδα αὐτῆς. —
τοῖς ὑμετέροις αὐτῶν ὀφθαλμοῖς.

127. The intensive pronoun αὐτός:

Σοφοὺς ὁμιλῶν καὐτὸς ἐκβήσῃ σοφός.
τρίτος αὐτός — ὁ πατὴρ αὐτοῦ. — ὁ αὐτός (122). — 158.

128. Demonstrative pronouns:	ὅδε ὁ ἀνήρ — ἥδε ἡ χείρ — ἐκεῖνο τὸ ὄρος.
	Τεκμήριον δὲ τούτου καὶ τόδε.
129. Relatives w. individ. force; ὅς etc.:	Ἔστιν Δίκης ὀφθαλμός, ὃς τὰ πάνθ' ὁρᾷ.
w. generic force; ὅστις etc.:	Μακάριος, ὅστις οὐσίαν καὶ νοῦν ἔχει.
Relatives assimilate to case of antecedent:	Ἄξιοι ἔσεσθε τῆς ἐλευθερίας, ἧς κέκτησθε.
the antec. a demonstr.:	Οἱ χρησμῳδοὶ ἴσασιν οὐδὲν ὧν λέγουσιν.
a noun:	Ἡριππίδας ἐπορεύετο σὺν ᾗ εἶχε δυνάμει.
Inverted assimilation:	Ἀνεῖλεν αὐτῷ θεοῖς οἷς ἔδει θύειν.
Anacoluthon instead of rel. construction:	Καὶ νῦν τί χρὴ δρᾶν, ὅστις ἐμφανῶς θεοῖς ἐχθαίρομαι, μισεῖ δέ μ' Ἑλλήνων στρατός;

The Cases.

THE ACCUSATIVE.

133. Accusative of External Object:	Ἐφυλάττοντο δὲ ἀμφότεροι ὥσπερ πολεμίους ἀλλήλους. — κακῶς ποιεῖν (λέγειν) τινά.
	Οὐδεὶς ποιῶν πονηρὰ λανθάνει θεόν.
	Ἠισχύνθημεν καὶ θεοὺς καὶ ἀνθρώπους.
	ὀμνύναι, ἐπιορκεῖν τοὺς θεούς — νὴ Δία.
137. Accusative of Internal Object, a noun of kindred etymology:	δεινὴν μάχην μάχεσθαι — δουλεύειν τὴν χαλεπωτάτην δουλείαν.
meaning:	μεγάλην μάχην νικᾶν — τὸν ἱερὸν πόλεμον στρατεύεσθαι.
an attribute (noun, adj. or pron.):	στάδιον ἀγωνίζεσθαι — Ὀλύμπια νικᾶν —
	πάντα νικᾶν — ἡδὺ γελᾶν — οὐδὲν φροντίζειν.
Two accusatives:	
135. external object and pred. accus.:	Δαρεῖος Κῦρον σατράπην ἐποίησεν (pass.?).
136. person and thing affected:	Ἀναμνήσω ὑμᾶς τοὺς κινδύνους (pass.?).
138. external and internal object:	Λακεδαιμόνιοι πολλὰ τὴν πόλιν ἠδικήκασιν.

139. Greek accusative (*os humerosque*):

κάμνω τοὺς ὀφθαλμούς, τὴν κεφαλήν — (τὸ) ὄνομα.
Βέλτιόν ἐστι σῶμά γ᾽ ἢ ψυχὴν νοσεῖν.

140. Acc. of extent (*how far? how long?*):

οὐ μεῖον ἢ μύρια στάδια — πολὺν χρόνον —
τριάκοντα ἔτη γεγονώς — εἰς Ἀθήνας.

141. Adverbial accusative:

οὐδέν, τί, (τὰ) πάντα, τἆλλα, τοῦτον τὸν τρόπον, τὸ λοιπόν, τὴν ταχίστην, ἀρχήν, πρόφασιν.

THE GENITIVE.

143. Possessive gen. (owner, author):

ἡ Κύρου στρατιά — ἱερὸς Ἀρτέμιδος — τὸ τοῦ Σόλωνος —
Κίμων Μιλτιάδου — ἐν Ἅιδου, εἰς Ἅιδου.

esp. w. εἶναι and γίγνεσθαι:

ἀνδρὸς σοφοῦ (ἐμόν) ἐστιν — πενίαν φέρειν οὐ παντός.
Βασιλεὺς ἡγεῖται ὑμᾶς ἑαυτοῦ εἶναι.

144. Objective gen. w. nouns den. action:

ἡ τῆς πατρίδος σωτηρία — δι᾽ αἰσχύνην ἀλλήλων.

w. judicial terms:

Ἁλῶναι τῆς κακώσεως τῶν γονέων — αἴτιος κακῶν.

w. certain verbs and adjectives:

Ἄνθρωπος ὢν μέμνησο τῆς κοινῆς τύχης — ἐπιμελής.
Ἦθους δικαίου φαῦλος οὐ ψαύει λόγος.

145. Partitive gen., wherever a relation of whole to part:

Οἱ σοφοὶ τῶν ἀνθρώπων — ἕτερον τῆς γῆς (τὴν γῆν!) —
Ὀλίγου σίτου ἐγεύσαντο — Σωκράτης τὸ φάρμακον ἔπιεν.

Note:

καινόν τι *aliquid novi*, οὐδὲν ἀγαθόν *nihil boni*.
ὁ λοιπὸς τοῦ χρόνου, τῆς γῆς τὴν πολλήν.

146. Gen. of quality w. numerals:

τεῖχος (τὸ) εὖρος εἴκοσι ποδῶν — ἐτῶν ὡς τριάκοντα.

147. separation:

Ἀπέχει ἡ Πλάταια τῶν Θηβῶν σταδίους ἑβδομήκοντα.

148. comparison:

Σιγή ποτ᾽ ἐστὶν αἱρετωτέρα λόγου.

149. material:

Οἱ στέφανοι οὐκ ἴων ἢ ῥόδων ἦσαν, ἀλλὰ χρυσίου.

150. cause w. verbs den. emotion:

Εὐδαιμονίζω ὑμᾶς τῆς ἐλευθερίας, ἧς κέκτησθε.
θαυμάσιος τοῦ κάλλους — σοφίας φθονῆσαί τινι.

151. price:

Τῶν πόνων πωλοῦσιν ἡμῖν πάντα τἀγαθ᾽ οἱ θεοί.
πολλοῦ *magno*, ὀλίγου *parvo*, μισθοῦ *for money.*

152. Gen. of time without attribute: *when?* with an attr.:	νυκτὸς καὶ ἡμέρας, θέρους, χειμῶνος, τοῦ μηνός (117). πολλοῦ χρόνου *for a long time* — δέκα ἡμερῶν *within.*

THE DATIVE.

155. Dative of Indirect Object:	Ἡ μωρία δίδωσιν ἀνθρώποις κακά.
156. advantage (disadv.):	Ἐνταῦθα Κύρῳ βασίλεια ἦν καὶ παράδεισος.
157. The ethical dative:	Μή μοι θορυβήσητε *pray* — οὕτως ἔχει σοι ταῦτα *you see.* πῶς ἡμῖν ἔχει; — *our darling?*
Dative of agent: = ὑπό w. gen.	Ἐὰν ἐκεῖ νικῶμεν, πάνθ' ἡμῖν πεποίηται.
reference:	τὰ ἐμοὶ πεπραγμένα — τί πέπρακται τοῖς ἄλλοις; Τῷ γὰρ καλῶς πράσσοντι πᾶσα γῆ πατρίς. (ὡς) συνελόντι εἰπεῖν — ἐμοὶ δ' ὄνομα Αἴθων (Gaio).
158. union, accompaniment:	Σοφοῖς ὁμιλῶν καὐτὸς ἐκβήσῃ σοφός. Θεῷ μάχεσθαι δεινόν ἐστι καὶ τύχῃ.
159. instrument:	ὀλίγῳ στρατεύματι — ναῦν αὐτοῖς ἀνδράσιν.
cause:	Οὐδεὶς ἔπαινον ἡδοναῖς ἐκτήσατο. Ἀβουλίᾳ τὰ πολλὰ βλάπτονται βροτοί.
(after verbs of emotion ἐπί may be added):	Χαίρεν ἐφ' ἡδοναῖς — θαυμάζειν ἐπὶ ποιήσει.
manner:	Οἱ Λακεδαιμόνιοι κρίνουσι βοῇ καὶ οὐ ψήφῳ. δημοσίᾳ *public,* ἰδίᾳ *privatim,* κοινῇ *jointly.*
160. degree of difference:	Πολλῷ κρείττον, πολλοῖς ἔτεσιν ὕστερον (πολύ, οὐδέν, τί).
time without ἐν, *dates*:	ταύτῃ τῇ ἡμέρᾳ — τετάρτῳ ἔτει — Παναθηναίοις.
with ἐν, *during*:	Ἐν νυκτὶ βουλὴ τοῖς σοφοῖσι γίγνεται.

Prepositions.

162, 163. Generally speaking, prepositions w. the gen.
w. the dat. } answer the question
w. the acc.

{ whence? whereof?
where? wherewith?
whither? how far?

USES AND MEANINGS.

		Genitive		Dative		Accusative	
with one case	ἀντί	instead of	τοῦ βελτίονος				
	ἀπό	away from	τοῦ ποταμοῦ				
	ἐκ, ἐξ	down from	τῶν ἵππων				
		from, out of	τῆς πόλεως				
		in consequence of	τῆς νόσου				
	πρό	before	τῆς θύρας, μάχης				
		in behalf of	τῆς πατρίδος				
	ἐν			in, at; during	τῇ πόλει, σπονδαῖς		
	σύν			with	Κύρῳ, τοῖς ὅπλοις		
with two cases	εἰς					into	τὴν πόλιν
	ἀνά					up, up along	τὸν ποταμόν
						over, through	τὸ πεδίον
	διά	through	τοῦ πεδίου			on account of	τὴν νόσον
	κατά	down from	τῶν ὀρῶν			down along	τὸν ποταμόν
		against	Φιλίππου			over, through	τοὺς ἀγρούς
						according to	τοὺς νόμους
	μετά	with	Κύρου			after, post	τὴν μάχην
	ὑπέρ	above	τῆς γῆς, κώμης			beyond	τὰ ὅρια
		in behalf of	τῆς πατρίδος				δύναμιν
with three cases	ἀμφί	[about, de]	τούτων	[about, on acct. of Ὀδυσῇ]		about	Ἀραῖον
							μέσας νύκτας
	ἐπί	upon	ἅρματος; ὄρους	upon	ταῖς ναυσίν	towards, against	Σοῦσα, τὰ ὅπλα
				in charge of	τῷ στρατεύματι	in quest of	ὕδωρ, λείαν
				dependency	τῷ βασιλεῖ	towards, against	
				because of	αἰσχραῖς ἡδοναῖς	friendly	τοὺς συμμάχους
				purpose	θανάτῳ. βλάβη	hostile	τοὺς Πέρσας

	Genitive		Dative		Accusative	
with three cases						
παρά	from (beside)	βασιλέως	by the side of, with	τοῖς Πέρσαις	to (the side of), up to	τὴν γέφυραν
	on the part of	θεῶν	near, at	τῷ βωμῷ	alongside of by and beyond, against	τὸν ποταμόν
					during	τοὺς νόμους τὸν πόλεμον
περί	on, concerning, de	τῆς εἰρήνης	[about, around	στήθεσσι]	about	Κῦρον, τὰ θεῖα
πρός	from, over against	τῆς Θρᾴκης	at, near	ταῖς πηγαῖς	towards	βασιλέα, τὴν ἕω
	by the side of	πατρός	in addition to	τῷ πόνῳ	with a view to	χάριν, ἀρετήν
ὑπό	from beneath	γῆς ἐλθεῖν	beneath, under	τῷ οἰρανῷ	to a place and	τὰ δένδρα, τὸ τεῖχος,
	under	γῆς οἰκεῖν	at the base of	τῇ ἀκροπόλει	under	νύκτα
	by (ab w. abl.) through	τῶν Ἑλλήνων λύπης, λιμοῦ	under	τυράννους		ὑφ' ἑαυτοὺς ποιεῖσθαι
			(sub w. ablative)		(sub w. accusative)	

The Voices and Tenses of the Verb.

165. Accusative (direct) Middle: λούομαι, ἐνδύομαι — παύομαι, φαίνομαι.
     Dative (indirect) Middle: ἀμύνομαι, μεταπέμπομαι, φυλάττομαι, ἄρχομαι.
     Dynamic Middle: παρέχομαι, ἐπαγγέλλομαι, πόλεμον ποιοῦμαι.
     Causative Middle: δικάζομαι, μισθοῦμαι, ποιοῦμαι, διδάσκομαι.

166. Personal **Passive** of intrans. verbs: ἄρχομαι, πιστεύομαι, φθονοῦμαι *mihi invidetur.*

167. Period of action — stage of action: φυγεῖν — φεύγειν — πεφευγέναι.
     The period of action is expressed solely by the indicative: ἔφυγον — ἔφευγον — ἐπεφεύγειν.

168. Durative **Present — Imperfect**:   Ξενίας ἀγῶνα ἔθηκεν. ἐθεώρει δὲ καὶ Κῦρος.
     Conative Present — Imperfect: Ἔπειθον, καὶ οὓς ἔπεισα, τούτους ἔχων ἐπορευόμην.
     Pres. and Impf. with perfect force: νικῶ, ἀδικῶ — ἥκω (ἧκον) — οἴχομαι (ᾠχόμην).
     Historical **Aorist**:   Ἦλθον, εἶδον, ἐνίκησα : *veni, vidi, vici.*
     Gnomic Aorist: Οὐδεὶς ἔπαινον ἡδοναῖς ἐκτήσατο — *omne tulit punctum.*

Pluperfect Aorist in depend. clauses: ἀπὸ τῆς ἀρχῆς, ἧς αὐτὸν σατράπην ἐποίησε fecerat.

Ingressive Aorist: ἐπολέμησα, ἐνόσησα — Ἱππίας ἔσχε τὴν ἀρχήν.

The **Future** ind. both ingressive: Σκεπτέον, ὅπως τὰ ἐπιτήδεια ἕξομεν.

and durative: Ὁ δίκαιος ἀνὴρ εὖ βιώσεται, κακῶς δὲ ὁ ἄδικος.

169. **Infinitives** and **Dependent Moods** denote merely

the stage of action: εἴπωμεν ἢ σιγῶμεν;

Aor. Imper.: one single action etc.: Μείνον παρ' ἡμῖν καὶ συνέστιος γενοῦ.

Present Imper.: repeated action, maxim: Τοὺς μὲν θεοὺς φοβοῦ, τοὺς δὲ γονέας τίμα.

170. **Participles**, relative time: ταῦτ' εἰπὼν ἀποβαίνει — ἀπέβη — ἀποβήσεται.

It is only in *indirect* discourse that optatives and infinitives express the *period* of action, **because then they**
represent the corresponding indicatives of the direct discourse:

Ἔλεγον, ὅτι διαβατὸς γένοιτο (*had been*; dir. ἐγένετο).

Ἐλέγετο δοῦναι Κύρῳ χρήματα (*to have given*; dir. ἔδωκεν).

The Moods of the Verb.

I. MOODS IN INDEPENDENT SENTENCES.

172. The **Indicative** of histor. tenses without ἄν,

a hopeless wish — present: Εἴθ' ἦσθα δυνατὸς δρᾶν, ὅσον πρόθυμος εἶ.

past: Εἴθ' εὕρομέν σ', Ἄδμητε, μὴ λυπούμενον.

The indicative of histor. tenses with ἄν,

1. unreality — present (*dicerem*): ἔλεγον ἄν, *I should say*, (but do not say).

past (*dixissem*): εἶπον ἄν, ἔλεξά ἄν *I should have said*, (but did not say).

2. past potentiality (The Potential Indicative — iterative ἄν):

θᾶττον ἢ ὥς τις ἂν ᾤετο (ᾠήθη) *you might have b.*

ἔπαισεν ἄν *he would sometimes strike.*

Accordingly, the indicative of *historical* tenses expresses three different relations: past reality, unreality, past
potentiality.

173. The **Subjunctive**: hortatory 1. p. — μή:
deliberative 1. p. — μή:
prohibitive 2. & 3. pp. aor.
subj.:

ἴωμεν eamus let us go.
τί ποιῶμεν; quid faciamus? what are we to do?

μὴ ποιήσῃς ne feceris do not do.

174. The **Optative**:
without ἄν: attainable wish — μή:
with ἄν: present potentiality — οὐ:
(The Potential Optative)

'Ω παῖ, γένοιο πατρὸς εὐτυχέστερος,
τὰ δ' ἄλλ' ὅμοιος, καὶ γένοι' ἂν οὐ κακός.
ἴσως ἄν τις εἴποι forsitan dixerit quispiam.

175. The **Imperative**. See above 169.
Prohibitions: 2. p.:
3. p.:

μὴ ποίει or μὴ ποιήσῃς.
μὴ ποιείτω or μὴ ποιήσῃ or μὴ ποιησάτω.

II. Moods in Dependent Clauses.

176. Dependence of Mood *may* be expressed after an *historical* tense and then only by means of the *optative* without ἄν (the Indirect Optative) [never by the subjunctive!]. Moreover, only the indicative expressing reality and the subjunctive are subject to this change, never the indicative denoting unreality or the potential moods.
Anticipation or Prolepsis:

Δέδοικα δ' αὐτήν, μή τι βουλεύσῃ νέον.

177. **Simple Sentences in Indir. Discourse**; 178. **Causal**, 179. **Interrogative** Sentences.

prince. tense: indic., ⎫ neg. οὐ,
hist. tense: mostly opt., ⎭
In Indirect Questions εἰ οὐ & εἰ μή:

Κῦρος ἔλεγεν, ὅτι ἡ ὁδὸς ἔσοιτο πρὸς βασιλέα.
Οἱ Ἀθηναῖοι τὸν Περικλέα ἐκάκιζον, ὅτι οὐκ ἐπεξάγοι.
Ἠρώτων εἴτε διδακτὸν εἴη ἀρετὴ εἴτε οὐ or εἴτε μή.
Ἤρετο εἴ τις ἐμοῦ εἴη σοφώτερος.

Interrogative sentences implying doubt (*deliberative subjunctive*):

prince. tense: subj, ⎫ μή
hist. tense: opt, ⎭

Ὁρῶ σε ἀποροῦντα, ποίαν ὁδὸν τράπῃ.
Ὁ Θηβαῖος ἠπόρει, ὅ,τι χρήσαιτο τῷ πράγματι.

180. **Consecutive** Clauses (ὥστε, ὡς):
actual result: ind, οὐ:
conceivable r.: inf, μή:

Ἦν ψῦχος δεινόν, ὥστε τὸ ὕδωρ ἐπήγνυτο.
Ἔχω τριήρεις ὥστε ἑλεῖν τὸ ἐκείνων πλοῖον.

181. **Final** Clauses (ἵνα, ὡς, ὅπως — μή):
princ. tense: subj.:
hist. tense: opt.:
Same after verbs of *fearing*:

After verbs of *caring* usu. fut. indic.:

Μὴ φθόνει τοῖς εὐτυχοῦσι, μὴ δοκῇς εἶναι κακός.
Ταῦτ᾽ εἶπον ἀνέστη, ἵνα περαίνοιτο τὰ δέοντα.
Δέδοικα, μὴ ἐπιλαθώμεθα τῆς οἴκαδε ὁδοῦ *ne*.
Ἐφοβεῖτο, μὴ οὐ δύναιτο ἐξελθεῖν *ne non*.
Σκεπτέον μοι δοκεῖ, ὅπως ὡς ἀσφαλέστατα **μενοῦμεν.**

182. **Hypothetical** Propositions: neg. *μή*. There are four types:

184. **First** Type: εἰ w. ind. ‖ ind.:
εἰ βούλει, δύνασαι: *si vis, potes.*
Εἰ θεοί τι δρῶσιν αἰσχρόν, οὐκ εἰσὶν θεοί.

185. **Second** Type: a) Present:
εἰ w. impf. ‖ impf. w. **ἄν:**
b) Past:
εἰ w. aor. ind. ‖ aor. ind. w. **ἄν:**
c) Mixed Forms:

εἰ ἐβούλου, ἐδύνατο ἄν: *si velles, posses* (sed non vis).
Φῶς εἰ μὴ εἴχομεν, ὅμοιοι τοῖς τυφλοῖς ἂν ἦμεν.
εἰ ἐβουλήθης, ἐδυνήθης ἄν: *si voluisses, potuisses* (sed —).
Οὐκ ἂν ἐποίησεν Ἀγασίας, εἰ μὴ ἐγὼ ἐκέλευσα.
Εἰ γὰρ σὺ μὲν παῖς ἦσθ᾽, ἐγὼ δὲ σὸς πατήρ,
ἔκτεινά τοί σ᾽ ἄν, κοὐ φυγαῖς ἐζημίουν.

186. **Third** Type:
εἰ βούλοιο, δύναιο ἄν: *si velis, possis.*
Οὐκ ἂν φορητὸς εἴης, εἰ πράσσοις καλῶς.

187. **Fourth** Type: 1) single fut. occurrence:
ἐάν w. subj. ‖ fut. or imper.:
ἐὰν βούλῃ (βουληθῇς), δυνήσῃ: *si voles (volueris), poteris.*
Ἐὰν δ᾽ ἔχωμεν χρήμαθ᾽, ἕξομεν φίλους.
Νέος ἂν πονήσῃς γῆρας ἕξεις εὐθαλές.

2) repeated occurrence:
a) in the present:
ἐάν w. subj. ‖ pres. ind.:
ἐάν βούλῃ (βουληθῇς), δύνασαι: *cum vis (volueris), potes.*
Ἢν ἐγγὺς ἔλθῃ θάνατος, οὐδεὶς βούλεται θνῄσκειν.
b) in the past:
εἰ w. opt. ‖ impf. (aor. — also w. *ἄν*: 172, 2).
εἰ βούλοιο (βουληθείης), ἐδύνασο: *cum volebas (volueris), poteras.*
Ξενοφῶν εἴ πού τι ὁρῴη βρωτόν, διεδίδου.

188. The protasis of one type is sometimes followed by the apodosis of another:

Δείξαιμι ἄν, εἰ μοί τινα βούλεσθε συμπέμψαι.
Οὐδ᾽, ἂν πολλαὶ γέφυραι ὦσιν, ἔχοιμεν ἄν, ὅποι σωθῶμεν.

189. **Concessive** or **Adversative** Clauses (*εἰ καί, καὶ εἰ, ἐὰν καί, κἄν*) are
conditional clauses: neg. *μή*:

Κεἰ μὴ πέποιθα, τοὔργον ἐστ᾽ ἐργαστέον.
Γελᾷ δ᾽ ὁ μῶρος, κἄν τι μὴ γελοῖον ᾖ.
Εἰ καὶ βασιλεὺς πέφυκας, ὡς θνητὸς ἄκουσον.

(*καί, καίπερ — οὐ* w. part. = *although*:
Εἰσηλθετε ὑμεῖς καίπερ οὐ διδόντος τοῦ νόμου — 203.)

190. **Temporal** Clauses:
a) actual event: indicative:

Ἐπεὶ πάντες συνῆλθον, ἐκαθέζοντο.

b) conceivable (expected) etc. event — single future or repeated occurrence (187):
princ. tense: future }
present } subj. w. *ἄν*:

Ἐπειδὰν ἅπαντα ἀκούσητε, κρίνατε.
Μαινόμεθα πάντες, ὁπόταν ὀργιζώμεθα.

hist. tense: past, opt.:

Κῦρος ἐθήρευεν, ὁπότε γυμνάσασθαι βούλοιτο.
Περιεμένομεν ἑκάστοτε, ἕως ἀνοιχθείη.
Διέβησαν πρὶν τοὺς ἄλλους ἀποκρίνασθαι.

Πρίν: affirm. princ. sentence — inf.:
negat. princ. sentence — finite verb,
histor. fact: indic.:
expected event: subj. w. *ἄν*:

Οὐκ ἐπαύσαντο πολεμοῦντες, πρὶν ἐξεπολιόρκησαν τὴν πόλιν.
Μὴ ἀπέλθητε, πρὶν ἂν ἀκούσητε (*pr. audiveritis*).

191. **Relative** Clauses:
a) *consecutive*: ind.; esp. fut.:
neg. *οὐ*:

Παιδές μοι οὔπω εἰσίν, οἵ με θεραπεύσουσιν
qui me colant. — οὐκ ἔστιν ὅστις οὐ ποιήσει.

b) *final*: fut. ind.:
neg. *μή*:

Ἡγεμόνα αἰτήσομεν, ὃς ἡμᾶς ἀπάξει abducat.
Ἔδοξεν ἄνδρας ἑλέσθαι, οἳ τοὺς πατρίους νόμους συγγράψουσιν conscriberent.

c) *hypothetical*: first type:
second type:

Ἃ μὴ οἶδα, οὐδὲ οἴομαι εἰδέναι.
Οἱ παῖδες ἂν ὑβρίζοντο, ὅσοι ἐνθάδε ἦσαν quicumque adessent.

third type:

fourth type:

1. single future occurrence:

2. repeated occ., present:

past:

192. Assimilation of Mood:

Verbal Nouns. Verbal Adjectives.

195. The **Infinitive** a noun and a verb:

197. 1) The subject of the infinitive the same as that of the leading verb (= nom. w. inf.):

2) Different subjects (= acc. w. inf.):

3) Indef. subject *one, a person, you, we*: Predicate qualifications agree with the word to which they relate:

199. There is an absolute infinitive **in:**

The **Participle** is used

201. as attribute and substantive:

202. as predicate:

Ὀκνοίην ἂν ἐμβαίνειν εἰς τὰ πλοῖα, ἃ δοίη.

Τῷ ἀνδρί, ὃν ἂν ἔλησθε, πείσομαι.

Νέος δ᾽ ἀπόλλυθ᾽, ὄντιν᾽ ἂν φιλῇ θεός.

Σφοδρὸς ἦν χαιρεφῶν, ἐφ᾽ ὅ,τι ὁρμήσειεν.

Εἴθε ἥκοις, ἵνα γνοίης.

Τὸ ἀκριβῶς τοῖς νόμοις πείθεσθαι.

Ὁμολογῶ ἁμαρτεῖν: confiteor me peccasse.

Ἔχω τριήρεις ὥστε ἑλεῖν τὸ ἐκείνων πλοῖον.

Σωκράτης ἡγεῖτο θεοὺς πάντα εἰδέναι.

Νοῦν ἔχειν δεῖ καὶ σωφρονεῖν.

1) Ἐρωτώμενος, ποδαπὸς εἴη, Πέρσης ἔφη εἶναι.

2) Νομίζω ὑμᾶς ἐμοὶ εἶναι καὶ φίλους καὶ συμμάχους.

3) Δίκαιον εὖ πράττοντα μεμνῆσθαι θεοῦ.

Ἔξεστιν ὑμῖν εὐδαίμοσι γενέσθαι or (ὑμᾶς) εὐδαίμονας γενέσθαι.

ὀλίγου, μικροῦ δεῖν — ἑκὼν εἶναι, τὸ νῦν εἶναι — ὡς εἰπεῖν, ὡς ἔπος εἰπεῖν — ὡς ἐμοὶ δοκεῖν.

οἱ παρόντες ἡγεμόνες, οἱ νῦν ὄντες ἄνθρωποι.

ὁ γραψάμενος τὸν Σωκράτη, ὁ οὐ πιστεύων.

ὁ βουλόμενος, ὁ τυχών, ὁ μὴ πιστεύων.

τυγχάνω, λανθάνω, φθάνω, οἴχομαι w. part.

Ἡ ψυχὴ ἀθάνατος φαίνεται οὖσα.

ὁρῶ, ἀκούω, οἶδα, γιγνώσκω, δείκνυμι, φαίνω.

Ὁρῶμεν πάντα ἀληθῆ ὄντα ἃ λέγετε.

203. The circumstantial Participle: appositive: genitive absolute:

accusative absolute:

> Οὐκ ἂν δύναιο μὴ καμὼν εὐδαιμονεῖν.
> Θεοῦ διδόντος οὐδὲν ἰσχύει φθόνος,
> καὶ μὴ διδόντος οὐδὲν ἰσχύει πόνος.
> δέον, προσῆκον, δόξαν, δεδογμένον, ἄδηλον ὄν.
> Κατακείμεθα, ὥσπερ ἐξὸν ἡσυχίαν ἄγειν.

204. Infinitive or Participle with **ἄν**: potentiality or unreality:

> Σὺν ὑμῖν ἂν οἶμαι τίμιος εἶναι.

205. Verbal Adjectives in -τέος: necessity, personal construction: impersonal construction:

> Οἱ συμμαχεῖν ἐθέλοντες εὖ ποιητέοι.
> Οἰστέον πᾶσι τὴν τύχην.

The Negative Particles.

206. οὐ *negantis*, μή *nolentis est*; hence
οὐ in statements, μή in wishes:

μή in conditions or equiv. phrases:
μή nearly always w. inf.:
after verbs of saying also οὐ:

> Ἐγὼ θρασὺς καὶ ἀναιδὴς οὔτ' εἰμὶ
> μήτε γενοίμην.
> ἃ μὴ οἶδα — ὁ μὴ δαρεὶς ἄνθρωπος οὐ παιδεύεται.
> Ὑπισχνοῦντο μηδὲν χαλεπὸν αὐτοὺς πείσεσθαι.
> Τολμῶσι λέγειν οὐδεμίαν μάχην γεγονέναι.

Two or more negatives of the same kind strengthen the negation:

Combination of negatives of a different kind neutralize it:

> οὐκ ἐρεῖ οὐδεὶς οὐδέν *no one will say anything.*
> οὐδεὶς οὐκ ἀποθανεῖται *every one will die, nemo non.*

οὐ μή w. aor. subj. } I am sure . . not:
or fut. ind. } (emphatic fut.):
μὴ οὐ w. verbs of fearing = *ne non*:
μὴ οὐ w. inf. after negat. phrases:

> Τὸν ἄνδρ' ἐκεῖνον οὔ τι μὴ λίπω ποτέ.
> Τοὺς πονηροὺς οὐ μή ποτε βελτίους ποιήσετε.
> Ἐφοβεῖτο, μὴ οὐ δύνατο ἐξελθεῖν.
> Πᾶσιν αἰσχύνη ἦν μὴ οὐ συσπουδάζειν *not to.*
> Οὐχ ὅσιόν σοί ἐστι μὴ οὐ βοηθεῖν δικαιοσύνῃ παντὶ τρόπῳ.

After neg. verbs of preventing, resisting etc. and denying etc. this μή οὐ is not rendered in English:

> οὐδὲν ἐδύνατο ἀντέχειν μὴ οὐ χαρίζεσθαι αὐτῷ.
> οὐδεὶς ἀντεῖπε μὴ οὐ καλῶς ἔχειν τοὺς νόμους.

Negatives used idiomatically:
οὐ w. finite verb after *to deny* etc.:
μή ψ. infin. after *to hinder* etc.:

> οὐκ ἂν ἀρνηθεῖεν ὡς οὐκ εἰσὶν τοιοῦτοι.
> ὁ φόβος τὸν νοῦν ἀπείργει μὴ λέγειν, ἃ βούλεται.

APPENDIX

CONTAINING

THE TRANSLATION OF THE GREEK QUOTATIONS USED IN THE SYNTACTICAL PART OF THE SHORT GRAMMAR.

The references to the Greek authors are as follows:
XENOPHON'S Anabasis is referred to by numbers only, *e.g.* *1, 3, 8,*
Mem. stands for his Memorabilia, Cyr. for his Cyropaedia. DEMOSTHENES
is quoted as D., HERODOTUS as Her., THUCYDIDES as Th., ARIS-
TOPHANES as Ar., LYSIAS as Lys., EURIPIDES as Eur., HOMER as
Hom., PLUTARCHUS as Plut., STOBAEUS as Stob., AESCHYLUS as
Aesch., AESCHINES as Aeschin., MENANDER'S Monostichi as Men. The
following are abbreviations for PLATO'S works: Leg. for Leges, Tim. for
Timaeus, Ap. for Apologia, Gorg. for Gorgias, Phaed. for Phaedo, Prot. for
Protagoras, Theaet. for Theaetetus, Lach. for Laches, Charm. for Charmides,
Rep. for Republic, Symp. for Symposium, Crat. for Cratylus, Menex. for
Menexenus.

TRANSLATIONS

---

114. 1. The omens were favorable. *4, 3, 19.*
Great gifts of fortune inspire fear. *Trag. fgm.*
(The Ancients believed that the gods were jealous of singularly fortunate men.)
2. Two excellent men have been killed. *4, 1, 19.*
Critias and Alcibiades could bridle their passions.
3. A portion of mankind do not believe in gods. *Leg. 948 c.*
The great mass of Athenians believe that Hipparchus was murdered while Tyrant. *Th. 1, 20, 2.*
4. What a shameful sight, an old, decrepit man-at-arms!
The soul is (an) immortal (being).
A sycophant is a scoundrel.
The mob is a terror (when ruled by unprincipled men). *Eur. Or. 772.*
5. (To will the same,) That is lasting friendship. *Sallust. Cat. 20, 4.*
This was another excuse. *1, 1, 7.*
(What the people in its meetings enacts by universal consent) That is law. *Mem. 1, 2, 42.*
Besides, he said, this is my native land. *4, 8, 4.*
This is perfect bosh, I declare. *1, 3, 18.*

   Note. — How do you define virtue ? *Meno 71 d.*

115. 1. Socrates was the first to say this.
Socrates cheerfully drank the hemlock.
We are quartered, with the blue sky above us, each ready at his post. *5, 5, 21.*
They reached Attica on the third day of their departure from Sparta. *Her. 6, 120.*
Epyaxa arrived at Tarsus before Cyrus. *1, 2, 25.*
The cities willingly contributed money. *1, 1, 9.*
It was already dark when they descended to the villages. *4, 1, 10.*
2. Our young men ought to be most ready to learn. *Leg. 812 e.*

116. 2. Some of them used their bows, and others their slings. *3, 3, 7.*
Thus they advanced, now fighting a little, now resting awhile. *4, 1, 14.*
Cyrus offered to Clearchus 10,000 darics. The general took the sum, and collected an army. *1, 1, 9.*

117. **1.** Of the seven wise men, Solon was the wisest. *Tim. 20 d.*
A wise man carries all his property within him. *Men. 404.*
Hither Xerxes retreated after his well-known defeat in Greece. *1, 2, 9.*
Cyrus promised to give 3 half-darics per month to each soldier. *1, 3, 21.*
2. A noble-minded man should bravely bear up with calamities. *Eur. fgm. 99.*
A soldier ought to fear his officer more than his enemies. *2, 6, 10.*
A lowly man, with justice on his side, triumphs over a mighty. *Eur.*

118. **1.** If you generals and captains will come to me, I am ready to tell you . . . *2, 5, 25.*
2. Three of the twelve companies were absent. *Hell. 7, 5, 10.*
3. Both the sons — on either side, on both sides —
every nation — every day — every year —
4. Feel shame before Zeus at whose shrine we are assembled. *Th. 3, 14, 1.*
My friend, whose son I educate, is dead.

119. **1.** Veracity (Honesty) is the best policy.
(It is always best to speak the truth.)
Sober second thought somehow is best. *Eur. Hipp. 436.* (*Gildersleeve.*)
Education is the most valuable treasure of man. *Men. 275.*
Chaerephon was my companion from boyhood years. *Ap. 21 a.*
2. Man is the measure of all things. *Theaet. 178 b.*
3. The sun was just setting. *7, 3, 34.* — It was already near sunset. *6, 4, 26.*

> Note 2. — The very Rule of the People was at stake. *Lys. 31, 32.*
> (The [reëstablishment of the] democracy was the prize of the contest.)
> He is the truly wise man, he the truly brave. *Menex. 248 a.*
> (He realizes our ideal of a wise and brave man.)
> It is just the foot-soldier that does the work on the field of battle. *3, 2, 18.*
> I am still (of) the same (opinion), whilst you change your mind. *Th. 2, 61, 2.*

120. the empire of the Persians — the Athenian people —
the present opportunity — according to the established laws —
We forget, I fear, that we are homeward-bound. *3, 2, 25.*
This region was called Western Armenia. *4, 4, 4.*
the upward march = from the coast to the interior of the country —
the men of that time — the return march — his former friendship —
his opponents at home — the battle of Plataeae.

121. All had their shields uncovered. *1, 2, 16.*

123. I will tell you the whole truth. *Ap. 20 d.*
Even the whole world (could) not (force a passage). *5, 6, 7.*
They have sinned against all the gods and all the citizens. *Lys. 14, 42.*
If the line were broken at any point, the breach would prove disastrous for
the entire phalanx. *4, 8, 11.*

They disabled in all about 200 ships. *Th. 1, 100.*
A happy man is at home everywhere. *Men. 716.*
An. 2, 5, 9: every road — all our way.

124. the blessing, advantage — the multitude — the majority —
those present — the present generation — the Ancients —
the word ὅπως — the saying "know thyself."
For youth silence is better than prating. *Men. 387.*

125. 1. a) I give myself to you as a slave and an ally. *Cyr. 4, 6, 2.*
A wise man carries all his property within him. *Men. 404.*
b) When Orestes was in exile, he persuaded the Athenians to restore him.
(Orestes persuaded . . . to restore him from exile.) *Th. 1, 111, 1.*
2. a) They told Xenophon that they were sorry. *5, 6, 36.*
b) Cyrus asked, on the ground that he was the king's brother, to have these
cities given to himself. *1, 1, 8.*
An. 1, 2, 8: in a contest with himself.

126. I give this to you, because you honor my mother. *Cyr. 1, 3, 7.*
You likewise, without exception, love your children. *D. 40, 8.*
You laugh at your own misfortune, and at mine. *Soph. El. 880.*
Astyages sent for his (own) daughter and her son. *Cyr. 1, 3, 1.*
Trust your own eyes, rather than this man's tongue. *Lys. 24, 14.*

127. 4. Associating with the wise, you will become wise yourself. *Men. 475.*
5. In all five generals were in command, (the fifth and) chief of whom was
Xenoclides.
(*Goodwin:* Xenoclides was general as the chief of five.) *Th. 1, 46, 2.*

128. 1. Proof of this is also the following. *1, 9, 29.*
That, then, is what you say. Now take this message from us to the king.
2, 1, 20.
So far Clearchus. Tissaphernes answered as follows.
2. Here I am. — I asked him where Socrates was. There, he said, he is coming behind you. *Rep. 327 b.* — Ships are coming yonder. *Th. 1, 51, 2.*
Note 1. — Choose your spokesman.
Note 2. — Agias and Socrates were among those put to death.
2, 6, 30.
Note 3. — It is characteristic of men that are shiftless and resourceless,
and worthless besides. . . . *2, 5, 21.*
He did not ask to see Menon, although he had come from Ariaeus who
was Menon's guest-friend. *2, 4, 15.*

129. 1. Justice hath an eye that seeth everything. *Men. 179.*
Blessed is the man of substance and of sense. *Men. 340.*
Note 2. — Sometimes and for some death is better than life. *Phaed.*
62 a.
Note 3. — No one contradicted. Whereupon he proceeded. *6, 5, 22.*

An. 3, 2, 10: the gods who are able, you know . . . who are, of course, able. . . .

An. 1, 6, 5 : Clearchus, who seemed to be the most prominent man, (because or inasmuch as he seemed to be . . .).

2. See that you be worthy of the freedom you possess. *1, 7, 3.*

Soothsayers understand nothing of what they say. *Ap. 22 c.*

Now I praise you for what you say and do. *3, 1, 45.*

These he made rulers of whatever country he subjected. *1, 9, 14.*

Herippidas marched out with what force he had. *Hell. 4, 1, 23.*

Note. — Apollo named to him the gods to whom he was to sacrifice. *3, 1, 6.*

3. Ariæus whom we were willing to make king, and to whom we gave, and from whom we received pledges (= with whom we exchanged pledges), is trying to injure us. *3, 2, 5.*

Where, then, is the man that joined us in the hunt, and whom you highly admired ? *Cyr. 3, 1, 38.*

What am I now to do, who am, 't is clear, but hated by the gods, and whom the Grecian host detests ? *Soph. Ai. 458.*

130. Who art thou ? And whence hailest thou ? *Soph. Phil. 56.*

Find out first who they are. *4, 8, 5.*

You know not what you do. *1, 5, 16.*

Note. — Now listen how the democratic government was put down. *Lys. 13, 4.*

132. They conquered the enemy. What victory have you gained ?

133. No one can hide his wickedness from God. *Men. 582.*

(No one that does wicked things escapes the notice of God.)

134. I cross a river, encounter a danger, cross a mountain, transgress the law, pass through the country, sail by an island.

135. Darius had made Cyrus a satrap. *1, 1, 2.*

Cyrus was appointed general. *1, 9, 7.*

136. I will remind you of the battles which your fathers fought. *3, 2, 11.*

We shall demand a guide and boats from Cyrus.

One sole day has robbed me of all my happiness. *Eur. Hec. 285.*

Note 1. — Aeaces had been despoiled of his sovereignty.

137. 1. to assume this command — to perform a most noble deed —

to be subject to slavery such as not even a slave would endure —

They are the authors of the greatest and most impious crimes. *Gorg. 525 a.*

I run the utmost risk — to undertake the sacred war —

Shall we return by the way we came, or by some other way ?

You will lead a happy life, if you master your anger. *Men. 186.*

2. to gain an Olympic victory = to win a prize in the Olympian games —

to laugh heartily — to treat with outrageous insolence —

to gain a complete victory — not to be a bit anxious —
to attend to the other business —
There is no man who succeeds in all he undertakes.　*Men.* 697.

138.　The king tortures us most cruelly.　*3, 1, 18.*
The Lacedaemonians have done our City many a grievous wrong.　*D. 18, 28.*

　　Note. — having been benefited in another way.　*Gorg. 520 c.*
　　having not been wronged in any way.　*1, 6, 7.*

139.　Like a god in face and form.　*Vergil A. I. 589.*
I have a pain in my head.　I have a pain in my eyes.
'T is better to be ill in body than in mind.　*Men. 75.*
Blind thou art in eyes and ears and mind!　*Soph. O. T. 371.*

140.　They were not less than 1000 miles away from Greece.　*3, 1, 2.*
No liar long (remains concealed) escapes detection.　*Men. 547.*

143.　the army of Cyrus — that saying of Solon — the affairs, cause, interests of
　　Greece —
the place is sacred to Artemis — Cimon, Miltiades' son — Pericles, son of
　　Xanthippus —
it is characteristic of shiftless and resourceless men — in, to the nether-world —
To bear poverty is not in the power of everyone, but in that of a wise man
　　(not everyone can bear, is capable of bearing).
Any man may err. — It is in my power.
See *2, 1, 11* : he thinks you are his, belong to him, are in his power.

144.　1. the deliverance of the country — the desire for pleasure —
because they were ashamed before each other and before Cyrus.　*3, 1, 10.*
2. If any man be found guilty of maltreating his parents, let him be put in jail.
3. The unlettered man hath eyes to see, but seeth not.　*Men. 438.*
Man that thou art, remember our common lot.　*Men. 8.*
4. He took his hand = he seized him by the hand.　*Hell. 4, 1, 38.*
We were disappointed in our expectation.　*Th. 4, 85, 2.*
We have seen many a black-letter day.　*D. 18, 253.*
(we have experienced many calamities.)

145.　1. the wise men (the wise among the men) — mortal men —
the best of all — which of us ? who among us ? — none of them —
Thebes in Boeotia (*modern :* Cleveland, Ohio) —
where on earth ? where in the world ? — late in the day —
to that pitch or degree of insolence.
Aristeus himself wished to be one of those who stayed behind.　*Th. 1, 65, 1.*
2. Those who had tasted of the honeycombs, lost their senses.　*4, 8, 20.*
Few tasted anything (took any food).　*3, 1, 3.*
Socrates drank the hemlock (he *emptied* the cup).

　　Note 2. — The remainder of the time — most of the country —
　　half (of) the food, half a loaf.

146. a journey of 3 days — a wall 20 ft. wide, and 100 ft. high. *2, 4, 12.*
When Proxenus died, he was about 30 years of age. *2, 6, 20.*

147. 1. Plataeae is (at a distance of) 70 stades from Thebes. *Th. 2, 5, 2.*
2. He who does no wrong, needs no law. *Antiphon.*

> Note 1. — we ask this of you — we ask you for this.
> They asked Cyrus for their wages.

3. Try to begin every task with the blessing of the gods. *Cyr. 1, 5, 13.*
The Athenians deprived Timotheus of his command. *Hell. 6, 2, 13.*
4. You shall hear from me all the truth. *Ap. 17 b.*

> Note. — On hearing the shouts, they did not stand their ground.
> *4, 4, 21.*

Listen to everything, and then pick out what is best for you. *Men. 566.*
While you are young, lend a willing ear to your elders. *Men. 384.*

148. 1. At times silence is preferable to speech. *Men. 477.*
Clearer than daylight. — No one loves anybody more than himself. *Men. 528.*
We can do this better than others. *Th. 1, 85, 2.*
2. Man is superior to animals by his intelligence. *Menex. 237 d.*
Second to none. — Pausanias reached Haliartus later than Lysander.

> Note. — gods are all-powerful — we defeated the Syracusians.

149. a garden of all sorts of trees. *2, 4, 14.*
shields (of wicker-work) covered with shaggy ox-hide. *4, 7, 22.*
The crowns were not of violets or roses, but of gold. *D. 22, 70.*

150. O thou wretched one !
I count you happy for the freedom you possess.

151. At the price of toil, the gods grant us all good things. (*Mem. 2, 1, 20.*)
A medical man he was, fully as good as many others. *Hom. Il. 11, 514.*

153. They condemned many to death for their Median sympathies.
(Many were condemned to death for Medism.) *Isocr. 4, 157.*

155. Folly leads man into mischief (gives trouble to man). *Men. 244.*
Obedience to the laws of the country is honorable. *Men. 372.*
There is no man but loves himself. *Men. 407.*

156. There Cyrus had a palace and a park. *1, 2, 7.*
Each one was born not merely for his father and mother, but also for his
country. *D. 18, 205.*
I have friends there. *Crito 45 c.*

157. 1. a) What do you want me to learn ? *Ar. N. 111.*
Pray, do not raise an uproar. *Ap. 20 e.*
I beg you to pay close attention to this. *D. 18, 178.*
b) How is our darling ?
My daughter, is the stranger gone at last ? *Soph. O. C. 81.*

c) Such is the case, you understand ?
In our opinion, Achilles deserves praise. *Eur. Hec. 309.*
2. If we be there victorious, the day is ours. *1, 8, 12.*
(all has been done by us, our task is finished).
3. *An. 3, 5, 15 :* to the west after crossing the river.
An. 6, 4, 1 : it is to the right as you enter the Pontus.
An. 3, 2, 22 : all rivers become fordable if we proceed to their sources.
To speak concisely, to be brief, to sum up. *3, 1, 38.*
(for one who has made the matter concise).
The man that is well off, is at home everywhere. *Men. 716.*
Let us return, if you please. *Phaed. 78 b.*

    Note. — Aethon is my illustrious name. *Hom. Od. 19, 183.*

158. 1. Associating with the wise, you will be wise yourself. *Men. 475.*
At daybreak. *2, 1, 2.*
'T is an awful thing, to be at war with God and destiny. *Men. 247.*
2. to follow with a small detachment —
to take the field (march out) with 2000 hoplites.
3. One ship they take, man and all. *Th. 7, 25, 4.-2, 90, 6.*
You were at the same place as these. *3, 1, 27.*

159. 1. No man ever reaped honor from enjoyment. *Stob. 29, 31.*
The king does with us what he pleases (treats us as he pleases).
2. Mortals mostly suffer harm through thoughtlessness. *Men. 15.*
The soldiers were indignant at the affair.

    Note. — to admire one as a poet (for poetic talent).
    to be proud of (or highly elated at) one's bravery.
    We should never take delight in shameful pleasures. *Soph. fgm. 841.*

3. in this way, thus — running, on the run, at full speed, — forcibly, in
    defiance of —
shouting, with a shout, — in silence, silently, quietly —
publicly, by public authority, at the public expense, as a state official —
privately, in a private capacity, — jointly, in common —
The Lacedaemonians pass judgment by acclamation, not by ballot. *Th*
1, 87, 2.
4. a little less than 300.
(Greece has become) weaker by an illustrious city. *Her. 6, 106.*
("Greece is reft of a renowned city," sc. Eretria. *Laurent.*)

160. 2. on this (that) day ; (on) the following day ; in the fourth year ;
in the following month ; at the celebration of the Panathenaea, at the Pana-
    thenaic festival.
During 70 years you were at liberty to leave the city. *Crito 52 e.*
Counsel comes to the wise at night. *Men. 150.*

163. 1. a) Ariaeus and his men (followers, attendants, etc.).
b) about midnight. c) about 50 years.
2. a) up the river, up stream ; over the plain ; upon the mountains.

b) all day long, throughout the day.

c) to the extent of one's power, at full speed ; in due proportion.

d) five each, five apiece, at the rate of five ; every day.

3. to choose the worse instead of the better, (prefer . . . to . . .);
we punish the men because we were insulted (for insulting us).

4. a) from the horse, on horseback ; (starting) from Sardis ;

b) from this time on, ever since that time ;

c) to be named after one ; to raise an army with this money ;
(he was praised) for his deed of daring.

5. a) through the center (middle) of the city ; to have in hand, be
working at.

b) at a distance of five stades ; after a long interval, a short time.

c) through (the medium of) an interpreter, by means of . . .

6. on this account, for this reason, therefore ; on account of, through treason ;
owing (thanks) to us, by help of us, through our fault.

7. a) into the city ; to march against (into the country of) the enemies.

b) till evening ; for the future.

c) to give, to use for some purpose ; about one hundred.

8. a) to flee (be banished) from the city ;
(to grow up from the earth) to be a natural product.

b) *a pueris,* from boyhood, childhood ; from ancient times, antiquity ;
from that time ; ever since.

c) as the state of things would require ; under present conditions ;
in consequence of this ; in every way.

9. a) at Athens ; among the Greeks ; to have taken refuge in fortified places ;
to be without honor among the fellow-soldiers ; on the Black Sea.

b) by night ; during the truce.

c) to be frightened ; to place one's hope in some one.

10. a) to ride in a chariot ; on top of the hill ;
towards Ionia ; to go home.

b) in the reign of Cyrus ; in my time ; our contemporaries.

c) by himself, alone ; by itself, on its own merits ;
as circumstances suggested.

d) to march four (men) deep.

11. a) on board the ships ; a city (situated) on the sea.

b) at the third signal ; thereupon.

c) those in command of the army ; local authorities ;
it rests with you, is in your hands ; to fall into the hands of the king ;
to delight in shameful pleasures ; on such terms ; on condition that ;
to lead to death, to execution ; by way of injury ; with a view to gaining ;
in honor of Patroclus, of Leonidas.

12. a) to mount a horse ; a road (leading) to Susa ;
to go or march to or against some one ; b) for three days ; for a long time.

c) to go out for plunder ; to send for water.

13. a) (down) from heaven ; (down) from the mountains ;
to leap down from the walls : to live underground ; to go beneath the earth.

b) to speak against some one.

14. a) down the river, down stream ; in the country ; by land and by sea ; those standing opposite : those whom they were facing.   b) at that time.

c) military matters ; to the best of one's power ; according to the laws ; in haste ; at one's ease ; little by little, gradually ; there fell about 6000 **men.**

d) one at a time, one by one ; man by man ; day by day, daily ; every year, annually.

15. to side with ; to fight in alliance with ; Cyrus and his attendants ; with tears ; amid dangers.

16. a) after the battle ; after this ; after daybreak, in the daytime.

b) of all things under God, the soul is nearest to Him.

17. to have come from the king ; to ask, learn something from **one.**

18. to be with (near) Clearchus ; among the Medes and among the Persians ; to cast anchor off the city ; to sacrifice at the altar.

19. a) to send an embassy to Philip ; to march along the sea ; to live on the coast.

b) throughout his whole life.

c) contrary to law, unlawfully ; contrary to his solemn engagement (oath) ; by far ; by so much ; so far ; by, within a little, by a small margin ; well disciplined compared with the others ; on account of his own strength.

20. to speak on, about the peace ; to contend for power ; to fear for one's throne ; to consider (as) very important, unimportant, all-important.

21. to wear twisted ornaments around the neck = to wear necklaces ; to fear for the whole city.

22. a) Cyrus and his followers ; (about) near the boundaries ; around the city.

b) about midnight ; about the time of full market = 10 or 11 o'clock, A.M.;

c) they are unjust towards us.

23. a) before the gates ; what is before one.

b) before the battle ; before daybreak ; our predecessors.

c) to prefer to many things ; to value very highly ; to fight for one's country.

24. a) I get praise from you ; the western wall ; to stand (looking) towards (facing) the river.

b) to side with some one ; to swear by the gods.

25. a) at Babylon ; at the source ; near the market-place.

b) in addition to the present trouble ; besides this.

26. a) towards the south ; to march to or against the king ; to make truce with some one.   b) towards evening.

c) not to be enthusiastic over the expedition ; he said in view of this, by way of answer ; wealth is nothing (worthless) compared with wisdom ; to be trained to be virtuous (for a virtuous life) ; for the sake of pleasing, as a favor.

27. a) the followers of Phalinus ; in arms, armed ;
with a shout ; with justice on his side, justly ;
with the help of the gods.

28. a) above the earth ; there was a hill above (= beyond) the village.
b) to discharge one's duties as a general in the interest of Philip
to fight for one's country ;
to be angry on account of what has happened.

29. a) to dwell beyond, on (the other side of) the Hellespont.
b) more than (upwards of) 50 years old.
c) beyond one's strength.

30. a) from beneath the earth he came to light ;
to dwell under the earth ; neither upon nor under the earth.
b) to be conquered by the Greeks ; to die at the hands of a murderer ;
to be maltreated by those who ought to treat one well ;
through grief ; to die of hunger ; to the sound of trumpet.

31. a) under the sky ; under the acropolis.
b) to be in, fall into the power of tyrants ;
to make subject (to oneself).

32. a) they went away under the trees ; to the foot of the hill.
b) at nightfall ; about the same time.

33. he has sent ambassadors to the king.

165. 1. b) The lawgiver makes laws (for others) ; the people make laws for
themselves (make their own laws).

168. 1. a) The Athenians send a ship to Delus (every year). *Phaed. 58 a.*
(The Athenians are in the habit of sending a ship.)
Xenias of Arcadia celebrated the Lycaea with sacrifices and athletic games.
Among the spectators of the contest was Cyrus. *1, 2, 10.*
b) I tried to persuade them, and those whom I succeeded in persuading, I
marched on with. *Cyr. 5, 5, 22.*

Note 1. — After the death of Darius, Tissaphernes falsely accused
Cyrus. *1, 1, 3.*

2. a) I came, I saw, I conquered. *Plut. Caes. 50.*
b) No one ever reaped honor from enjoyment. *Stob. 29, 31.*
He bears away the palm who rightly tempers the useful with the pleasant.
Horace A. P. 343.
c) At the sound of trumpet, with shields forward and spears in rest, they
advanced. *1, 2, 17.*
Darius summoned Cyrus from the province of which he had appointed him
satrap. *1, 1, 2.*

Note. — Cyrus saw the camp where the Cilicians had kept watch and
ward. *1, 2, 22.*
The same persons (*Gr. 66, 2*) that were formerly wont to do him
homage, did so on this occasion also. *1, 6, 10.*

d) You went to war for a mere bagatelle. *Th. 1, 140, 4.*
On the death of Pisistratus, Hippias became ruler. *Th. 6, 54, 2.*
(took the reins of government, succeeded in the Tyranny).
3. I think we ought to see that we get our provisions. *1, 3, 11.*
An honest man will lead a happy life, a wicked man a wretched one.

    Note. — I am going (willing, intend) to explain to you. *Ap. 21 b.*
No one was likely (could be expected) any longer to sell provisions.
3, 1, 2.

4. Xenias and Pasion have indeed deserted, but not escaped us,
(they are gone, but not out of reach). *1, 4, 8.*
Speak the word, and it shall at once be done. *Ar. Plut. 1027.*
Now is no more the time to advise, but to be advised. *Crito 46 a.*
(It is no longer time for forming a plan, but for having a plan ready.)

169. 1. Are we to speak, or to continue silent? *Eur. Ion 758.*
    3. Stay with us, and be our guest (share our hearth). *Eur. Alc. 1151.*
Fear the gods, honor your parents, and obey the laws. *Isocr. 1, 16.*

170. 1. a) Associate with the wise, and you will be wise yourself.
(Associating with the wise, you will . . .) *Men. 475.*
    b) Do what is right, and you will have the gods to fight for you.
(Having done . . . , you will . . .) *Men. 126.*
    c) The Greeks had already crossed the river, when suddenly Mithradates
       makes his appearance. *3, 4, 2.*
I say all this after much thought and deliberation. *D. 21, 191.*
    d) The barbarian marched upon Greece with the intention of subjugating it.
       Th. 1, 18, 2.

172. 1. Well, why so silent, child? Silence doth not profit thee. *Eur. Hipp. 297.*
You shamefully wronged those whom you ought least to wrong. *Crito 54 c.*
    2. O that you were able to do as much as you are prone to do! *Eur.*
      Heracl. 731.
(*Thompson*: Would that your power were proportioned to your zeal!)
O that we had not found thee, O Admetus, in distress! *Eur. Alc. 536.*

    Note. — Would that Cyrus were alive! *2, 1, 4.*
O that I had departed life before! *Soph. El. 1131.*

    4. And when anyone seemed to be remiss at work, Clearchus would occa-
      sionally strike him. *2, 3, 11.*

173. 1. Let us go! — Well, let us say it then!
What we blame (in others), let us not do ourselves! *Gnom.*
    2. Are we to speak or hold our peace? Or what are we to do? *Eur. Ion.*
      758.
Shall we call it force, or shall we not? *Mem. 1, 2, 45.*
    3. Let not this incident discourage you. *5, 4, 19.*

174. 1. My son, may'st thou fare better than thy sire! *Soph. Ai. 550.*
May I not get what I desire, but what is best for me! *Men. 366.*

I think it is time to break up camp.

My son, may'st fare thou better than thy sire,
but else be like him, and thou wilt not be base. *Soph. Ai. 550.*

176   He indicated the place where wine lay hidden.   *4, 5, 29.*

He related to his friends how the trial of Orontas was conducted.   *1, 6, 5.*

177   The plaintiff says I'm a wanton, violent man.

Cyrus admitted that his expedition was intended (that the march would be) against the king of Persia.   *1, 4, 11.*

The news was that Cyrus had fallen, and that Ariaeus, who had taken flight, was at the halting-place.   *2, 1, 3.*

178.   As the Athenians were not signally victorious, they fancied they were defeated. *Th. 7, 34.*

The Athenians abused Pericles because, although he was then general, he did not lead them out. *Th. 2, 21, 3.*

The Greeks wondered that Cyrus was not seen anywhere, and that nobody else had come (with a message) from him.   *1, 10, 16.*

I beg you will remain with us, because I would not listen to anybody more eagerly than to you. *Prot. 335 d.*

179.   **1.** We ask you what is to be done.   *2, 1, 16.*

He inquired from Medosades if this were true.   *7, 2, 25.*

I will tell you, then, of what hopes I were to deprive myself (if . . .). *2, 5, 10.*

Xenophon did not in the first place ask (at Delphi) if it were more expedient for him to set out for Asia than to remain at home, but tried to ascertain how he could reap most honor from his journey.   *3, 1, 7.*

2. I see you wavering which path in life to choose. *Mem. 2, 1, 23.*

The Theban was at a loss how to act under the circumstances,
(how to deal with the matter, what to make of it). *Hell. 7, 4, 39.*

180   **1.** There was a severe cold so that the water froze.   *7, 4, 3.*

I have enough triremes for capturing their boat.   *1, 4, 8.*

The soldiers raised a great shout so that the enemies should hear it.

2. a) They do everything so as to escape punishment. *Gorg. 479 c.*

Cyrus inspired all (his visitors) with such sentiments as to be more attached to himself on their departure than to the king.   *1, 1, 5.*

b) The Deity is of such a nature as to be everywhere.
(The Deity is by nature omnipresent). *Mem. 1, 4, 18.*

Who wields such power of eloquence as to prevail upon you?

c) They did not shoot far enough to reach us.   *3, 3, 7.*

This has not happened so long ago that you could be ignorant of it. *D. 59, 91.*

d) The Heracleans made great promises to Timasion on condition that the Greeks should sail off.   *5, 6, 26.*

They said they would restore the corpses on condition that we do not burn their homes.   *4, 2, 19.*

Note 1. — On the following day Tissaphernes failed to come. **So**
that the Greeks began to feel uneasy. *2, 3, 25.*

181. 1. Don't envy fortune's favorites, lest you be considered base.
As he said this, he at once arose to do the necessary business. *3, 1, 47.*
Abrocomas burnt the vessels to prevent Cyrus from crossing. *1, 4, 18.*
2. We shall forget, I fear, that we are homeward bound. *3, 2, 25.*
He feared he would not be able to get out of the country. *3, 1, 12.*

Note. — *An. 1, 3, 17 :* I would hesitate to embark in the ships that
Cyrus would give us.

3. I think we ought to see that we stay here with least danger to ourselves.
1, 3, 11.
Cyrus sought for means and ways of shaking off his brother's yoke for good,
(how he might no longer in all his life be subject to his brother). *1, 1, 4.*

Note 1. — I hope it isn't (though I'm afraid it is) too harsh a thing
to say. *D. 16, 21.*
You will again do, I fear, what has so often brought you harm.
The difficulty is not, I dare say, in escaping death, but in escaping
wickedness. *Ap. 39 a.*
Surely I will never leave that man !
As for the good-for-nothings, you won't make them better, that's sure,
(sc. by presenting them with a crown). *Aeschin. 3, 177.*

Note 2. — We fear, we have missed both at once. *Th. 3, 53, 2.*
Beware lest thine be but an empty plea. *Soph. El. 584.*
(beware lest thou art putting forth an empty plea).
Take heed lest thou involve thyself in grief. *Soph. El. 581.*

184. If gods do aught that is base, they are not gods. *Eur. fgm. 294, 7.*
If you have done a dreadful deed, you're bound to suffer dreadful pain.
Soph. fgm. 18.
Curb thy tongue, or thou shalt smart for it. *Eur. fgm. 5.*
(if thou dost not restrain thy tongue, thou wilt have trouble).

185. a) Without light, we should be like the blind. *Mem. 4, 3, 3.*
(if we had not light, we should be . . .)
Without Chrysippus, there would be no stoa. *Diog. Laert.*
b) Agasias would not have done this, had I not commanded him. *6, 6, 15.*
If only 30 votes had gone over to the other side, I should now stand ac-
quitted. *Ap. 36 a.*
c) Had you not come, we should be going to the king. *2, 1, 4.*
For if thou wert my child and I thy sire,
I should have slain, and not now banish thee. *Eur. Hipp. 1042.*

Note. — Being himself a continental, Agamemnon would have had no
insular possessions, had he not had also some sort of a navy. *Th. 1, 9, 4.*
If thou wert not my father, I should (at once) reply : thou art not
right in mind. *Soph. Ant. 755.*

186. If in short one were to say this, he would be right. *Th. 1, 70, 9.*
If I must either do or suffer wrong, I would rather suffer wrong than do it.
Gorg. 469 c.

> Note. — If I were you, I should take an oath like the Argives.
> *Phaed. 89 c.*

187. **2. I.** I shall come to you to-morrow, God willing. *Lach. 201 c.*
If in your youth you toil, you will be happy in your age. *Men. 388.*
If we have wealth, we shall have friends. *Men. 165.*
While fortune favors you, you'll number many friends. *Ovid Tr. 1, 9, 5.*
II. a) When deeds are wanting, all speech is manifestly empty talk.
D. 2, 12.
When death raps at the door, there's none that wants to die. *Eur. Alc. 671.*
b) Wherever Xenophon found a morsel to eat, he would distribute it. *4, 5, 8.*
No one that complied with Cyrus' request, and rendered him a service, would
ever have his zeal go unrewarded. *1, 9, 18.*
An. 2, 3, 11: When any seemed to be idle, Clearchus would occasionally
pick out the right man, and strike him.
An. 1, 9, 19: Whenever Cyrus found anyone to be a just and skilful man-
ager, he would never deprive him of his territory.

188. **I.** This I can show, if you will send some one along with me. *5, 6, 7.*
Even if there are many bridges, we shall not know whither to escape. *2, 4, 19.*

189. E'en though I (trust not =) shrink, yet must the deed be done. *Aesch.
Cho. 298.*
A fool grins where grins are out of place. *Men. 19.*
(A fool laughs even though there be nothing to laugh at).

190. **2.** When all were assembled, they took their seats ; it was midnight, when
this meeting was held. *3, 1, 33.*
3. What grave will welcome me to rest, when I shall die ? *Eur. Iph.
T. 625.*
Judge not until you've heard me out. *D. 4, 14.*
We all are mad, when in a fit of anger. *Philem. 156.*
Cyrus went hunting in his park, whenever he wished to take some exercise,
and train his horses. *1, 2, 7.*
Let us not wait till the enemies outnumber us ; but let us advance while we
think we may yet easily get the best of them. *Cyr. 3, 3, 46.*
4. a) They crossed the river before the others had declared their intention.
1, 4, 16.
Many a man dies before it appears of what stuff he was made. *Cyr. 5, 2, 9.*
b) They did not sail away until they had forced the city to surrender.
Hell. 7, 4, 18.
Do not depart until you have heard the whole story. *5, 7, 12.*
The Corinthians refused to sail along before they had attended the Isthmian
games.

191. **2.** **something** which did not happen — which will not happen —
which cannot happen — which would not have happened —
which could not have happened —
which I pray may not hap- which I beg we shall never do —
pen —
which I forbid you to do —

3. a) Strange that you give us nothing. *Mem. 2, 7, 13.*
(You who give nothing to us, do a strange thing).
b) I have as yet no chiidren to take care of me. *Lys. 24, 6.*
Who so mad as not to wish to be your friend ? *2, 5, 12.*
Impossible for you to have your youth restored ! *Eur. Heracl. 707.*
c) We will ask Cyrus for a guide to lead us back. *1, 3, 14.*
The people voted that a committee of 30 be chosen to compile the ancestral
laws by which they were to be governed. *Hell. 2, 3, 2.*
4. a) What I do not know, I do not think I know. *Ap. 21 d.*
Neither listen to, nor look at things that do not concern you. *Men. 19.*
b) (If we were wise) we should not attempt to do what we did not understand. *Charm. 171 e.*
c) I for one should be loath to embark in the ships that Cyrus would give
us. *1, 3, 17.*
d) Answer what I am about to ask you. *Lys. 12, 24.*
I shall obey whatever man you choose. *1, 3, 15.*
God's favorites die young. *Gnom.*
All Midas touched, was turned to gold.

192. **1.** I wish you would come that you might know.
Let every man practise the trade he knows. *Ar. Vesp. 1431.*
Would he not treat us with the utmost cruelty, that he may inspire fear in all
men ? *3, 1, 18.* (Would he not have recourse to any plan, that . . .)
2. If the good were born good, we should keep them in the citadel out of
the way of harm (that no one might corrupt them). *Men. 89 b.*
If in reality I happened to be a foreigner, you would pardon me for speaking
in my native dialect, and after the fashion of my country (if I spoke in the
very accent and manner in which I should in that case have been brought
up). *Ap. 17 d.*

193. **1.** a) Socrates said : " The gods know everything."
Socrates said that the gods knew everything.
b) " Do not retire from your post."
I ask you not to retire from your post. *D. 38, 24.*

194. **6.** Now hear the other side, that you may learn . . . *2, 5, 16.*

197. **1.** Cyrus thinks he has been wronged by us. *1, 3, 10.*
I confess that I did wrong : I plead guilty.
2. Socrates believed that gods knew everything, or
Socrates believed the gods to know everything. *Mem. 1, 1, 19.*

Note.—A man should go to school, and be taught and get sense. *Men. 96.*

3. Being asked of what country he was, he said he was a Persian. *4, 4, 17.*
I think you are my country and my friends and my allies. *1, 3, 6.*
When fortune smiles, 'tis meet that we should well remember God. *Men. 118.*
You can have success. *D. 3, 23.*
They were eager each to be first. *Th. 2, 65, 10.*
Cyrus sends word to Xenias to come with the others. *1, 2, 1.*

198. 2. 'Twere better for a youth to hold his peace, than to be prating. *Men. 387.*
Master your anger by calm reflection. *Men. 381.*
The plaintiff is at an advantage (over the defendant), because he is the first to speak. *D. 18, 7.*
Who dares much will blunder much. *Men. 724.*

199. 1. a) But now it is time to depart. *Ap. 42 a.*
You ought to be brave. *3, 2, 11.* Compare *3, 2, 15.*
b) Protagoras used to say that man was the measure of everything. *Crat. 386 a.*
Whatever you do, think that some god or other is looking at you. *Gnom.*
If you honor God, you may hope to be successful.
Be jealous for your fair name, rather than greedy of wealth. *Men. 285.*
What will prevent him from going wherever he pleases? *D. 1, 12.*
Learn to submit to the power of your masters. *Men. 727.*
She knows not how to bend in trouble. *Soph. Ant. 472.*
2. Everything is easy for God to accomplish.
You are the quickest of all to form a judgment on the matter of discussion. *D. 3, 15.*
Among all Cyrus was the most fit for governing. *1, 9, 1.*
3. He allowed the Greeks to plunder the villages. *2, 4, 27.*
They chose Dracontius to take charge of the race-course. *4, 8, 25.*
4. (To be constantly calling to mind, and harping upon the favors one has conferred) is almost as bad as throwing them up to one. *D. 18, 269.*
They have not spoken a word of truth, I dare say. *Ap. 17 a.*
If it depends on them, you are done for. *Hell. 3, 5, 9.*

201. The assembled generals : the generals present —
to those Thracians who live on the other side of the Hellespont —
the accuser of Socrates —
a chance comer, the first to come, anyone —
he that wishes, whoever likes, the first that offers, anyone —
he that does not believe, an unbeliever.

202. 1. a) The soul is evidently immortal. *Phaed. 107 c.*
I came, as it happened, with a horse. *Symp. 221 a.*
They continued fighting seven days in all. *4, 3, 2.*

They reached the city before the Persians. *Her. 4, 136.* They entered
unperceived. *Th. 2, 2, 3.*

b) I never ceased to pity you : I never ceased pitying you. *3, 1, 19.*

I shall not endure life. *Eur. Hipp. 354.* (I cannot endure to live.)

Don't grow tired of obliging a friend. *Gorg. 470 c.*

Stop talking. *Eur. Hipp. 706.* I stop the enemy from laughing.

c) You did well to tell me (in telling me) beforehand.

(Cyrus asked the gods to let him live) until he should outdo (both friend
and foe) in returning like for like. *1, 9, 19.*

You do wrong to break the truce and go to war. *Thuc.*

By leaving behind a certain Mede, he obliged Cyaxares. *Cyr. 3, 3, 1.*

d) I am delighted to hear (at hearing) you talk so reasonably. *2, 5, 16.*

They are glad to be honored : delight in being honored. *Eur. Hipp. 8.*

I wouldn't be sorry to hear it : (at) hearing it.

This I am not ashamed of saying : I say this without a blush. *Cyr. 5, 1, 21.*

2. a) I saw Cato sitting — I heard Socrates say (saying).

We see that all you say is true. *5, 5, 24.*

They did not know that Cyrus had fallen. *1, 10, 16.*

If you are caught (in) doing this, you shall die. *Ap. 29 c.*

We suffer that man to increase his power. *D. 9, 29.*

b) I was the first to announce that Cyrus was approaching. *2, 3, 19.*

This much will become clear : Philip's is a most selfish policy. *D. 2, 8*

(Ph. will be convicted of doing, proved to do all for himself.)

> Note 2. — Know that thou art mortal.
> We see that we are unable to get the upper hand. *Th. 1, 32, 5.*
> Note 3. — I am not conscious of being wise. *Ap. 21 b; see 22 c.*

203. **2.** The gift that God bestows, no envy can prevent,
the gift that God withholds, no labor can secure. *Gnom.*

(If God should bestow, not bestow a gift . . .)

3. a) The reason why I say this, is because I want you to agree with me
(I wish that to seem good to you which seems so to me.) *Phaed. 102 d.*

As their attack was sudden, they captured many slaves. *6, 3, 3.*

They made a noise to signify their approval of Agasias' speech.

(for the purpose of showing that A. had spoken well.) *6, 1, 30.*

b) There will be no one to lead us. *2, 4, 5.*

The Athenians prepared for war. *Th. 2, 7. 1.*

c) (My inner voice) often checked me in the middle of a discourse,
(it stopped me from continuing while discoursing). *Ap. 40 b.*

This was done while Conon was general. *Isocr. 9, 56.*

d) If you do what is right, you will have the gods to fight for you. *Men. 126.*

Taste, and you too will find that these things are sweet. *Cyr. 1, 3, 5.*

No pluck, no luck ! (One can't succeed unless one toil).

e) For, many although well-born are base. *Eur. El. 551.*

You entered without the law to warrant you : without the warrant of the law.

(although the law does or did not allow it).

4. Here we lie idle, as though we could afford to take our ease. *3, 1, 13.*
Did those who failed to help when help was needed, escape safe and sound ?
(those who neglected the duty of rescuing). *Alcib. 1, 115 b.*
Philon demands a place in the Senate, although he has no claim to one.
Lys. 31, 32.

204. In your company, I think, I should be esteemed everywhere. *1, 3, 6.*
(If I should remain with you . . .)
Aristippus asked Cyrus for about 2000 mercenaries and their wages, saying
(*Gr. 203, 3 a*) that in this way he would worst his opponents. (See
Goodwin's note on this passage, *1, 1, 10.*)

205. 2. We have to humor those who are willing to help us. *Mem. 2, 6, 27.*
Each must endure his fate (carry his cross).
Punishment is due to the evil-doer.
(Evil-doers should be punished). Compare *2, 5, 18.*

206. 1. Shameless and reckless I neither am nor may I ever be! *D. 8, 68.*
(I shameless and reckless ? Neither am I nor may I ever be!)
2. It is not possible — he said it was not possible —
why did you not come ? — since this did not happen —
whence there is no escaping.
3. May I not get what I desire, but what is best for me! *Men. 366.*
Don't envy fortune's favorites, lest you appear to be base.
We shall forget, I fear, that we are homeward bound. *3, 2, 25.*
4. a) If you don't curb your tongue, you'll smart for it. *Eur. fgm. 5.*
What I know not, I do not think I know. *Ap. 21 d.*
No rod, no reason ! *Men. 422.*
(An unchastised man is not well bred).
b) They promised that the fugitives would not get into trouble. *Hell. 4, 4, 5.*
They have the audacity to say that no battle has taken place. *Lys. 14, 5.*

> Note 1. — Some would not even deny that they are such (spies).
> *D. 9, 54.*
> Note 2. — Clearchus barely escaped being stoned to death.
> (C. had a narrow escape from death by stoning). *1, 3, 2.*
> Fear forbids the mind to tell what it would fain reveal. *Eur. fgm 68.*
> No one ever denied that the laws were all right.
> I do confess the deed, and I disown it not. *Soph. Ant. 442.*
> The king forbade anyone to shoot until Cyrus should have hunted to

his heart's content. *Cyr. 1, 4, 14.*
5. No one will say anything. Everyone shall die.
6. a) As for the good-for-nothings, you won't make them better, I am sure.
Aeschin. 3, 177.
b) He feared he would not be able to get out of the country. *3, 1, 12.*
c) 'Tis a want of piety in you, not to come to the aid of Justice. *Rep. 427 e.*
All were ashamed not to lend a helping hand. *2, 3, 11.*
(Out of shame they all lent a helping hand, or
Not to be put to shame, they all joined in the work).

HOMERIC DIALECT.

213. 1. Accus. : go ye to the tent. *I. 1, 322.*

Gen. : they are marching through the plain. *I. 2, 801.*

she came up from the grey sea. *I. 1, 359.*

wine was drawn from the casks. *O. 23, 305.*

Dat. : dwelling in heaven. *I. 2, 412.* upon the topmost peak. *I. 8, 3.*

the arm fell upon the ground. *I. 5, 82.*

to force the Achaeans back to the seashore. *I. 18, 294*

3. above others quick at running. *O. 3, 112.*

more than other mortals, he offers sacrifices to the gods. *O. 1, 66.*

4. out they went : they disembarked.

they dismissed (= satisfied) their hunger. *O. 1, 150.*

on came the darkness (darkness set in). *I. 1, 475.*

fools, that devoured the kine of the Sun above. *O. 1, 8.*

5. cut down by the Ciconians. *O. 9, 66.*

having escaped (from) the day of doom. *O. 9, 17.*

6. upon a golden staff. *I. 1, 15.*

7. among them he arose (= to address them). *I. 1, 68 (O. 1, 28).*

to hold in one's hands. *O. 3, 281.*

214. 1. and many a man shall one day say. *I. 6, 459.*

(thus one day some will say). *I. 6, 462.*

such men I never saw nor shall I ever see. *I. 1, 262.*

2. and thus shall many a one say. *I. 4, 176.*

Them could we but seize, we might win for us great renown. *I. 5, 273.*

well, now depart, provoke me not, that thou mayest depart in safety. *I. 1, 32.*

Would that the earth forthwith were to swallow him up ! *I. 6, 281.*

3. Easily may a god, who will, bring a man home safe from afar. *O. 3, 231.*

And if again a god shall wreck me on the wine-dark sea, I shall be patient still. *O. 5, 221.*

Zeus watches over all men, and chastises those that sin. *O. 13, 214.*

O Friends, however sad, we shall not yet go down to the mansions of Hades, until our destined day arrive. *O. 10, 174.*

As when smoke issues from a city, and rises into the upper air, from an island afar-off which foes beleaguer, thus from Achilles' head a blazing flame rose heavenwards. *I. 18, 207.*

Where the billow might have swept me away. *I. 6, 348.*

4. O lord Zeus, may my Telemachus be blest among men and may he get whatever in his heart he desires. *O. 17, 345.*

5. Thereupon, at once returning to your native land, you shall build your father's mound, and perform the funeral rites, full many, as are his due, and give your mother to a husband. *O. 1, 290.*

BEGINNING & INTERMEDIATE GREEK

A Greek Reader for Schools
C. E. Freeman and W. D. Lowe

Includes ✦ selected excerpts from Aesop to Plato ✦ introductions ✦ notes ✦ vocabulary ✦ index of proper names.

iv + 142 pp. (1917, Reprint 1994) Paperback, ISBN 0-86516-267-0

> ...we have found no better means to introduce students to some smashingly good stories...
>
> —S. L. Pearce
> Jesuit High School

Herodotus
The Wars of Greece and Persia
W. D. Lowe

This fascinating introduction to Herodotus includes ✦ student notes ✦ vocabulary ✦ illustrations.

Illus., 144 pp. (1913, Reprint 1990) Paperback, ISBN 0-86516-054-6

> ...the passages from Greek history complement the ancient history studies and add a certain element of prestige to a student who is reading the original.
>
> —Frank P. Raispis
> St. Ignatius College Prep

Plato: Apology
James J. Helm

The revised edition of this popular textbook features ✦ same page vocabulary and grammatical notes ✦ sentence diagrams ✦ principal parts of verbs ✦ word frequency list ✦ complete vocabulary.

viii + 127 pp. (1981, revised 1997) Paperback, ISBN 0-86516-348-0

Appian Civil Wars, Book I
J. L. Strachan-Davidson

This reprint of the Oxford edition features ✦ Greek text ✦ notes.

vii + 150 pp. (1902, Reprint) Paperback, ISBN 0-86516-021-X

Plutarch's Life of Pericles
Hubert Ashton Holden

This text features ✦ an extensive apparatus criticus ✦ marginal notes ✦ chronology of events ✦ vocabulary ✦ four indices.

lxii + 303 pp. (1894, Reprint) Paperback, ISBN 0-86516-026-0

> This commentary can be used with profit by the advanced student of Greek who knows Latin.
>
> —Gail Smith, *The Classical Outlook*

Bolchazy-Carducci Publishers, Inc.

1000 Brown Street, Unit 101
Wauconda, IL 60084
Phone: 847/526-4344
www.bolchazy.com

Meleager: The Poems
Jerry Clack

An excellent introduction to Meleager's 132 epigrams.

Includes ✦ notes ✦ vocabulary ✦ proper name and epigram sou indices

vii + 160 pp. (1992)
Paperback, ISBN 0-86516-254-9

Asclepiades of Samos and Leonidas of Tarentum
The Poems
Jerry Clack

Includes ✦ introduction ✦ Greek text ✦ commentary
✦ index of proper names ✦ selected bibliography ✦ glossary

A manageable text (c. 800 lines) for an undergraduate Greek class.

280 pp., (1999)
Paperback, ISBN 0-86516-45

Dioscorides and Antipater of Sidon
The Poems
Jerry Clack

Hellenistic Epigram for the Classroom

Includes ✦ annotated Greek text ✦ introduction to the lives an works of the two poets ✦ glossary ✦ selected bibliography
✦ index of proper names ✦ list of the sources of the poems

vii + 219 pp. (2001)
Paperback, ISBN 0-86516-511-4

Bolchazy-Carducci Publishers, Inc.

1000 Brown Street, Unit 1
Wauconda, IL 600
Phone: 847/526-43
www.bolchazy.cc

INTERMEDIATE GREEK TEXTS / GREEK REFERENCE

Theocritus: Select Poems
Kenneth J. Dover

Dover's selections with accompanying introduction and extensive notes provide insights into both the writing and the context of the poet.

The best commentary available for students.
—Thomas Hubbard, University of Texas, Austin

lxxii + 323 pp. (1971, Reprint 1994) Paperback, ISBN 0-86516-204-2

Luciani Vera Historia
C. S. Jerram

Vera Historia is the only English-language commentary in print. It includes ✦ introduction ✦ Greek text ✦ vocabulary ✦ notes ✦ delightful illustrations.

Ideal for a second-year course in classical Greek, Lucian's prose style and use of Attic Greek parallel that of early Plato, so teachers may consider this text as a substitute or counterpoise to Socratic dialogues.
—Casey Fredericks, *The Classical Journal*

Illus., xxiii + 79 pp. (1879, Reprint 1990) Paperback, ISBN 0-86516-240-9

Greek and Latin in English Today
Richard Krill

Help students build vocabulary as well as knowledge of history and culture. Successfully tested with hundreds of students.

FEATURES ✦ essay on European Linguistics and the Greek Alphabet ✦ teaches students the Greek alphabet transliteration ✦ helps students appreciate the ancient languages ✦ teaches basic Latin and Greek vocabularies

Book: vi + 250 pp. (1990, Reprint 1998) Paperback, ISBN 0-86516-241-7
2 Cassettes: (1993) ISBN 0-86516-248-4

Handbook of Greek Literature
H. J. Rose

A brief yet comprehensive survey of Greek literature from Homer to Lucian.

454 pp. (1950, Reprint 1996) Paperback, ISBN 0-86516-321-9

Schoder's Slides: Ancient Greece from the Air
Raymond V. Schoder, S.J.

Complete Set of 175 slides: ISBN 0-86516-SLIS; *Set of 35:* ISBN 0-86516-SLID; Slides can be ordered *individually,* (minimum of 10 slides), ISBN 0-86516-SLI1; *Contact us for a complete inventory of slides.*
Use of these slides in publications is restricted by copyright ©1987, Bolchazy-Carducci Publishers, Inc.

Bolchazy-Carducci Publishers, Inc.

1000 Brown Street, Unit 101
Wauconda, IL 60084
Phone: 847/526-4344
www.bolchazy.com

The Living Voice of Greek Literature

Read by **Stephen G. Daitz**

in the Restored Pronunciation of Classical Greek

Pronunciation and Reading of Ancient Greek: A Practical Guide

Two cassettes contain explanations of the pronunciation of the vowels and consonants and the pit
accents of ancient Greek, and also present a method for reading Greek poetry that integrates the pit
accents with the rhythm based upon syllabic quantity.

(1980) booklet and 2 cassettes, Order # 23660

A Recital of Ancient Greek Poetry (2nd ed., revised and augmented)

These four cassettes contain selections from the *Iliad*, the *Odyssey*, the lyric poets, and Greek traged
and comedies. Each is read first in English and then in original Greek. An accompanying booklet co
tains an introduction and complete Greek text.

(1999) booklet and 4 cassettes, Order # 23600

The Iliad of Homer

Complete program consists of four parts each with six cassettes and corresponding Greek text w
English translation.

(1990) Part I (Books 1-6), Order # 23810; (1991) Part II (Books 7-12), Order # 23817
(1992) Part III (Books 13-18), Order # 23824; (1992) Part IV (Books 19-24), Order # 23830

Selections from the Greek Orators

Speeches of Gorgias, Perikles, Lysias, Isokrates, and Demosthenes are read on cassette.

(1988) booklet and 2 cassettes, Order # 23690

The Odyssey of Homer

Complete program consists of four parts each with six cassettes and corresponding Greek text wi
English translation.

(1996) Part I (Books 1–6) Order # 23850; (1997) Part II (Books 7–12) Order # 23860
(1998) Part III (Books 13–18) Order # 23870; (1999) Part IV (Books 19–24) Order # 23880

Euripides' Hekabe

Euripides' testament to the devastations of war—for both conquered and conquerors; hauntingly rel
vant to today's world.

(1981) booklet and 2 cassettes, Order # 23650

Aristophanes' Birds

> *...Daitz's reading in Ancient Greek of Aristophanes' comedy marks a major effort in
> the quest of restoring a living voice to ancient Greek literature.*
> —*Library Journal*

(1983) booklet and 2 cassettes, Order # 23670

Plato's Portrait of Sokrates

Includes Plato's *Apology* (entire), *Krito* (entire), and *Phaedo* (selections).

(1988) booklet and 2 cassettes, Order # 23695

Bolchazy-Carducci
Publishers, Inc.

1000 Brown Street, Unit 1(
Wauconda, IL 6008
Phone: 847/526-43
www.bolchazy.co